ENGLAND UNDER QUEEN ANNE

RAMILLIES

AND THE

UNION WITH SCOTLAND

QUEEN ANNE IN THE HOUSE OF LORDS
(FROM THE PICTURE BY TILLEMANS IN KENSINGTON PALACE)
BISHOPS ON THE LEFT. ARMADA TAPESTRIES ON THE WALLS
(Reproduced by gracious permission of His Majesty the King)

ENGLAND UNDER QUEEN ANNE

RAMILLIES

AND THE

UNION WITH SCOTLAND

BY

GEORGE MACAULAY TREVELYAN, O.M.

REGIUS PROFESSOR OF MODERN HISTORY IN THE
UNIVERSITY OF CAMBRIDGE

* *

WITH MAPS

LONGMANS, GREEN AND CO.
LONDON ◆ NEW YORK ◆ TORONTO
1932

LONGMANS, GREEN AND CO. LTD.

39 PATERNOSTER ROW, LONDON, E.C. 4
6 OLD COURT HOUSE STREET, CALCUTTA
53 NICOL ROAD, BOMBAY
36A MOUNT ROAD, MADRAS

LONGMANS, GREEN AND CO.

55 FIFTH AVENUE, NEW YORK
221 EAST 20TH STREET, CHICAGO
88 TREMONT STREET, BOSTON
128–132 UNIVERSITY AVENUE, TORONTO

BIBLIOGRAPHICAL NOTE

First Edition . . . . *October 1932*
New Impression . . . *October 1932*

TO THAT TRUE SCOT

JOHN BUCHAN,

A PLEDGE OF

'UNION' AND FRIENDSHIP

PREFACE

THE public has very kindly received my first volume on *England under Queen Anne*, entitled *Blenheim*, and I hope this continuation entitled *Ramillies and the Union with Scotland* will be regarded with similar indulgence. Before I am likely to publish the third, and I trust last, volume, the world will have been gratified by the appearance of the authentic Life of Marlborough by his distinguished descendant. After that I trust his *manes* will be appeased for all the detraction he has suffered, in life from the Tories, and after death from one Whig. This volume shows him, at least in my estimation, at the summit of his career and performance,—Ramillies, Oudenarde and the reconquest of Belgium,—and also at the beginning of his decline, not indeed in military genius, in which he never declined so long as he took the field, but in political and diplomatic grasp of the realities of the European situation and of the possibilities of war and peace. It stands here recorded how he won the war that but for him would have been lost ; and how he failed to make the peace.

This volume is a rope twisted of three strands—the war, English politics and the Scottish problem. The close interconnections of the three are the special interest and difficulty of the historian.

The chapters devoted to the war show Marlborough in his full glory at Ramillies and Oudenarde ; the tragedy of our unsuccessful Peninsular War, when we had on our side neither a Wellington nor the sympathies of the Spanish people ; the romantic comedy of Peterborough ; our first heroic defence of Gibraltar ; the plucking of Minorca like a ripe orange, as the fruit of Mediterranean supremacy ; the firm establishment of our naval power in the world ; the

great episodes of Turin and Toulon ; the thwarted invasion
of 1708 ; and the whole scheme of the war by land and sea,
stretched from Lisbon to the threatening camp of Charles XII
in Saxony, held in the grasp of Marlborough's capacious
mind, so often marred by the failure of allies and lieutenants,
but on the whole so wonderfully successful.

At home English politics move to the old tune, the
harsh discord of ' those vile enormous factions,' Whig and
Tory, 'the merciless men of both parties,' struggling with
rude old English vigour for the favour of Queen Anne and
of her subjects, yet throwing up all the while fruits of real
statesmanship, the winning of the war, the Regency Act
and the Scottish Union.

The making of Great Britain, the Union of the English
and Scottish Parliaments, proved no less important in its
ultimate effect of reconciling the two peoples on terms of
equality and justice than in its immediate result of preventing civil war and the severance of the two Crowns.
Scottish politics, religion and society then differed so
greatly from English, that I have thought it best to
introduce the history of the Union by two chapters on the
State of Scotland in Queen Anne's reign, answering to the
four chapters on the English scene with which my previous
volume began.

As contrasted with our treatment of Ireland and our
dealings with America, the Scottish Union stands out in
the Eighteenth Century as a thing apart, an unwonted and
surprising act of wise Imperial initiative. The men who
made the Union of 1707 (Marlborough, Godolphin, Somers
and Harley for England, Queensberry and Argyle for
Scotland) were not selfless patriots—it was not an age pro-
ductive of such. They were shrewd, worldly men, capable
of looking the real facts of a situation in the face. And
they studied the interest of their respective countries all
the better because, unlike Fletcher of Saltoun, they could
do so without too much zeal. They were, moreover, free
from the religious and political fanaticisms of the previous
century, which had so often stood in the way of agreement
by mutual concession. In the age of Anne, religious and
political passions were already cooling ; they were no longer

liquid lava, though they were not yet stone-cold, as they became under the first two Georges. The moment was, therefore, favourable for great artificers to mould the future shape of the body politic.

The action of these courageous but wary statesmen was based, not on theory, but on sound information and calculation of all the forces on the board. Such was the method of the Whigs and Tories who made the Revolution Settlement of 1689, the Act of Settlement of 1701 that fixed the Succession on the House of Hanover, and half-a-dozen years later this Union with Scotland. These three settlements, on which the British Constitution has rested ever since, are parts of a single scheme ; they were all of them made in the same spirit of compromise between parties, churches, and nations, and therefore they were never overset. The not very idealistic statesmen of that Augustan age laid the foundations of modern Britain more wisely and well than the passionate Cavaliers and Roundheads of an earlier time had been able to do. It was the heroic idealists—Laud, Hampden, Cromwell, Montrose—who had rough-hewn the issues of controversy, but the terms of settlement were drawn up by their prudently compromising successors in the reigns of William and Anne. The Scottish Union was a piece of their most characteristic and successful work.

I should like to express my gratitude to the Duke of Buccleugh and Earl Spencer for placing the MSS. of Boughton and Althorp freely at my disposition, and to the numerous friends who have helped me in the Scottish affair, especially Dr. Meikle of the National Library, Edinburgh. I have already, in the Preface to *Blenheim*, rendered thanks to the authorities of the Bodleian, of the Rijks-archief at The Hague, and to those who so kindly helped me at Gibraltar, for assistance that has been valuable to me in preparing both this and the former volume. Col. Goldney kindly had a tracing made for me of an early eighteenth-century plan in the Engineers' House, Gibraltar, on which Map II in this volume is partly based.

NOTE ON METHODS OF DATING

Readers will note the difference between the New Style (N.S.) and Old Style (O.S.) of reckoning dates. Until 1752 the English at home always used the Old Style, after 1700 eleven days behind the New Style of Gregory XIII's Calendar, which was current in all continental countries except Russia. Our sailors, on service at sea and on coast operations like the taking of Gibraltar, generally used the Old Style familiar at home. Our soldiers in the Netherlands and Spain generally but not always used the New. Diplomats abroad most of them used the New, but some the Old. *I employ the O.S. for home affairs ; and for affairs outside England I use the N.S. or put the double date, thus—Aug.* $\frac{2}{13}$.

Anne came to the throne on March 8, 1702—at least, so we say now. But our ancestors called it March 8, 1701. For, with them, the New Year began not on January 1, but on March 25. March 24, 1701, was followed after midnight by March 25, 1702. This is confusing to modern students of old documents, who are liable to get a year out in affairs occurring in January, February or early March, particularly in Parliamentary affairs, as the normal session was held in winter, astride of the two years. The Lords' and Commons' Journals of Anne's reign change from 1701 to 1702 only on March 25. *All modern histories, including this book, begin the new year at January* 1.

CONTENTS

CHAPTER I

CONTENTS

CHAPTER XII

CHAPTER XIII

CHAPTER XIV

CHAPTER XV

CHAPTER XVI

CONTENTS

ILLUSTRATIONS

FRONTISPIECE

QUEEN ANNE IN THE HOUSE OF LORDS.
From the original painting in the Royal Collection at Kensington Palace.
By kind permission.

MAPS

RAMILLIES
AND THE
UNION WITH SCOTLAND

CHAPTER I

AFTER BLENHEIM

The position at home and abroad. Libels on Marlborough : his real
character. Marlborough at Berlin. The Montagu-Churchill marriage.
The Parliamentary Session of the winter 1704–5. Public Records.
'The Tack.' Harley and St. John. The Place Bill. The Aylesbury
Case. Quarrel of the Queen with the High Tories. The General
Election of 1705. The Whig tide begins to rise.

IN the winter following the famous victory on the Danube,
our countrymen took stock of the new situation.   Blenheim
had saved Germany from immediate conquest by France ;
it had dealt the first serious blow to the prestige of Louis
and his soldiers ; it had given a world-wide value to the
British army and to the name of Marlborough ; and it had
renewed the fainting courage of the Allies to continue
their uphill struggle with good hope of success.   But the
war was very far from won.   The objects for which the
sword had been drawn were as yet unattained.   England,
Holland and Austria, as signatories of the Treaty of Grand
Alliance, had bound themselves to drive the French out
of Italy and the Spanish Netherlands.   Three years had
passed since then, but the Spanish Netherlands and Italy
were still in the hands of France.

Henry St. John, the Secretary at War, wrote in the
summer of 1705 : 'we want seven years' success to be as
far advanced in Flanders as King William was when he
began.' [1]   Ramillies was destined to reduce the seven years
to as many months, but at the time when St. John wrote so
despondently no one could foresee Ramillies, or could even
be sure that Marlborough would ever again be allowed to

attack the enemy in the field.   For, in the very year after
Blenheim, not only did the Imperialists fail to support his
great designs on the Moselle, but the Dutch Generals again
forbade him to give battle on their frontiers.

But if the lesson of Marlborough's genius at Blenheim
had been taught in vain to those in Holland and Germany
who refused to learn, it had its full effect in our island.
Bishop Burnet was not the only man whose ' heart was so
charged with joy he could not sleep ' on the night when the
news came through.[2]   In manor house, farm and workshop
a race of country-folk, who commonly heard and thought
about little save their own quiet occupations, were stirred
by the strange tidings from the Danube, which opened
wider vistas to the imagination, recalled fireside talk of
King Harry at Agincourt and Queen Bess at Tilbury, and
pointed forward to a future of illimitable magnitude for
their country and their children, dimly descried like the
sun rising behind the mist.   There was little fear that
England would be misled by militaristic ideals or dreams
of continental expansion in Europe, for her very prejudices
were anti-military.   But Blenheim knit her determination
to trust Marlborough and to win the war.   Although
party politicians were still at odds on that issue, the central
body of public opinion was now fixed, and the Queen
exerted the great power of the Crown to give effect to the
national resolve, overriding the factions of partisans.   The
union of Crown and people in support of Marlborough was
the secret of the General Election of 1705, which sealed
the doom of Louis XIV's ambition.   Only after the *annus
mirabilis* of Ramillies and Turin had given the essential
victory to the Allies in 1706, did new situations arise at
home and abroad.

Popular content with the war and with Godolphin's
Ministry was increased by an accident of nature—a series
of abundant harvests.   Between 1702 and 1708 wheat was
more often below than above thirty shillings a quarter—
less than half the terrible price of seventy-two shillings a
quarter to which it suddenly rose in the year of Malplaquet,
when the war became rapidly unpopular.   But during the
critical early years of Anne's struggle with Louis, common

folk in England had enough to eat, both those who bought
their food, and those who ate their own produce. In up-
land parishes the fare in cottage and farm was plentiful,
whenever the crop had been good on the common field of
the village. In those days even well-to-do gentlemen fed
their large households off their own estates : ' we now buy
nothing but sugar and spice in the market, having all
eatables and drinkables at home,' wrote Yorkshire Squire
Molesworth.*

Yet the same gentry, who rejoiced in the rustic plenty
with which during these years their tables were loaded from
their own fields, gardens and coverts, groaned over the
miserable prices of all they sold. The seamy side of good
harvests is portrayed in a letter to Thomas Coke from
another Midland squire, in the Christmas after Blenheim :

It has been thought proper by the legislators to charge four
shillings in the pound upon land, but at the same time I don't hear that
anything is done to enable the owners to pay so great a tax. Never
was less money stirring, or commodities, except foreign, cheaper.
The best beef is but $2\frac{1}{4}d$. a pound, mutton $2d$., wheat $3s$. a bushel,
and all other grain proportionable ; nor can, for want of vent, any of
these things be sold in quantity. Cattle and sheep are sent to fairs
and return unbought, and it's reckoned good market when two or
three strike of corn will go off. The Midland Counties must
inevitably be ruined for want of sale of their goods, and by the
Receivers [tax gatherers] sending that little money away in specie,
that should circulate here.[3]

Had it not been for Marlborough's success on the
Danube, these outcries against the Land Tax would have
taken such effect in the House of Commons as might well
have paralysed the conduct of the war. Actually the
Godolphin Ministry had been reprieved by the news of
Blenheim, but their position was still one of anxiety and
danger when Parliament met in the last week of October
1704 to hold its annual session. The ' Triumvirate,' as
Marlborough, Godolphin and Harley were now called, had
the confidence of the Queen and of the country, but they

* Sept. 25, 1708. Two years later Molesworth writes : ' Our garden is as
empty as it used to be when we had a Scotch Presbyterian gardener.' So Andrew
Fairservice had his prototype in real life ! *H.M.C. Clements* (1913), pp. 239, 247.

had no majority of their own in either House of Parliament. The Cabinet had ceased to represent the Tory party as a whole, and had not yet absorbed any Whig elements to take the place of the High Tory Ministers dismissed in the previous May.* How should the narrow basis of the Ministry be broadened ? The breach with the High Tories was unbridgeable, and the Whigs, who agreed with the Cabinet's policy at home and abroad, demanded, as the price of Parliamentary support, admission to office and to royal favour. The Triumvirate, though most unwilling to share power with the Whig chiefs, were beginning to feel the necessity to do something at least in that direction.

Meanwhile a combination of the two oppositions, Whig and High Tory, was prophesied in various quarters. Defoe, in his new capacity of secret confidential adviser to Harley, warned the Secretary of State that, in the session now beginning, the Whigs would no longer be ' worded in a fool's paradise,' and that ' the two ends would be reconciled to overthrow the middle way,' unless one of the two extreme parties were propitiated by the Moderate Government. ' The Whigs of King William's reign expected to come into play again,' and were saying to each other that Harley must first be turned out from the Speaker's chair, then ' worked out ' from the Secretary's office, and Godolphin driven from the Treasury. Defoe, in thus warning his patron of his danger, urged him to make friends with Somers, the former Whig Chancellor, ' whom all allow to be a great man. United, what may you not do ! Divided, what mischief must ensue to both, and the nation in general ! ' [4]

But there were difficulties of which Defoe, in his lowly station, knew little. The Queen had the strongest prejudice against Somers, as indeed against all the five Lords of the Whig Junto. Moreover, she still moved in the constitutional ideas of former reigns. She conceived the Crown as choosing servants irrespective of party, and leaving them to make what bargains they could with the Houses of Parliament. She would never admit that her Cabinet must be in some sort representative of a majority in Parliament.

* See *Blenheim*, pp. 335–337.

Nor in this was she singular. The need to adjust the composition of the Ministry to the character of the House of Commons was not an accepted theory of the day, although the troubles towards the close of the last reign had illustrated the necessity to the full, and had finally made a considerable impression on the mind and conduct of William III.

In these circumstances, the Duchess of Marlborough,* on behalf of the Whig party, kept up all autumn a double pressure, by word of mouth on ' poor unfortunate Mrs. Morley,' who still loved ' dear, unkind Mrs. Freeman,' and by letter on her husband still in the field. At the end of October 1704, before the session began, Marlborough replied from Germany to his wife's political demands : ' while I live I will meddle with no business but what belongs to the army '—surely one of his less candid assertions. But a fortnight later he capitulated, informing her : ' I have writ to my Lord Treasurer as you desired concerning the Dukes of Buckingham and Newcastle. I can refuse you nothing.' Already, before Parliament met, Harley had put himself into friendly correspondence with the great Whig magnate, the Duke of Newcastle, whose word was law at election time in various boroughs of Notts and Yorkshire, whose ' estate is so very great he would certainly be of use ' to the Ministry, and who was not one of the notorious Junto so much dreaded by the Queen. Harley saw in Newcastle a solid buttress for the system of moderate non-party government, which he desired to establish under the shield of the royal authority. It was beginning to be understood that the Privy Seal might soon be taken from the High Tory, Buckingham, and given to

---

* At this period of her life, intellectually her prime, Sarah must have been a more attractive and a nobler creature than the grim fury into which she assuredly degenerated. Otherwise, not even a friend, who owed his Peerage to her advocacy, could have written as Lord Hervey wrote of her to Sir R. Cocks in July 1704 : ' Did you know her but half as well as I have the happiness to do, she would make you think of her as one said of the sea, that it infinitely surprised him the first time he saw it, but that the last sight of it made always as wonderful an impression as if he had never observed it before. She hath a most acute and elevated understanding, equally partaking of the solid as well as the shining faculty, a mind so richly furnished with all those amiable talents of prudence, justice, generosity, constancy and love of her native country that she ought to have been born in the golden age !' *Hervey, L.B.,* I, p. 205.

Newcastle, though the change did not actually take place till the following spring.[5]

The Whigs had recently learned much in the school of adversity. Their action was decided by the counsels of the closely united Junto and its advisers ; Whig party discipline, though sometimes weak in William's reign, was strong under Anne. So the party had the sense to wait in patience for the inevitable hour of its return. It made no alliance with the High Tory malcontents. But it continued its pressure on the Ministry, lifting its hand to threaten but not to strike. That winter, Wharton declared that he ' had now the Lord Treasurer's head in a bag.' The Lords of the Junto could dictate the policies, though they could not yet share the perquisites of government. Their young henchman, Robert Walpole, was already recognized as the ' leader ' of the Whigs in the Lower House. ' He will always either be laughing or talking,' a colleague complained ; but the cheery and irresponsible covert-side manner of the Norfolk squire masked a shrewd and cautious instinct for the real chance in politics.

And so, when the House met, Harley, though principal Secretary of State, was allowed still to occupy the Speaker's chair, in order to prevent the otherwise certain choice of a more pronounced Tory. The session began without a government defeat, and, as it went on, the violence of the High Tory attack on policies common to the government and to the Whigs, soon drew together all to whom the success of the continental war was the first of political objects.[6]

Oct. 24 1704

High Church anger was directed all this winter, with ever-increasing personal bitterness, both against the Queen herself and against her servants. In a celebrated pamphlet entitled the *Memorial of the Church of England*, Godolphin and Marlborough were denounced as renegades, ' who owe their present grandeur to the protection of the Church, and who with a prevarication as shameful as their ingratitude, pretend to vote and speak for it themselves, while they solicit and bribe others with pensions and places to be against it.' Godolphin, though brought up a Tory, was stung by these attacks into a hostility to the Church clergy surpassing that of the Whigs themselves. For all his apparent placidity, he was less patient of abuse than laughing Wharton. As early as September 1704 he wrote to Harley ' a discreet clergyman is almost as rare as a black swan ' ; and in the following September, ' I have heard of several insolences of the clergy, which are really insufferable and next door to open rebellion, and I don't find the least notice taken of it, or the least thought or disposition to reprehend any of them.' In that sentence we have the germ of the impeachment of Sacheverell four years later.[7]

From this time also we can date the bitterness of the High Tory vendetta against Marlborough, with those tales of his avarice, meanness and treachery which the genius of Swift, a few years later, stamped upon the national consciousness so indelibly that the great Whig historian of the Nineteenth Century became, in a manner, their dupe. ' The spirit of lying,' wrote Marlborough in May 1705, ' runs away with more Torrys than ever I had the honour to know.'

His covetousness was very remarkable [wrote one of these sage critics] ; as he was riding one day in Flanders, and had only a pair of linen gaiters on, they were extremely wet so that they could not be taken off without tearing ; he bid his servant that took them off to take care to rip them in the seam that they might be sewed up again.

Monstrous, indeed ! But worse still, his spelling was bad.

This man who made so great a noise in the world, had the fewest qualifications. Learning he had none, for he could not spell English.

We are told, on the authority of the same critic, that the Duke was guilty of spelling *Cardinal* as *Cardonel*, like his secretary's name ! * On another occasion, in 1705, Joshua Barnes, Professor of Greek at Cambridge, brought to the War Office an edition of Anacreon, which he wished

---

* Specimens of his actual spelling can be seen in his letters to Heinsius as printed in the Appendix, p. 407, below. It is no worse than the spelling of the great majority of educated men in his period, and much better than that of most ladies, *e.g.* Lady Wentworth's letters in the *Wentworth Papers*: ' The Duke of Molbery,' ' the Queen of Prushee,' ' Gibletor ' (Gibraltar), ' yousles,' etc. Or compare the letter of James Gordon to the Earl of Seafield—' I am necessitat once mor to trobubell your Lordsip, that ye vill be pleassed to speck to hir Majesty the Quan of Great Breatten, to proquar on letter to is Majesty the King off Suadlan,' etc. *Seafield*, 1912, p. 370. For Marlborough's generous style of living on campaign see p. 62, below.

to dedicate to Marlborough, not without hope of such modest reward in guineas as a Cambridge Professor might then expect from ' the great.'

Mr. St. John, who was Secretary at War, was then in the room, the Duke comes up to him : ' Dear Harry, here's a man comes to me and talks to me about one Anna Creon, and I know nothing of Creon, but Creon in the play of Oedipus, prithee do you speak to the man.' Mr. St. John said the Duke never gave the man any, but he was forced himself to pay him.

Disgraceful indeed that we should have our battles won by a fellow who has not heard of Anacreon and has his linen gaiters slit at the seam !   But nations at war have to make what shift they can.   The gentlemen who were most eager in spreading such pitiful gossip belonged to a class we should now call ' defeatists.'   After the news of Blenheim one of these said it was true a great many men were killed and taken, but that to the French King was no more than a bucket of water out of a river.[8]

Against the coffee-house chat of his political enemies we may set the partial but well-informed evidence of the only human being to whom he ever revealed himself.   In the muniment room at Althorp lie two papers, written by Sarah, Duchess of Marlborough, in the last month of her life, a fierce old woman of eighty-four, with one tender spot left in her withered heart, where she kept still fresh the memory of her dear lord, dead more than twenty years since :

I have read Lediard's History [of Marlborough] which I never did before. . . . It begins with some verses of Mr. Addison's very true and very pretty. . . . Everything I have yet read is so true of the late Duke of Marlborough that I could not read it without wetting the paper.   But then in the Dedication he says as much of the present Duke, who is the reverse of his grandfather in every particular, which makes me quite sick.   (October 4, 1744, to Mr. Mallet.)

The Duke of Marlborough never had any vanity, and therefore living so many years with great employments he left a great estate, which was no wonder he should do, since he lived long, and never threw any money away ; and money was for many years at 6 per cent. And I have heard him solemnly swear, when it was of no signification

to do it to me, that he never in the whole reign of Queen Anne sold
one commission, title or anything to anybody, when he had so much
favour from Queen Anne.   He had a great deal of compassion in his
nature, and to those that he had been long acquainted with he gave
money out of his own pocket to those that were poor, though they
were not of his opinion.   For I was directed by him to pay some
pensions when he was abroad, and have letters to prove the truth
of it from the persons.

He was naturally genteel [she adds] without the least affectation,
and handsome as an angel, tho' ever so carelessly drest.

Marlborough was not a scholar or a student, but he
won the heart of educated posterity by confessing that his
knowledge of English history was drawn from Shakespeare's
plays.   Sarah had no more learning than he : when, after
her husband's dismissal, indignant Whigs compared his ill
treatment by the Tories to the ingratitude showed to the
great general Belisarius, she asked Burnet who that worthy
was and why he had fallen into disfavour.   The Bishop, with
his usual tact, blurted out that one reason of his decline in
the popular esteem was that he had 'a brimstone of a wife.'

While Parliament was sitting in November and early
December, the Duke was still abroad.   Having at length
finished the campaign of 1704 which he had begun on the
Danube and ended on the Moselle,* he spent several weeks,
in spite of headaches and bad health, in riding and driving
fifteen hours a day over nearly a thousand miles of German
roads deep in mud, on his annual winter's task of persuading
prickly Princes to hire out their troops again for service
next year.†   The victor of Blenheim was a powerful as
well as a charming advocate, but he was expected to appear
in person to win his cause.   So the far journey to Berlin
had to be accomplished before he could return to England
to receive the thanks of his own countrymen.

* See Chapter III, pp. 48–52, below, for the Moselle campaign in the autumn.
† Even luxurious travelling was not in those days comfortable.   In August
1704 Lord Fermanagh wrote to Lady Cave : ' Deare Daughter, I'me glad to hear
you are all well after your hot journey, for I am sincible that a glass chariot is an
inconvenient way of travelling in the month of August, but tis Beauish, and that
makes Amends to your sex especially when overgrown with pride.'   *Verney Letters
of 18th Cent.*, I, p. 218.

In Berlin lay the keys of Italy, and only Marlborough could turn them.   Richard Hill, the English envoy at the Court of Savoy, appealed to him to save Turin from capture. It was true that since last summer ' the Princes of Italy fear the Duke of Marlborough's coming, especially the Court of Rome ' ; it was true that the authorities at Genoa and Leghorn had been frightened by the news of Blenheim and by the cruises of the English fleet into a friendly be-haviour towards our merchant ships.   But these favourable symptoms would quickly disappear if the French overcame the last resistance of Savoy-Piedmont.   And in Hill's opinion that event was certain unless help could be devised by England.   ' We have not soldiers enough in Piedmont,' he wrote to Marlborough, ' to put a garrison in Turin.' The Emperor's letters pointed to the same conclusion : he could send no more Austrian troops to Italy because the Hungarian rebels, with whom he obstinately refused to come to terms, were pressing him hard at home.   He called instead upon Marlborough to find somewhere the troops to relieve their Savoyard ally.   Could not Frederick I of Prussia be persuaded to hire out another 8,000 men to England, and send them into the valley of the Po in the early spring ?

But there were difficulties in the way of aid from Prussia. Frederick lived in constant alarm from the presence beyond his eastern frontier of Charles XII of Sweden, with his victorious army and unaccountable temper.   The King of Prussia detested the Emperor and the Austrians ; and he had for more than two years past been engaged in a bitter diplomatic wrangle with the Dutch government over the will of their late Stadtholder William III, to whose property he claimed to be heir.   But if Holland and Austria were ill thought of at Berlin, England was in high favour. Frederick had on hand a design to introduce a German translation of the English Book of Common Prayer, *mutatis mutandis*, as the form of service in his dominions, and so unite his Lutheran and Calvinist subjects.   The golden opinions which the Prussian troops had won at Blenheim had aroused the martial pride of the Court of Berlin ; and the ever provident Marlborough, throughout all the pre-

occupations of his Danube campaign, had found time to
' write often to the King and please him extreamly.'

So when, in the last week of November, the tired
traveller reached Berlin, he was welcome there as no other
man in Europe.   In a few days Marlborough had calmed
the King's anger against the Dutch, allayed his fears of
Sweden, and negotiated a Treaty by which 8,000 Prussian
bluecoats were to cross the Alps, and England and Holland
were to pay 300,000 crowns for their year's service.   Marlborough, by his painful winter's journey to Berlin, had
provided bare salvation for Turin in 1705, and prepared
the means by which the French were expelled from Italy
in the following year.

Coming back by way of the Court of Hanover, where
it was always well to pay one's respects, he sailed from
Holland with the captive Marshal Tallard as his companion
on the yacht, and landed in England on December 14, 1704,
at the critical moment of the session, and in no good
humour with the High Tories.   ' I find,' he had written
from Hanover, ' that only zeal and success is capable of
protecting me from the malice of a villainous faction.' [9]

That winter, the victor of Blenheim, aided by his wife,
brought to completion a private treaty which further
strengthened his political position between Whig and
Tory.   His two elder daughters had already been well
and usefully disposed of to Sunderland and to Godolphin's
son ; it was now the turn for his favourite younger
daughter, Lady Mary Churchill.   Tradition says she had
set her heart on a private gentleman, but in that age even
favourite daughters of ' the great ' were no more permitted
to carve for themselves than Princesses of the Blood.   In
March 1705, before Marlborough left for the spring campaign, he saw her married to John Montagu, whose father,
Ralph, was thereupon made first Duke of Montagu.   Ralph
was a clever ruffian, of the worst Restoration school in
public and private affairs, but he was a man of immense
possessions, which made him a political power apart from
party.   Marlborough and he both found their advantage
in the alliance, though even the Churchills dared not ask of
the Queen all the rewards demanded by their new relation.

The marriage of the young people does not seem to have been unhappy. John Montagu, who succeeded to the Dukedom in 1709, was a pleasant dilettante, liked by almost everyone except his mother-in-law Sarah, who wrote him down a fool. He is still remembered in Northamptonshire as a planter of mighty avenues, and, like his unscrupulous old father, was a wise patron of the arts. He inherited the finest modern town house in London ' for stateliness of building and curious gardens '—Montagu House, on the site of the present British Museum—while the finest example of French architecture of the period to be found in rural England was Boughton House, near Kettering, which his father had built in William's reign, and adorned with splendid French tapestries, hung in panelled rooms that vied with the chambers of Wren's Hampton Court. It is to be hoped that these splendours, and an agreeable husband, consoled the beautiful Mary Churchill ; and by the look of her in her pictures, at the head of her band of pages, she seems to have found her greatness very tolerable.*

When the winter session of 1704–5 began, the fate of the Godolphin Ministry seemed to hang in the balance. It lacked a majority of its own in either House, and it was liable to attack both from the Whig and the High Tory side; it was strong only in the glamour of Blenheim and in the favour of the Queen. Anne was persuaded to intervene actively on behalf of her servants. Her speech to the Houses exhorted them to be ' entirely united at home,' because ' our enemies have no encouragement left but what arises from their hopes of our divisions. 'Tis therefore your concern not to give the least countenance to those hopes. I hope there will be no contention among you but who shall most promote the public welfare.' Anne had lost all enthusiasm for the Occasional Conformity Bill, because

* Boughton House, including the furniture, is to-day (1932) probably the most perfect and unaltered example of a great mansion of the time of William and Anne, both outside and within. For Mary Churchill's marriage and her relations and houses see also *Dict. of Nat. Biog.*; *H.M.C. Buccleugh*, I (1899), pp. 351–357 ; Thomson's *Memoirs of Duchess of Marl.* (1839), II, pp. 8–16 ; Strype's *Stow's London*, Bk. IV, p. 85.

she could think of nothing but the war, while the High
Tories were so angry at the repeated rejections of their
favourite measure that they could not think about the war
at all. The misunderstanding was therefore complete
between the Queen and the loyalists who, only two years
before, had ecstatically hailed the advent of their crowned
pupil.

Further to protect her Ministers, Anne revived during
this session an old custom of Charles II. She attended
unofficially the most important debates in the House of
Lords. The Merry Monarch had found it ' as good as a
play ' to watch Shaftesbury denounce the royal policies,
with his politic eyes asquint at the face of his sovereign,
standing ' incognito ' with his back to the fireplace. If
Anne, seated on the same spot, got less amusement she got
as much instruction from the debates to which she listened.
What she heard increased her indignation with Nottingham
and her old High Tory friends, while the Whig chiefs
seized the opportunity to mitigate her prejudices against
themselves by defending her Ministers before her face.
Her Majesty's presence caused such crowds to jostle for
admission that their Lordships ordered

That Sir Christopher Wren, Her Majesty's Surveyor General, do
forthwith take care and give order for the making of a gallery over the
lobby door across the House with four benches.[10]

Wren was also engaged at the instance of the House of
Lords in another work of particular interest to historians.
He was fitting up in the Tower of London apartments
suitable for the preservation of the National Archives. A
committee of their Lordships had discovered that ' a
mountain of broken records,' Plantagenet and Tudor, were
perishing by ' cartloads ' under the leads of the White
Tower and in Caesar's Chapel.

While Wren was thus engaged in providing quarters
for ' the chronicles of wasted time,' he may well have been
visited at his work by an *habitué* of the Tower, Isaac Newton,
Master of the Mint ; there were giants on English earth
in those days.

Meanwhile a first consignment of the State Papers of the

Middle Ages was being edited at the public expense by Thomas Rymer ; the mighty tomes of his *Foedera* continued to appear, year after year, from 1704 until the end of the reign. The systematic publication of our historical records had begun, and the way was being prepared for the great antiquarian movement of the Eighteenth Century.[11]

But while the Queen watched the proceedings of 'the great' among the Armada tapestries in the Upper House, St. Stephen's Chapel was the scene of the most critical act of the session. For, although only the lesser political leaders were in those days to be found in the House of Commons, it was there and there alone that taxes could be voted to carry on the war. At the end of the last session Nottingham and other High Tories had said in their wrath that next time the Commons should 'tack' the Occasional Conformity Bill to supply.* That Bill, aimed against the Dissenters and the Whig influence in Corporations and Parliamentary elections, had been lost in the Lords in two successive sessions, after passing the Tory House of Commons with enthusiasm. It had become the touchstone of party feeling. It was hoped that by putting it in the same Bill as the Land Tax, the financial mainstay of the war, the Lords would be compelled to pass it. Before Parliament met in the autumn of 1704, William Bromley, member for Oxford University, summoned a series of meetings of the high-flying party at the Fountain Tavern. There the fox-hunters over their October ale decided on the policy of the tack, which would certainly please the dons and the clergy, but might be less agreeable to the Queen and the nation. Those who put it forward argued that if the House of Lords were compelled to choose between passing the Occasional Conformity Bill and throwing out the war taxes, they would pass the two together. But in fact this was by no means certain. For their Lordships, without distinction of party, had pronounced 'tacking' to be unconstitutional, and in defence of its corporate privileges the Upper Chamber might prove as regardless of the national interest as the Tackers themselves.

* *Coxe,* chap. xx, vol. I, p. 229. For the Occasional Conformity Bill see *Blenheim,* pp. 277–280, 330–332.

Early in the session, the motion to tack the Occasional
Conformity Bill to the Land Tax was proposed by Bromley,
Nov. 28 and backed by Sir Edward Seymour and Sir John
1704 Packington, the Worcestershire Baronet, famous
for his quarrels with Lloyd the Whig Bishop of
that region. But otherwise there are few names of
any distinction in the division list of the Tackers. On
this question the Whig opposition was swelled by the
Moderates and the Ministerial Tories, including Mr.
Secretary Hedges, Henry St. John the Secretary at War,
Sir Simon Harcourt, Henry Boyle one of the members
for Cambridge University, and the cadets of the Houses of
Harley and Godolphin. The fine Tory soldier, Cutts the
' Salamander,' told the House that the Tack, involving as
it would the loss of the chief war taxes, ' would give
the French King almost as great advantage as we had
gained over him at Blenheim.' In the critical division it
was defeated by 251 votes to 134.

The excitement in the country was such that the division
list, contrary to the usual custom, was published and closely
scrutinized. The Tackers' names were noted down for
denunciation by war-patriots of all parties in the coming
General Election. Marlborough wrote to Godolphin that,
according to the laws of war, as the Tackers gave no quarter
they should be given none ; and Godolphin wrote to the
Duchess Sarah : ' I shall never think any man fit to continue in his employment who gave his vote for the tack.'
The Tackers replied by giving the name of ' Sneakers ' to
those Tories who had refused to support Bromley's motion.
Sneakers and Tackers went to the polls next April, hating
each other worse than either hated the Whig party—the
tertius gaudens.

An examination of the division list shows how complete had been the split in the Tory ranks from the Cheviots
to Land's End. The forty Tory members for the Cornish
Boroughs, not unevenly divided between the Godolphin
and the Seymour influence in those parts, showed a small
majority against the Tack. Oxfordshire, whose representatives had initiated the policy under pressure of the clerical
dons upon Bromley, was one of the very few counties

that was solid for the Bill. An election song of the following spring comments thus :

> Perusing the list of the Tackers in print,
> And carefully marking what Members were in't,
> Some names I observed to most counties did fall,
> But Oxford afforded no fewer than All.
> Nine Members, Nine Tackers ; and had there more been,
> And their number as great as their spirits were keen,
> A desperate risque we had presently run
> Of the League being broke and the Nation undone.
> But will this agree with their courtship, thought I,
> When the Queen was harangu'd and extoll'd to the sky,
> On her way to the Bath by the literate fry ? *
> Or can we imagine it mightily sutes
> With thanks for her gift of the Tenths and the Fruits ? †
> Unless it be grateful in sons of the Church,
> Their best benefactors to leave in the lurch ;
> And when for their sakes she had lessened her store,
> To shut up the purse and supply her no more.

After the defeat of the Tack, the ' Occasional Bill,' in a slightly modified form, was passed by the United Tory vote in the Lower House. But in the Lords it was thrown out as a matter of course, after a debate kept up chiefly to instruct the listening Queen. Marlborough and Godolphin for the first time ventured to vote openly against the Bill which they had now managed to out-manœuvre in three successive sessions.[12]

On the day after the defeat of the Tack in the Commons, Daniel Williams, a famous nonconformist divine, in close alliance with ' the monied interest' on the London Exchange, wrote to congratulate Harley, whose old family connections with Puritanism served him in good stead in his rôle of secret middleman between the Whig and Tory supporters of the war.

God hath honoured you above any [wrote Daniel Williams in reference to Harley's part in the Act of Settlement of 1701] in procuring the settlement of the Protestant Succession. The Bill against Occasional Conformity is apt as well as intended to undermine it, and

* Oxford's loyal reception of Anne on the way to Bath in 1702. See *Blenheim*, pp. 213-214.
† Queen Anne's Bounty.

the best part of the present Ministry in the State as well as the Church.
Nay, had you seen the tottering state of our stocks last night you would
[have seen ?] the crisis the apprehended success of our violent men
would cast us into.[13]

Defoe's reports to Harley of his journeys through
England were giving his patron a broader idea of English
public opinion and of English interests than any that found
its way to High Tory chiefs or Whig aristocrats. The
more pity that Harley was so slovenly a speaker and writer,
so furtive a colleague, so uninspiring a leader, so inferior in
all the publicity of politics to the brilliant St. John. For it
was Harley and not St. John who understood his countrymen.
Harley had Chatham's vision of the real workaday England
that was hidden from partisan politicians and fashionable
place-hunters. But he had not Chatham's power of
expressing the vision that he saw. He understood the need
for national unity, the futility of party and sectarian per-
secutions and slogans of hate. This unfitted him to be the
popular spokesman either of Whigs or Tories, but it fitted
him, by patient delving underground, to keep Marlborough
and Godolphin in office until they had beaten France.

St. John, at present doing the nation good service as
Secretary at War, and still writing to Harley as ' dear
master,' was destined at the end of the reign to resume his
former rôle of High Tory orator and afterwards, for six
months, to act as the Pretender's secretary. After that
irreparable act of folly, bitterly and vainly repented, Bolingbroke spent his later years in preaching with his pen
Harley's gospel of national reconciliation, an unconscious
convert to his rival's point of view. People who admire
Bolingbroke's *Patriot King* do not always realize that the
doctrine is the doctrine of Harley, against which the most
brilliant episodes of St. John's active life had been a protest.
Queen Anne, so long as she was guided by ' the Triumvirate ' of Godolphin, Marlborough and Harley, was ' the
Patriot King ' of Bolingbroke's later dreams, the protestant
sovereign above party, and above aristocratic cliques, freely
selecting the ministers of the Crown with thought neither
for Whig nor Tory, but only for the common good. It
was not the ultimate form of the Constitution, which

developed instead on the lines of the Party Cabinet, with the monarch in the background. But it had its moment of realization ; its truest success was not in the early years of George III when America was lost, but in the early years of Anne, when the great war was won.

The heavy defeat of the Tack at the end of November was the true moment of crisis in the session, but danger Dec. and discomfort were still the lot of the Ministry, 1704- placed like a football between two teams of rough Mar. and angry players. As the session went on, the 1705 ball came more and more into the possession of the Whig side, as Godolphin grew into an ever-closer understanding with the Lords of the Junto. The affairs of Scotland, which had in the last few months passed completely out of his control into a highly dangerous state, were debated in the Lords, and a vote of censure on the Lord Treasurer's handling of Scotland seemed certain, when Wharton crossed over to the Bench where Godolphin sat and, in a whispered conversation, exchanged pledges with him, and 'diverted the whole debate.' * So, too, when the Whigs in the Lower House threatened to join with the Tackers to invite over the Electress Sophia of Hanover to reside in England as prospective heir—always a favourite measure of Opposition throughout the reign— Godolphin induced the Lords of the Junto to call off their hounds in the Commons, because of the extreme uneasiness that any such proposal would cause to the Queen.[14]

A similar manœuvre defeated the Place Bill. The High Tories, persuaded that the Tack had been defeated by placemen and place-hunters, moved that all who Jan. 27 held paid office under the Crown should be excluded 1705 from the Commons.† The Whigs, not being yet in office, were tempted, as the Opposition was always tempted, to vote for this popular cure for 'mercenary

---

* See pp. 245–246, below.

† The Tackers 'found themselves so much mistaken in their numbers that they are still more and more incensed against the Ministry, who they say have debauched their party from them. And therefore they are not likely to make much difficulty of excluding any place man out of the House.' Vernon to Duke of Shrewsbury, Jan. 10, 1705. *Boughton MSS.*

Parliaments.' But Walpole had his cue, acted as teller
for the ' Noes,' and brought up just enough Whigs to vote
with Government and defeat the Tackers' Place Bill by six
votes.   If it had become law, not only would the Godolphin
Ministry have been destroyed, but incidentally the growth of
the English Constitution would have been diverted into a
totally different channel, since the House of Commons
would have deprived itself of all direct communication with
Ministers of the Crown.   If the House of Lords alone had
been allowed to offer seats to Ministers, our Constitution
must have become even more aristocratic, and the conflict
between an irresponsible House of Commons on one side
and a high-born Executive on the other would have become
more and more dangerous to the peace and efficiency of
Government.[15]
     Meanwhile the House of Lords, under Whig guidance,
was holding a prolonged enquiry into naval administration.
The political object of the enquiry was twofold : first to
diminish the glory of Admiral Rooke by an inquest upon
his year's work at Gibraltar and Malaga, which his High
Tory admirers had unwisely set up against the achievement
of the victor of Blenheim ; and in the second place to
discredit the general administration of the Admiralty as
conducted by a Tory Board, presided over by Marlborough's
brother, George Churchill, a better Tory than himself.
Except as a political manœuvre, a form of Whig pressure
on the Ministry, little came of the enquiry, beyond a
collection of evidence about the Gibraltar campaign and
the state of the Navy, very useful to future historians.
     The Committee reported that the difficulty of finding
sailors for the Royal Navy in spite of Bounties and the
Press Gang lay in the higher rates of wages paid by the
Merchant Service.   The administration of the Naval
Board was shown to be defective, and the debt of the Navy
had risen by a million and a quarter in two years, out of
all proportion to the very moderate debts in other branches
of the administration.   Such were the complaints made by
the Lords' Committee, but they had few positive remedies
to recommend.[16]   The proposed economy of serving out
three quarts instead of one gallon of beer a day to each man

before the mast would, they reported, only save £21,000, and would be ' taken as a discouragement to the seamen.' *

At length the distemper of partisanship came to a head, and a clash between the two Houses on the famous Aylesbury case of Ashby *versus* White put a sudden end to the session. The modern reader may find amusement and instruction in the social and political, as well as in the legal aspects of this great constitutional quarrel over a straw, when a cobbler's vote shook the State and dissolved a Parliament.

In the reign of Victoria the trial of Election Petitions was made over, none too soon, to the Judges and Law Courts of the land. But in Stuart times the right of trying disputes about alleged corruption or false returns at elections was one of the privileges most cherished by the House of Commons. Indeed, so long as the Judges were the removable nominees of the Crown, it would have been dangerous for the liberty of Parliament to allow Election Petitions to be tried before tribunals presided over by Scroggs or Jeffreys. After the Revolution there was less need for distrust of the Law Courts, but the Commons still clung to their ancient privilege and abused it shamefully. When a new Parliament met, the question whether Whigs or Tories were in the majority was brought at once to two tests of party strength, the voting for the new Speaker and the voting on the first batch of Election Petitions. No one pretended that justice was done on the evidence. Sir Edward Seymour, the veteran leader of the Tories of the South-West, once exclaimed in the House, ' If the Lord should be extreme to mark what was done amiss by us in the matter of elections here, Mr. Speaker, the Lord have mercy on us all.' The conduct of the Tory majority in this matter after the General Election of 1702 had been grossly partisan ; and the conduct of the Ministerialist and Whig majority on the following Parliament of 1705 was

---

* The seamen on service usually received money in lieu of part of the gallon due to them, which we are told was more than they wished to drink. And in the Mediterranean and hot climates where beer would not keep, ' each man may have in lieu of one gallon of beer, one pint of strong sound wine for each day '— which I suppose they watered ! *H. of L. MSS.* (1704–1706), pp. 222–223.

destined to be no better, when, as Burnet himself confesses,
' Most of the controverted elections were carried in favour
of the Whigs.   In some few they failed, more by reason
of private animosities than by the strength of the other
side.'[17]

Such a system of dealing with Election Petitions encouraged returning officers to act with unfairness.   If they
thought that their party was likely to be strong enough
in the new House of Commons to bear them out, some of
them cared little what they did.   And so it happened at
Aylesbury, in the General Election of December 1700,
when the Mayor White and other Tory constables had
struck off the register several Whigs who were entitled by
law to vote, including a certain cobbler named Ashby.*

Incidents of this sort were common all over the country,
and nothing said.   But Aylesbury was one of the boroughs
in Buckinghamshire where the indefatigable Whig orga-
nizer, Lord Wharton, was building up an interest.   He
induced Ashby to bring an action against White for
defrauding him of his vote.   ' I do not think,' said Sir
Edward Seymour in the House of Commons, ' there was
virtue enough in the cobbler of Aylesbury, nor had he
purse enough, if a Lord had not acted that part.'   To
which Lord Hartington replied ' I think the liberty of a
cobbler ought to be as much regarded as of anybody else :
that is the happiness of our constitution.'[18]

Under such distinguished patronage, Ashby brought
his action at the Assizes and won it.   The Assize Court
ordered his name to be restored to the Register of Voters.
But the Tories and the House of Commons denied the
jurisdiction of any Law Court in any electoral matter.
Mayor White found himself supported by all the Tories
of England, as cobbler Ashby by all the Whigs, and their
respective moves in a long series of lawsuits spreading over
four years were dictated to them by rival coteries of ' the
great.'

White appealed to the Queen's Bench to quash the
proceedings of the Assizes, on the ground that only the

---

* By some accounts he was a cobbler, by others an ostler ; like many people
in the country towns of those days, he may have had more than one occupation.

House of Commons had the right to decide cases of a claim
to electoral franchise.   Three out of four of the Queen's
Bench Judges decided in favour of White, the House of
Commons and the Tories ; but the contention of Ashby,
the Assize Court and the Whigs was upheld by no less a
dissentient than Lord Chief Justice Holt.   The doctrine
that Holt laid down was this : Election Petitions, he allowed,
were the proper business of the House of Commons, with
which no Law Court could interfere ; but a man's individual right to vote was a piece of his property, and if it
were taken away he must needs have his remedy in the
ordinary Courts.   Otherwise, argued Holt, what redress
has a man defrauded of his vote if there is no Election
Petition ?   His case will never come before the House of
Commons and he will have no remedy if he is debarred
from suing at the Assizes.   Holt was too cautious to add
what all the world was saying, that in electoral cases the
House of Commons seldom did justice according to the
evidence.

In reply to the Lord Chief Justice it was urged that
Election Petitions, admittedly subject to the jurisdiction of
the House of Commons alone, frequently involved questions
of the right of individuals to vote.   Both classes of questions
must, therefore, come before one tribunal, and that tribunal
could only be the House of Commons.   Ashby *versus*
White was indeed a nice case on which constitutional
lawyers are still divided, but no longer, as in Anne's reign,
on party lines.

The next stage in the proceedings had more serious
consequences.   Ashby and his Whig patrons had been
beaten in the Queen's Bench, but since the Lord Chief
Justice had pronounced in their favour, they carried up
their case to the House of Lords as the Supreme Court of
Appeal.   This was in the winter before Blenheim, three
years after the original wrong had been done to Ashby.
It was the custom in the Lords for the whole House to vote
on judicial matters—not merely the Law Lords as in our
more scrupulous age.   The Whigs had normally a small
majority in the House, but on this occasion it was swelled
by many Tory Peers who felt that they must stand up for

the jurisdiction of their Chamber, and curb the encroach-
ments of the Commons. Jealousy between the Houses
was often a stronger motive than party feeling itself. Holt's
opinion, therefore, was upheld in the House of Lords, and
that of his three learned brothers was upset by a vote of
55 Peers to 16, a majority greatly in excess of that normally
at the service of the Whigs.

In the serious feud between the Houses that arose from
this decision, the real grievance of the Tories and of the
Lower Chamber lay in this, that the supreme Law Court
in the land was a party interested in the suit, that it was
moreover a political assembly of Whig inclination, and that
in its corporate capacity it was the rival of the Commons
House.* In these circumstances it was but natural that the
Commons should take their stand on the somewhat mystical
ground that the privileges of Parliament are not derived
from the Common Law, but have an independent source
which renders them exempt from the jurisdiction of the
House of Lords as Court of Appeal. The cobbler's vote
had become a point round which revolved the subtlest
questions of legal philosophy and the angriest passions of
national politics.

As soon as it was known that the Lords had decided in
favour of Ashby, St. Stephen's Chapel was in an uproar.
Honourable Members declared that the Upper Chamber
was abusing its judicial powers to make away with the
privileges of the Lower House. The Lords replied by pub-
lishing their decision and their reasons for it, broadcast,
appealing to public opinion, which was prevalently on their
side. The unfairness of the Commons in the electoral cases
was too well known, and the subjects of the land preferred
to have their franchises protected in the ordinary Law Courts
where, since the Revolution, political bias was less marked.

So far the affair had gone in the session that ended in

* On the other hand it was quite possible this session for a High Tory to get
personal justice from the House of Lords in its judicial capacity. A Whig had
called Jack Howe, a ' Papist and Jacobite.' Howe as a Privy Councillor sued him
for *scandalum magnatum* and got £400 damages in the Queen's Bench. The
defendant carried it to the House of Lords, who divided on the question and
upheld the judgment of Lower Court by 48 to 35 votes. *Add. MSS.* (L'H.)
17677, AAA, f. 87 ; *H. of L. J.* xvii, p. 635.

April 1704. In the following winter it came to a final
crisis. Encouraged by Ashby's success in the House of
Lords, Wharton put up five other humble citizens of
Aylesbury to imitate his example. White had deprived all
these men of their votes, and they now sued him in the Law
Courts as Ashby had done, and as the Lords had declared
he had a right to do. The Commons, when they heard it,
were beside themselves with anger. They had not touched
Ashby, but they called the five new litigants to the Bar of
the House, voted them guilty of breach of privilege,
Dec. 5   and caused them to be arrested upon warrants
1704   signed by Speaker Harley, who must secretly have
regarded the whole business as very unfortunate. The five
prisoners, three of whom could not even write their names,
may well have found their detention in Newgate an exhilar-
ating change from the life in the slums of Aylesbury : they
were feasted like aldermen on dainties from the richest
tables of London, while the coaches-and-six of the Whig
aristocracy blocked the street with visitors, come to encourage the latest champions of the cause for which
Hampden died in the field, and Sidney on the scaffold.
The Commons, hearing of these fine doings, moved their
prisoners from Newgate to the direct custody of the
sergeant-at-arms.

A motion was then made in the Queen's Bench for a
habeas corpus to release the five. It was argued that they
had broken no law in bringing an action which the House
of Lords, the final Court of Appeal, had declared to lie in
the similar case of Ashby. This might be true, but the
Commons replied with equal truth that no Law Court had
the right to release prisoners whom the Lower House chose
to arrest for alleged contempt of its privileges. The Queen's
Bench again decided for the Commons, Chief Justice Holt
again dissenting.

Then came the final crisis. The Whigs moved for a
writ of error to bring the matter before the Lords. The
Mar.   Lords petitioned the Queen to grant leave for the
1705   writ of error to be brought in. If she acceded and
allowed the case to be brought before the Lords, they
would undoubtedly order the prisoners to be released and

the Commons would no less certainly refuse to give them up. The two Houses would be in open and violent conflict. The constitutional comedy might lead to a national tragedy. If, on the other hand, the Queen refused the writ of error, she would disoblige the Peerage and would appear to many of her humbler subjects to be refusing them justice and protection against the tyranny of the Commons.

Fortunately a third course was open to the embarrassed lady. The Commons had, before Christmas last, voted the supplies for the year 1705. She therefore brought the stormy session to an end by proroguing Parliament on March 14. Three weeks later she dissolved it, hoping, not in vain, that a General Election would lay this and many other questions to rest, and that a new Parliament would find the Houses in better agreement with one another and with her Ministers.

April 5 1705

As soon as the Houses were prorogued, the five men of Aylesbury automatically recovered their freedom, for the Commons claimed no power to keep people in prison between one session and the next. When the new Parliament met neither House wished to revive the quarrel. The questions raised were left undecided in the sense that neither had the Commons admitted the right of the Law Courts to protect men in their electoral franchises, nor had the Lords admitted the right of the Commons to imprison the men of Aylesbury. Yet in substance the Commons had lost the first case and won the second. For the men of Aylesbury got back their votes by order of the Law Courts, but the Commons had kept them in prison till the end of the session. Neither the liberty of the subject nor the privilege of the Commons had suffered any dangerous wound.[19]

Ever since the New Year, all England had been astir with expectation of a General Election, due that summer under the Triennial Act. As early as January 'some neighbouring gentlemen desired to shoot' the well-stocked woods of Thomas Coke, member for Derbyshire, while he was away on his Parliamentary duties, and 'against election time no gentleman that asked' was denied. In March

'pamphlets fly thick as hail in order to influence the elections.' From the dissolution on April 5 to the
polling, the country was kept for two months in fierce
political agitation. It was not then usual to hold
public meetings or to make speeches to crowds ;
but canvassing, bribery and pressure of every sort became
the business of the countryside and of the market-place.[20]

April–
June
1705

The Queen was induced by her Ministers to prepare the
defeat of the Tackers by small but significant concessions
to the Whigs, enough to give her loyal subjects a lead in the
disposal of their votes, and enable Moderate Tories to use
Her Majesty's name against the High Church candidates,
as in the last election they had used it against the Low.   In
April, therefore, several Lord Lieutenancies and subordinate
Government posts were taken from High Tories and given
to men more Whiggishly inclined, while the Whig Duke of
Newcastle, in pursuance of plans laid long before by Harley,
was made Lord Privy Seal in place of the Jacobitical Duke
of Buckingham.* The Queen was unwilling as yet to go
further, but it was already understood between Godolphin
and the Junto that if the elections went well the Great Seal
should be taken from Wright and put into Whig hands.
The Tackers, by their reproaches against the Queen in
pamphlets† and in common talk, themselves confirmed the
popular belief that the Crown was against them, an impression that proved fatal to every party in turn, at every General
Election throughout the reign.[21]

Politics, especially at election time, had an important
part in the friendships, quarrels and sports even of quiet
country gentlemen.   In most counties the Tory squires
were more numerous than their rivals, but the Whigs were

---

* See p. 5, above.

† The famous *Memorial of the Church of England*, by Dr. James Drake, was
much talked of at election time, and in the early autumn was presented at the Old
Bailey and at the order of the court burnt by the common hangman.   The
Memorial (p. 5) complains that 'contrary to these fears they [the Dissenters] found
the Head of the Church inclined not only to forgive but to forget past injuries,
and that instead of punishment they meet not with so much as a rebuke or a
reproach, but comfortable speeches and kind assurances from the Queen herself,
and good countenance from some of her Prime Ministers, etc.'   The language of
the *Memorial* against the 'Prime Ministers,' Godolphin and Marlborough, is much
stronger, *e.g.* p. 6, above.

almost everywhere formidable. On the racecourse, as the Verneys complained, ' the Whigs have the best horses, since they have all the money,' and Wharton was almost as eager for victory on the turf as at the polls. In a society thus constituted, the open breach in the Tory party between ' Tackers ' and ' Sneakers ' could not fail to ensure a considerable measure of electoral success to the Whigs.[22]

The policy of the Tackers and their friends was to say nothing about the war, but to appeal to the country on the Church in Danger. Ministerialists and Whigs sought to turn the issue on to the war, then at the height of its popularity. The question was which of these two potent forces —Church-feeling, or war-patriotism—was the stronger with borough-owners, forty-shilling freeholders and town corporations ?

Sir John Packington had a banner carried before him whereon was painted a church falling with this inscription *For the Queen and the Church, Packington.* As they were marching through the Foregate street in Worcester they met the [Whig] Bishop's coach in which was a nonconformist teacher going to poll for the captain, but the horses at sight of the Church (as it was believed) turned tail, overturned and broke the coach and very much bruised the holder-forth's outer man, and this raised no small admiration that the Bishop's horses should be afraid of a church.

In Chester the Whig mob cried ' down with the Church,' and ' when about sixty of the clergy headed by the Dean came to poll, they said hell was broke loose and these were the devil's black guard ! ' They then proceeded to break the windows of the Cathedral.

In such places, where the issue was a fair fight between the Church and its opponents, the High Tories were usually successful. But many shires, boroughs and borough-owners were thinking chiefly about the war. The great popular constituency of Middlesex unseated two Tackers and chose two Whigs in their room : from Brentford, where the poll had been taken, triumphal processions of the new members and the army of freeholders who had returned them, set off, some on horseback and some in boats, to parade the streets and the river of the capital, crying out ' No Jacobites,' ' No French Government,' ' No wooden

shoes.' The London crowd that watched them was in full
sympathy ; the City chose four Whigs, and Westminster
got rid of a member who had voted for the Tack.*

At Coventry the High Tory candidates led the mob to
overpower the constables, seize the Town Hall and hold
it against all comers for the three days of the election.
Venturesome Whigs who attempted to force their way in
to record their votes, were knocked down and dragged
along the ground by the hair, or stunned and carried off for
dead. But the members thus elected were unseated by a
vote of the House of Commons. In the boroughs of
Wiltshire the defeated Tories complained of bribery ;
Marlborough town ' was grown as corrupt as any other,'
and at Bedwyn the voters ' were all in an uproar and will
have £6 a man,' which the Whigs were able to supply.
It was noted that the Quakers everywhere, in spite of their
pacific principles, voted for the war party, rather than
commit themselves to the tender mercies of the High
Church zealots. Only in some regions like Dorset, the
village clergy were so ' temperate ' that the Dissenters ' had
nothing to complain of' and therefore would not bestir themselves politically.[23]

At Cambridge the Whigs and Ministerialists had on
their side the Heads of Houses, including the powerful
but unpopular Bentley, and the University's magnificent
Chancellor, the proud Duke of Somerset. These authorities, desiring the overthrow of the High Tories at the
coming election, made the most of the Queen's visit on
April 5, when she stayed at the Lodge, and dined in state
in the hall of Trinity College. The occasion was seized
to confer Honorary Degrees on Lords Sunderland, Orford
and Wharton of the Whig Junto, and the Queen knighted
Isaac Newton, her Master of the Mint, who was prospective
Whig candidate for the University, which he had on some

---

* Early in Anne's reign pamphlets occasionally appeared, vainly recommending
a redistribution of seats more in accordance with wealth and population. It is
remarkable that such reformers calculated that not only western England but also
northern England was over-represented (Middlesex and the Capital of course
under-represented) ; whereas redistribution in 1832 meant an increase in north-
country representation, owing to the Industrial Revolution. *Somers' Tracts*,
XII, p. 410.

former occasions represented in Parliament.   But the High
Churchmen were not to be thus overawed.   At the election
next month they spoke contemptuously of Newton as
' a late made knight ' and, according to the Whig Bishop
of Ely, ' it was shameful to see a hundred or more young
students encouraged in hollowing like schoolboys and
porters, and crying *No Fanatic, No Occasional Conformity*
against two worthy gentlemen that stood candidates.'   The
two ' worthy gentlemen ' were Newton himself and
Godolphin's son Francis, who were handsomely beaten by
a Tacker and another High Tory.   The cry of ' No fanatic '
raised against Isaac Newton by a mob of young gentlemen
about to take holy orders has its humorous side.   Newton
was right at the bottom of the poll, but he had consented
to stand too late and too reluctantly and had refused to
canvass ; it was said that the majority of the residents
had voted for Godolphin and Newton, but had been outvoted by the non-residents, who were for the most part
country parsons.

Oxfordshire was staunch to its nine Tackers, except
that Marlborough's influence in his new estate where the
foundations of Blenheim Palace were being laid, enabled
him to secure the return of Cadogan, his jolly Irish Quarter-
master General, as one of the two members for Woodstock.[24]

The South-West had proved a Tory stronghold at the
election three years before, when the interests of Godolphin,
Sir Edward Seymour and Sir Jonathan Trelawny, Bishop
of Exeter, were exerted all on one side.   But now Seymour's
' Western Empire ' was challenged in Cornwall by
Godolphin ; and the hopes of Whigs, Moderates and
Ministerialists were further raised by the desertion from
the High Tory cause of Trelawny himself and others of
his Cathedral clergy.   Trelawny was still the aspiring and
active prelate he had been when James II had sent him to
the Tower, and his was still a name with which to conjure
in Cornwall.   Patriotism and self-interest now combined to
make him join with the rising tide of Moderatism and
Whiggism.   Largely owing to his change of side, one of the
two Cornish county seats was carried by a Whig, and a fair
proportion of the Cornish boroughs went on this occasion

the same way—though the hold of Seymour and the Tackers on Exeter City could not be shaken. Two years later Trelawny was moved from the poor Bishopric of Exeter to the rich Bishopric of Winchester.

The movement among the abler clergy towards moderate views, as the path alike of promotion and of good sense, was not confined to Trelawny. Wake, whose learning had so well defended the Bishops in their constitutional quarrel with the Lower House of Convocation,* was Dean of Exeter, and had exerted himself on the side of his Bishop at the General Election. Immediately afterwards the Queen made him Bishop of Lincoln, and he was destined ten years later to become Archbishop of Canterbury. In 1705 the place that Wake vacated as Dean of Exeter was filled by the Sub-dean, Lancelot Blackburne, who had taken the same line in local politics ; Blackburne also rose under the Hanoverians to be Archbishop of York. This well-rewarded defection from the hot gospel of the High Church on the part of the leaders of the rising generation of clerics was ominous of much, and Queen Anne was *particeps criminis.* Her simultaneous promotion of the venerable High Churchman, Dr. Bull, to the remote see of St. David's, where he was too old to do duty, was not held in Tory circles to atone for her kindness to the Exeter rebels.[25]

Before midsummer the Grand National Pantomime of the General Election was over, but though it might seem mere clowning to an amused or cynical spectator, the elections had decided the fate of Europe and of Britain. The new House of Commons was not only certain to push on the war in the manner that Marlborough wished, but it was capable of dealing wisely with the very dangerous question of the relation of England to Scotland, now come to the decisive crisis of its long history. The Tory Parliament just dissolved had on the whole served the country well, but it would never have steered the barque of the Scottish Union through the clashing rocks. In the new Parliament, Whigs and Ministerial Tories formed a

June
1705

* See *Blenheim*, pp. 286–287.

solid phalanx that dominated both Houses and gave free play to the policies of Marlborough and Godolphin, Queensberry and Somers.

When the election results were examined, it was agreed that High Toryism had suffered a defeat, but the strength of parties could not be precisely stated in days when many members had no distinct allegiance. The Whigs claimed that the figures were 240 Whigs, 200 Tories and 73 ' who act for the Court and will hold the balance.' Godolphin reckoned that in a particular division there voted 160 Whigs, 190 Tories and 100 ' Queen's servants ' ; others reckoned the Tory Opposition at 170. In any case Whigs and Courtiers would act together and the tone of the new House of Commons would be different from the last. Of 134 who had voted for the Tack, not more than 80 sat in the new Parliament, many having met defeat at the polls. Their enemies the ' Sneakers ' had also suffered owing to the division in the Tory ranks, and the Whigs had gained at the expense both of extremists and moderates.[26]

The Ministry made haste to come to terms with the Whigs before the Houses met. Walpole was given a seat on the much criticized Admiralty Board. Sunderland, Marlborough's son-in-law and his representative on the Whig Junto, was sent to Vienna in state, to congratulate the young Emperor Joseph on his accession after his father Leopold's death. Argyle was sent as High Commissioner to Scotland.

The disposal of the Great Seal was more difficult, owing to the unwillingness of the Queen to give it to an avowed member of the Whig party, though she realized that so hot a Tory as Wright could no longer hold it. On July 11, 1705, after the result of the General Election was known, she wrote to Godolphin:

I wish very much that there may be a moderate Tory found for this employment [the Great Seal]. I must own to you I dread the falling into the hands of either party, and the Whigs have had so many favours showed them of late, that I fear a very few more will put me insensibly into their power, which is what I'm sure you would not have happen to me no more than I. I know my dear unkind friend [Sarah] has so good an opinion of all that party that she will use

all her endeavour to get you to prevail with me.   I do put an entire
confidence in you, not doubting but you will do all you can to keep
me out of the power of the *merciless men of both parties.*

But Godolphin felt obliged to support Sarah's request that
the Great Seal should be entrusted to the hands of the
moderate Whig, Sir William Cowper, an able lawyer and
an agreeable man.   The Queen in despair appealed to
Marlborough to protect her against the insistence of his wife
and of his colleague, but she received from him the following reply from abroad : ' If I had the honour of being with
you, I should beg on my knees that you would lose no time
in knowing of my Lord Treasurer what is fit to be done,
that you may be in a condition of carrying on the war, and
of opposing the extravagances of these mad people ' ; if not,
she must send again for Rochester and Nottingham, and be
contented to lose the war.   At length she surrendered to
this reasoning, urged by the combined remonstrances of her
three friends ; in October, Cowper became Lord Keeper
of the Great Seal.   The stage was thus set for the new
Parliament, and for the decisive actions of the reign at
home and abroad.[27]
    Henry St. John took the new situation philosophically.
He thought the High Tories had overreached themselves
and must pay the penalty, till the war was won.   He wrote
to his intimate Tom Coke, the Tory Squire of Derbyshire,
to ask :

What temper you find gentlemen in ; whether they will think it
reasonable to support the Queen, who has nothing to ask but what we
are undone if we do not grant ; and who, if she does make use of
hands they do not like, has been forced to it by the indiscretion of our
friends.   The real foundation of difference between the two parties
is removed, and she seems to throw herself on the gentlemen of
England.*

* A letter that does credit to the writer ; more so than his letters to the same
correspondent during the same years on another common pursuit.   ' As to whores,
dear friend, I am unable to help thee.   I have heard of a certain housemaid that
is very handsome ; if she can be got ready against your arrival, she shall serve for
the first meal.'   And again, ' Really Tom, you are missed : whoring flags without
you.'   There were blemishes in St. John's make-up for the two parts which he
loved to play alternately—leader of the High Church Party and moral philosopher.
H.M.C. Coke (1889), pp. 49, 61, 63.

CHAPTER II

THE DEFENCE OF GIBRALTAR
(Oct. 1704—April 1705)*

THE formation of the Portuguese Alliance of 1703, that opened to the English Grand Fleet the magnificent harbour of Lisbon, had been followed next year by the capture of Gibraltar and the sea fight off Malaga.† These events speedily led to the substitution of English for French naval control of the Mediterranean and prepared the way for the Peninsular War, the great ' side show ' which some of our statesmen like Nottingham regarded as being the war itself. The effort to replace the Bourbon Philip by the Austrian Charles at Madrid absorbed, every year, more and more of England's man-power ; gave an excuse for the prolongation of the war after it had been won in Germany, Flanders and Italy ; and finally ended in failure. But the retention of Gibraltar and Minorca under the British flag gave to England those naval bases south of the Bay of Biscay, without which her maritime power in the Mediterranean could never have been established.

The winter months of 1704–5 witnessed the great effort of France and Spain to recover Gibraltar, with all the vicissitudes of six months' siege full of perilous chances. The defence of the Rock by stout old Eliott for George III is better remembered, because it flames as a bright deed in the darkest hour of Britain's world-defeat, while the similar achievement of Anne's soldiers, sailors and marines was but one laurel leaf in the Queen's crown of victory.

The Eliott of this first defence of Gibraltar by the

---

* *For Maps for this chapter see Map of Europe, No. X, at end of the volume, and Maps I and II, pp.* 36 *and* 40, *below.*

† *Blenheim*, pp. 298–304, and Chapter xix.

British was not himself a Briton.   Prince George of Hesse
Darmstadt, the best type of German aristocrat and soldier,
was a loyal servant of ' Charles III,' the Austrian candidate
for the throne of Madrid ; but he had the good sense,
wanting to Charles's other German advisers, to appreciate
how entirely the chances of success in Spain depended on
friendly co-operation with the English.   He knew the
English well, having served with them in Ireland.*   By his
tact, knowledge and firmness he was as well fitted as any
foreigner could be to command the garrison of Gibraltar.
Even so, the fact that King Charles had set a compatriot of
his own over a force consisting almost wholly of subjects of
Queen Anne caused friction, which would have been fatal
but for Hesse's temper and prudence.

After the battle of Malaga, the Grand Fleet started home
from Gibraltar at the end of August 1704, leaving Hesse
with 1,900 English marines and 400 Dutch, sixty great guns
and as many gunners, all lent by the navy.   In return,
Admirals Rooke and Byng proposed to carry off the brass
cannon and the wine of the fortress.   Hesse insisted on
keeping them, in view of the coming siege.   The two
Admirals departed, in high dudgeon.   Fortunately, their
ill-humour did not communicate itself to Admiral Leake,
who was left on the station with a winter squadron based on
Lisbon, to co-operate with Hesse for the safety of the Rock.

This absurd incident had its serious consequences.
Arising from Hesse's quarrel with the Admirals, there grew
up a movement in the garrison directed against his authority.
At the head of the malcontents was Fox, the Brigadier of
the marines.   Hesse had, perhaps unwisely, appointed as
Governor of the town an Irish Catholic exile called Nugent,
who had been made a noble of Spain by the late King.
Nugent was now, in the name of ' Charles III,' raised to
the rank of a Spanish Major-General.   Fox was furious to
find himself thus placed under yet another foreigner, one
of the conquered Irish !   The personal dispute involved
the political question, whether Gibraltar was to be treated

---

* He had been at William's side on Boyne banks when the famous cannon ball
had wounded the King's arm.   Another had brought down Hesse's horse, causing
William to cry out.' The poor Prince is killed.'

as an English fortress or as a Spanish town of King Charles. The quarrel waxed hot, and might well have been fatal to the defence, had not Fox and Nugent both been killed on duty early in November. The besiegers' cannon impartially solved the problem and enabled Hesse to make a fresh start. He had learnt his lesson, and for the future appointed none but Englishmen. Brigadier Shrimpton succeeded Nugent as Governor of the town ; he and Captain Bennet, the chief engineer of the garrison, became Hesse's loyal supporters until the siege was raised.

Two successive conspiracies to deliver up the place to the enemy were brought to light. The first was of Spanish origin, but the leader of the second was Major Lawrence of the marines, who moved in good English society at home, but who, according to Hesse, had inherited the feud begun against his authority by Byng and transmitted by Fox. Lawrence's treason was discovered in time ; he was tried by court martial, condemned to be shot, but reprieved and eventually reinstated. Like Benbow's action at sea, these ugly incidents remind us that officers' discipline, afloat and ashore, was not yet what it became under Nelson and Wellington, and that the treachery of the age was not confined to statesmen in correspondence with St. Germains. Hesse had reason to regret that he had not allowed the Admirals to go off with the wine, for he deplored the frequent drunkenness and insolence of the English garrison, though he was always loud in praise of their obstinate and tireless valour.[28]

If the French had attacked Gibraltar from the sea, they could not have failed to retake it. The three miles of coast between Europa Point and the Old Mole invited assault ; its defences, at best old-fashioned and inadequate, had been ruined by Byng's bombardment, and could not have withstood such another ordeal or resisted a landing in force. Twice Admiral Pointis was about to attack from sea, and twice Leake came swooping from Lisbon in the nick of time to scatter and destroy his squadron. And when Leake was away the French ships were either themselves absent at Cadiz, or were unable to attack on account of foul weather. The very defects of Gibraltar Bay as an

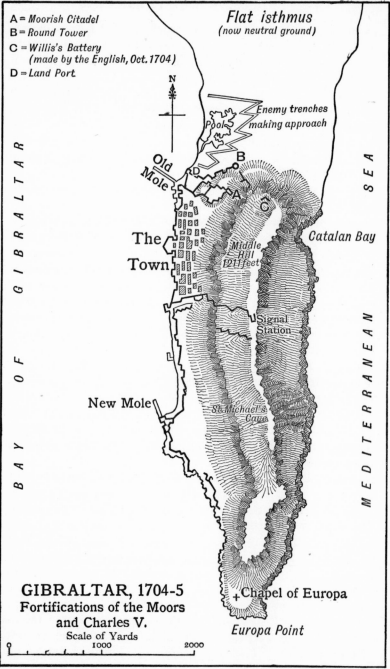

MAP I

A = *Moorish Citadel*
B = *Round Tower*
C = *Willis's Battery*
    (made by the English, Oct. 1704)
D = *Land Port*

Flat isthmus
(now neutral ground)

N

Enemy trenches
making approach

Pool

Old
Mole

B

D

A

C

BAY OF GIBRALTAR

SEA

Catalan Bay

The
Town

Middle
Hill
1211 feet

Signal
Station

New Mole

St. Michael's
Cave

MEDITERRANEAN

GIBRALTAR, 1704-5
Fortifications of the Moors
and Charles V.
Scale of Yards
0   1000   2000

+*Chapel of Europa*

Europa Point

anchorage helped England that winter.   Leake's relieving
squadron was more at home in a gale than the half-hearted
seamen of the French blockade.   'The English,' wrote
Marshal Tessé from the besiegers' camp, 'show us the
way to keep the sea in all weathers, for they sweep to and
fro over it like your swans at Chantilly.'   Gibraltar was
saved by 'the battle and the breeze.'

The protection that Leake gave Gibraltar on the sea
side, intermittent as it was, could never have been given at
all if Lisbon harbour had not been at his disposal owing to
the Portuguese Alliance.   It would have been impossible to
relieve Gibraltar three times in one winter from bases on
the other side of the Bay of Biscay.   Plymouth and Portsmouth were too far away.   But Leake, able to winter snugly
at Lisbon, set himself there with all his energies to prepare
one relief expedition after another for the Rock, fitting out
his hard-used squadron once more to take the winter sea,
and once more to face the foe, while he loaded up transports
with soldiers, food, ammunition, tools and tackle for Hesse's
use.   He was well supplied from home, where the Ministry
fully realized both the importance and the difficulty of
saving Gibraltar.   Men and stores from England were
constantly arriving at Lisbon, and were thence convoyed
to the besieged fortress.

Without supplies from England, Leake could have
done little.   He complained that he had to 'make bricks
without straw,' because the Portuguese docks and magazines
were empty of all necessaries, and the native officials were
unfriendly and inactive.   To make matters worse, John
Methuen, the able envoy who had negotiated the Treaty of
Alliance and had more influence at King Peter's Court than
any other Englishman, was jealous of the Admiral and
began to put obstacles in his way.   However, the two
made up their quarrel just in time to save Gibraltar, for
each had that object very earnestly at heart.   Leake
deserves a high place in England's gratitude.   As a young
Captain he had cut the way through the broken boom
and relieved Londonderry ; as a middle-aged Admiral his
energy, daring and forethought saved Gibraltar.[29]

These favourable conditions at sea made it just possible

that Hesse might succeed in holding against great odds
the northern land-front.   Nature, indeed, had made the
place potentially impregnable on the north, but man had
as yet done little to avail himself of these abundant natural
means of defence.   There were as yet no galleries or gun-
emplacements hollowed out in the precipice.   The virgin
Rock still rose unpolluted into ether, as when Odysseus
and the Tyrians had seen it long ago.   But its huge feet
narrowed the enemy's way of approach to the northern
wall of the town, and the flat land there available for the
batteries of the besiegers was yet further diminished by a
large straggling pool.   The French and Spanish trenches
were carried first up to the northern edge of the pool, then
round it under the lee of the rock, and finally spread out on
the ground between its waters and the town.   The front
trenches, whence the breaching batteries fired, were scarcely
two hundred and fifty yards from the Land Port, as the
gateway in the northern curtain was called.*   They were
enfiladed by the musketry of the English in the Round
Tower, and in the lines connecting the Round Tower with
the Land Port.†   A battery, erected at the end of the
Old Mole, also greatly disturbed the enemy.   And the
whole system of his trenches was subject to a plunging fire
of round-shot, sometimes from the sea when Leake's
squadron was in the Bay, and always from Willis's Battery,
far overhead on the land side ; in October 1704 that
enterprising officer had, with the aid of the seamen and their
ropes, erected the battery still called after his name, at a
level never reached before, so making the first real attempt
to bring the Rock proper into the scheme of defence for
the town.   Such were the positions of besiegers and
besieged during Gibraltar's ordeal of six months.

---

* In Eliott's siege in George III's reign, the enemy trenches were much
further away, on the north side of the pool or 'inundation' as it was then called,
which had been by that time artificially enlarged.   On the other hand, a more
serious attack was then made from the sea, by the ' floating batteries,' etc.

† Later known as the King's Lines.   *See Map II, p.* 40, *below.*   The scarp
had not then, nor for long afterwards, been cut so as to render it impossible,
as it is now, to scramble up from the sea level to the King's Lines.   The spot
where the Round Tower stood has been largely, though not entirely, cut away
by this later scarping.

Admiral Pointis was detached with a squadron from the French Grand Fleet at Toulon, with orders to assist the siege. Late in September 1704 he landed in Gibraltar Bay three thousand French infantry and a siege train, who joined themselves to the nine thousand Spanish troops already arrived overland. The siege was forthwith begun, but Pointis himself sailed on to Cadiz, and only occasionally appeared in the Bay to join in the operations. All October the trenches crept slowly forward round the pool under the fire of the English. By the end of the month the breaching batteries were posted and in full play. Pointis returned with his squadron and prepared to attack the sea front. And five hundred Spanish soldiers, who had sworn on the Sacrament never to return without having taken Gibraltar, went round, past Catalan Bay, on the steep eastern side of the Rock, whence, near its southern end, they scrambled by night to the top of the great ridge. Their guide was a patriotic goat-herd, Simon Susarte, well acquainted with the passages of the precipice. From its summit rope-ladders were let down to help the ascent of the rear-guard. It was such a feat of guerilla war as suited the national genius. They slept in the magnificent shelter of St. Michael's Cave. It had been agreed that Gibraltar was to undergo a triple attack—from the sea, where 3,000 men were to be landed at the New Mole ; from the trenches ; and by surprise from this mountain ambush above. Success was regarded as certain, and not without reason. But on the very day before the grand assault was to be made, Leake came sweeping into the Bay, destroyed the French men-of-war that he found there, and prevented, by a few hours, the attack that would almost certainly have put an end to the English possession of Gibraltar.

Oct. 29
Nov. 9
1704

Next morning, the five hundred Spaniards, mast-headed on the Rock, looked down in vain to see any movement among their compatriots and allies below. Though deserted, they did not lose courage, but marched northwards along the crest of the heights and overpowered the guards at the Signal Station and on the Middle Hill. The English in the town below, perceiving an enemy force where they had

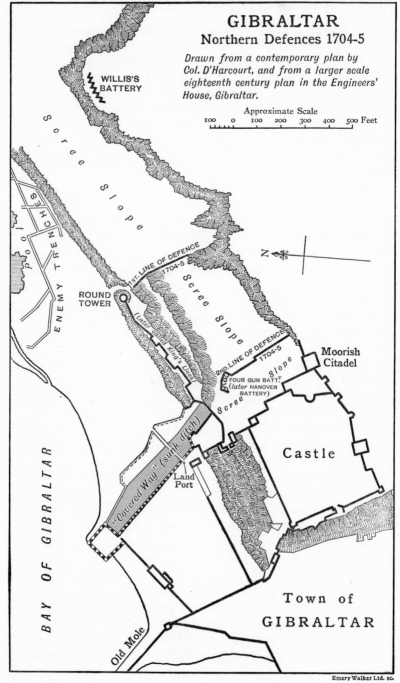

MAP II

GIBRALTAR
Northern Defences 1704-5

*Drawn from a contemporary plan by
Col. D'Harcourt, and from a larger scale
eighteenth century plan in the Engineers'
House, Gibraltar.*

Approximate Scale

100   0   100   200   300   400   500 Feet

WILLIS'S
BATTERY

S c r e e   S l o p e

P o o l

ENEMY TRENCHES

1ST. LINE OF DEFENCE
1704-5

ROUND
TOWER

(Later called King's Line)

S c r e e   S l o p e

N

2ND. LINE OF DEFENCE 1704-5

Moorish
Citadel

FOUR GUN BATT.Y
(later HANOVER
BATTERY)

S c r e e   S l o p e

S c r e e   S l o p e

Castle

Covered Way (sunk ditch)

Land
Port

B A Y   O F   G I B R A L T A R

Town of
GIBRALTAR

Old Mole

Emery Walker Ltd. sc.

least expected it, sent up some companies of marines. With characteristic improvidence, the Spaniards had forgotten to bring with them their spare ammunition, but they put up a gallant fight.   Some two hundred were captured ; the rest were killed by the English musketry or driven over the edge of the precipice.   Many fell headlong and perished, but a few scrambled safely down the limestone gullies by the harsh aid of the cactus and other shrubs that broke the sheer descent, and so returned alive to Catalan Bay.

Such was Leake's First Relief of Gibraltar.   He remained some weeks, lending much-needed aid to the defence, although the winter storms often rendered his presence in the Bay both difficult and dangerous.   At length, at the beginning of December, he sailed back to Lisbon to convoy stores and men arrived there from England for Gibraltar.

All winter the siege went sullenly on.   The rain fell in torrents, flooding the trenches.   King Philip's soldiers, without shoes or pay, and with a plentiful lack of food, powder and provisions, waded about knee-deep in mud.   Half the besieging army perished of disease and exposure.   But the Spaniards are never more tenacious than in the defence or attack of towns, and they stuck fiercely to their task, venting their ill-humour on their allies.   ' If it were not proclaimed death for a Spaniard to fall out with a Frenchman, they would be killing each other every day.'   But the defenders, too, suffered scarcely less from disease and exhaustion : by the middle of November Hesse had only a thousand tired sailors and marines to man the walls ; they daily dragged themselves up to repair the ever crumbling breaches and replace the overturned cannon, of which forty were dismantled by the enemy fire.   It was a rivalry in stubborn endurance, a war of attrition.*

Not a day too soon came the Second Relief, the arrival from England by way of Lisbon of food, stores, ammunition

---

* The reason why the enemy would not storm the breaches they were perpetually making in the curtain between the Old Mole and the Land Port, was that in front of it ran a ' covered way,' that is, a deep broad ditch below the level of the ground, at the bottom of which palisades were placed and which was swept from end to end by the fire of guns placed for the purpose.

and 2,000 Regulars of the Guard and Line, under the
able command of Brigadier Shrimpton. By luck and
Dec. $\frac{8}{19}$ Leake's guardian care, they had just escaped capture
1704   by the ships of Pointis, watching for them off Cadiz.
Lord Galway, the Huguenot commander of the English
at Lisbon, had had the public spirit and generosity to
weaken his own forces for the Portuguese campaign, in
order to speed on these and other troops to save Gibraltar.
After this second relief the besiegers lost heart ; before the
end of the year the Spanish General reported that he had
lost 4,500 men by desertion. They had been starved and
exposed beyond human endurance.

Anger and shame at the failure to retrieve Gibraltar
from the heretic seamen were spreading through the towns
and villages of Castile, among a race that lacked neither
pride nor courage. National feeling was so strong that the
Court of Spain dared not, if it would, give over the siege.
Louis, also, still desired, though with less personal passion,
to retake the key of the Mediterranean for the House of
Bourbon. But co-operation between Versailles and Madrid
was no longer harmonious ; the honeymoon of France and
Spain had ended in sour mistrust. The Queen's favourite,
the Princess des Ursins, had ventured to defy the trucu-
lent French Ambassador, the Duc de Gramont, and had
championed the cause of Spain for the Spaniards. She
had ceased to play her part as agent for the Court of France
and had chosen, instead, to become the faithful servant of
her mistress and of the country that learnt to look to her for
salvation. Louis, therefore, had recalled her from Spain.
The feeble King Philip, who depended for health, happiness
and policy on the bright young Savoyard he had married,
was obliged, in appearance at least, to support his Queen's
feud with his grandfather on behalf of the Princess des
Ursins. Since her enforced departure, the Court of Spain
had sulked, and the French Ambassador soon found that
he had no more influence after the Princess had gone than
when she was present to thwart him. Moreover, her
energetic spirit was now lacking in the royal counsels. All
went to rack and ruin, and Gibraltar with the rest.

The only point on which the King and Queen were agreed with the Duc de Gramont, was to obtain from Louis the recall of the Duke of Berwick from the command of the French forces in Spain—an error that nearly cost them the crown.   Berwick had refused to alter his military plans to suit the fancies of the Ambassador or of the Queen.* He left Madrid for France in November 1704, and, until the Princess des Ursins returned eight months later, there was no person of character and ability of either sex in charge of the civil or military affairs of Spain.   In place of Berwick, Louis sent Marshal Tessé, a pleasant courtier and a great writer of literary letters from the front.   He was excellently suited to negotiate the return of the Princess des Ursins, a task to which he devoted himself with tact and zeal. But it fell to him also to take over the bitter business in the plague-stricken, water-logged trenches before Gibraltar, which needed a different kind of man.[30]

The mutual hostility between French and Spaniards was not confined to Court circles.   The armies and the peoples shared it to the full.   At Christmas, Tessé complained that the march of the French reinforcements to the siege was impeded by the Spaniards, jealous lest it should be said that their allies had retaken the Rock which they themselves had lost.   From this motive the Spanish General, the Marquis Villadarias, whom Tessé was to supersede, determined to make a grand assault on Gibraltar on February 7, three days before the arrival of his supplanter with further French reinforcements.   This attack was very nearly successful, for the Spaniards fought with a furious zeal of patriotism, doubly on their mettle against the French at their side and the English in their face.   They afterwards averred that they were badly supported by the French infantry, desirous that Gibraltar should fall not to Villadarias but to Tessé.   Whether the charge were true or not, the jealousy of the two Latin nations was one of the causes why the Rock, by so narrow a margin, remained in the hands of England.

* The Queen called Berwick ' un grand diable d'Anglais, sec, qui va toujours tout droit devant lui.' Tessé, Mém., II, p. 137. Berwick was the soldier son of James II and Arabella Churchill ; he was well worthy to be Marlborough's nephew.

The grand assault was delivered not against the covered way and the curtain down below, but on the higher ground. The objective was the Citadel, a Moorish castle built in the Fourteenth Century or earlier, but since often repaired. Its ancient walls were of great thickness, but the bombardment had made a breach 'very easy to enter,' Brigadier Shrimpton reported to Marlborough.* The fall of the Citadel would have ended the siege, but to get to it the storming party would have first to carry two lines of outer defences. These lines were neither of them very formidable obstacles : they consisted of rough limestone walls, breached in many places by the cannon ; they ran parallel with one another up the steep slope to the foot of the precipice, on the top of which stood Willis's Battery, well out of harm's way. The first of these lines started uphill from the neighbourhood of the Round Tower, the principal advanced post of the defence. The second line started from an emplacement for a Battery of Four Guns, known in later days as the Hanover Battery.†

The ground traversed by these lines, where the fate of Gibraltar was to be decided by hand-to-hand fighting, consists of a steep limestone scree, overgrown to-day by wild olives and brushwood. The advance guard of the French and Spanish had climbed up at night on to this uncouth battleground, where they lay unperceived in the clefts till the grey of dawn. At the given signal, they rushed the first line, and captured the Round Tower by firing and hurling rocks upon its defenders from immediately above their heads. Thence they advanced, scrambling along over the scree, till they came to the second line, which they also carried, capturing the Four-Gun Battery. Over fifteen hundred picked infantry of France and Spain, flushed with success, were now coming on, and their leaders were within forty yards of the Castle

Feb. 7
(N.S.)
1705

---

* Shrimpton added : 'Had they attacked us at the same time on the covert way, the north bastion and the curtain [down below], we should have found it very hard to have kept them out.' *Add. MSS.* 9115, f. 14.

† See *Map II, p.* 40, *above.* Lieutenant (now Capt.) E. S. M. Goodwin and I, in 1928, discovered the lost traces of this second line of stone wall running up the slope from the Hanover Battery. It is marked in old maps, but has to be looked for carefully among the brushwood that to-day covers the steep scree.

breach, the key to Gibraltar.* The surprise had been ably managed, and the English reserves were still tumbling out and mustering in the streets of the town below. But Captain Fisher and seventeen marines held the enemy at bay for a few precious minutes. They were overpowered at last, but not before the approach of several hundred of the Guards and Line ; some came running up from the town, some climbing up from the covered way, against which the enemy, by a grave error, had made no containing attack. The first reinforcements to arrive were led by Lieutenant-Colonel Moncal, a Huguenot refugee. For another ten minutes the men of the three nations shot and stabbed each other in the twilight of the winter dawn, sliding and falling on the slippery limestone and rolling together down the slope. At length the French and Spaniards began to give way. They were pushed back out of the Four-Gun Battery, back over the lines they had captured, and back out of the Round Tower which had been in their hands for sixty minutes. About four hundred men had fallen in the mêlée.

Gibraltar was never again in such danger, but it was still far from safe. Tessé arrived with three thousand infantry fresh from France ; and a few days later Shrimpton reported to Marlborough that the garrison was reduced to 1,800, that they 'had not half the rest that nature requires,' that they were losing between twenty and forty every day by the cannonade, that the battalion of Guards was reduced to 250 ragged and weary men. Yet Tessé was convinced that only an attack from the sea would overcome the resistance of the garrison. The rain, a good ally to England, still fell in torrents, filling the trenches with water and the grave-pits with men. Louis at Versailles was anxious to save his soldiers and have done with the siege, but the government at Madrid was still obstinate.

It was agreed that one last attempt should be made.

---

* 'Came over the hill as far as the Four Gun Battery and were possessed of that too, which is within 40 paces of the Castle breach which is very easy to enter and that is the last opposition on that side.' Shrimpton to Marlborough. *Add. MSS.* 9115, f. 14.

Pointis was positively ordered, much against his will and judgment, to sail out from Cadiz and attack Gibraltar. But the foul weather again delayed the attack from the sea, and the unhappy French Admiral was beating about in the mouth of Gibraltar Bay, his squadron already scattered by wind and wave, when out of the mist, out of the heart of the gale, burst upon him Leake's squadron, come from Lisbon in despite of wind and weather to save the Rock once again and once for all.

It was not a battle but a chase. Of five French three-deckers surprised at the mouth of the Bay, one struck without a fight, two were boarded and taken, and Mar. $\frac{10}{21}$ two were driven ashore and burnt. Those ships 1705 that were far enough away to escape past Malaga made straight for Toulon. In this brilliant little action the Dutch, in Leake's opinion, did even better than the English ; but the Portuguese, ' those that durst get anything near, did more harm than good. One of them, mistaking the *Pembroke* for the *Lys*, gave her a broadside, but did little damage.'

For another month the Spaniards insisted on remaining before Gibraltar, but every hope of success had now disappeared. Ships not only from Portugal but from Italy were now pouring supplies into the town, unchallenged. Louis was impatient to cut his losses, and Tessé was in a hurry to be gone. At length, as April was drawing near its end, the tired English watched the foe drag his cannon from the trenches, and his columns wind away and vanish behind the northern hills already green with spring. Silence and solitude at length settled on the desolate flats of the Isthmus, the Aceldama where so many thousands of French and Spaniards had died since last those hills were green. Five thousand men marched away, in the track of at least an equal number of deserters, who had gone before to avoid death by starvation in the trenches. In the opinion of Tessé, the King of Spain might still, like his ancestors before him, have ' the best infantry in the world, and the most capable of enduring and suffering,' if only he would pay, clothe and feed them !

The Spaniards, as they retired, looked back, embittered

by more than the loss of so many brave comrades. That
skyward pointing Rock, symbol of Mediterranean lordship,
was in alien hands. So once had the departing Moor
looked back and sighed. Life is brief, and Empire only
a little longer.[31]

APPENDIX TO CHAPTER II

THE MARINES

THE marines, who played the principal part in the land-defence of
Gibraltar, had only been formed as a special branch of the Service at
the beginning of Queen Anne's reign (see *Blenheim*, p. 410, note).
It is remarkable how soon they acquired two reputations that clung
to them for many generations—a reputation for good, honest, modest
service and character, and a reputation among snobs of being socially
less smart than the army. In 1708, Chatham's grandfather, old
Governor Pitt, of the Pitt Diamond, wrote home from Madras to
his son Robert :

I take notice of the employ you have pitched upon for my son Thomas.
I wish you had bought him a very good employ in the English guards,
though it had cost three times the money, for, being in Marines will oblige
him to live a great deal in sea-ports, where the associations are none of the
best. (*H.M.C. Fortescue (Dropmore)*, 1892, p. 36.)

To this add Steele's delightful account of 'the honest rough
relation at the lower end of the table, who is a lieutenant of Marines,'
and his 'plain goodsense,' in No. 79 of the *Tatler*, October 11, 1709.
The idea of the marines had not changed very much in old England
between Anne's reign and Victoria's, when Meredith described the
services, qualities and treatment of Crossjay's father in the *Egoist*.

CHAPTER III

THE CAMPAIGNS OF 1705

Marlborough's disappointments on the Moselle and in the Netherlands. Imperialist negligence and Dutch obstruction. Forcing of the Lines of Brabant. Louis's first offer of peace.

So great had been the moral effect of Blenheim that throughout the following year Marlborough was confident that the enemy would give way, whenever assaulted in a position not absolutely impregnable. 'The French will always be forced whenever they are attacked,' he wrote to Heinsius.* Yet owing to Imperialist negligence, Dutch obstruction and personal jealousy, this precious year slipped by unused. The French were given a breathing space in which to recover their morale, and though the events of 1706, the *annus mirabilis* of the war, showed that the breathing space had not been sufficient, such delay might easily have been fatal to the liberties of Europe. Two factors saved the situation, Marlborough's inexhaustible patience that never allowed anger to disturb courtesy or calculation, and the increasing strength of England's will to conquer.

When, early in September 1704, Marlborough crossed the Rhine in pursuit of the armies he had defeated on the Danube,† there were still two months before him ere he need go into winter quarters. The Allies sat down before Landau, which had again fallen into French hands the year before. The siege operations were committed to Prince Lewis of Baden who conducted them with a lethargy that

---

* September 5, 1705. See Appendix A, below.

† See *Blenheim*, p. 400. *For this chapter see Map IX, The Netherlands, with Moselle inset (end of volume).*

gave the first practical signs of his determination to pay out the English General for having fought the battle of Blenheim without his knowledge. ' The Prince of Baden is now sufficiently revenged for our robbing him of a share of the glory of the victory of Blenheim,' wrote an English officer in November ; ' he has spun out the siege till the left wing of horse, to which that action was chiefly owing, is entirely ruined. We have not above twenty horses a troop left.' [32]

Marlborough and Eugene were to cover the siege, but as the French armies, even those that had not been in Bavaria, were much too frightened to attempt anything that autumn, the Duke determined to use the occasion for a cross-country march into the Moselle valley. Eugene was left to protect the slow operations of Prince Lewis until Landau at length surrendered. If Marlborough could arrive on the Moselle by surprise, he could take Trèves and Trarbach and establish bases for his great design of an invasion of France next spring by way of Thionville and Metz. For more than a year past he had thought of the Moselle as the short cut to final victory.* No such lines of fortresses as stood so thick in the Netherlands barred the way up that river into the heart of France. If he took Saarlouis and Thionville he would open what he himself described as ' the true route by which to pass on and reduce them to reason.' If once he reached Metz, military men observed that his mere presence there would compel the French to evacuate Alsace, that he would be in the rear of their position in the Netherlands, and that he could ' raise contributions even to the gates of Paris.' [33] In the autumn of 1704 he set out to prepare the ground with his small raiding force. Next spring he calculated he would have 90,000 English, Dutch and German troops for the great design. And indeed if Vienna and the Hague had not failed to make any reasonable effort to support him, he might very possibly have finished the war in 1705 by the route of the Moselle.

The Duke had been ailing all summer on the Danube and was a victim to ague and headache on the Rhine. Early in October he wrote to Sarah, ' I am so very lean that it is

* See *Blenheim*, pp. 316–317.

extreme uneasy to me,' and, 'your care must nurse me this
winter or I shall certainly be in a consumption.'   But he
never thought of sparing himself or resting on his laurels.
His march by cross-country roads from Landau to the
Moselle lay through wooded hills which he described as
'mountains,' 'the terriblest country that can be imagined
for the march of an army with cannon.'   But he was
favoured with 'extraordinary good weather,' so that Colonel
Blood's engineering skill brought the guns through.
Oct. $\frac{13}{24}$ The French were successfully surprised and made
1704   no resistance in Trèves.   Trarbach surrendered
after a short siege, and the Moselle, from its junction with
the Saar downwards, was occupied and fitted up with allied
bases for the great enterprise next spring.[34]

Having done his military work for the year, the Duke
started off early in November, not yet for home, but on his
self-imposed diplomatic mission to Berlin.*   If Woodstock
Manor was a good year's pay, it had been faithfully earned.

Next spring Marlborough came abroad betimes, eager
to win the war by the way of the Moselle.   It has been
remarked that in every year when he started out with high
hopes he was destined to disappointment, and that in those
years when he crossed the sea with the worst forebodings
he was nobly successful.   This curious fact is not to be
attributed to mere chance.   Success in one campaign made
the Dutch and Austrian authorities indifferent for the next,
whereas after a little misfortune they were more apt to fall
in with Marlborough's plans.   When he reached the Hague
in April 1705, the States General, who the year before had
let him take so large a part of their army to the Danube,
refused to send more than a small portion of it to co-operate
with him on the Moselle.   When in May he reached the
scene of operations, he found that the magazines which he
had formed at Trèves and which the Dutch had undertaken
to fill with stores, were still half empty : the States Com-
missary had gone over to the French with the money he had
embezzled.

At the same time it became apparent that the Austrians
and the German Princes of the Rhine had equally failed him.

* See pp. 9-10, above.

Their promised armies were not forthcoming on the Moselle. Prince Eugene was heart and soul for Marlborough's plan, but he was back in Italy, and his influence at Court had waned with the passing of the danger that had made it supreme the year before.

The Jesuits and reactionaries were once more in the ascendant at Vienna, while Lewis of Baden ruled the war plans of the German Princes. The death of the Emperor

April 24
May 5
1705

Leopold threw matters into still greater confusion that summer, though hopes were entertained that the succession of his son, Joseph, a great admirer of the Duke, might improve the prospects of the Alliance another year. For the moment every form of obstruction was supreme. The negotiations with Hungary broke down, and, by an almost incredible piece of obscurantism, the Viennese Chancery began to address Queen Anne in formal documents as ' Serenity ' instead of ' Majesty,' denying the title of lawful queen to the sovereign to whose effectual aid last year the Hapsburgs owed it that they still occupied their throne ! This was too much even for Secretary Harley's furtive caution : he charged Stepney to let the young Emperor know in good set terms what was thought of this piece of bureaucratic impertinence, and of the ' practices ' of the Prince of Baden and the Viennese enemies of England, which had ' obliged the Duke of Marlborough to quit his design on the Moselle.' [35]

Though left with less than half the troops he had hoped to command, Marlborough did not at once abandon the enterprise. But he was not only ill supported but stoutly opposed. Louis XIV, recognizing the serious danger of his country, had applied this year to the right quarter. Villars had been sent to stop the invasion of France by ' Malbrook.' * The Marshal had chosen and prepared a strong position at Sierk, barring the passage up the Moselle to Thionville. The river on one side, ravines and deep forests on another, prevented hostile approach, and on the only weak side Villars had thrown up entrenchments. Marlborough could not attack so strong a post with his inadequate force, but he pushed through the mountain

* On Villars see *Blenheim*, p. 317.

defiles to its foot, and challenged the enemy to come out and give battle. Villars was not to be drawn ; for all his gasconades and cheerful self-laudation he had a perfect grip on reality, and knew when to be prudent and when to be bold. He despised his fellow Marshals, but he did not, like Villeroi, despise Marlborough.

The Duke, unable to force the position at Sierk, hoped to turn it by east and south, and was about to lay siege to Saarlouis, when in the middle of June he received serious news from the Netherlands. Villeroi had made a push, recaptured Huy on the Maas and was besieging Liège. The Dutch called on Marlborough to come back and save them. So he turned sorrowfully away from his ' true route ' into France, to ' take the bull by the horns ' amid the tangle of Netherland fortresses.[36]

He never saw the Moselle again. His allies had not the heart or the brains to let him win the war where it could be won most quickly. The Dutch would fight on their own border and nowhere else. The idea of a ' united command,' of an allied war-plan, was equally repugnant to the provincialism of Austria and the Princes of the Rhine, busy each with their own little campaigns. Only England, since the General Election had disposed of Marlborough's opponents, was eager to fight wherever he chose. The localism of the Allies set bounds within which he must confine his schemes. When his achievements are compared to those of Frederick or Napoleon, the limitations of his authority as a commander must never be forgotten.*

---

* Marlborough's own account of the reasons that induced him to abandon the Moselle campaign will be found in the following ill-constructed but coherent sentence, written on June 30, 1705, to the Duke of Shrewsbury. It comes from the Duke of Buccleugh's MSS. in Boughton House : ' By the failure of our friends in all they have promised me on the Moselle I have been oblig'd to march back to the Meuse. I was 15 days together in the Camp of Efft [before Sierk] without being join'd by any troupes but what were in the English and Dutch pay, tho' I was to have been considerably reinforced by the Germans emediatly upon my taking the field, and finding already a scarsety of forage, by the unseasonable cold weather, which had destroy'd all the grase and oates, with no manner of hopes of being suplied in any reasonable time with horses and carriages promis'd for bringing up our great artillery for the sige of Saar Lewis, where if we had been once posted we shou'd have been plentifully suplyed with subsistence out of Lorraine, all these disappointments obliged mee to yield to the pressing instances of the [Dutch] States and their Generals to come to their relief.'

Henceforth the Duke had to devote himself to the direct conquest of the Spanish Netherlands and their fortresses by frontal attack ; he could no longer hope to turn that whole region from the south.   Under these conditions the first obstacle to be overcome was the so-called Lines of Brabant. At the beginning of the war the French had erected this barrier, and after Marlborough's first successes in 1702 had fallen back behind it.   It ran from the sea to the Maas, from Antwerp to Namur.   In some sections of the Line great rivers formed the obstacle, but for the most part it was an earthwork, not unlike Wellington's lines of Torres Vedras, but in length more nearly resembling Offa's Dyke.

The Dutch generals had forbidden him to attack it in 1703.*   They were of the same opinion in 1705.   But this time he ' perfectly bubbled them into it,' as his Chaplain, Francis Hare, wrote home, ' drawing them into it as you would manage children.'   He promised that ' if he saw the Lines strongly guarded he would not opiniatre the matter,' and it was agreed that the Dutch troops were only ' to second and follow him if he succeeded, to help him to make his retreat if he miscarried, but not to share the danger with him.'   The French were misled by a demonstration made some miles further south by Overkirk, Marlborough's one friend among the Dutch generals that year.   There was therefore only a handful of men guarding the Lines at Elixem.   The English marched secretly to that point, passing across William's old Landen battlefield at dead of night.   It was nearing dawn when they reached the famous entrenchment, protected by the waters of the Little Geete on its front.   The red-coated infantry stormed the bridge at Elixem, made for the earthworks, and ' were over before one thought they were at them,' and so ' with the loss of half a dozen men passed those Lines which was thought would have cost at least as many thousand.'

But the enemy had taken the alarm, and the rising sun shone on the swords of thirty-five squadrons gallop-
July $\frac{6}{17}$ ing up from the south, with infantry following
1705   behind ; they might yet recover the ground, while the bulk of the allied foot was still filing over the bridges and

---

* *Blenheim*, p. 316.   *See Map IX, Netherlands, below.*

pontoons, and mounting the breaches which the sappers were hastily making in the rampart. The finest part of the Bavarian army that had escaped from Blenheim, the heavy cavalry in their black cuirasses and helmets, were supported by French, Spanish and Walloon horse. The variegated masses of their new uniforms blazed like the fields of tulips in Holland.

The moment was critical, but the English cavalry and dragoons were already well across the Lines, and had deployed in time. The allied cavalry were hastening to support them. With the Duke himself in their midst, Cadogan's horse and the other red-coated squadrons charged straight into the Bavarian ranks. Then was proved what Blenheim had shown already and Waterloo was to show yet again, that cuirassiers in armour could be overcome by the free swing of the sword in the hands of men clad only in broadcloth. After a hot action of two hours, the enemy horse galloped away and the infantry were glad to form hollow square and escape in that order from the cavalry of Britain. Standards, kettle-drums, cannon, and over 3,000 prisoners remained as trophies of the field. Lord John Hay, at the head of his Scots Greys, had taken ' with his own hands ' the principal enemy general engaged, the Marquis d'Alègre. Marlborough had been in the mêlée ; an enemy officer had struck at him so eagerly that in delivering the blow he lost his balance, fell off his horse and was taken. ' I asked my lord,' wrote Orkney, 'if it was so : he said, " It was absolutely so." See what a happy man he is. I believe this pleases him as much as Hogstet did. It is absolutely owing to him.'

The success indeed had been so great and had been so cheaply won that even the Dutch generals that morning were fain to congratulate the Duke, though they nourished against him a bitter grudge for the poor part they themselves had played. In the streets of Tirlemont the victorious English were cheering ' Corporal John,' and calling aloud to him to lead them in pursuit of the flying foe. It was only ten in the morning, and though they had been marching all night the veterans of William's wars called out to their officers that they knew the country well and that

they could all be in Louvain before dark. The retreating
enemy were watching Tirlemont over their shoulders,
in terror lest they should see the redcoats emerge from
it on to the Louvain road. If the Duke had pushed
on that day, he might have reconquered much of the
Netherlands at a rush. But for such a venture he must
be sure of the full co-operation of the Dutch army. His
personal enemy, General Slangenberg, was at his side in
Tirlemont, among the excited English regiments shouting
to be led forward ; he agreed with the Duke that they ought
to continue their advance on Louvain, and went back,
ostensibly to get the agreement of his Dutch colleagues.
But the army of the States was already pitching its tents,
and the men were weary after their night march in rear of
the English. What precisely passed between Marlborough
and the Dutch generals is uncertain ; but the golden
moment to advance was not seized. Whether the Duke's
decision to halt was right or, as many of his friends thought,
wrong, in either case the motive was his belief that he could
not sufficiently depend on the active support of his allies.[37]

So the enemy were permitted to rally behind the Dyle
at Louvain, and to save Brussels and Flanders for another
year. But their famous Lines of Brabant were abandoned
for good ; in September, fatigue parties from Marlborough's regiments levelled such long stretches that
nothing more was heard of the Lines in the strategy of the
war. The Spanish Netherlands must henceforth be defended, not by a continuous outer line of rivers and earthworks, but by the strength of its fortresses and by the skill
with which the defending army could manœuvre among
them so as to baffle Marlborough's endeavours to bring it
to an action. In their endeavours to avoid a battle the
French had powerful allies in the Dutch generals and the
civilian Deputies, through whom they spoke the word of
doom to one project after another which the Duke laid
before them. A full catalogue of their refusals in the next
few weeks would weary the reader. Matters came to
Aug. $\frac{7}{18}$ a head when a final opportunity to defeat the enemy
1705   at Overyssche, which the Duke's skill had brought
about, was as usual prohibited by the Dutch generals

and Deputies. Overkirk alone besought his colleagues to permit the attack. 'That beast Slangenberg,' as the Reverend Francis Hare called him, 'was very noisy,' and roundly abused the Commander-in-Chief to his face. It was not cowardice, but jealousy, that moved the Dutchman, who had two years before shown himself a brave soldier at the battle of Ekeren.

After the open scandal of this scene, the Duke saw that he could accomplish nothing with such men. 'As it is ordered by Monsieur Slangenberg,' he wrote to Portland, 'I have not the tenth part of the authority I had last year.' With his usual calculating forethought, he adopted a policy which sacrificed any further hopes for that campaign, in order to secure a free hand in the following year. With apparent humility the greatest soldier of the age begged that his Dutch subordinates would themselves frame the plans for the use of the allied army, which he, for his part, undertook to carry out.

I have so good an opinion of this army [he wrote to Heinsius on August 27], that I think they are able to execute whatever their generals will resolve ; besides we have yet two months before we ought to think of winter quarters. I beg you will believe and assure others that I will with all cheerfulness endeavour to make everything succeed that shall be proposed to me.

And a week later he writes from Tirlemont :

The resolution I have taken of being governed by your generals the remaining part of this campaign gives me a great deal of quiet, so that I am drinking the Spa waters.*

The veiled irony of this courteous strike by the Commander-in-Chief was not lost on the world, and least of all on the Dutch Government and people. It was supported by representations from Queen Anne to the Pensionary that 'we cannot but impute the disappointments that have lately happened to their placing less confidence in the Duke of Marlborough this year than last.' The indignation of all England was shared by more than half Holland. The Duke of Shrewsbury, on his way back from his long

* See Appendix A, p. 409, below.

residence in Italy with his new Duchess,* halted in Amsterdam and noted the temper of the people.

> The Duke of Marlborough [he wrote in December 1705] is beloved by the people of that city ; besides his success and personal merit, they think, as being a stranger so well established elsewhere, he cannot be dangerous to their liberty.   He may do them good, but can do them no hurt.   They are so enraged against Slangenberg for his being his enemy, as well as a Jesuited Papist, that had he come to Amsterdam this summer, after he hindered the battle, he would have been de Witted.

The conduct of the Dutch generals was approved only by that party among their countrymen who were for patching up a peace with France without first recovering the Spanish Netherlands.   And so, in the winter of 1705–6, Marlborough won his cause at the Hague.   The States, pressed by Heinsius from above and by the people from below, agreed that Slangenberg should not be sent into the field next year, and that Deputies and generals should be chosen who were friends to Marlborough, and should be given instructions to agree to all that he might propose.[38]

Hardly less hopeful for the prospects of 1706 was the effect produced by the allied failure on the light mind of the French Marshal, and the stupidity of his chief, the Minister for War.   In September Chamillart from Versailles wrote to Villeroi in the field :

> I have a mediocre opinion of the capacity of the Duke of Marlborough.

Blenheim he attributed ' to chance alone.'   Villeroi replied in the same tone that the English general was ' a mortified adventurer.'   The idea was taking possession of the French official mind that Blenheim might be avenged by a battle in the Netherlands.   Among the military authorities on both sides a new mentality was growing up, which led speedily to Ramillies when the new campaign opened.[39]

Louis was not, however, so confident of military victory that he could any longer despise those diplomatic arts of which, in his wiser moments, he was so great a master.

* *Blenheim*, p. 202.

His hot fit of pride, which had plunged Europe into war, had been cooled in the waters of the Danube. Before the war began he had been so confident of victory that he had planned to divide the Spanish Netherlands between France and the vassal House of Wittelsbach.* But in the autumn of 1705 he made tentative peace proposals to Holland, adumbrating the erection of the Spanish Netherlands into an independent state,—though how its true independence should be guaranteed was left dangerously vague. The Austrian candidate was in no case to be sovereign either of the Netherlands or of Milan : Louis suggested that Charles might receive Naples and Sicily in compensation for the loss of the rest of the Spanish Empire. But since Austria had no fleet, Southern Italy held on such terms would be merely a pawn in the hands of the House of Bourbon for the good behaviour of the House of Hapsburg. So long as the armies of France and her allies remained in the Milanese, they could seize Southern Italy whenever they wished, and no Austrian troops could get there at all without the war-like intervention of the Maritime Powers. Savoy-Piedmont would similarly become a vassal of France, surrounded on both sides by her power.

Louis' proposals were therefore quite unacceptable, but there was some alarm felt lest the peace-party in Holland would seek to detach their country from the Alliance as a result of this offer. Actually Buys, who represented a reasonable and loyal party more inclined to peace than Heinsius, considered that, if Louis would also give up the Milanese, the terms proposed were not so bad. But it was only the military events of 1706 that made any such an arrangement possible.

England, unlike either Holland or France, was in a mood of growing confidence, her finances stable, her population contented, and her will to conquer confirmed at the recent General Election. Therefore, in August 1705, Marlborough and Godolphin implored Heinsius not to listen to the French proposals. These were the weeks of the Duke's most aggravated trouble with the Dutch generals, but even then he was confident of ultimate victory. He

* *Blenheim*, p. 137.

and Godolphin laid down to Heinsius not only the doctrine
that Holland must have a strong barrier in the Netherlands,
on which point the Dutch statesman was well agreed, but
also that Milan must go to the Austrian candidate. So
much had been in William III's plan for the new Europe
as expressed in the Treaty of Grand Alliance of 1701, and
it was ultimately realized at Utrecht. But the two English
statesmen went further: already in 1705, before the reconquest of the Netherlands and Italy, they pledged themselves to the dogma of 'no peace without Spain.' On
August 18 Godolphin wrote to Marlborough about Louis'
offer :

> If England had lost a battle at sea and another at land, I think they
> would still despise such a peace, and I believe you may depend upon it
> they will never consent to any peace that leaves Spain and the Indies
> or either in the hands of the Duke of Anjou.

Marlborough sent this on to Heinsius. His own
comment was :

> You know as well as I do that England can like no peace, but
> such as puts King Charles in the possession of the Monarchy of Spain ;
> and as for yourselves, I think you ought to have garrisons in Antwerp,
> Namur and Luxemburg, besides I think the Duke of Savoy should be
> our particular care.

At the moment that Marlborough wrote thus, ' King
Charles ' and his allies occupied neither Milan, Naples,
Sicily, the Netherlands, nor any foot of land in ' Spain and
the Indies ' except Gibraltar. It was a month later that
Barcelona was added to his actual possessions.

In these letters of Marlborough and Godolphin we
recognize their admirable determination to win the war,
which next year at Ramillies and Turin put France in its
proper place for the Eighteenth Century ; but we see also
their concentration of purpose on an impossible object,
which William had never contemplated. No word is said
in Marlborough's letters about the Grand Alliance Treaty
of 1701 and the moderate programme that the Stadtholder-
King had there laid down. The Portuguese Treaty of 1703
had taken its place in determining the new war-aims of

England : Spain herself and her undivided Empire must
be won for the Austrian candidate.*

Marlborough was not one to name impossible terms and
then do nothing to secure them.   In the winter of 1705 he
made an even longer tour of Germany than the year before,
laying the plans that won Italy for the Allies in the following
year.   First, on a visit to Dusseldorf, he persuaded the
Elector Palatine to send his troops to Italy.   Thence in a
' very tedious journey,' including six days' sail on the Danube
to avoid the winter roads, he reached Vienna in the middle
of November.   The young Emperor Joseph was on ill
terms with Prussia and Holland, but he worshipped Marlborough, and affairs were adjusted for the coming campaign.
Thence the pacificator of the Allies travelled north to Berlin
and there completed the work, and with it the arrangements
for the effective relief of the Duke of Savoy.[40]

---

* See *Blenheim*, pp. 302–303, on the Portuguese Treaty, 1703 ; see Appendix A,
p. 407, below ; *Coxe*, chap. xxxviii, I, pp. 453–456 ; *Geyl*, pp. 8–10, on Dutch
views of the offer ; *Legrelle*, IV, pp. 364–374, on a later and more formal stage of
these offers of Louis, made through the Marquis d'Alègre in Holland during the
winter months of 1705–6.   The Marquis was to offer Marlborough ' two million '
for a peace on these terms ; but the Duke was less venal than Louis and others
supposed.

In January 1706 James Vernon, our envoy at Copenhagen, reported to Harley
a dinner-table conversation indicating how much some of England's friends and
allies would be averse to the undue aggrandisement of the House of Austria :
' The Envoy of Sweden had invited to dine with him the Imperial, Dutch and
Prussian Ministers and myself.   After dinner one of the company said that the
affairs of Spain looked towards a general revolution [by that time Peterborough
had taken Barcelona].   The saying of that provoked the Swede to such an excess
of passion as would have surprised me to see in Poussin himself [the French Envoy].
He told us the Princes of Europe would never suffer that monarchy entire in the
House of Austria ; that there would be a stop put to that career ; that he could
not imagine what England and Holland meant to drive things so far and not be
satisfied with a Treaty of Partition. . . . The Prussian Envoy was by all this
while and contradicted none of his allegations.   The rest of the company stared at
the furiousness of the orator.'   *H.M.C. Portland*, IX, p. 220.

APPENDIX TO CHAPTER III

A Jacobite Nobleman visits Marlborough

Some readers may be interested in the following picture of Marlborough in private life, near the close of the campaign of 1705. It is written by his old friend Thomas Bruce, Earl of Ailesbury, a Jacobite living abroad in Belgium, with friends in both armies, though mainly on the French side. Marlborough made court to him, partly for old friendship's sake, partly, one suspects, so as to have friends among the more moderate of the Jacobite nobility. Ailesbury crosses into the allied lines to see Marlborough by special invitation.

Towards the middle of September (1705) Count Oxenstierra, my great friend and correspondent, wrote to me desiring I would come to Tirlemont, for that I had sufficiently mortified my Lord Marlborough for going from his promise (the year before) given to my wife. I went in one day in my post chaise with my own coach horses, and passing over the plain of Landen I awakened by the horrible stench of dead horses on both sides, the road passing through the Dutch line. . . . All the dead horses are to rot above ground, and the sickness was much amongst the horse in the camp of the Allies, as well as in the French.

Count Oxenstierra was quartered in a convent of Nuns and my Lord Marlborough just without the gates. My host invited several of our nation to sup with me. The next morning he carried me to my Lord's, who was in business, and the Generals in Chief and of the auxiliary troops were also attending, but he sent for us two into his chamber, and it being post day that morning, he desired Count Oxenstierra to amuse me as well as possible until dinner time, and at his little table, a great word with him, he seldom having a great one save Sundays. He embraced me much and made me many protestations. At dinner, sitting by me, he would continually take me by the hand, but politickly (at which he was great master) putting his hand under the napkin.

That night My Lord Orkney gave me a vast supper, and of consequence much company of all those he knew that had a regard for me. He had the hautboys of the regiment of footguards, and . . . a great number of books with the best airs, and all sorts of instruments, and of all countries, fit for hautboys, and the symphony was admirable. And who should come in but my Lord Marlborough, with this expression (for he was not invited, as not supping) : ' My Lord Orkney, do not take it ill if I say I come here for the sake of this Lord,' pointing to me. He was perfectly merry, and for him ate much and drank heartily, and we all found the effects of the excellent wine and I never saw more mirth. The next day he asked me where I dined. I told him where he was to dine—at Count Oxenstierra's. ' I shall not be so happy,' said he, ' for I am condemned to dine with base company, and shall have as base dinner.' The three States Deputies of the Army had invited him, and that year they were three sad fellows and great pedants, and continually thwarting him.

The next day we were all invited to My Lord Albemarle's at Landen. That morning Marechal Overkirk posted his troops and auxiliaries, the left line of the Army, in review, and my Lord Marlborough promised to come, but we going to see him in the morning he entertained us and the company so long that I put him in mind of going. He whispered in the ear that it was very indifferent to him. At last he went in his chaise for one person and one horse ; and in getting up he set foot on ground again, and told me he had forgot to shew me the plan of his house and gardens at Woodstock [Blenheim], and so went up again, and in pointing out the apartments for him and lady, etc., laid his finger on one and told me *'that* is for you when you come and see me there,' and yet it was he that out of policy and by a timorous temper, that kept me on this side [viz. in exile], together with my Lord Godolphin, and yet both in their hearts wished me most well. I asked him who was his Architect (although I knew the man that was). He answered ' Sir Jo. Van Brugg.' On which I smiled and said : ' I suppose, my Lord, you made choice of him because he is a professed Whig.' I found he did not relish this, but he was too great a courtier for to seem angry. It was at my tongue's end for to add that he ought as well to have made Sir Christopher Wren, the Architect, Poet Laureate. In fine, I understand but little or nothing of this matter but enough to affirm (by the plan I saw) that the house is like one mass of stone, without taste or relish.

Memoirs of Thomas, Earl of Ailesbury (Roxburghe Club, 1890), vol. II, pp. 584–587.

Marlborough kept high state on his campaigns. At Althorp are to be seen the great ' pilgrim bottles ' of silver, for carrying wine on pack animals, and the vast silver wine cooler, all beautifully engraved with his arms and the Imperial eagle of his German Princedom. These travelled with him, as also did a large screen, also at Althorp, of Chinese work but with figures in European clothes of the period, given him by the grateful Emperor after Blenheim. These details of his campaigning outfit recall Drake served on silver plate in the cabin of his ship, rather than the Spartan simplicity of Frederick the Great and Charles XII.

CHAPTER IV

PETERBOROUGH TAKES BARCELONA

ALREADY in August 1705 Marlborough and Godolphin had laid it down to Heinsius that there could be ' no peace without Spain.' They were soon to be strengthened in this resolve by the news that Peterborough had taken Barcelona ; that the eastern seaboard of the Peninsula was rapidly falling into the hands of the Allies ; and that next year a twofold advance could be made on Madrid from Portugal on one side and Catalonia or Valencia on the other.*

It is in keeping with the fantastic character of Peterborough's career that his one great achievement as a soldier probably did more harm than good to his country and to the world. Had he failed in the attempt on Barcelona, the Allies must have abandoned all serious intention of placing ' Charles III ' on the throne ; in that case the men and money that England so long continued to lavish in Spain could have been profitably used elsewhere, in Flanders, Toulon or Canada ; or else peace might have been arranged years earlier on terms at least as good as those of Utrecht.

Before Peterborough's feat changed the situation, the prospects that ' Charles III ' would ever be crowned in Madrid seemed small indeed. The capture and successful defence of Gibraltar, valuable as it proved to England's future in the Mediterranean, served little to promote the military and political conquest of Spain, and only made the inhabitants of Andalusia more than ever loyal to King Philip in their anger against the occupation of the Rock by the heretics.

* For this chapter see Map X (Europe) at end of book, and map of Barcelona, p. 69, below.

On the Portuguese border, the campaign of 1705 brought small success to the allied cause. The Huguenot, Ruvigny, Earl of Galway, had taken up the command on that front,* but though a competent and gallant soldier, he could make nothing of the situation. The English complained that the Portuguese were ' utter strangers to all warlike preparation ' and were still ' wavering in their resolutions.' The money promised by the Maritime Powers to maintain the Portuguese regiments was duly forthcoming, but since it was not administered by English or Dutch hands, ' the army is never paid nor can be depended on, but all the money is lost and swallowed up among the Hidalgos and officers.' Our Envoy, John Methuen, was blamed by the subordinates in his office because he did not expostulate more strongly with King Peter. Methuen himself, in writing home, admitted the badness of the Portuguese army, particularly of its officers, but spoke of its ' noble train of artillery.' Much of the army existed only on paper, and the remainder was of little use. The Portuguese regiments had not, as in Wellington's day, the advantage of English officers. Galway took the field early in April 1705 with 12,000 of these doubtful allies, and 5,000 Dutch and English. But he could accomplish nothing beyond the capture of a few small towns on the Spanish frontier before the heats of June set in, when the Portuguese ' thought it high time to be at home ' ; flocks of deserters set the example and the whole army had shortly to follow.†

But, just when Galway was returning disconsolate to Lisbon, the English fleet came sailing into the harbour, June $\frac{9}{20}$ 1705 bringing large reinforcements from home, under the command of Charles Mordaunt, third Earl of Peterborough. They were not, however, to land in Portugal : their instructions were to go on to Italy and relieve the Duke of Savoy, or failing that to take Cadiz or Barcelona.‡

To modern naval and military historians the selection of

---

* See *Blenheim*, p. 404.

† See note [41], below. In the autumn, after the heats were over, Galway took the field, but failed to capture Badajos, where he lost an arm in the trenches.

‡ They had two sets of instructions, see *H. of L. MSS.* (1706–1708), pp. 361–364.

Peterborough for the command of the expedition has seemed
strange. Why, they ask, did Marlborough, the sage professional soldier, with his reticence, patience and forethought,
choose for the execution of his own favourite plans of
amphibious warfare in the Mediterranean a man of slight
experience or training in the profession of arms either by
sea or land, a man well known to be everything that Marlborough himself was not—quarrelsome, boastful, light-
minded, over-busy with tongue and pen, changing his plans
and his friends as readily as he shifted his shirt, sudden in
resolutions but unable to hold a course, ever shooting out
his lively imagination to the other end of Europe and itching
to follow in person, leaving the tasks of yesterday half done ?
A generous patron of poets and a witty and charming talker,
Peterborough was loved by men of letters, to whom his
reputation with posterity has owed much: but Swift could
not forbear writing of his friend that he was ' the ramblingest,
lying rogue on earth.' Why did Marlborough, of all men,
choose such an one as commander-in-chief of the land and
sea forces of the expedition ? *

We have no record of the reasons that induced the
government to select Peterborough. But something perhaps
may be divined. Although in the course of political intrigue
he had once attempted to do Marlborough a base injury,
he was now on good terms with the Duke, and in familiar
correspondence with Sarah, to whom he was paying political
courtship with some success. What was known of him was
by no means wholly to his disadvantage. He had played so
spirited a part in the preparation and conduct of the great
adventure to Torbay, that William for a while had thought
highly of him, and, if he had had any steadiness or sense to
balance his active qualities, he would have been one of the
real rulers of England during the King's reign. But his
irresponsible gambols in political life soon lost him the confidence of William, of his Whig party colleagues and of the
country as a whole.

* His commission made him sole commander of the military forces of the
expedition ; and admiral and commander-in-chief of the fleet, jointly with
Sir Cloudesley Shovell. Rooke was not again employed, because the High Tories
had set him up as rival to Marlborough. See *Blenheim*, p. 420.

Quiet men such as Marlborough often admire those sons of Mercury who are most unlike themselves. He had the generosity to acknowledge the genius that underlay all Peterborough's nonsense. It is true that in the course of a year this strange Commander-in-Chief exhausted even Marlborough's patience, chiefly by his endless letters of complaint about everything, and abuse of everyone, till in September 1706 the Duke wrote to Godolphin ' It is a misfortune to have to do with so ill a man.'[42]

But, after all, he took Barcelona. No one else whom Marlborough could have chosen would have taken it under the circumstances : not Galway, not Stanhope—not Ormonde certainly ; Ormonde, moreover, was no longer available for service abroad, being Lord Lieutenant in Dublin. Yet the choice was limited to the not very long list of British grandees. For the object was to find, not merely a general to command a few regiments, but a grand seigneur who would supervise the naval, military and diplomatic course of the armament in the Mediterranean, and represent England in the counsels of the Allies. For such a part a great nobleman was required, according to the ideals of an age when war was less professional and more aristocratic than it has since become. Whatever his reasons, Marlborough chose Peterborough for the post, and the consequences were what they were to all the parties concerned.*

The armament commanded by Peterborough and Sir Cloudesley Shovell, having put in to Lisbon in the middle of June, was joined there by a Dutch fleet. It was further increased by two regiments of English dragoons supplied by Galway, ever generous to lend his troops to others where the service would benefit. ' Charles III ' and his German courtiers also came on board, and the allied fleet, thus royally loaded, set sail for the Mediterranean. At Gibraltar the recruits fresh from England and Ireland were exchanged

* At the beginning of Anne's reign, Peterborough was a Whig and Marlborough a Tory. Yet, in the later years of the reign, Tory propaganda for party purposes exaggerated the genius of Peterborough and the faults of Marlborough in a manner that affected national opinion for two hundred years, and found its echo in the writings of Macaulay.

for the veterans of the garrison, who sailed on, to add the
laurels of Barcelona to those of the defence of the Rock.
The hero of that defence, Prince George of Hesse, himself
joined the expedition.

The Prince of Hesse Darmstadt had great influence in
Catalonia, which he had governed successfully under the
late King of Spain. But he felt no enthusiasm for an attack
on Barcelona. He knew, indeed, that the Catalans hated
the Spaniards and French, but he knew their ways too well to
believe the tales of an army of 12,000 men already in the field.
Moreover, he well remembered the strength of Barcelona,
which in 1697 he had himself held for nearly two months,
against a French army of 26,000 men commanded by
Vendôme. But the stories of the Catalan rising had fired
the imagination of the English home government, and had
made the gallant young 'Charles III' as anxious to put
himself at its head as ever was Prince Charles Edward to
appear among his loyal Highlanders. In vain Hesse advised
a landing in Valencia, where horses abounded, and whence
an immediate advance should be made on Madrid. The
enemy forces, he pointed out, were concentrated in Catalonia
and on the Portuguese frontier, so that the path from
Valencia to Madrid lay open. Peterborough sometimes
favoured this bold project, at other times was all for the
voyage to Italy to save the Duke of Savoy. In any case, he
had ceased to wish to go to Barcelona.* But the royal wishes
of ' King Charles ' probably carried more weight at a Council
of War than those either of Hesse or of the Commander-
in-Chief, particularly since Charles never varied in his desire
for the Catalonian adventure, and Peterborough's plans
changed from week to week. All were agreed that it was
useless to attack Cadiz. A series of Councils of War resulted
in the decision to attack Barcelona.[43]

Though Barcelona would have ranked as a fortress of
the third class in the Netherlands, its defences were stronger
and in better condition than those of any other city in Spain.
The garrison, under a zealous Governor, Count Francisco
de Velasco, consisted chiefly of Spanish troops, ill fitted for

---

* Peterborough favoured the Catalonian project for a few days in July (see his
letter in *Künzel*, pp. 576–577) ; but, as usual, he very soon changed his mind.

field operations, but certain to fight with stubborn courage in defending the walls of a town. The Allies had no regular siege train, but the guns of the fleet could be landed and could blow a breach, provided an approach could be made. But on the north-east side, where alone it was possible for the assailants to disembark without opposition, marshes spread over land now covered by modern suburbs. The general officers of the Allies, after the first survey, declared that batteries could not be erected on such ground.*

On the opposite side of Barcelona the ground was firm and the defences of the town were less complete, but that side was protected by the Citadel, the famous fortress at Monjuic, crowning a steep hill that rose 575 feet straight out of the sea. The only weakness in its situation as a citadel was that it stood to the town as an Italian campanile stands to its church, a little apart, so that communications might be cut by surprise. But for three weeks after the day when the allied armament arrived in Barcelona roads, no one proposed to attack Monjuic.

Fifteen battalions of foot were at once landed on the north-east of the town, followed by dragoons and cavalry. But there were as yet no cannon and no plans for a siege. King ' Charles III ' came ashore, greeted by the shouts of nobles, priests and peasants from the neighbouring villages ; and it was known that the population held down by the garrison in the city was heartily on the same side. Hatred of the Spaniards, who encroached on their provincial rights, had been the heritage of the Catalans from of old, and hatred of the French had received fresh fuel during their occupation of Barcelona in the last war. None the less did consternation prevail among the allied soldiers when they found that the Catalans had nothing requisite for waging war, except enthusiasm and a few old

Aug. $\frac{11}{22}$
1705

---

* ' The workes which we must attack are in very good condition, but the ground through which our attack must be carried is for the most part a bogg.' *P.R.O., S.P.*, 94, 75, Council of War of August $\frac{16}{27}$. It is true the French in 1697, not being able to take Monjuic, had taken Barcelona by attacking the San Pedro and New Bastions on that side, but they had 26,000 men, a proper siege train and engineers, they approached by land, not from the sea, and in any case it cost them 10,000 men to take the place.

muskets. The 'army of 12,000' had vanished through the gate of dreams, after the manner of tales told by exiles. Some companies of 'Miquelets,' as the patriot banditti were called, consented to take their allies' pay so long as it lasted, but refused to submit to their allies' discipline.

MAP III

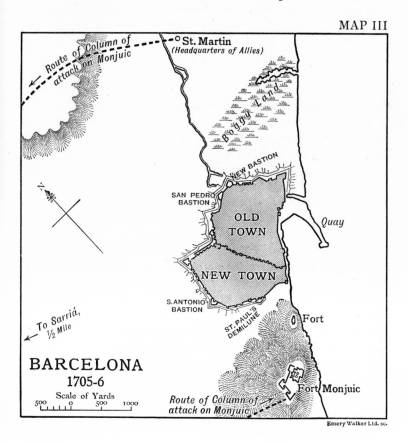

BARCELONA
1705-6

Scale of Yards
500   0   500   1000

St. Martin
(Headquarters of Allies)

Route of Column of attack on Monjuic

NEW BASTION

SAN PEDRO BASTION

OLD TOWN

NEW TOWN

Quay

S. ANTONIO BASTION

ST. PAUL'S DEMILUNE

Fort

To Sarriá,
½ Mile

Route of Column of attack on Monjuic

Fort Monjuic

Emery Walker Ltd. sc.

The next three weeks were occupied by a series of Councils of War, held by the quarrelsome chiefs of the expedition, while the army that had been somewhat hastily set ashore did nothing in particular, except prepare to re-embark. The General Officers at the council-board were unanimous against attempting the siege, and called for an immediate departure, preferably for Italy. Peterborough sometimes supported his officers' views with warmth, but not always, for he was incapable of a fixed resolution. The naval captains, bitterly incensed against his association with Shovell in command of the fleet, supported their Admiral against him, and declared they would gladly lend guns and gunners to begin the siege.

But if there was sullen heat between army and navy, there was fire and fury between the German courtiers and the English soldiers. ' Charles III ' was determined not to desert the Catalans, and was in terror lest the whole force should be diverted to Italy, with fatal results to his own chances of a throne. His civilian courtiers joined in the feud against Peterborough ; in particular the odious Prince of Lichtenstein ' gave himself most horrible ayrs ' at these ' ugly debates.' On one occasion he threw a stool at my Lord Peterborough's secretary's head.'

After a number of plans, too wearisomely many to record, had been adopted and rescinded by successive Councils of War, it was finally determined, on Peterborough's proposition, ' with great reluctance to march to Tortosa and Tarragona, for it was now too late to think of going to Valencia,' or, for the matter of that, to Italy. A worse decision could scarcely have been reached. The Catalans of the neighbourhood had been incited to rebellion by the landing and were now to be deserted to the Spanish vengeance, without a shot fired against Barcelona. The other rival projects of an advance on Madrid by Valencia, or the rescue of the Duke of Savoy, hopeful at one time, had been ruined by delay. The decision to march against two minor cities of Catalonia was, as everyone knew, merely intended to save the face of the commanders who had been unable to agree on any profitable course.[44]

Aug. 31 / Sept. 11 / 1705

Suddenly, Peterborough became conscious of these unpleasant truths. The fault was, in part at least, his own. He had gone very far in opposition to an attack on Barcelona. He had even caused Colonel Richards to write to Hesse, warning him that the troops would mutiny if an attack were ordered contrary to the known opinion of their Generals and the decision of the Council of War.[45] Yet he now realized that the hazard must be run: that secrecy and promptitude must take the place of Councils of War ; and, best of all, he saw the one way in which Barcelona might even yet be attacked with some chance of success.

Deserters had given the English General information ' of the ill state and condition of Monjuic.' Since only the other side of the town had so far been threatened, the Spaniards had ceased to take thought for their citadel. A long and difficult march would have to be made from the allied camp in order to reach it, but if the march were conducted at night the surprise would be all the more complete just because so arduous a manœuvre would seem to the enemy impossible. Peterborough made up his mind. If his resolutions soon sank into their own ashes, they burned fiercely while they were alight. He could carry through nothing that required a month's plan ahead, but an enterprise conceived and executed in forty-eight hours had an excellent chance in his hands.

His confidant at the moment was Colonel John Richards, a Roman Catholic officer of artillery, who, being unable to hold an English commission, had seen service under Venice and Poland, and was at present serving the Portuguese in order the better to help his native countrymen. His heart was entirely English, and his professional abilities were supported by a calm and excellent judgment, and by a thorough knowledge of the language and character of the Spaniards. He could see all round his chief, whom he declared to be ' so very inconstant as not to remain two days in the same sentiments.' His unprejudiced evidence, based on a first-hand knowledge of the facts quite unequalled by that of any other witness, solves the controversies, and disposes of the rival legends, which have so long obscured the events of the capture of Monjuic.*

Early on Saturday, September 12, Peterborough and Hesse met, and agreed on the details of the retreat to Tarragona. But in the course of the next twenty-four hours Peterborough had changed his mind and came to the resolution to attack Monjuic, apparently on no other prompting but that of the information of deserters. He disclosed his

* See Appendix at end of this chapter. p. 79.

intention to Richards and sent him to Hesse to ask for
another conference. The meeting took place. No
Sunday, one was present except Peterborough, Hesse and
Sept. $\frac{2}{13}$ Richards. The German and English generals
1705 agreed to sink their recent feuds and to co-operate
in a surprise attack on the Citadel. No fourth person, not
even the King, was to know whither the expedition was
bound, until it was on the point of departure.

At six on Sunday evening, a thousand picked infantry,
of whom eight hundred were English, started off under
Peterborough and Hesse, as though they were marching to
Tarragona in accordance with the still unrescinded decision
of the Council of War. At the last moment, 'King Charles'
was informed of the real destination, and sent a note after
Hesse to wish him God-speed. A great circuit had to be taken
by way of Sarriá. The night march was wearisome, through
a dozen miles of difficult country. The guides made
mistakes. Time was lost. And the sun was on the
Monday, point of rising out of the sea as the tired vanguard
Sept. $\frac{3}{14}$ dragged itself up the steep slopes by which Monjuic
1705 Fort can be approached from the side of the land.
The surprise was not complete. The 500 Neapolitan infantry
who were defending the place saw the English coming and
opened fire, but there was not time to send reinforcements
from the town before the British grenadiers flung themselves into the 'covered way,' as the broad open ditch of
the fort was technically called. Here, a great part of the
garrison were encamped in their tents. They were 'un-
nested from thence,' and driven up the scarp and across the
unfinished outer works of the Citadel, to take refuge in its
'Dungeon,' a 'little square fort of four bastions,' which
they held against the first assault of the grenadiers. A
good day's work had already been accomplished while the
disc of the sun was still on the waves, and while Peterborough and Hesse were still some distance behind with the
belated supports.

Arrived at last on the spot, the two chiefs divided their
tasks. Peterborough rode down the hill again to find and
bring up the reserve under James Stanhope. Hesse
marched with a detachment to the left to cut off communi-

cation with the town, whence reinforcements were momently expected. He made the mistake of passing close to the Dungeon by a route where he and his men were exposed unprotected to the Neapolitan fire. A musket-ball hit him in the right thigh, and he bled to death in less than half an hour. So perished the defender of Gibraltar, the wisest head among the allied chiefs in Spain.

The moment of crisis had come. Peterborough was away at the bottom of the hill, trying to find the strayed supports. Less than half the thousand, who had marched from camp the evening before, were now in the outer works of Monjuic. They were unnerved by Hesse's fall ; they saw nothing either of Peterborough or of the reserves ; they expected each minute to be cut off by a sortie from the town ; they had had nothing to drink all night and the heat of morning was already becoming intense; they were deceived by a ruse of the enemy in the Dungeon, who pretended to fraternize and then shot them down. Panic seized the veterans of Gibraltar. ' The officers with their swords in their breasts could not stop them,' and they fled, 'in a greater consternation than ever I saw Englishmen,' as Richards bears witness. The Neapolitans emerged from the Dungeon and reoccupied the outer works.

But the fugitives had not reached the foot of the hill before they were met by Peterborough. He was no professional soldier, but he had in him the quick temper for such an emergency. Falling ' into the horriblest passion that ever man was seen in,' he cowed the panic and led the runaways back up the slopes to recover the works they had just abandoned. Richards at the moment feared the rashness of the act, for the enemy were seen to be coming out in force from Barcelona, and the English were a mere handful. But onward and upward went the fiery little lord, ' a skeleton in outward figure,' without knowledge of war, without fear of death, and no man was so base as not to follow him. The Spaniards coming up from the town, hearing that Hesse and Peterborough were both on the spot, assumed that the Commander-in-Chief would not have come without the main body of his troops, and too prudently turned back upon their traces. The English stormed the outworks of

Monjuic for the second time that day and the Dungeon was once more closely besieged, though by a force so tiny and so far isolated from the rest of the army that a determined attack from the city must have sealed its doom. But Velasco, though he had obstinacy, had no enterprise, and permitted the Catalan 'Miquelets,' when they arrived on the scene, to seize a small fort between the Citadel and the town and so further interrupt communications.

When heavy firing had been heard at dawn coming from the slopes of Monjuic, the allied fleet and army had been as much surprised and puzzled by the sound as were the garrison and inhabitants of Barcelona. Wonder, excitement and suspense continued until Richards arrived in camp, having galloped back with a request from Peterborough to the Admirals that they would land ammunition and cannon, to bombard the Dungeon and so complete the capture of the Citadel. Guns were sent ashore, and a few days later a lucky shot from a mortar plumped into the magazine ; the explosion that followed killed the Neapolitan Commandant and his principal officers as they sat Sept. $\frac{6}{17}$ at dinner, and blew away one of the bastions of the 1705 Dungeon. A prompt surrender followed. Monjuic had fallen.

All now was eagerness and activity among the Allies, ashore and afloat. Quarrels between nations, services and persons were laid aside. Councils of War were no longer held. The bulk of the army remained on the north-east side of the town, but the siege batteries were erected at the foot of the Monjuic hill, to breach the curtain of the town wall between St. Paul's demi-lune and the Saint Anthony bastion. No regular approach trenches were made and the siege was conducted by the handy-men of the ships' crews in a manner that would have shocked Vauban or Cohorn ; but it sufficed to overcome the inert resistance of Velasco. The breaching cannon all came from the decks of the men-of-war, and, in the absence of carriages and horses, were dragged and lowered into position over the steep and broken ground by parties of shouting sailors, in high good humour at their trip ashore. Richards and Major du Terne, the most expert artillerymen in the army, directed the jolly tars in their somewhat primitive siege operations. They had ' no authority to command or money to pay ' the service of the Catalan peasants, whose presence only made confusion worse confounded, but by the help of the sailors they got ' fifty-eight great guns into battery.' And though ' our master-gunner, Silver,' was blown to pieces by the enemy fire from the town, an effective breach was made.

Meanwhile, tidings came in that every city in Catalonia, except Rosas on the French frontier, had declared for ' King Charles.' The news of the capture of Monjuic had been the signal for the rising of the Province.

To avoid a storm and sack, a capitulation was signed. On the morning of October 14, Velasco and his garrison were to march down, under treaty, to the quayside and be transported by English ships to Rosas. But as the Allies were waiting for them to appear, a frightful uproar broke out inside the town. The tocsin clashed in the steeples of Barcelona, while its fiery citizens, long held in check by the severe measures of the Governor, rose on the garrison as it filed through the streets, drove it into one of the bastions, and was on the point of killing Velasco and every Spanish soldier and sympathiser within the walls.

Oct. $\frac{3}{14}$, 1705

The English army made haste to enter. By the admission of ' King Charles ' in his letter to Queen Anne, they and their General behaved admirably, refusing every temptation to plunder, and saving the lives of Velasco and his men at great risk to their own. James Stanhope, who had already seen much service for so young a man, told Burnet that he had never been in a hotter place than the streets of Barcelona that morning, ' from the shooting and fire that was flying about in that disorder.' Peterborough, as he rode up the street, met the beautiful Duchess of Popoli, flying with dishevelled hair from her pursuers ; dismounting from his horse, he led her out of the town by the hand, the bullets of the Catalans flying round him, and one passing through his wig. According to Carleton, it was more than an hour before he returned from placing her in safety ; if this were true, more credit would be due to his officers and men than to himself for averting a general massacre. But, like much else reported by Carleton, it is highly doubtful. On the better evidence of Richards' diary we know that the Duke and Duchess of Popoli were accommodated together in Peterborough's quarters.[46]

The moment Barcelona had fallen, the quarrels of the allied chiefs broke out with fresh vigour. Hesse, the man who best envisaged the need for good understanding between Germans and English in Spain, had been removed for ever from their counsels. Poverty exacerbated ill temper. The English Government had sent out the expedition short of money to pay the troops, and now the expenses of a successful revolution were superadded. Peterborough had exhausted his private credit, never large, for in peace or war he was always in debt. The ' King and Court without a farthing ' looked to England to pay everything, and were furious when cash was not forthcoming. ' Never,' wrote Peterborough in November, ' never was prince accompanied by such wretches for ministers. They have neither money, sense nor honour.' And again, ' We are at a full stop for want of money ; a sum proportionable to such a design would in two months secure Valentia and Aragon, or carry us to Madrid.' *

Even without the money Valencia and Aragon were secured. The fall of Barcelona set all eastern Spain aflame with civil war, and the Carlists, as the partisans of ' Carlos III ' may be called, acted with greater energy than their opponents, under the stimulus of the success in Catalonia. The revolution spread from one town to another along the eastern seaboard. Peterborough was not likely to be behindhand and took a prominent part in the partisan warfare of surprise marches, bluffs, ruses and revolutionary onslaughts
Dec.   which in the course of the winter won all Valencia
1705– for the Carlist cause. He was in his element in
Feb.   such work, and while we need not swallow whole-
1706   sale all the gallant stories told about him to the
British public by his admirers, Dr. Freind and Captain Carleton, there is no reason why they should all be rejected as intrinsically impossible. The historian has no such

* P. to St., p. 2 ; P.R.O., S.P., 94, 75 (October 28 and November 2, 1705).

judicious guide as Richards to enable him to distinguish truth from falsehood in regard to Peterborough's performances in the Valencian campaign.*

Thus, by the spring of 1706, Philip V at Madrid had been placed between two fires—the war conducted from the base at Lisbon by the English, Dutch and Portuguese armies ; and the war conducted from Catalonia, Aragon and Valencia by another English army and by the Carlists of eastern Spain. Communication between the two wars was kept up by way of Gibraltar, by means of the English fleet, no longer challenged by the French fleet port-ridden in Toulon. But the enemy at Madrid had the great advantage of the central position, from which the French and Spanish forces could move in either direction against the widely divided armies of the Allies.

No Carlists had been found in the neighbourhood of Vigo, Cadiz, Gibraltar or on the Portuguese border, but they were found in plenty along the Eastern coast of Spain. The fall of Barcelona would have had little effect had it not been the capital of the Province most disaffected to Philip V. The Catalans stood in relation to the Castilians much as the Hungarians stood to the Austrians. They were a different race, and they were proud of medieval privileges and liberties which the Castilian Kings ignored, just as the Austrian Emperors ignored the ancient constitutional rights of Hungary. The Catalans therefore were hearty allies of the English, and loyal subjects of ' Carlos III.' Much support was also found for him in the Spanish provinces of Aragon and Valencia, where the Carlist party was moved by ancient

---

* One story told by *Carleton* (p. 110) is, I fear, intrinsically probable. It refers to this first winter in Barcelona : ' I was one day walking in one of the most populous streets of that city, where I found an uncommon concourse of people of all sorts got together ; and imagining so great a crowd would not be assembled on a small occasion, I pressed in among the rest, and after a good deal of struggling and difficulty, reached into the ring and centre of that mixed multitude. But how did I blush when I found one of my own countrymen, a drunken grenadier, the attractive loadstone of all the high and low mob and the butt of all their merriment ! It will be a thing not a little surprising to one of our country to find that a drunken man should be such a wonderful sight.' The poor fellow, very probably one of those who had saved Gibraltar, had few comforts in Spain :

' Dead or living, drunk or dry,
Soldier, I wish you well.'

provincial jealousy of Castile and of the King in Madrid. It was a civil war waged by the Spain of the Mediterranean seaboard against the Spain of centre and west.

But the will of Castile, the heart of Old Spain, proved stronger and more unanimous than the will of the Carlists of Valencia and Aragon. The enthusiasm of the Catalans for Charles was indeed stubborn enough, but Catalonia only a single province. To the majority of the Spaniards the English and Dutch armies were unpopular as heretics, and the Portuguese as ancient enemies and former subjects. It is true that they hated the French, but they hated the Dutch, English and Portuguese even more. In the winter of 1705–6 this was not yet clear, but the events of the next two years made it so, or showed it to be so. By 1707, if not before, the great mass of the nation identified Philip with Spanish nationality and Charles with alien conquest. Once that opinion had hardened, Charles's cause was doomed. For, as Napoleon found a hundred years later, the Spaniards were the most formidable civilian population in the world in guerilla warfare, though little use as troops of the line. If Napoleon's armies of 200,000 could not police Spain, still less could Galway's or Peterborough's armies of ten or twenty thousand. Diplomats could meet at the Hague or Utrecht and decide what Princes should bear rule over Italian and German States, but the throne of Spain could no more be disposed of against the will of the Spaniards than the throne of England against the will of the English. Therefore the capture of Barcelona, though it evoked a great popular rising for Charles along the coast, was a misfortune for that very reason, because it led the Allies, excusably enough, to believe that they could dispose of Spain, and because it pledged them in honour not to desert the Catalans and Carlists. Nevertheless the whole gigantic enterprise proved to be standing on a false foundation.

APPENDIX TO CHAPTER IV

PETERBOROUGH'S PART IN THE CAPTURE OF MONJUIC

COLONEL JOHN RICHARDS has left two accounts of the origin and execution of the attack on Monjuic—a *Diary* written at the time, and a *Narrative* written within a couple of years at latest. He was no blind admirer of Peterborough, of whom he speaks in the *Narrative* as ' so very inconstant as not to remaine two days in the same sentiments.' But his unbiassed evidence, the only first-hand evidence extant on the subject, makes it quite certain that the idea of the attack on Monjuic emanated from Peterborough, not from Hesse. The contrary statements by Leake and Martin are not first-hand, and come from naval sources, for good reason prejudiced against Peterborough.

Col. J. Richards' *Diary* (B.M. *Stowe MSS.* 467, f. 38) says :

Sat. 13th Sept. [Sat. was really the 12th (N.S.)] The Council of flags having concluded it was too late in the year to go upon the expedition to Savoy, and the King of Spain having consented to this march [to Tarragona] my Lord [Peterborough] sent for me very early this morning, where in the presence of the Prince of Hesse we resolved to march on Tuesday next [to Tarragona].

Sunday the 14th Sept. [Sunday was really 13th.] Notwithstanding the former resolution of a march, my Lord Peterborough being resolved by several deserters of the ill state of Montjuic the citadel of Barcelona, he proposed to me the surprisal of it this night by escalade, and afterwards the Prince who approving thereof a detachment of 400 grenadiers and 600 musqueteers was ordered to rendez-vous at 4 o'clock at the prince's quarters, where I likewise sent the necessary ammunition and scaling ladders. The secret was communicated to no living creature, not so much as to the King [he was told last thing as the expedition started, as his letter in *Künzel*, p. 666, shows]. We marched all night being forced to make a grand tour.

Monday the 15th [really 14th]. The getting up the hill [Monjuic] was painful to us that were already tired by the length of the march, and what was worse our guides mistook the way. The grenadiers went one way, and musqueteers another, the Prince and my Lord a third, and all wrong. It was therefore break of day before we came in sight of the citadel, so that we were discovered by the enemy.

Substantially the same with some differences of detail is the other account given by Richards in his *Narrative* (*Stowe MSS.* 471, f. 15) :—

It was the 13th of the said month that my Lord Peterborough was pleased to communicate to me certain informations which he got from divers deserters of the citadel of this town situate upon a hill on the farther side of the city. He ordered me to the Pr. of Hesse to appoint a time of conference with him.

It was then resolved to attack, and my Lord promised if he carried it that he would then form the siege of the town ; and in case they did not, that then the Prince should concur with him in all future operations projected by them ; and in the meantime great assurances of mutual friendship passed between them, which I was very glad to see, for not long before there appeared in their conduct nothing less.

I was the only person present at this Conference. The secret was mightily recommended, in so much as it was resolved that the King should know nothing of it. Sunday the 14th [really 13th] in the evening we marched with 500 grenadiers supported by 500 foot, the necessary ammunitions and some scaling ladders, towards Montjuic by a long way about.

See my article in the *Cambridge Historical Journal*, 1931, for further quotations from Richards as to the fighting for Monjuic, on which he is the best authority, and for further discussion of the value of his evidence as against Col. Parnell's opinions. It is worth noting that while the naval men, like Leake and Martin, who had good reason to hate Peterborough, chose to believe that the idea of attacking Monjuic came from Hesse and not from Peterborough, the military men held exactly the opposite opinion. Col. Edgworth (*H. of L. MSS.* (1706–8), p. 510) told the House of Lords ' That it was the opinion of all the camp that Earl Peterborough communicated the design to no person whatsoever, but that the Prince of Hesse went thither as a volunteer.'

CHAPTER V

THE VICTORY OF 'MODERATION'

Godolphin, Harley, Cowper and the Junto. First Session of the new
Parliament, winter 1705–6. The Regency Act and the Hanoverian
Succession. Settlement of the question of 'Placemen' in the House
of Commons. The Court of Hanover : Sophia, George, Leibnitz and
England.

WHEN the new Parliament assembled in the autumn of 1705
it was clear that the Godolphin Ministry, as a result of the
General Election in the summer,* would sail henceforth
in smoother waters. 'Moderate men looked big.' The
principle of 'Peace at home and war abroad' was triumphant, owing to the joint efforts for three years past of the
Queen on the throne, of Godolphin at the Council Board,
of Harley in the Lobby, and of Marlborough winning battles
oversea.

Hitherto, though Anne had been the least willing to
move, all four had kept step in their march away from High
Tory policies. But now that the victory of Moderation
was won at the polls, the difference of view as to the proper
means to maintain and exploit it begins to be perceptible in
the correspondence between Secretary Harley and Lord
Treasurer Godolphin. The Treasurer was prepared to
advance further than the Secretary along the road of Whig
alliance. The Queen, indeed, had always been loath to
acknowledge that because she had quarrelled with the High
Tories, she must therefore make friends with the Whigs.
In July 1705 she had written to Godolphin, imploring him
to 'keep me out of the power of *the merciless men of both*

* See pp. 26–31, above.

parties.' * And three months later Harley begins, in his letters to the Treasurer, to lay down principles very similar to those of their royal mistress.

I take it for granted [he writes to Godolphin in September], no party in the House can carry it for themselves without the Queen's Servants join with them. The foundation is, persons and parties are to come to the Queen, and not the Queen to them. The Queen hath chosen rightly which party she will take in. If the gentlemen of England are made sensible that the Queen is the head, and not a Party, everything will be easy, and the Queen will be courted and not a party.

Therefore the High Tory opposition must not be completely alienated by too eager a court paid to the Whigs.

The embodying of gentlemen (country gentlemen, I mean) against the Queen's service is what is to be avoided.

Whiggish policies will, in Harley's opinion, ' shock more persons than they will gain.' Already the great ' trimmer ' of the reign was preparing to redress the balance against the Whig predominance that he foresaw and dreaded.

But Godolphin thought otherwise. He had not the Secretary's cold indifference to abuse. He was indignant with the conduct of the High Tories, and especially was he vexed by the hue and cry of the clerical pamphleteers against the person of the Lord Treasurer. Moreover, he wrote to Harley that the Government with its middle party of 100 ' Queen's Servants ' could only obtain a majority in the Commons by courting the 160 Whigs, who could be more easily appeased than the 190 Tories.

For every one we are likely to get from the 190 we shall lose two or three from the 160. And is it not more reasonable and more easy to preserve those who have served and helped us, than those who have basely and ungratefully done all that was in their power to ruin us ? . . . As for the clergy, they always say themselves it is easy for the Queen to get them into her interests. I think so, too, if they be once thoroughly satisfied which is the right way to preferment.†

---

* *Add. MSS.* 28070, f. 12.

† The last remark, certainly unfair on the clergy as a whole, though true of individuals, shows Godolphin's growing animosity against their profession, see pp. 6–7, above. This letter of Godolphin's of March 1706 reads like an answer to

These two letters may be read to mean merely that
Godolphin would go on to become a Whig, and Harley go
back to remain a Tory.   But there is more in the difference
than that.   Harley, like Queen Anne, believed that the
advent of pure party government could and should be
avoided in England.   Godolphin believed that the hard
facts of House of Commons life were making party government inevitable.   Harley preached, while it was still con-
ceivably practicable, the doctrine afterwards advocated by
Bolingbroke in an age too late, of the ' Patriot King,' a
monarchy governing by its influence in Parliament, but
detached from party ties.

This difference of policy between Harley and Godolphin
was connected, whether as cause or effect, with a decided
preference on the part of the Whigs themselves for the
Treasurer over the Secretary.   Somers and Wharton, the
grave and the gay, were equally at home in driving bargains
with Godolphin in whispered colloquies on the benches
of the House of Lords.   But Harley was suspect to every
Whig, whether on account of his sly and furtive manner, or
because they already had wind of the drift of his thoughts
and saw in him the secret but dangerous enemy of their own
power.

The Whig distrust of Harley is intimately revealed to us
in the private diary of Sir William Cowper, elevated
to be Keeper of the Great Seal with the promise of a
peerage to follow.   Cowper in office soon overcame
the Queen's original prejudice against him, and won golden
opinions with all men, both by his obliging manners, very
different from those of his predecessor Wright, and by his
disinterested refusal to accept the customary ' New Year's
gifts ' from the counsel practising at the Chancery Bar.   He
felt that these perquisites, though they might be sanctioned
by antiquity, smacked of corruption, the more so as they
were estimated to range between fifteen hundred and three
thousand pounds every year.   The chiefs of the other
Courts resented his scrupulosity and refused to follow his

Oct.
1705

Harley's of September 1705, although, in fact, the Parliamentary session had
intervened between the two letters.   *H.M.C. Bath*, I, p. 74 ;   *H.M.C. Portland*, IV,
p. 291.

example.   But the public sided with Cowper against the other judges, and his good deed was celebrated in bad verse by Ambrose Philips—the poet whose nickname of Namby-Pamby has added a word to the language * :

> He the robe of justice wore,
> Sullied not as heretofore,
> When the magistrate was bought
> With ' Yearly gifts.' [47]

Cowper was disposed, by his easy temper and by the political conditions of the hour, to make himself agreeable to his Tory colleagues in the Cabinet.   He was even on friendly personal terms with Rochester, the leader of the highest Tory opposition, whom he declared to be ' a good-natured man, though hot.'   But Harley he could not away with.   From the first he suspected him of trickery and secret opposition.   In the early days of January 1706 the Secretary gave a dinner to Marlborough, Godolphin and the Whig Chiefs.   It was to be a great occasion, ' to re-concile Somers and Halifax with Harley.'

Secretary Harley [writes Cowper] took a glass, and drank to Love and Friendship and everlasting Union, and wished he had more Tokay to drink it in (we had drank two bottles, good, but thick).   I replied his White Lisbon was best to drink it in, being very *clear* :   I suppose he apprehended it (as I observed most of the company did) to relate to that humour of his, which was never to deal clearly or openly, but always with reserve, if not dissimulation or rather simulation ;   and to love tricks even when not necessary, but from an inward satisfaction he took in applauding his own cunning.   If any man was ever born under a necessity of being a knave, he was.

The Whig Chiefs, in fact, thought of Harley much as their successors thought of Shelburne.   And Godolphin was beginning to harbour similar suspicions.   How indeed could he not suspect hypocrisy when Harley wrote to him ' I have united my very soul to you.   I have no other views, no other passions than to be subservient to your lordship.'   The Secretary protested too much.[48]

---

* It was Ambrose Philips who, in celebrating the happy accession of the House of Hanover, was inspired by the soaring of the stocks to personify ' property ' as a racial deity of our island :

> ' O Property !   O Goddess, English born ! '

One function of government, according to the ideas of the time, was to identify and prosecute the anonymous authors of violent Opposition pamphlets. The ' freedom of the press,' released indeed from censorship, was still limited by the fear of the consequences of publication. Two years back Whig pamphleteers had suffered prosecution by the Godolphin Ministry ; now it was the turn of their rivals. The author of the High Church *Memorial of the Church of England*, Dr. James Drake, had not yet been identified.* In August 1705 Marlborough had written to Godolphin from the field :

> In this camp I have had time to read the pamphlet called *The Memorial of the Church of England*. I think it the most impudent and scurrilous thing I ever read. If the author can be found I do not doubt he will be punished ; for if such liberties may be taken of writing scandalous lies without being punished, no Government can stand long. Notwithstanding what I have said, I cannot forbear laughing, when I think they would have you and I pass as fanatics ; and the Duke of Buckingham and Lord Jersey for pillars of the Church ; the one being a Roman Catholic in King James's time, and the other would have been a Quaker or any other religion that would have pleased the late King.

Cowper found Secretary Harley slack in this business of detecting the author of the obnoxious pamphlet, and unwilling to employ his private agents and sources of information against a brother Tory. Investigations and proceedings dragged on for a year, in the course of which Dr. Drake, though not positively convicted, was worried into a fever that killed him ; and poor Ned Ward, the Tory public-house poet, a reprobate rather dear to posterity, expiated his *Hudibras Redivivus* in the pillory, where he suffered from the London mob, whom he had satirized, much more severely than Defoe had formerly suffered in a similar elevation.† Whether or not Harley's slackness in these acts of

---

* See pp. 6 and 26 note, above.

† It is probably to this occasion (1706) that Pope refers in the line :

'As thick as eggs at Ward in pillory,'

for Ned Ward appears in another passage of the *Dunciad* (I, l. 233 ; III, l. 34). In May 1706 the Rector of Sutton, condemned to stand in the pillory for a libel on Marlborough, was, on full submission, begged off by Sarah, the Duke approving. *Coxe*, chap. xlii The physician, Dr. Joseph Browne, was also sent to Newgate as the author of *The country parson's advice to the Lord Keeper*. (*Rosebery Pamphlets, Edin.*)

party vengeance had been at all due to humanity and good sense, it was regarded as mere double-dealing by Godolphin and the Whigs, who were destined ere many years were out to have their fill of prosecuting a more famous ' Doctor ' than Drake.[49]

The new Parliament met at the end of October 1705, and the first business in the Commons was to choose a Speaker. It had been known for some time that the Tory Opposition would put up Bromley, the leader of the Tackers. His opponent was to be John Smith, an out-and-out Whig. After the custom of the time, speeches were made in ' Billingsgate language,' blackening the lives and characters of the rival candidates for the Chair. The House was re-minded that in the late King's reign Smith had unpatriotically voted for a standing army in time of peace. On the other hand Bromley had, fifteen years before, published a foolish book of youthful travels which was held to reveal the extent of his Jacobitism, and more certainly revealed the limitations of his intellect. His enemies had it reprinted and circulated in time to influence the division—one of Harley's sly tricks, it was said.* Smith was chosen by 248 votes to 205. Not all the supporters of Government had realized that they were expected to vote for a Whig Speaker, and fifteen office-holders had voted for Bromley ; one of them, a Secretary of the Admiralty, was dismissed by way of example, in order that the Ministerial-Whig Coalition might in future rely on the votes of all Her Majesty's servants.[50]

The Queen's Speech was Whiggish. The first draft had been drawn up by Godolphin in his own hand and, as was

---

* The new edition was, indeed, a knavish piece of work. It contained a new Contents Table with such headings as : ' The Author compared with our Saviour, and wants of his Height, a hand's breadth by measure, p. 107.' ' The Author kissed the Pope's slipper, and had his blessing though a Protestant ; but not a word of religion, p. 149.' ' Eight pictures take up less room than sixteen of the same size, p. 14.'

In *The Dyet of Poland, a Satyr*, a Whig review of political personalities, published in 1705 (*Rosebery Pamphlets, Edin.*), we read of *Bromsky* (= Bromley) :

' In foreign parts he travelled much in vain,
Just made a book and so came home again ;
Tells us he saw a bridge at Rochester ;
And when he was at Chatham—he was there,' etc.

usual with all royal messages to either House of Parliament, was passed at a Cabinet with Anne present. She urged on the Houses the necessity of a Treaty of Union with Scotland; she spoke with bitter indignation of those who said the Church of England was in danger under her government ; and she declared that ' we have great grounds of hope that, by the blessing of God upon our arms and those of our allies, a good foundation is laid for restoring the Monarchy of Spain to the House of Austria.' The news of the fall of Barcelona had just arrived, and the salvoes of guns firing to celebrate the event had been heard by Members as they rode into London for the new Parliament. The Whig and Ministerial newspapers urged the necessity and practicability of conquering Spain for ' King Charles,' and foresaw in the consequent trade with Spanish America a means of making good more than all that the war would cost. On military expenditure a perpetual stream of lamentation flowed through the Opposition press ; it was said that the nation was ruined and, very unjustly, that ' the Dutch had expended nothing on the war.' Both statements the Whig and Ministerial newspapers denied. The High Church papers had also, for some time past, been carrying on a campaign of abuse of the Scots, to prevent the project of Union : the *Rehearsal* averred that the Privy Council and magistrates of Edinburgh had caused our Saviour to be burnt in effigy —a story contradicted by the Whig *Flying Post*. Harley, who, for all his doubts as to the future, was still substantially loyal to the government policies of the hour, wrote to Marlborough :

I hear the ill-intentioned in Holland give a very wrong turn to the part of the Queen's Speech which relates to the monarchy of Spain, as if that was to eternize the war, when there cannot be a clearer proposition than that it is the only way to a secure peace.[51]

After both Houses had replied to the Queen's Speech, welcoming the sentiments she had expressed, the Commons plunged eagerly into the attractive business of Election Petitions. As usual, party was the first consideration, and evidence a poor second. The loudest clamour arose over the St. Albans election, a close-run thing, in which the personal canvass of the Duchess of Marlborough, who often resided there, had turned waverers in favour of the Whig Admiral Killigrew. Bromley, in the House, ventured to compare her to Alice Perrers, the politically-minded female favourite of Edward III's dotage—a comparison not calculated to please the Queen. After a stormy debate the seat was voted to the Admiral.[52]

Since the General Election the High Tories had lost control of the Commons. Seymour and Bromley were reduced to impotence : the formidable old patriarch of the West was sinking to his grave, and Bromley had not the parts to hold attention without a majority behind him. The more important leaders of the Tory Opposition sat in the House of Lords, which became the principal scene of political skirmishing in this Parliament.

In December 1705 Rochester moved that the Church was in danger, on the ground that the Ministers and Bishops and, it was implied, the Queen also, had gone over to the enemy. In the debate that followed, the Whig Bishops bemoaned the attacks made on them by their own clergy in Convocation and elsewhere. The Bishop of Ely, with experience of Cambridge,

complained of the heat and passion of the gentlemen of the Universities, which they inculcated into their pupils, who brought the same fury with them to the parishes when they came abroad, to the great disturbance of public charity.

The Tories complained of the multiplication of Dissenting Schools and Academies, although the Dissenters paid for these entirely themselves, and were, moreover, excluded by law from the Universities. The Whigs replied that since the Toleration the Dissenters had ' softened their tempers and concurred zealously in serving all the ends of Government,' better, indeed, than those who attacked them. A large majority in both Houses voted that the Church had been rescued from imminent danger by King William the Third of Glorious Memory, and that ' whoever goes about to suggest and insinuate that the Church is in danger under Her Majesty's administration, is an enemy to the Queen, the Church and the Kingdom.' The Queen herself, a diligent listener under the Lords' gallery, was more than ever alienated from her old friends when she heard them accuse her of indifference to the Church she so truly loved. At no moment was she nearer to the Whigs—at least, at no moment was she further removed from the heart of Toryism.*

The High Church fared ill this session, for Convocation, meeting at the same time as Parliament, was broken up by another violent quarrel between the moderate Bishops in the Upper House and the high-flying majority in the Lower. Tempers were further exacerbated by an open protest, signed by the Moderate minority in the Lower House, in favour of the Episcopal authority. The Queen at length intervened on the same side, declaring that ' she was resolved to maintain her supremacy, and the due subordination of Presbyters and Bishops as fundamental parts thereof.' She supported the right of the Archbishop to prorogue the sittings of the Lower House, which the extreme high churchmen had denied.†

Another question raised before Christmas by the Opposition in the House of Lords was our relations with the Allies. The reckless Lord Haversham, a recent convert from Whig to Tory intransigence, moved for an enquiry into the misconduct of Prince Lewis of Baden and the Dutch generals in thwarting Marlborough during last summer's campaign.

---

* *Parl. Hist.*, VI, 479–509 ; *Burnet*, V, pp. 235–238 (435) ; *Cowper*, pp. 25–26. The Tory Dartmouth, in his notes to Burnet, gives us an intimate account of the humours of the debate : ' This dispute rather than debate was brought on by Lord Rochester's passion, without consulting anybody, and was as ill-timed as it could well be, for we all knew the Queen was little satisfied with the hands she was fallen into, and the Whigs wanted nothing more than an opportunity to justify themselves in relation to the Church. I happened to sit by Lord Godolphin, when Lord Rochester accepted Lord Halifax's challenge, and I said to him (not thinking it would go further) that I believed a scene between Hothead and Testimony would be very diverting. He was pleased with the conceit, and told it to all about him, knowing nothing damps a debate more than turning it to ridicule ; and it had such an effect that everybody was ready to laugh, when either of them spoke.'

† See *Blenheim*, pp. 284–287, on the Convocation Controversy. For the Convocation of 1705–6, see T. Lathbury, *Hist. of Convocation*, pp. 398–399, and *Burnet*, V, pp. 247–249 (442). The Lower House complained to the bishops of Defoe's *Review* and Tutchin's *Observator* as licentious publications ; of the immorality of the theatre ; and of the public services held in London by Unitarians, who enjoyed no legal protection under the Toleration Act.

The feeling in the country on this subject was naturally very bitter. Political poets, some of whom hated the Dutch more than they loved the Duke, were writing satires entitled 'The Dutch Deputies' :

> Mechanicks, base Republicans, controul
> The vast designs of Marlb'rough's thoughtful soul.
> See now, they doubt and stop the conquering hand
> That gave them victory at his wife's command.

Such popular diatribes were very well, but a motion carried in the House of Lords condemning our allies would have ugly repercussions abroad, and would not help to make things better in the field next year. There was indeed much ground for complaint, but the man who had most right to complain had most to lose by Haversham's motion, which was purely mischievous in intention. Both Houses voted an address to the Queen to maintain good correspondence with the Allies.[53]

The party manœuvrings of this winter in the Lords, paltry and ephemeral as for the most part they were, chanced to produce a measure fraught with great consequences for the future of England. The Regency Act not only supplied the machinery by which in fact the House of Hanover came unopposed to the throne in 1714, but removed from the Act of Settlement clauses which must have proved a bar to the growth of our national system of Parliamentary Cabinet government. The story is as curious as its outcome was important.

The leaders of Opposition, as they watched the sun of their party's fortunes, which had risen so splendidly at the Queen's accession, sink in a fog of war and Whiggery, were so shaken with rage against the Queen and her servants that their conduct this winter became both eccentric and dangerous. The Scottish Jacobite, Lockhart, then in London, wrote home to the Duke of Atholl that ' sure since the siege of Jerusalem, never was there such a divided, I may rather say, sub-sub-divided nation ' as England, and that rather than see the Whigs come into power the Tories would rise in rebellion. The Scot did not understand South Britain, where civil war was more alien to native custom than in his own country. But one phrase in Lockhart's letter came very near the mark. After observing that the Whigs and Tories regarded the question of the Succession from the point of view of party interest alone, he added :

They don't so much value in England who shall be King, as whose King he shall be !

The steadfast Jacobite had been moved to utter this epigram by the spectacle of the chiefs of the High Tory Opposition, led by Lord Haversham, moving in the House of Lords that the Hanoverian successor be invited over to reside in England until the Queen's death.[54]

Rochester, Jersey and Buckingham, who supported Haversham's motion, were half Jacobite. But Rochester was also on good personal relations with Sophia, the Dowager Electress of Hanover, statutory heir to the English throne. In October 1705 he had been given to understand, by a correspondent in Hanover, that her regard for him was undiminished ; that she would be very willing to come to England ' whenever the Queen and Parliament call her,' and that her son, the reigning Elector George, ' though exceeding modest on this point,' substantially agreed with his mother.[55] Rochester was tempted to gratify his anger with his niece Anne, who, as was well known, abominated the idea of the ' Successor ' setting up a rival court in England in her lifetime. The Queen once wrote to Marlborough that to have Sophia, or the Elector George, or even the Electoral Prince over here was ' a thing I cannot bear, though but for a week.' Rochester and Nottingham, seeing themselves entirely out with the reigning sovereign, who was not expected to live for long, were tempted to sacrifice all chance of royal favour from Anne in order to build up a strong claim on one of her possible successors. The plan was a shrewd one, but in 1705 it was premature, for in fact the poor invalid Queen lived for almost another decade. It was only when she was really sinking to her grave that the Whigs played the same game, more boldly, more sincerely, and with very much greater success.

There was another point in this move of the Opposition
Lords. If the Ministers and the Whigs accepted the proposal to invite over the Electress or her son, they would ruin
themselves with Queen Anne. But if they opposed it, would
they not ruin themselves with the nation ? Could they not
then be denounced by the High Tories as disloyal to the
Protestant Succession ? And even if that charge were not
very widely believed in England, might it not at least find
credence in Hanover, and teach Sophia and George to think
that Nottingham and Rochester were their only honest
friends ? The personal connection of the Whig chiefs with
their future sovereign was at that time less close than it soon
afterwards became. As to Marlborough and Godolphin, all
Europe knew that in the last reign they had been no less
Jacobite than Rochester, and very much more so than Nottingham, who was as consistent a Hanoverian as Wharton
himself. It seemed, therefore, by no means impossible in
1705 to persuade the House of Hanover that Whigs and
Ministerialists were less good friends to the Protestant
Succession than the calumniated High Tories.

It was a clever trap, and Godolphin and his Whig allies
only escaped from it by a bold and energetic movement.
They refused to vote that the Successor should be invited
over in the Queen's lifetime. But, at the instigation of the
ever-ready Wharton, they turned the flank of the High
Tories by proposing a Regency Act, which provided a
practical machinery to ensure the Protestant Succession
upon Anne's death.

The Lords of the Tory Opposition complained in their
speeches that the Queen's presence in the Chamber was a
constraint on the freedom of debate. Nevertheless she continued to sit there and listen with ever-growing indignation.
She heard the Duke of Buckingham prove the necessity of
inviting over Sophia on the ground that Anne's faculties
might soon give way, and she become ' as a child in the
hands of others.' But most of all was she astonished
and outraged to hear Nottingham and Rochester support
Haversham's motion. When they had been her Ministers,
they had indoctrinated her with the belief that the Whigs, in
proposing to invite over the Successor in her lifetime, had

designed to depose her. They themselves now pressed the
policy of the invitation. Wharton, in high spirits,
Nov. 15 chaffed Rochester, Jersey and Buckingham on their
1705 ' miraculous conversion ' to the Hanoverian interest,
opposed the invitation, and suggested instead the outline of
the Regency Bill. This important Act of State was forthwith
drawn up by the Ministers with the help of Lord Somers.
The great Whig constitutional lawyer enjoyed so little of
Anne's favour that he was never again Lord Chancellor,
but his wisdom and experience were at the disposal of the
Ministers of the Crown. Though still in a private station, he
took an active part in framing and passing both the Regency
Act and the Treaty of Union with Scotland.[56]

Although the Regency Act of the winter of 1705–6 was
the outcome of party manœuvring, it was none the less of
capital value to the future of England. It brought the Act
of Settlement up to date, and supplied means to put it into
force at the critical moment, when the Hanoverian successor
would still be abroad. It provided that the Privy Council
should not be dissolved by the demise of the Crown,
but should continue to sit and should at once proclaim the
successor. A Regency of ' Lords Justices ' was to rule the
country until Sophia or George had time to cross over from
Hanover and assume the government in person. The ' Lords
Justices ' were to consist of the holders of the seven principal
offices of State * at the moment when Anne should die, and
other persons to be named by the successor. Parliament
was not to be dissolved by the Queen's death, as was then
the law unless otherwise provided, but was to meet at once
and was to sit for six months. These arrangements would
leave the Pretender little chance of slipping on to the throne
through the confusion and paralysis of government. When
the test actually came, the precautions proved practical and
adequate. Another Act, passed at the same time, naturalized
the Electress Sophia and her issue.

The High Tory Opposition could only murmur that

* The Archbishop of Canterbury ; the Chancellor or Lord Keeper ; the
Lord Treasurer ; the Lord President of the Council ; the Lord Privy Seal ; the
Lord High Admiral ; the Lord Chief Justice. The Tory Opposition in the Lords
voted to omit the Lord Treasurer, out of spite to Godolphin, and to substitute the
Lord Mayor of London ; but they were outvoted.

these measures were unnecessary. The Jacobites among them were fairly hoist with their own petard, overreached by their own cunning. When the Regency Bill went down to the Commons it lay there for some time ' by a secret management that was against it.' Hanover and the High Tories were in communication. The Electress, who had never had any particular preference for the Whigs and was irritated by the Queen's attitude of obvious personal hostility, continued to agitate behind the scenes for an immediate invitation to England. She wrote to the Archbishop of Canterbury expressing her willingness to come over when asked; the letter found its way into print, causing a high debate in the Commons, and alienating Queen Anne more than ever from her Hanoverian kinsfolk.

Sophia, a lively and adventurous lady of seventy-five, was not afraid of making a little trouble in England. A jaunt to the famous island, to ' shine there ' awhile as the much-courted ' Successor,' would amuse her declining years. By habit and affection she was less deeply rooted in Hanover than was her son George. If her heart was not ' entirely English,' neither was it entirely German—or Dutch. If she had lived to reign, ' Queen Sophy ' would have been popular.

So the High Tories in the House of Commons moved the invitation to the Successor to come to England, in place of the Regency Act. There was some danger lest the Whig private members should break away from the orders of the Junto and vote for the invitation, which used to be the Whig policy and was to be so again half a dozen years later. But the excellent discipline of the Whig party held good, the invitation was voted down, and the Regency Bill became law.[57]

The main purport of the new Act was scarcely more important to the future history of England than were two of its minor provisions, altering certain provisions in the Act of Settlement of 1701. That measure had fixed the succession on the Electress and her heirs, being Protestants, but had decreed certain limitations on the power of the Crown, to come into force whenever the House of Hanover actually succeeded.* One of these limitations provided that

* See *Blenheim*, pp. 119-121, for the text of these limitations.

all matters and things relating to the well government of this Kingdom, which are properly cognizable in the Privy Council, by the laws
and customs of this Realm, shall be transacted there and all resolutions
taken thereupon shall be signed by such of the Privy Council as shall
advise and consent to the same.

This clause was intended to put an end to the recently
developed system of government by the secret consultations
of a Cabinet.   But it was repealed by the Regency Act
before it ever had the chance to become operative.

Cabinet Government with secret consultations was thereby allowed to continue.   But such a Cabinet might exist
and yet all its members might be disconnected from the
House of Commons, as the United States Cabinet is disconnected from either House of Congress.   Such was the
old ideal of the English Constitution, as conceived by many
Members of Parliament for many years both before and
after the Revolution.   The desire to get rid of the ' Royal
Servants ' from the House of Commons was always strong
with the Opposition members of the day, whether Whig or
Tory, who regarded ' placemen ' in the House as persons
bribed by the Court to vote them down.   Only gradually
did the idea spread that the House of Commons was in
future to be, not as heretofore the focus of opposition, but
itself the seat of governmental power.

The fact that, before the Premiership of Walpole, the
most important Ministers sat in the Lords, still rendered
the Commons suspicious of Government as such, and
jealous of Ministerial influences in their midst.   Therefore
the Act of Settlement of 1701 had contained a provision
that, as soon as the House of Hanover should succeed to
the throne—

No person who has an office or place of profit under the King, or
receives a pension from the Crown, shall be capable of serving as a
member of the House of Commons.

When the Regency Act was introduced it was felt by
Ministerialists to be a fitting moment to repeal this provision.   The House of Lords was strongly of that opinion,
though in fact the repeal has proved a chief cause of the
ultimate predominance of the Lower House.   It is a

curious fact that the Commons of February 1706 were far less enthusiastic to liberate themselves from a self-denying ordinance, which would have isolated their House from the real government of the country.   The Ministerial Tories, indeed, were all for the repeal of a provision which would drive them either from office or from the Commons on the Queen's death.   But for that very reason the High Tory Opposition were all for maintaining the clause.   The Whigs were divided, but the pressure of the Junto Lords and of party discipline was exerted to make them vote for the Government.   After many debates and divisions, and a formal conference between the two Houses, a compromise was at length agreed upon.   After the House of Hanover had come to the throne, certain offices should no longer be held by Members of the House of Commons.   But the holders of other offices, including the principal political offices of State, though they must on taking office resign their seats, might be re-elected to the House of Commons. The electors were to judge of the propriety of their continuing to sit there.   This arrangement, repeated in the Act of 1707 that established the Union with Scotland, held good until recent years, when it has been modified almost out of recognition.

In the course of the debates on this subject, the Lords, who had certainly shown the higher statesmanship, reminded the Commons that

To enact that all persons employed and trusted by the Crown shall, for that reason alone, become uncapable of being trusted by the people, is in effect to declare that the interest of the Crown and of the People must be always contrary to each other ; which is a notion no good Englishman ought to entertain.

The matter at issue could not have been put into wiser words.   In spite of the memory of former strife between Stuart Kings and Parliaments, in spite of the future theories of Montesquieu,* the more closely the executive

---

* Montesquieu's mistaken belief that English liberty was secured by the separation of the executive and legislative, was widely spread by his authority, not without important results in America and France.   His error was largely due to the survival of the tradition against ' placemen in the Commons,' which died very hard.   Montesquieu, who visited England about 1730, was a generation or more behind the times in his analysis of the English Constitution as it had then become.

and legislative were identified, the better for the government
of the country, the better even for its liberties.   The separation of executive and legislative in the American Constitution
of to-day, involving the frequent hostility of Congress to
the President and his Cabinet for party reasons, has many
very grave consequences to the United States and to the
world at large.   If, on the accession of the House of
Hanover, ' placemen ' had been excluded from the House
of Commons, consequences of a not dissimilar kind would
have arisen in England.   This was prevented by the
Regency Act of 1705–6.[58]

If Anne had died about this time, Sophia would have
succeeded unopposed to the throne of England—(Scotland
was another matter)—and she would not, like her son in
1714, have been primarily dependent on Whig support.
She had no intention of identifying her cause with either party
in the State.   She believed that the Whigs must perforce be
loyal to the House of Hanover, and that her care should
be to conciliate the less certain loyalty of the Tories.   A
Princess brought up in the ideas of the Seventeenth rather
than of the Eighteenth Century, she did not care about
her ' Parliamentary title,' but claimed ' hereditary right,'
although she allowed that Parliament could exclude Roman
Catholics.   The point was perhaps too fine to be very
important, but it showed her to be, like William III before
her, rather Royalist than Whig in political theory.

Neither was she greatly prepossessed by ardent Whigs
who came over to pay court at Hanover, such as Toland the
pamphleteer.   Poor Toland, a useful champion of freedom
of thought in religion, like many useful champions of unpopular causes, was not personally attractive, and lacked
the worldly wisdom needed to make himself agreeable to
Sophia.   Her philosophical friend was not Toland but
Leibnitz.

She liked better such humble visitors as ' Mr. Warden
of Gloucestershire,' who came in 1704 ' to tell her how
many good friends she hath in his county.   And Her
Highness is very dexterous,' the English Resident reported,
' in pleasing them that come so far to be pleased, and hath

used him so civilly that he says he does not doubt but by
the relation of the good usage he hath received he shall send
twenty more gentlemen out of Gloucestershire with more
business than he hath himself.'

Godolphin, though he had heartily supported the
Regency Act, was never, like the Whig chiefs, in personal
correspondence with Hanover. He and Marlborough
lived always under the cloud of their Jacobite past. What
either of them would do in case of a disputed succession was
always regarded as uncertain by the Whigs, and by the
Court of Hanover, although the Duke was assiduous there
in his visits at the end of each campaign. Anne's views
about the Succession were regarded as even more doubtful.

In the early summer of 1706 Lord Halifax was sent out
on a mission to Hanover to make all smooth there on behalf
of the Whig party and the Ministers. He carried with him
the text of the Regency and Naturalisation Acts, and a
Garter for the young Electoral Prince, afterwards George II.
But Sophia was too sore on the question of her foiled visit
to England, and too certain of Whig fidelity in any case, to
be at pains to display much enthusiasm. Addison, recently
made an Under-Secretary of State for his poem on Blenheim,
came to Hanover in the train of Halifax. Sophia had heard
of his rising reputation as a wit and a man of learning and
looked forward to hearing him talk. But his shyness and
silence in a Court circle disappointed her.

She had no such difficulty with Mrs. Burnet, who came
over the next year to present her good husband's compliments. Sophia liked the Bishop's wife and made to her
the following remarkable confidence :

> She believed that if the Queen died to-day, she should succeed
> to-morrow, and her children after her. But the Queen might live
> twelve years and things might change. And she knew not how fit
> her son, a stranger to all, might be.

If the Whigs did not quite know what to make of Sophia
herself, they began now to make better progress with her
son the Elector. Halifax and he were shut up together
alone ' to converse in very ill French.' The Whig chief
reported to Godolphin that

The Elector was much more easy and familiar than I expected, and took up new airs of good humour, as they that know him say, but I think him very dry.   I have been wonderful fortunate, for this victory of Lord Marlborough [Ramillies] has made their coun-tenances much more gracious than I think I should have found.

So long as his mother lived, George was still in the back-ground in transactions about the English succession, but he was the ruler of Hanover, and as such felt a steady enthusiasm for the war and for the English Alliance.   He had already learned that the England of Marlborough and the Whigs was a more valuable ally than Holland, and when disputes arose he took their side against the Dutch.   But he sus-pected the Tory Opposition of indifference to the war.   He knew and cared less than his mother about English domestic affairs, but he was eager to court England as the defender of German interests against France.   Therefore he was more drawn to the Whigs than to the Tories.   The circumstances in which, six years later, Bolingbroke brought the war to an end, greatly increased these prepossessions in the mind of the future George I.[59]

Wiser than either the Electress or her son was their faithful friend, the philosopher statesman Leibnitz.   A letter that he wrote in August 1706 to Davenant, the pamphleteer of the Ministerialist Tories, shows his clear grasp of prin-ciples and their relation to the actual situation :

Princes who govern according to law are for the most part those who have the greatest authority, or at all events the most durable. This English maxim deserves to be that of all nations.   After having been saved by your good principles and your money, it is right that we should go to school to you—I mean you as you now are and not as you were sixty years ago.   You have learnt to your cost that you may push liberty too far.   Hence I hope that people will be wiser now, and will not suffer themselves to be dazzled by exaggerated Republican principles at a moment when the fear of arbitrary power will be diminished by the humiliation of France.   [Ramillies had just been won.]   The Whigs are at this moment on good terms with the Court.   We are not sorry for it ; for we seek and desire the welfare of the nation and the agreement of parties in one same principal object, which will also be the security of the Succession.[60]

CHAPTER VI

Ramillies

In May 1706 the war had been raging for four years, but the Allies had made little progress towards the reconquest of the Netherlands and Italy from the French, which they had declared in the Treaty of Grand Alliance to be essential to the future safety of Europe. The enemy battle-fleets had indeed been driven from the sea, and a terrible blow had been dealt at Blenheim to the arms of France. But her military prestige had made a partial recovery, owing to the failure of the Allies to profit by their great opportunities in 1705. Taught by that failure, the Dutch Government was ready next spring to defer to all Marlborough's wishes in the field. But the Republic, though loyal to the Allies, was staggering under financial burdens heavier than she could bear. England had greater powers for taxation and borrowing, and her newly elected Parliament was ready to see them used to the full. But not only had she now, with the Spanish war on her back, to raise British armies twice the size of those of 1702, but the mercenary Princes of Europe were crying aloud to Marlborough for April– the full payment of arrears. The Kings of Prussia May and Denmark refused to let their men march to the 1706 Rhine or Flanders on any other terms.

In the case of Prussia, the demand for money was not the only trouble. English influence had so far kept Frederick true to the distasteful alliance with Austria and Holland. But, since the effect of Marlborough's last visit to Berlin had worn off, an intrigue among the courtiers against Lord Raby, the English Resident, threatened to detach Prussia from all participation in the war. The Elector of Hanover, also, kept back his troops till the tension between his mother and Queen Anne was somewhat relaxed. The Emperor Joseph, sunk in bankruptcy, yet still refusing to make terms with the Hungarians, urged Marlborough to carry out his favourite scheme of invading France by the Moselle. But the Duke declined to embark again on a project which, however rightly conceived, depended for its success on the active assistance of Lewis of Baden; for that Prince, more sullen and secretive than ever, still commanded the Imperial forces in the neighbourhood of Landau.

The Alliance was stale and sick ; another year of failure would bring on the first stages of dissolution. The tonic of victory was needed, yet the coming campaign was not unlikely to end in positive defeat. The fall of the Duke of Savoy, and the final expulsion of the Austrians from Italy, seemed imminent. On April 19, Vendôme, before Eugene had arrived from Vienna, beat the Imperialists at Calcinato, and drove them into the mountain recesses above the Lago di Garda. Only Eugene's arrival prevented their complete dispersion. Some of the troops who suffered this reverse through want of Austrian preparedness, were the Prussian and Danish contingents that Marlborough had obtained for Italy. King Frederick at Berlin made it another grievance against Vienna and the Alliance.

Marlborough, meanwhile, was planning to carry his own army across the Alps, and fight an Italian campaign, ' which had been a fine jaunt indeed,' as his English officers said.* The Dutch statesmen, ashamed of the obstructiveness of their generals last year, were singularly accommodating to a plan that would have doubled the distance of the Danube march. They only bargained that no native Dutch regiments were to go.

---

* ' Upon our taking the field, the Duke of Marlborough ordered six hand-mills for grinding corn to be delivered to every British regiment, Horse as well as Foot. This occasioned a report that he designed to march on to Italy, to the relief of the Duke of Savoy, which had been a fine jaunt indeed. But whatever his Grace's design was, it is still a mystery, for we never had occasion of hand-mills in Flanders.' *Parker*, pp. 108–109. This makes me doubt Col. Cranstoun's statement that Marlborough only intended to take the British Cavalry with him to Italy. *H.M.C. Portland*, IV, pp. 440–441.

I am to have a meeting next Sunday [the Duke wrote, to Godolphin, from the Hague], with some Burgomasters of Amsterdam, for those I have consulted here dare not agree to what I propose unless I can persuade them to approve of it.

The idea had, indeed, many attractions for Marlborough. To co-operate once more with Eugene, and, on some battlefield among the vines and mulberries on the banks of the Po, to deliver Italy from the French power ; then, to carry out in person his own schemes for amphibious warfare in the Mediterranean ; above all, to attack Toulon, in connection with the redoubled activities of Galway and Peterborough in Spain ; here was another back door to victory, not barred by Netherlands fortresses, or blocked by the jealous incompetence of Lewis of Baden.

But suddenly came ill news that dispersed for ever his dream of riding ' to Italy an Hannibal.' At the beginning of May 1706 Prince Lewis was attacked by Villars, defeated and hurled back across the Rhine. Germany was threatened, and, in the then mood of Prussia, Hanover and other States, could Germany be trusted even to defend herself ? The Dutch broke off all talk of letting Marlborough go to Italy, greatly to the relief of Godolphin, who ' could never swallow so well the thoughts of your being so far out of reach, and for so long a time.'

With a heavy heart, the Duke took the field on the Netherlands border once more, to resume there, as he supposed, the dreary round of marches and counter-marches.

In Flanders [he wrote to Sarah], where I shall be forced to be, I am afraid the whole summer, there will be very little action, for the French will not venture in this country. . . . It is impossible for my dearest soul to imagine the uneasy thoughts I have every day in thinking that I have the curse at my age of being in a foreign country from you, and at the same time very little prospect of being able to do any considerable service for my country or the common cause.

To Godolphin, he wrote :

The little zeal that the King of Prussia, the King of Denmark and almost all the other Princes show, gives me so dismal thoughts I despair of good success.

And finally, on May 15, he wrote once more to Sarah, ' my

being here in a condition of doing nothing that shall make a noise, has made me able to send ten thousand men to Italy.' [61]

Eight days later he had won Ramillies, making, 'on that loud Sabbath,' such another ' noise ' as Blenheim itself.

The Alliance was saved, because Villeroi had come out to fight. The motives of a step so contrary to the true interest of France that Marlborough had conceived it to be impossible can be read in the letters that passed between Villeroi in the field, King Louis at Meudon, and Chamillart, the Minister of War, at Versailles.

We have already seen that, at the close of the last uneventful campaign, Chamillart and Villeroi had conceived ' a mediocre opinion ' of Marlborough as ' a mortified adventurer,' and had agreed to attribute Blenheim to ' chance alone.' * How far their master had been led to share these views is uncertain, but the terrible strain of the war upon the finances and prosperity of France induced King Louis, on May 6, 1706, to bid Villeroi take the offensive, even at the risk of a battle. The King wrote to his favourite Marshal that he must have peace, and that, in order to induce his enemies to accept his terms, they must be attacked in every seat of war, and so compelled to believe that his resources were by no means exhausted.† In pursuance of this policy, he ordered Villeroi to cross the Dyle, to lay siege to Léau, and, if necessary, to give battle to Marlborough.‡

The mistake in this line of policy was the resolve to attack ' everywhere ' (*partout*). Louis had already that year attacked with success in Italy and on the Rhine, and with still undetermined results in Catalonia. The Alliance was suffering from internal dissension and war-weariness, which these displays of French power would enhance. But to attack also in the seat of war where Marlborough was in command was a fatal error, probably induced by the belief

---

* P. 57 above.

† ' *Je ne vois rien qui puisse mieux les déterminer à venir à un accommodement qui est devenu nécessaire, que de leur faire voir que j'ai des forces suffisantes pour les attaquer partout.*' Pelet, VI, p. 18.

‡ See Map IX, The Netherlands, etc., at end of volume.

in the ' mediocrity ' of the English general, which Chamillart and Villeroi had been fostering all winter.

In obedience to the royal orders, Villeroi, on May 19,
crossed the Dyle from Louvain to Tirlemont, coming into
the open field to besiege Léau, and to challenge Marlborough, who expected no such good fortune. The Elector
of Bavaria and the officers of the French army rejoiced in the
prospect of a battle. There was a marked similarity to the
situation before Blenheim, except that Villeroi had none of
Tallard's just hesitations. This was the second time, in
Marlborough's opinion, when his own fortunes and the
liberties of Europe were saved by the unwillingness of his
opponents to stay within their lines when the game was in
their hands.

Reinforcements under Marsin were meanwhile moving
to join Villeroi, and it was thought that he might at least
have waited till they came.* But he was deceived as to the
forwardness of Marlborough's preparations ; he knew that
the Prussians and he believed that the Danes had not taken
the field. The Duke, however, on hearing that Villeroi
had crossed the Dyle, persuaded the Danes to make forced
marches to the front, partly by pledging his own credit for
the arrears due to their government, partly by appealing to
the soldierly spirit of the generals in command, who came
without awaiting orders from the hucksters in Copenhagen.
The splendid cavalry of Denmark rode into camp one day
before the battle, very much as the Ironsides from the
Eastern Association rode into the bivouac before Naseby.

But where were the Infantry of Prussia—the bluecoats
who had borne up the allied right at Blenheim ? To Raby
at Berlin, Marlborough wrote, on May 21 :

> If it should please God to give us a victory over the enemy, the
> Allies will be little obliged to the King for the success : and if, on the
> other hand, we should have any disadvantage, I know not how he will
> be able to excuse himself.

Yet, on the 22nd of May, as he sat giving his last direc-

---

* Whether Marlborough's threat to besiege Namur acted as a further inducement
to Villeroi to come out from behind the Dyle, is not certain. His orders from
Louis were to come out in order to besiege Léau, and it is these orders that he pleaded
in apology after the battle. See *Pelet*, VI, p. 40.

tions for the morrow's march, which he well knew would be interrupted by the second great battle of the century, this Duke was at the pains to dictate and sign another letter to Berlin, to beg a pension for the widow of a brave Prussian officer recently dead.   It was not only his Englishmen for whom he had a large human heart.   How many of the great commanders of history would have had the combined humanity, industry and *sang-froid* to write such a letter at such a time ? [62]

Marlborough, as soon as he heard that the French had come out from behind the Dyle, moved south-westward from Tongres, meaning to march round the sources of the Little Geete, and attack the enemy in the neighbourhood of Judoigne.   Villeroi, who had been joined by Marsin's cavalry, though not yet by his infantry, was moving to meet the Allies, intending to occupy the plateau of Ramillies, the water-shed that stands between the marshy upper courses of the Mehaine and the Great and Little Geete.   It was a fine position, where either he could await the allied attack, or decide to move eastward to take the offensive himself. The two great hosts were converging on the same spot, each with a burning desire to try the issue of battle.

Soon after three o'clock on Whit-Sunday morning, Marlborough's men were afoot, moving westward through a dense fog, over ways slippery with recent rain. May 23 The gigantic Irishman, William Cadogan, the best (N.S.) 1706 of the Duke's excellent staff-officers,* had been sent far ahead to scout.   At eight o'clock he discerned, through the rising mist, the vanguard of the enemy, already occupying the high grounds around Ramillies.   His aide-de-camp, galloping back, found the English and Dutch armies halting for a rest ; at the news that the enemy were within their reach they sprang eagerly to arms.   In a few minutes they had crossed ' the old line '—the once famous Lines of Brabant, which they had stormed and levelled the year before.

By ten o'clock the Duke had reached the front, accompanied by his staff, by the Field Deputies of the States and

* See Appendix at end of this chapter, p. 120.

by the veteran Overkirk, the finest of their generals, who was to win high renown for himself and the Dutch soldiery that day. The mist had by this time totally dispersed, and a splendid sight rejoiced Marlborough's eyes. There lay the rich reward of all the patience with which he had endured frustration at the hands of fools for twenty months past. For there, stretched over four miles in battle array, stood sixty thousand men—the long, white lines of the French infantry, the Bavarians in blue and red, the Swiss foot from the mountain cantons, the many-coloured troops of French, Spanish and Walloon horse, and whole brigades of Louis' magnificent Household Cavalry,* the red-coated gens-d'armerie prominent in their midst. All were resplendent in new uniforms, indicating to Europe that neither the resources nor the ambition of Louis were yet exhausted. Marlborough wrote of them to Godolphin as ' all the best troops of France,' and afterwards told Burnet ' the French army looked the best of any he had ever seen.' And the same remark was made that morning by French officers, confident of victory. The total of allied horse and foot was equal to those of the enemy. Marlborough had more cannon, but the French, magnificently equipped by their master for the last great effort that was to give victorious peace to Versailles, had been supplied with a number of three-bore field pieces, new invention of which they were so careful that they had c ʃed them over from observation until they arrived on the fie 1 of Ramillies.[63]

Ϡut if, in numbers and equipment, the two armies were appɾ ximately equal, a marked superiority in morale and discip ine lay, as the event proved, on the side of the Allies. The s aleness perceptible in the diplomatic Alliance of Princes had not infected the armies of the various nations who fou ʒht under Marlborough's command. The Danes had only just arrived in camp, without the leave of their trafficking Court, but the Duke knew that he could trust them and the Dutch cavalry as if they were his own English. Acting on that principle, he pitted Danes and Dutch against the Household Cavalry of Louis at the spot where the battle

* Students of this battle must remember that the *Maison du Roi* were the *Household Cavalry* while the *Régiment du Roi* (at Autre Eglise) were infantry.

MAP IV

SCOTS GREYS

REGIMENT
DU ROI

L'Église

Little Geete

PLATEAU DE JANDRENOUILLE

ALLIED SWISS
who retired
Ramillies

DUTCH

DANISH CAVALRY

Franquée
FOUCE

R. Mehaigne

...h, Calcutta, Bombay & Madras.

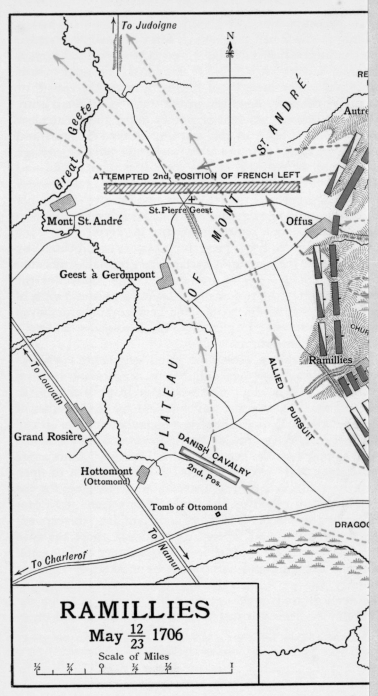

To Judoigne

N

ST. ANDRÉ

RE

Autre

ATTEMPTED 2nd. POSITION OF FRENCH LEFT

Mont St. André

St. Pierre Geest

Offus

Geest à Gerompont

To Louvain

Grand Rosière

Ramillies

CHUR

PLATEAU OF MONT

DANISH CAVALRY
2nd. Pos.

Hottomont
(Ottomond)

ALLIED PURSUIT

Tomb of Ottomond

DRAGOO

To Charleroi

To Namur

RAMILLIES

May $\frac{12}{23}$ 1706

Scale of Miles

½   ¾   0   ¼   ½   I

Longmans, Green & Co. Ltd., London, New York, Toro

was to be lost or won.   To his redcoats he assigned the part of
holding in check half the enemy's force by their appearance
and conduct on the right wing ; and the fear that the French
generals had of ' les Anglais ' rendered this policy most
effectual.*   The memory of Blenheim made the victory of
Ramillies the most complete in the war.   The allied army
went into action, confident of victory under their matchless
chief.   The French in the morning wished to fight and
redeem the recent past, but after two hours' gallant exchange
of blows they returned to the after-Blenheim mood, and
cried out that they were betrayed.   Their moral recovery
had been superficial, and the reaction was to be doubly
disastrous.   Moreover, the army had weak spots, in particular the Walloon regiments in Spanish service.

The vast, rolling, hedgeless plateau, cultivated by
peasants and their draught cattle, was green that morning
with the young corn of mid-May.   The nature of the
ground enabled the two armies to enjoy a splendid view of
each other, while the Allies for several hours deployed
over the great arena to match themselves against Villeroi's
host, already in position.

The Frenchmen's line, four miles long from Taviers to
Autre Eglise, was very similar in length and tactical
character to that other line of theirs from Blenheim to
Lutzingen.   Their right was bounded by the marshes of
the Mehaine and its tributaries, which confined the area of
the battle on the south, as on the former occasion it had
been confined by the marshes of the Danube.   Once more
the French right-centre occupied a broad stretch of open
country, unbroken by any obstacle, an arena clear for the
manœuvres of cavalry ; the flanks of this arena were protected by the villages of Taviers and Ramillies (corresponding to Blenheim and Oberglau), and once more the twin
villages stood too far apart from one another to command
the field between, and both might be masked by vigorous
infantry attacks, while the allied horse broke through on
the open ground in the centre.   But on this occasion the
field for the decisive cavalry charge was not covered on its

---

* On May 6 Louis had written to Villeroi : ' avoir une attention particulière à
ce qui essuiera le premier choc des troupes anglaises.' *Pelet*, VI, p. 19.

front by any natural obstacle like the marshes of the Nebel. On the undulating plateau of green corn, two miles in breadth between Taviers and Ramillies, Marlborough would seek the decision of the day.*

Further north, Villeroi's left, between Ramillies and Autre Eglise (like the French left around Lutzingen which Eugene had kept in play), was strong with natural obstacles, not as on that former occasion, forested hills, but the marshy bottom of the head-waters of the Little Geete, and the steep slopes leading thence to the villages on the height above. The orchards and enclosed grounds round Offuz and Autre Eglise further added to the strength of that wing.

The position chosen by Villeroi was well known for its strategical importance as a water-shed between the rivers, and had often before been surveyed by military men. When, therefore, Marlborough studied it through his telescope that morning, the Netherlanders in his company felt competent to assure him that the morass of the Little Geete was impassable, and that the enemy's left could not be assailed. The Dutch Deputies and generals had that year received strict orders not to interfere with his plans, but Deputy Goslinga personally disliked him and, civilian as he was, thought himself the better soldier. He was vexed when the Duke, in spite of his warning, ordered an attack to be made on the enemy's left with the strength of the English and Danish foot, supported by the horse under General Lumley. Marlborough's secret was in his own breast. It was a feint, to draw the enemy's troops away north. But sham attacks are most effectual when those conducting them think they are real. When Orkney and his English regiments crossed the Little Geete, they fully intended to carry the French position. Being themselves deceived, they deceived Villeroi and so enabled the battle to be won at the other end of the field.

Marlborough himself had placed his batteries, many of

---

* This open part of the battlefield is still exactly as it was. But the villages, though still quite rustic, have been to some extent rebuilt and enlarged, and the marshes near them have been drained. English visitors from Brussels who prefer their battlefields unvulgarized by pyramids and panoramas, and are prepared to find out the site for themselves without a guide, can be commended to try Ramillies and Oudenarde.

them along the edge of the bank overlooking the Little Geete. Between one and two o'clock the cannon opened fire on both sides, and, before three, the English and Danish infantry moved down under cover of the cannonade into the slippery bottom of the valley. They struggled over the marsh, which had been proclaimed impassable, and mounted the opposite slope in face of a heavy fire from the villages and enclosures of Autre Eglise and Offuz. Behind them Lumley, ' with very great difficulty,' brought the British squadrons through the soft ground in the valley bottom.

The two villages on the heights above were strong positions, defended by infantry of good reputation, the Régiment du Roi in Autre Eglise, and the Swiss and other French in Offuz. But the English drove them back from hedge to hedge and house to house. Villeroi, thoroughly alarmed, gave his personal attention to that wing and strengthened it with large bodies of horse and foot that ought to have been taking part in the decisive struggle to the south of Ramillies.

The feint had done its work. When the struggle for Offuz and Autre Eglise was at its hottest, Marlborough's aides-de-camp galloped up one after the other to call off the attack. Foreseeing the anger and incredulity with which the orders to retreat would be received, the Duke took the precaution to send ten messengers to Orkney, one of them being Quarter-Master Cadogan himself.*

It needed good troops to disengage themselves from the conflict in Offuz, return unbroken down the long slope and across the morass with the triumphant French close on their rear, and then to form up once more along the eastern edge

---

* ' I endeavoured to possess myself of a village,' wrote Orkney, ' which the French brought down a good part of their line to take possession of, and they were on one side of the village, and I on the other ; but they always retired as we advanced. As I was going to take possession, I had ten aide-de-camps to me to come off, for the horse could not sustain me. We had a great deal of fire at this, both musquetry and cannon ; and indeed I think I never had more shot about my ears. And I confess it vexed me to retire. However, we did it in very good order, and whenever the French pressed upon us, with the battalion of Guards and my own I was always able to make them stand and retire. Cadogan came and told me it was impossible I could be sustained by the horse if I went on then, and since my Lord could not attack everywhere, he would make the grand attack in the centre, and try to pierce there, which, I bless God, succeeded.' *E.H.R.*, Ap. 1904.

of the ravine, presenting a sulky and formidable face to the
foe. There the strength of English infantry stood for the
next hour, while the battle was being decided to the south.
Half Villeroi's army, horse and foot, watched them from
the other bank of the Little Geete, not daring to cross the
marsh, and rendered useless for service elsewhere.

But the thin red line, thus reformed along the ridge,
was only a façade. Behind them to the east, the ground
sloped away into a shallow valley, so that the troops of the
second line were hidden from the observation of the French.
As soon, therefore, as Lumley's cavalry had retired up the
hill again out of the enemy's sight, squadron after squadron
of English and foreign horse wheeled sharply to the south,
and trotted off to the field of real decision between Ramillies
and Taviers. The outcome of these proceedings was that,
while Villeroi had weakened his southern battle, Marlborough was strengthening his by drafts from the north.
The advantage of this shuffling of weight was the more
easily gained, because the allied communications were
shorter than the French, since their line of battle was
convex and the French concave.

The manœuvre of the false attack, by which the enemy
was deceived, sounds a simple device. A schoolboy might
think of it. But it required a great general and a fine army
to carry it out. The honours must be divided between
Marlborough and his men. Orkney in particular must be
praised for keeping his head and his temper at a moment
of confusion, peril and sharp disappointment, when some of
his subordinates were so angry that they swore Cadogan
had invented the orders to retreat.[64]

The victory was to be won on the southern half of the
battlefield, an open and gently undulating water-shed, unprotected by any obstacle in front, but flanked by the villages
of Ramillies and Taviers. More than half Marlborough's
troops on this wing consisted of the blue-coated Dutch army
under Overkirk ; some of its regiments were natives of the
Republic, while others were drawn from Protestant populations as far distant as Scotland, Switzerland and Scandinavia. The polyglot Dutch army made up in discipline,

and to some extent in religious zeal, for what it lacked in racial unity.

On the extreme south wing, a detachment of Dutch infantry, after dislodging an enemy outpost from the hamlet of Francqnée, attacked Taviers, a post of some natural strength, being in those days more than half surrounded by the marshlands of the swiftly flowing Mehaine and its tributaries. Villeroi had neglected to occupy it in sufficient force, and he was now far away at Offuz, attending to the English. The meagre French garrison in Taviers was quickly overpowered by numbers. Villeroi's lieutenants attempted to repair their chief's error by sending the troops nearest at hand to recover the village, French dragoons, supported by Swiss infantry and by some regiments in the service of the dispossessed Electors of Bavaria and Cologne. The reinforcements came on against Taviers, happy-go-lucky, without any concerted plan of mutual support. Leaving their horses picketed, the dragoons in their heavy top-boots plunged knee-deep through the marsh, only to meet a disgraceful repulse on the outskirts of the village. Those dragoons who escaped out of the marsh were driven into it again by the Danish cavalry, or fled from the field on foot, leaving their horses to be taken. The Swiss perished fighting in the village. A few companies of French and Electoral infantry were held together by Colonel de la Colonie, who has narrated the affair in detail. His little force remained in the marshlands till the day was lost, when they escaped across the Mehaine southwards to Namur, on a different line of retreat from the rest of the army.[65]

Owing to this initial success of the Dutch infantry, the fire from Taviers, instead of galling the flank of the allied cavalry, galled the flank of the French. For this reason the Danish horse were able to fight their way round the extreme right of the enemy's squadrons. They 'slipped in between the enemy's right and Taviers, and flanked them.' After driving a number of the enemy's horse and foot into the marshes west of Taviers, the Danes in full career of victory galloped on for a mile or more to the west, till they reached the curiously shaped mound called the 'Tomb of

Ottomond,' a landmark visible from many points of the battlefield. There they formed a new line, facing northwards against the right rear of Villeroi's whole position.[66]

This manœuvre of the Danes on the flank was decisive of the day, because the Allies had been able to hold their own in the centre. The Household Cavalry of France had failed, after a gallant effort, to break the troops opposed to them in the open ground between Taviers and Ramillies. In that spacious arena both sides had placed the chief strength of their horse, interlined with foot according to the tactics that had won Blenheim. 'The foot on both sides,' it was reported, 'often stopped the squadrons in their career.' But too many of the French infantry had been withdrawn northwards by Villeroi, in his alarm at Orkney's attack. And when he returned to the true scene of decision there was no time to revise his arrangements.

The Maison du Roi, though inadequately supported by foot, after a severe struggle broke through two lines of Dutch horse, whom at the beginning they outnumbered. But Marlborough, as usual, was found at the point and at the moment of danger. Just to the south of Ramillies the onslaught of the Household Cavalry threatened to pierce the allied line, but the platoon firing of four regiments of foot, placed there by Marlborough, gave the first check to the triumphant charge,* and the advent of the fresh cavalry from the north turned the tide of war.

This affair was doubly the most critical of the day's doings, for not only was the line almost broken, but Marlborough himself barely escaped death or capture. When

---

* The Scottish private's rude verses narrate this crisis. (*Remembrance*, p. 377.)

> ' Two times our horsse was put to the worsse
>   Which Mallberie weel did see.
> To Overquerke he spake, who could it not help,
>   " Your horsse had need of suplie."
> Four regiments of foot in haste were called up
>   And set on the left of our horsse.
> This was the third time the horsse was engagding,
>   And the French was put to the worsse.
> The French coming down ready to fall on
>   Our foot shot at them with ball,
> The which did them grieve and sadly mischieve,
>   Many horsse and men their did fall.'

the French cavalry broke through the Dutch, he had been surrounded and cut off from his friends. The splendid charger he rode carried him out from the ring of foes, but in leaping a ditch it flung him to the ground. He scrambled to his feet and ran for safety, encumbered by his heavy wig and jack-boots. General Murray was bringing up some allied Swiss infantry to his rescue. His mounted pursuers, who had recognized the identity of the Milord sprinting in front of them, rode after him so furiously that they could not draw up, and were impaled on the Swiss bayonets. Bare victor in the race, he clambered on to the horse supplied by his aide-de-camp, Captain Molesworth, the only man on his staff who was present.* Before the Duke's leg was well over the saddle, Colonel Bringfield, who was holding the stirrup, had his head torn from his body by a cannon ball. The incident struck the imagination of England and Europe. Our newspapers seized on it as the symbol of Ramillies, as they had seized on ' Tallard in the coach ' for Blenheim. A monument to Bringfield in the north aisle of Westminster Abbey recalls the tale to posterity. His widow and children were, at Marlborough's special request, befriended by Sarah and pensioned by the Queen.[67]

Meanwhile, Ramillies itself saw the hottest fighting of all. The village and the enclosures around it were packed by a score of French and Swiss battalions and a dozen cannon. It was assailed by a corresponding force of allied infantry under the Dutch General Schultz, including the Scots and other nationals in the service of the States, and the English battalions of Mordaunt and Churchill.† John Campbell, the brilliant young Duke of Argyle, who had already acted as Queen Anne's High Commissioner to her Scottish Parliament, was destined for many years to play a prominent and varied part in the wars and policies of Britain, and to be retrospectively imagined by Sir Walter as the sympathetic patron, in the evening of his days, of Davie and Jeanie Deans. Not even the Jacobites dared

* The ' Dick ' Molesworth of the Yorkshire Squire's family, mentioned in *Blenheim*, p. 32.

† The presence of these English infantry in the fighting round Ramillies has not been noticed by modern authors, but is proved by Orkney in *E.H.R.*, Ap. 1904, p. 315 ; *H.M.C. Portland*, IV, p. 310.

whisper that he ever spared to expose himself to danger.
As Brigadier of the attacking Scottish infantry, he

was himself the second or third man who with his sword in his hand
broke over the enemy's trenches, and chased them out of the village
of Ramillies.   He received three shot upon him, but happily all blunt.

The fight for the village swayed forward and back, along
the streets and among the hedgerows, but Marlborough
brought up more and more troops from his right to his
centre, and at half-past six in the evening the enemy finally
gave way.   The two English battalions drove three French
battalions into the morass surrounding the springs of the
Little Geete.   The Scots drove before them the famous
Regiment of Picardy.

> With good hearts and our screwed baginets
> We advanced on a deal of rye,

wrote the regimental bard, himself a private in the ranks,

> And all our bregade they proved pretie lads,
> And the French they proved but kie.

> Our brigade in platouns did fire their guns.
> From hedge to hedge we beat off the dogs.

And so the gallant defenders of Ramillies, who were ' cattle '
and ' dogs ' only in the rough parlance of the camp, had
met their match at last, and were rolled out of the village
enclosures to mingle with the general rout in which the
whole army was now involved.[68]
    The cavalry of the Maison du Roi had well borne up the
European fame of their corps, but after nearly two hours of
charging and counter-charging they were overborne by the
numbers of horse and foot whom Marlborough's tactics
had collected for their destruction.   The Dutch horse had
rallied round the reserves brought up fresh and eager from
the right.   The French were fighting with intervals between each squadron, when the allied cavalry, in a single
wave of unbroken length, surged through the gaps, surrounding and destroying each body of horse piecemeal.*

* The French Colonel, De la Colonie, has left an account of the Dutch cavalry
charge that won the day, of which he witnessed the southern end from his station
behind the marsh.   It is to be noted that the trot, not the gallop, was, as at Blenheim,

At this critical moment the French became aware that in the rear-flank of their whole army, the formidable cavalry of Denmark was drawn up in a new battle array. At the same time the infantry defending Ramillies were pouring out from the enclosures with Dutch, Scots and English hot on their traces. The right half of Villeroi's army was broken at every point. Suddenly the French morale collapsed, and a defeat was turned by misconduct into the catastrophe that decided the war. 'We had not got forty yards on our retreat,' writes the Irish captain, Peter Drake, 'when the words *sauve qui peut* went through the great part, if not the whole army, and put all to confusion. Then might be seen whole brigades running in disorder.'

From their position of advantage near the 'Tomb of Ottomond' the Danish squadrons swept on to the disordered crowds, 'and did not forget how their poor natives were sacrificed at Calcinato in Italy ; so that when their generals bid them halt, they drove on, Jehu like, giving no quarter, and cutting them to pieces for several miles ; but our brave English boys were more merciful and granted quarter.'

Isolated companies of French musketeers strove to stem the tide in hollow ways and hedges ; where the allied cavalry had outridden their infantry supports, such resistance met here and there with local success. But Villeroi completely failed in his attempt to form a fresh line of battle facing southwards, stretching from Offuz to Mont St. André. For this purpose he had drawn the Spanish and Electoral horse from the neighbourhood of Autre Eglise to the high ground near St. Pierre Geest. But the infection of defeat had reached these reinforcements, and they refused to face the oncoming tide of Danish and English cavalry. According to the French official account, the whole 'fifty squadrons' of the left wing, who had not yet struck a blow,

the pace of the decisive charge : ' I saw the enemy's cavalry advance upon our people, at first at rather a slow pace and then, when they thought they had gained the proper distance, they broke into a trot to gain impetus for the charge. At the same moment the Maison du Roi decided to meet them, for at such a moment those who await the shock find themselves at a disadvantage. . . . The enemy profiting by their superiority in numbers, surged through the gaps between our squadrons and fell upon their rear, while their four lines attacked in front.' *Colonie*, pp. 312–313.

were seized with panic, and rode in terror through the
flying infantry, whose retreat they had been drawn up to
protect.   Here, near the cross-roads of St. Pierre Geest,
the Elector of Bavaria and Marshal Villeroi were almost
captured by General Wood when, at the head of the English
Dragoon Guards, he crashed at a gallop into the Bavarian
horse, capturing their kettle-drums and two Lieutenant-
Generals.*

One reason for the failure of Villeroi to re-form his
unused troops in a new line, was the mistake he had made
in leaving his baggage close behind his front, instead of
sending it some miles to the rear, as was the custom of
prudent commanders about to give battle.   Waggons as
well as fugitives encumbered the ground over which the
troops of the French left wing had to move to their new
positions.   And, after the retreat had become general,
further disaster and confusion resulted from the block of
waggons breaking down in the mud of the deep sunken
ways through which the country roads ran to Judoigne.
The artillery could not pass, and every one of Villeroi's
fifty cannon were taken.[69]

Meanwhile, the English foot, whom Marlborough's
orders had balked of their victory two hours before, were
pouring once more across the ravine of the Little Geete.
This time they met no resistance worth the name in Offuz.
The panic, spreading northwards, had reached the extreme
verge of the battle, where, in and around the village of Autre
Eglise, the infantry of the Regiment du Roi had their post.
When Lord John Hay's Dragoons, the ' Scots Greys,' fell
upon two battalions of them, ' à la hussarde, sword in hand,
and at a gallop,' they flung down their arms and the
famous regiment was made prisoner.   In all parts of the
field the British cavalry were now charging at a gallop,
having no longer need of the measured trot, their usual
tactics to preserve the close order of their ranks against an

---

* ' Both these assured me, the day after the battle, that the Elector himself
and the Marshal de Villeroy were in the crowd and not ten yards from me, when
they two called out to me for quarter and that they narrowly escaped.   Which
had I been so fortunate as to have known I had strained Coriolanus, on whom
I rode all the day of battle, to have made them prisoners.'   General Wood's letter,
in *Boyer* (ed. 1707), V, p. 82.   Confirmed by *H.M.C. Hare* (R. 13, pt. 9), p. 211.

unbeaten foe. One French regiment after another was broken up, scattering in fragments to hide and run through the night. Eighty standards were taken, pledges of the disruption of an army.[70]

The shades of night were now beginning to fall, but there was no halt in the chase. The clatter of war rolled far away, leaving the darkened battlefield at peace under the stars, with no sound save the heavy groans of the wounded. The stream of flight and pursuit poured through the streets of Judoigne and the surrounding hamlets, thence on without a pause towards Louvain and the line of the Dyle. Only behind that river could the hunted mob hope for safety. The English horse and foot, like the Prussians at Waterloo, not having borne the worst heats of the day, undertook the joyous burden of the pursuit.*

Since resistance was no longer to be feared, each regiment hunted on its own, but all striving in the general direction of the Dyle. ' All night we knew nothing of one another,' wrote Orkney, ' and Mr. Lumley and I had resolved to march straight to the Dyle to their lines. But here we are, endeavouring to make a camp and form in some order. For we look like a beaten army.' Several English detachments halted at break of day at Meldert, nearly fifteen miles from Ramillies. Marlborough rode through the night till his guide lost the road ; then he lay

* Writers for the English public, such as *Boyer* (1706, V, 83), gladly recognized that the Dutch, ' both horse and foot, bore almost the whole brunt of the day.' The Scottish Cameronian Colonel Blackader, who disliked the English, and had declared that their heavy losses at Blenheim were a punishment for their sins, had an equally ready explanation for Ramillies : ' The English had but small part in this victory. They are the boldest sinners in our army, therefore God will choose other instruments. Also the English have got a great vogue and reputation for courage and are perhaps puffed up from it ; and so God humbles their pride, as it were, by throwing them by.' ' Give me grace, o Lord, never to forget this great and glorious day at Ramillies.' *Life of Col. Blackader*, 1824, p. 280.

The pursuit was so immediate, rapid and continuous for the next ten days on end, that some of the thrifty Scots soldiers who had thrown down their ' wallets ' containing their ' stockings and linens,' when ordered to attack the village of Ramillies, never saw them again.

> ' Some was left behind our walats to bring
> And foloued as far behinde.
> Some walats was lost whatever they cost
> And no redress we did find.'
> *Remembrance*, p. 385.

down on the open ground upon his soldier's cloak, calling
on Deputy Goslinga to come and share it with him, ' which
I did,' says the Dutchman, ' for a quarter of an hour.'   And
so, halving his modicum of comfort with a civilian who
loved him not, racked with headache but glad at heart, he
fell asleep—hoping that Sarah would be pleased.[71]

Scenes of that flight through the darkness were deeply
bitten into the memories of the pursued.

> Though the enemy appeared no more that night [wrote the Irish
> Captain Drake], we halted not till the break of day near Louvain,
> when we crossed the river, dispirited and weary, having been on our
> feet twenty-four hours without the least rest.   It was indeed a truly
> shocking sight to see the miserable remains of this mighty army of
> seventy thousand men reduced to a handful.

All their fifty cannon, their tents, their baggage, even
the sacred ' *marmites* ' of the regimental cooks had been left
far behind on the field.   The fugitives who reassembled
at Louvain had for the most part flung away their arms.
There the beaten generals ' held a sort of tumultuous Council
of War, by flambeau-light in the market place,' where they
decided to throw the stores from the magazines of Louvain
into the Dyle, and be off, after a few hours' rest, for Brussels.
Thus without a blow they abandoned the line of the river
which a fortnight before Marlborough had feared would
be his boundary for all that year.   The beaten army never
stopped until it had reached the protection of Lille.

The numbers killed and taken were not so great as at
Blenheim, but the disbandment was even greater.   The
Walloon regiments deserted *en masse*, many of them joining
the Allies.   Spaniards and Bavarians had had enough of
campaigning.   Great numbers even of the French failed to
rejoin their colours.   The killed, wounded and prisoners
in the battle were estimated for Villeroi's army at some
13,000 men, but his losses by desertion may have doubled
that number.   Probably half the splendid army that he had
set in array was lost to him, and the remainder were a
demoralized remnant, unable for months to look the foe in
the face.   Marlborough had all summer before him, in
which to reconquer the Belgian fortresses without having to

fear any serious interruption by a field army.   And his own regiments had suffered far less than at Blenheim, having lost some 4,000 in killed and wounded. ' The consequence of this battle,' he wrote to Godolphin, ' is likely to be of greater advantage than that of Blenheim, for we have now the whole summer before us, and with the blessing of God, I will make the best use of it.'

No wonder Villars wrote of Ramillies as ' the most shameful, humiliating and disastrous of defeats.' ' How many misfortunes,' he wrote to Madame de Maintenon, ' would have been avoided, if I had been allowed to act, and if safety and inaction had been enjoined on the Marshal de Villeroi.'   All Villars' bright hopes of invading Germany were dispelled, and most of his troops were drafted off to Flanders.[72]

In England the news came like a thunderbolt of joy. Nothing had been expected from that quarter for weeks to come, and nothing good that year.*   When the strange tidings reached London that the French army was no more and that Marlborough was advancing by forced marches on Brussels, ' most people move about as in a dream or ecstasy, God does so many marvels for us.'   The reception of the news in the countryside was thus dramatized in the Whig *Observator* :

Countryman—Come, Joan, make haste, bring us a full jug of October, clean glasses, clean pipes and some Moore's tobacco.   Here, Tom, Jugg, everybody !   Come and hear the good news.   Master, before we finish here's a good health to the Duke of Marlborough. Nay let it go round.   Everybody must drink it.   I am sure we have no Tories or High-flyers in this house.   And now, Master, one more health to Mr. Overkirk, the Dutch general, who behaved himself so bravely in this action.

Meanwhile a happy woman was reading these words :

Monday.   May 24.   11 o'clock.   I did not tell my dearest soul, in my last, the design I had of engaging the enemy if possible to a battle, fearing the concern she had for me might make her uneasy ;

* Defoe, though a supporter of government and of the war, had written in his *Review*, published on May 18, O.S., just before the news of the battle reached England, ' The prospect of the campaign is nowhere promising, they say, but in Spain.'

but I can now give her the satisfaction of letting her know that, on Sunday last, we fought, and that God Almighty has been pleased to give us a victory.   I must leave the particulars to this bearer, Colonel Richards, for having been on horseback all Sunday, and after the battle marching all night, my head aches to that degree it is very uneasy to me to write.   Poor Bringfield, holding my stirrup for me, helping me on horseback, was killed.   I am told he leaves his wife and mother in a poor condition.   I can't write to any of my children, so that you will let them know that I am well, and that I desire they will thank God for preserving me.   And pray give my duty to the Queen, and let her know the truth of my heart, that the greatest pleasure I have in this success is, that it may be a great service to her affairs ; for I am sincerely sensible of all her goodness to me and mine.   Pray believe me when I assure you that I love you more than I can express.[73]

APPENDIX TO CHAPTER VI

CADOGAN AND MARLBOROUGH'S STAFF

WHEN, in the last years of the reign, the petty malice of the Tory pamphleteers against Marlborough reached its height, it became their custom to ascribe his successes to the advice of his staff, especially of Cadogan.   ' It has always been the peculiar happiness of Colossus [Marlborough] to have the command of a great many more able and experienced heads in the trade of war than his own.'   *Oliver's pocket looking-glass or great modern Colossus*, 1712.   ' His conduct, of which we have heard so much, is all owing to Cadogan's advice.'   *Character of Present Ministry*, 1712.

In reality, William Cadogan was an excellent Quarter-Master-General—tireless, patient, and devoted to the essential and difficult problems of transport and supply.   But the Duke was his own Chief of Staff, and his civilian secretary, Adam Cardonnel, was therefore of great importance in the military hierarchy.   See the essay on Marlborough's Staff in Fortescue's *Historical and Military Essays*, based on the staff papers of Capt. King.   At Oudenarde Cadogan commanded the vanguard in a difficult operation with ability and success.

CHAPTER VII

THE CONSEQUENCES OF RAMILLIES

The Belgian Revolution. Brabant and Flanders recovered. England, Holland and Austria as masters of the Spanish Netherlands. Their quarrels. Marlborough refuses the Governorship. The *Condominium*. The Dutch Barrier and the English Succession. Battle of Turin. The French expelled from Italy. The war won.

THE battle of Ramillies had been fought on Sunday, May 23, 1706.* The next fortnight witnessed the revolution that secured the sovereignty of Belgium to the House of Austria for three generations. The allied army moved westward from the battlefield by forced marches on the line of Louvain, Brussels, Gavre and Bruges, causing the remnants of the French field-army to retreat southward to Lille, lest it should find itself cut off to the north of the Bruges Canal. In the ordinary course of things the Dender, the Scheldt, and the Lys rivers, and the Brussels and the Bruges canals could each have been held by the French, as the Dyle had been held, and would have afforded matter each for a year's campaign ; they were now crossed one after the other, as fast as the allied infantry could tramp over the bridges of ' copper boats,' laid by the cavalry scouting in advance. So, too, the fortresses of Malines, Ghent, Bruges, Oudenarde and Antwerp could each have held out for months of siege. Yet before the end of the first week of June, all these places, together with Alost, Lierre and Damme, had followed the example of Brussels, opened their gates to detachments of allied troops, and proclaimed Charles III as their sovereign, without a shot fired or a trench dug.

---

* In this chapter of foreign happenings I use the new or continental style of dating, or else give both styles. *See Map IX, The Netherlands, etc., at end of volume.*

The Duke's letters to Sarah record his feelings :

May $\frac{16}{27}$. I have been in so continued a hurry ever since the battle of Ramillies, by which my blood is so heated, that when I go to bed I sleep so unquietly that I cannot get rid of my headache, so that I have not as yet all the pleasure I shall enjoy of the blessing God has been pleased to give us by this victory. . . . We have done in four days what we should have thought ourselves happy if we could have been sure of it in four years.

May $\frac{20}{31}$. We are now masters of Ghent, and to-morrow I shall send some troops to Bruges. So many towns have submitted since the battle, that it really looks more like a dream than truth. My thoughts are now turning to the getting everything ready for the siege of Antwerp, which place alone in former years would have been thought good success for a whole campaign.

Five days later, Antwerp surrendered without a blow. Meanwhile, on June 3, the Duke resumed :

Every day gives us fresh marks of the great victory, for since my last we have taken possession of Bruges and Damme, as also of Oudenarde, which was besieged the last war by the King, with sixty thousand men, and he was at last forced to raise the siege. In short, there is so great a panic in the French army as is not to be expressed. Every place we take declares for King Charles. . . . I am so persuaded that this campaign will bring us a good peace, that I beg of you to do all you can that the house at Woodstock may be carried up as much as possible, that I may have a prospect of living in it.

Meanwhile, the Scottish Cameronian colonel, Blackader, was expressing in his diary similar gratification in a different language :

May $\frac{15}{26}$. They have abandoned Brussels and all Brabant. The Lord is taken heart and hand and spirit from our enemies.

May $\frac{16}{27}$. Passing the canal [of Brussels] at Vilvoord. No resistance from the enemy, though we thought, happen what might, they would have defended the canal.

May $\frac{19}{30}$. A fatiguing march this Sabbath. All day I met with what I fear and hate in this trade, viz. cursing, swearing, filthy language, etc., yet though it was a hell around me, I bless the Lord there was a heaven within. We are still pursuing our victory, and they

are still fleeing before us.   There is certainly something in this affair
beyond human working.

May 24
June 4.   Marching   still   forward.   Crossing   the   Lys   above
Ghent.   Still no enemy to be seen.   Bruges, Antwerp, and in
short all Brabant and Flanders almost yielded.   What the French
got in a night by stealth at the King of Spain's death, they have lost
again in a day.   That old tyrant who wasted God's church is about
to be wasted himself.

Although the main strength of the army crossed the
Brussels canal to the north of the city, Marlborough was
officially received in the capital on May 28, and many of our
officers were found in its streets on errands of business or
pleasure.   After Ramillies, as before Waterloo, the Hotel
de Ville and the Guild Houses of the Grande Place * looked
down on the red-coated gentlemen, the Dobbins, Major
O'Dowds and George Osbornes of an earlier day, but of
much the same breed, temper and background of experience.
After the campaign was over, in the winter of 1706–7, we
are told that there was ' great mirth ' in Brussels, ' with
great and numerous company, and there was an excellent
opera, and balls at the theatre that began at midnight, and
where there was great play.   The ladies were all masked.
There were continued suppers,' the English taking the lead
in all the gallantry and expense.[74]

The Belgian revolution, launched by the victory of
Ramillies, had a political aspect that softened the character
and speeded the pace of Marlborough's conquest.   The
government of the Spanish Netherlands had been carried
on by the Elector of Bavaria through his Lieutenant, the
Marquis of Bedmar, nominally on behalf of Spain, but for
four years past really on behalf of France.   The Elector
was personally liked by the aristocracy, but Bedmar's
rule had been marked by arbitrary acts, in contravention
of the ancient liberties of the land, as set forth in the
charter of the ' Joyous Entry,' and the French soldiers were
insolent and unpopular.   The burgher corporations of the

* Many of them, rebuilt after the French bombardment of 1695, looked the
same in 1706 as in 1815 or to-day.

Netherlands cities had never wholly forgotten the heritage of freedom for which their ancestors had struggled against medieval Counts of Flanders, Kings of France, Princes of Burgundy, and later against Alva and the Spanish power. The losing battle had never been quite lost nor the flame wholly extinguished. What was left of these rights was now in more danger from Louis XIV than from the moribund monarchy of Spain. Flanders and Brabant seemed on the way to become mere provinces of France. The French-speaking Walloons had no more wish for that than had the Flemish-speakers along the Dutch border. Similarly, the Flemings had no wish to be subjected to their cousins, the Dutch. Although Belgium, as the home of two races, had little national self-consciousness, its great civic traditions and liberties made it anxious to remain a unit independent both of Holland and of France.

With this end in view, the Estates and the Cities, on the news of the total defeat of the French arms at Ramillies, hastened to proclaim Charles III as the rightful King of Spain, and to throw themselves on the protection of Marlborough. Charles, who had no troops of his own in the Netherlands, and seemed destined to live either in Madrid or in Vienna, would, they hoped, make an excellent King Log. Meanwhile, Marlborough and his redcoats would protect them from oppression by the Dutch, their fellow-subjects of long ago, but for many years past their jealous and successful rivals in trade.

Four days after the battle, the representatives of the Three Estates of Brabant completed a negotiation with Marlborough, resulting in the proclamation of Charles III by the Estates, and the recognition of the liberties of Brabant by the victorious English General. In the name of Queen Anne and of the Dutch Government, the Duke solemnly assured the great ecclesiastics, nobles and burghers who came on deputation to his camp, that 'there would not be the least change in regard to religion, and that His Catholic Majesty would renew the Joyous Entry of Brabant, as it had been granted by his predecessor, Charles II, of glorious memory.' At the same time he issued a proclamation to his army that everything in Brabant and Flanders would have to be paid for, and that looting and marauding would be punished by death.*

On these terms, the Estates of Brabant, and a few days later the Estates of Flanders, and the municipalities of all the great cities of the region, proclaimed Charles III and made the Dutch and English armies welcome. Such prompt action by the native rulers of the land, which forestalled actual military compulsion, had a moral effect on the garrisons of the fortress cities, formed partly of French troops and partly of Belgians in the Spanish service. The native soldiery, following the lead of the civic authorities, opened the gates to the Allies and declared for Charles III, and in very few cases were the French either in numbers or in mood to prevent them. In this manner, by June 6, every town in Belgium north of the line Bruges-Ghent-Brussels, with the exception of Dendermonde, had fallen to the Allies, besides Oudenarde further to the south. Even the noble Spaniard, the Marquis of Tarazena, Governor of Antwerp, decided that Charles III was now his King, and by opening the gates of the city saved Marlborough many precious months which he must otherwise have wasted

---

* The army seems to have been impressed by the solemnity of the proclamation. The private who was chronicler of the Scottish regiment thus paraphrased the Duke's words (*Remembrance*, p. 383) :

' King Charles the thrid he is now procleamed
    The right King of Spain for to be.
This Spanish speybae [Pays Bas] it belongeth now all
    To His Catholick Majestie.
Therefor at large we now discharge
    Al spoiling of this countrie,
To prevent milroding or stealing or robing
    Under the pain of your death.
If this country ye wrong ye are to hang
    And afterwards reckon your skaith.'
And now afterhind the bouers [peasants] did come in,
    With enough of provision to sell.
The price of meat and drink was agreed on, I think
    And for everything money we tell.

       *   *   *   *

Our officers to the fair town of Brussels
    Right frequently made their repaire.

An English officer writes home on June 2 : ' The common people of the Low Countries seem very much rejoiced at the change ; the priests and gentry but very reserved.' *H.M.C. Coke* (1889), p. 71.

before its walls. ' My Lord Duke was received at Antwerp,' we are told, ' with one piece of ceremony which was
odd enough, the magistracy of the town marching before
him with lighted flambeaux though in the middle of the
day, which is looked upon as the greatest mark of honour
they can show, and which they seldom, or ever, have
bestowed upon their Dukes of Brabant.[75]

So far, no siege operation had been necessary. But the
remainder of the campaign, from the latter part of June to
the first week of October, was devoted to the four successful
sieges of Ostend, Dendermonde, Menin and Ath. In these
places the French had prevailed over the Belgians in the
garrison, resistance had been organized and fresh troops had
been thrown in.

The decision of Marlborough to begin with the siege of
Ostend had both military and political significance. The
capture of its port would open a direct line between England
and the army at the front. This shortening of Marlborough's communications proved invaluable to him in all
the later stages of the war : for example, the grand operations which resulted in the capture of Lille in 1708 could
never have been carried through if supplies from England
had still been forced to go round by way of the Dutch ports
and the long overland route. Godolphin, with his purely
political intelligence, hoped that the Allies would begin by
taking Dunkirk, the headquarters of the French privateers
so much dreaded by the English merchants. But when
Marlborough assured him that Dunkirk could not possibly
be approached till both Ostend and Nieuport had fallen,
he at once, as always, bowed to his friend's superior knowledge of war. Ostend had indeed been second only to
Dunkirk as a nest of privateers, and its capture converted
it into the chief port of entry for English cloth into the reopened markets of the Spanish Netherlands. Holland had
her eyes on it as the most desirable of all places to be
acquired under cover of her new Barrier—a point on which
both England and Austria would have much to say.

The summer siege of this water-girt fortress, which had
been taken by Spinola in 1604 only after the passage of

three years and the loss of 80,000 men, was accomplished by Marlborough in three weeks, with a loss of 500. His rapid success was due in part to the half-heartedness of some Walloon regiments in the garrison, and partly to the co-operation of the English squadron, which bombarded Ostend from the sea, while the Duke's land batteries fired from a narrow frontage on the sand dunes of the coast. On all other sides the fortress was completely protected by marshes and inundations.[76]

From Ostend, which fell on July 6,* Marlborough moved inland to Courtrai, which offered no resistance. He was now joined by the Prussians, whose king, after Ramillies, had no longer any thought of deserting the Alliance. Six thousand good French troops composed the garrison of Menin, a small town just inside the French territory, regarded as one of Vauban's greatest masterpieces of fortification. It was besieged and carried before the end of August. The French field-army was close at hand, but did not dare to attack the lines of circumvallation which Marlborough constructed to cover the siege.

Henceforth till the end of the war Corporal Trim was kept busy with his spade. In these sieges, following one after the other in the campaigns of the next half-dozen years, the British grenadiers of the different regiments, and the infantry as a whole, were constantly and severely engaged, losing many more men in a hundred forgotten assaults and sallies, on scarp and counterscarp, half-moon and ravelin, than ever they lost in the four famous battles of the war. Captain Parker writes of his own regiment at Menin : ' Here we paid for our looking on at Ramillies. Having had two captains and five subalterns killed, and eight officers wounded, among whom I was one.' And foremost in these desperate encounters was the Duke of Argyle, who

* Marlborough, Godolphin and the Dutch had, in June and July, a plan for a ' descent ' to be made somewhere on the coast of France, Godolphin hoped against Rochefort. But though the preparations got some way, it came to nothing. It was hoped to get all the Protestants of south France to rise ; the invaders were to proclaim that they ' came only to restore the people to their liberties and *to have Assemblies of the States as they had anciently.*' It is fortunate that this design of interference with the internal affairs of France was not, in fact, attempted. *Dispatches*, II, pp. 579, 682 ; *Burnet*, V, p. 266 (453) ; *Coxe*, chap. xlvi, vol. II, pp. 45–47.

exposed himself more like a young subaltern than a grave statesman, on whom so largely rested the burden of guiding the Union Treaty through two Parliaments.[77]

Scotland was indeed well represented among Marlborough's men, in that year when Great Britain was being forged on the anvil of policy at home. As the siege of Menin drew to a close, there died of fever at Courtrai the young Colonel of the Scots Greys, Lord John Hay, son of the Marquis of Tweeddale, another statesman of the Union. Lord John, as the Duke wrote, was 'generally regretted through the whole army.' In the three brief years of his Colonelcy, on the banks of the Danube and by the Belgian streams, he had founded the European reputation of his regiment and its 'terrible grey horses,' which Napoleon was one day to watch careering through the ranks of his army as through a field of corn, at Waterloo.[78]

Meanwhile, Louis was hastening up reinforcements at the expense of his strength in Italy and on the Rhine, and calling back from beyond the Alps one of his best Marshals, the Duke of Vendôme, to take Villeroi's place and repair the situation in the Netherlands. It is more than probable that if Vendôme had been left in Italy, that peninsula would not have been lost by France in the autumn. In a dozen different ways Eugene's victory at Turin was prepared and rendered possible by Marlborough's victory at Ramillies.

On the fifth of August, 1706, Vendôme reported to Chamillart, the Minister of War, the state of things that he found on his arrival at Valenciennes, near the Netherlands border of France.

With regard to the troops in the Spanish service, no one can answer for them ; but that grieves me far less than the sadness and dejection that appears in the French army. I will do my best to restore their spirit. But it will be no light matter for me to do so, for *everyone here is ready to take off his hat at the mere name of Marlborough.**

From the capture of Menin on the French border, the Duke turned back against Dendermonde, which alone held

---

* 'Tout le monde ici est près d'ôter son chapeau quand on nomme le nom de Marlborough.' *Pelet*, VI, p. 94.

out in the middle of the newly conquered Belgian territory, barring the navigation of the Dender and the Upper Scheldt to the Allies. It was a place of immense natural strength owing to the water which, in any normal year, prevented all approach. During the French invasion of 1667, when the other Low Country fortresses fell like ninepins, Dendermonde, safe behind its inundations, had successfully defied Louis in person. The old King now comforted his courtiers with the assurance that 'only an army of ducks could take it.' This sense of security was so great that the garrison had been left 'inconsiderable, sickly and half-starved, and the fortifications very ill-conditioned.' It had been loosely blockaded by the Allies since June. Seven weeks without rain gave the Duke a chance that he did not let slip. When the garrison of Menin marched out on August 25, he at once ordered an attack in force upon Dendermonde and, owing to the unusual drought, took it after a week's siege. He was not a day too soon. On September 6th, the day after its surrender, the weather broke and it rained for four days on end. Marlborough saw in this the finger of Providence ; still more surely did Colonel Blackader :

Even the people of this country say that God fights for us ; for old men at seventy years observe they never saw such a drought, or the waters so low about the town.[79]

Returning in the direction of the French border, the Duke sat down before Ath. Vendôme was close at hand, near Valenciennes, with a great army collected from all the other fronts to guard the grand entry of France. Much indeed had changed in a few months. Here at the gate was the 'mortified adventurer' whom Louis, Chamillart and Villeroi had challenged to battle in the lightness of their hearts. The lesson at last had been learned. When Vendôme enquired whether he was to oppose the Duke's operations at the risk of a conflict, Louis sharply forbade him. 'He attacks places,' wrote the King, 'in the hope of enticing you thither.' So the siege of Ath went on without interruption save from the rains. The Scottish private thus chronicles the routine :

And the nixt day in the trenches we lay,
   And our officers bought us the brandie.
We keept the trenches and held in the Frenchies,
   And beat them back when they sallie.

On October 2nd Ath fell—the large French garrison being
made prisoners of war.   Marlborough had hoped to take
Mons before retiring into winter quarters, but the Dutch
did not wish to venture on so large a task so late in the year,
and Marlborough himself finally confessed to Harley that
' the continued rains we have had for several days past have
made it almost impracticable to undertake another siege.'
The glorious campaign of 1706 was at length brought to an
end.[80]

The conquest of the Spanish Netherlands had not been
Marlborough's only task in that eventful summer.   While
he was planning marches, sieges and the taking in of towns,
he was at the same time engaged, in spite of his headaches
and other symptoms of advancing years, in an equally
arduous but much less decisive series of operations in the
regions of diplomacy.   Here he was fighting on a triple
front ; his task was to reconcile the claims of England, of
Holland and of Austria to each other, and to the possibilities
of a peace with France, which everyone now considered
to be close at hand.   The Duke was a very able statesman
and diplomat, as he had shown at the making of the
Grand Alliance, and on many occasions since.   He spoke,
too, with immense prestige, as the personal incarnation of
British power and allied victory ; he was Wellington and
Castlereagh in one.   But he had not the twofold authority
in England and Holland that had been wielded by the
Stadtholder-King, nor had he the strong intention to get
peace in spite of every obstacle, which had inspired William
in his dealings with friend and foe at Ryswick.   The Duke
showed no such pacific initiative now as the King had shown
then.   He had the qualities William lacked, for he could
not only plan, but win a world war ; but he was to fail
where William had succeeded, for he could not make a
world peace.   Indeed, he can scarcely be said to have tried.
He was not prepared to advise any sacrifices to induce the

French to accept the main consequences of the beating he had given them. For years past he had been writing to Sarah, declaring, probably with the sincerity of the moment, how much he longed for victory that should allow him to return from the wars and live with her in retirement at St. Albans or at Blenheim. But now that victory had come, he seemed to care little how long the war went on, and to have no other recipe for ending it than ever more extensive military operations.

Some expressions in the correspondence between Marlborough and Godolphin are singularly unpacific, as when the Treasurer wrote in July 1706 :

I don't think the Dutch are very reasonable, to be so much in pain about their barrier, as things stand ; but it is plain argument to me they think of joining their interest to France, whenever a peace comes, and for that very reason the longer we can keep it off, the better.

In August the Duke replied :

It is publicly said at the Hague that France is reduced to what it ought to be, and that if the war should be carried further, it would serve only to make England greater than it ought to be. In short, I am afraid our best allies are very fond of a peace.

In the same month Marlborough wrote to Heinsius :

As a good Englishman, I must be of the opinion of my country, but both by treaty * and in interest we are obliged to preserve the Monarchy of Spain entire.

The news that the Allies were in Madrid seemed that summer to justify the policy of ' no peace without Spain.' That claim emanated from Marlborough and Godolphin, but the Dutch were in full agreement. Not only Heinsius, but in 1706 even his political rival, Buys, the head of the moderate party in foreign affairs, fell in with the demand for the cession of the whole Spanish Empire to Charles. By so doing, they hoped to buy England's support and Austria's acquiescence in the matter of Holland's own claims for a

* The Treaty with Portugal, 1703, *not* the Treaty of Grand Alliance, 1701 ; see *Blenheim*, pp. 146, 302–303.

good Barrier in the Netherlands. But that was not their sole motive. The Dutch had fears on their own behalf that a French Bourbon at Madrid would endanger the position of the overseas trade of Holland in the lands of the Spanish Monarchy.

But in 1706 the difficulties of the Allies were not due to the rock ahead of 'no peace without Spain,' on which they were all fatally agreed ; the immediate question that divided and perplexed them was how to deal with the Spanish Netherlands, the magnificent trophy that Marlborough had laid at their feet. The bear had been killed, and the hunters at once fell out over the spoil. England, indeed, hastened to disclaim for herself any desire to occupy Ostend or any other town in the Netherlands after the war was over. This important declaration, made by Marlborough in June with Godolphin's full concurrence, greatly relieved the fears that both Dutch and Austrians had felt on that score, and put the Duke in a strong position to act as mediator between them.[81]

On the subject of the Spanish Netherlands the ideas of Austria and Holland were diametrically opposed. William and Marlborough had found this out in negotiating the Treaty of Grand Alliance in 1701. They had therefore drawn up Clause Five in terms purposely obscure ; the vague phraseology was not due to bad drafting, but was adopted so that all parties could sign the Treaty of Alliance, postponing the question of the future of the Spanish Netherlands until its reconquest had first been secured. In June 1706 the time had come when some meaning had to be given to the unintelligible verbiage of the Fifth Clause.*

The ideas of the Austrian Court were, as usual, simple in their utter selfishness. The Emperor Joseph, acting on behalf of his younger brother King Charles, absent in Spain, claimed that reconquered Brabant and Flanders should at once be put under a governor named by himself,

* ' Et afin de procurer cette satisfaction et cette sûreté [to the Emperor Leopold and to the States General] les Alliez feront entr'autres choses leur plus grands efforts pour reprendre et conquérir les Provinces des Païs Bas Espagnols, *dans l'intention qu'elles servent de Digue, de Rempart, et de Barrière pour séparer et éloigner la France des Provinces Unies.*' See *Blenheim*, pp. 146–147.

who should forthwith collect all the revenues ; that England
and Holland should go on fighting for the new regime at
their own expense till the war was over, and then withdraw
entirely from the Spanish Netherlands. If the Dutch
wanted a Barrier, they must seek it in fortresses to be won
from the territory of France. This highly legitimist
argument ignored the fact that neither of the Hapsburg
monarchies, neither Austria nor that shadowy nonentity
the Spain of 'Charles III,' had supplied a soldier or a
dollar to recover Belgium or to hold it now that it was
recovered.

The views held at the Hague and Amsterdam were very
different from those of Vienna. With the help of England,
Holland had reconquered the Spanish Netherlands from
France. The general had been English, but half the money
and much more than half the troops had been supplied by
the Dutch. At the decisive battle of Ramillies their bluecoats had borne the burden and heat of the day. All that
they asked for themselves, as the prize of victory in the
world war, was a secure barrier in that region against French
invasion, and some compensation from the revenues of
Belgium for the ruin that the Dutch finances had undergone
in the cause of Belgian liberation from France. The spoils
of the ocean and the lordship of the Mediterranean and
Atlantic were tacitly conceded by the countrymen of Tromp
and de Ruyter to the countrymen of Blake. As the resources
of the little Republic failed under the stress of the long war,
the Dutch quota of warships and their tale of men in Spain
grew less year by year, and those of England greater. But
in the Low Countries the States General maintained 120,000
of their own troops, supplying by far the greater part of the
garrisons of the reconquered towns, as well as most of the
field army. Having fought their way into the Spanish
Netherlands at a cost ruinous to their own prosperity, the
Dutch refused to march out again without some compensation for their sacrifices and some security against the
armed return of the French power.

The Dutch therefore claimed that the government of
Brabant and Flanders should be vested in themselves till
the war was over, and that after the peace they should

continue to garrison Barrier Fortresses stronger than those which had fallen so easy a prey to Louis in February 1701.* They intended, moreover, that their military occupation of this Barrier should carry with it trade advantages.

Between these irreconcilable claims of Austria and Holland it was Marlborough's task to mediate. While claiming nothing for herself in the Netherlands after the war, England rightly claimed to share with Holland in the government of Belgium so long as the war should last. But in other respects Marlborough was more inclined to the Dutch than to the Austrian view, during the weeks immediately before and after the battle of Ramillies. The Emperor's claims on behalf of King Charles for instant possession, put forward by his emissary Count Goes, were brushed aside in June, and England and Holland proceeded to act together as caretakers of the reconquered provinces for Charles for the duration of the war, pending permanent arrangements to be made about the Dutch Barrier.

The Emperor saw that he must do something to divide England and Holland. Therefore, with considerable astuteness, he changed his original intention and at the end of June offered the Governorship of the Spanish Netherlands, in the name of King Charles, to Marlborough himself. It was an apple of discord indeed. The Duke had every reason to desire the post. It would greatly facilitate his military operations ; it would enable him to keep the Belgians loyal to the Alliance, for they trusted in him and in England, and feared oppression by the Dutch ; moreover the Governorship, perhaps the greatest post a subject could fill in Europe, was worth £60,000 a year even in the money of that day. The Queen and Godolphin rejoiced at the honour done to their friend and to England in his person. Marlborough hoped and wished to accept. But in a few days he found that acceptance would mean a breach with Holland that must be fatal to the Alliance. The rage of the States General broke out in a stormy sitting at the Hague, and Heinsius had great difficulty to control their passion. He plainly told Marlborough that Holland could not thus forgo her rights in

* See *Blenheim*, pp. 137–138.

the territory which she had done so much to reconquer, and which constituted her main interest in the war.

Reluctantly, yet with perfect temper, the Duke declined the splendid gift.* The Emperor never forgave him for having refused, and the Dutch never forgave him for having wished to accept. The days of his confidential friendship with Wratislaw on one side and Heinsius on the other were at an end.

Marlborough himself had received a wound in the house of his friends which he felt for years to come. Ever since William had sent him to the Hague in 1701, he had done more than any English statesman to cement the friendship of England and Holland, contending against the strong current of anti-Dutch feeling that prevailed in his own party at home. He had won the war for Holland by cordial co-operation, bearing with much from her Generals and Field Deputies. He knew that he was trusted and even loved by the Dutch common people, and he had hoped that their statesmen would be ready to confide to him their interests in Belgium. He expected too much of human nature, forgetting the intensity of Dutch sensitiveness about the Netherlands.

Unfortunately, like Cæsar and Cromwell, though he refused the crown, he never abandoned the hope that some day he might be permitted to wear it. He dreamed that the Governorship might yet be his. The weak spot in his character was his proneness to double-dealing learnt in the dynastic intrigues of English politics. It led him now to aspire secretly after the great post which he had so magnanimously refused. The half-hearted pursuit of a personal ambition continued for several years to hamper the initiative of his action as diplomatist. His chance of mediating successfully between Austria and Holland on the Barrier question was thereby sensibly reduced. The thick atmosphere of mutual suspicion involved all the relations of England, Holland and Austria, and Marlborough no longer towered gigantically with his head above the cloud. He too was

---

* So much is now understood of the Duke's real character that it is perhaps superfluous to point out that a man whose chief motive was avarice would not be likely to refuse £60,000 a year for any consideration of the public interest,

involved in it, suspected by all parties, not wholly without reason.*

By the middle of July 1706 the English and Dutch completed the negotiations for their joint control of the Spanish Netherlands, which had been interrupted by the Emperor's offer of the Governorship to Marlborough. A *condominium* of England and Holland was established over Belgium for the duration of the war, after which it was to be handed on to the direct rule of Charles III, subject to the reservation of a Dutch Barrier, the extent and nature of which had still to be settled. George Stepney, who could no longer endure the political atmosphere of Vienna and had made himself unpopular with the Imperial advisers by his constant demand that they should come to terms with the Hungarian rebels, was summoned away to Brussels to act there as England's representative in the *Condominium*. The Dutch resented the presence of an Englishman as their colleague, while the Belgians had little confidence in Stepney, since Marlborough, in whom they had put their trust, had, as they conceived, deserted them and left them to the tender mercies of Holland. The Dutch expected the inhabitants to contribute heavily towards the cost of the war and the maintenance of the garrisons. A letter of Marlborough to Stepney that winter indicates the milder and wiser policy that he would have pursued if he had been allowed to become Governor of the Netherlands.

The Condominium [he writes] contained nothing contrary to the known laws of the country. However, our chief aim ought to be to

---

* The facts and arguments on which this view is based will be found in Marlborough's correspondence, but more particularly in the late Roderick Geikie's posthumously published work *The Dutch Barrier* (Cambridge Press, 1930), ably completed by Mrs. Montgomery. See in particular chaps. I and II and App. A. This work of a fine Cambridge scholar of the last generation, whom I had the privilege to call my friend, throws a flood of light on these complicated transactions. Coxe's view of Marlborough's conduct is too uniformly favourable. See *Add. MSS.* 7058, f. 55, for Marlborough's letter of July 12 declining the Governorship. See also *Klopp*, XII, pp. 86–96, *Coxe*, II, pp. 548–549 (at end of chap. lxxii.).

Professor Basil Williams, in his *Life of Stanhope*, p. 62, shows that Stanhope, British envoy at the court of Charles III of Spain, had, on his own account, been pressing Charles to grant the governorship to Marlborough. Charles was not enthusiastic, but fell into line with the Emperor's policy and confirmed the offer.

satisfy the people and make them easy under the present administration, so that the collecting at present a little money more, or less, ought not in my opinion to come in competition in a matter of this moment, especially considering when we take the field, we shall be able to leave but small garrisons in the great towns, and must depend in some measure on the faithfulness of the inhabitants.[82]

Marlborough foresaw that the hatred of the Belgians for the departed French might soon be turned into regret, as actually occurred with serious military results in 1708, when the ' great towns ' of Bruges and Ghent changed sides again.

Indeed the rule of the Allies was not popular for long. The Spanish Netherlands had been saved from ultimate absorption in France, but the immediate gain in liberty was not very marked, and the material conditions were worse than before Ramillies, because the war had now been moved into the heart of Belgium. The rival armies cut down the trees, burned the farms, carried off the cattle and carts of the peasantry in the ordinary course of military operations. Behind the front, the English indeed paid handsomely for all they wanted and the inhabitants ' loved the English officers and soldiers.' But the thrifty Dutch brought all their supplies by water from Holland, while they exacted heavy regular contributions towards the war.*

Stepney warned Heinsius that ' the people would be driven to despair when they apprehend they are treated too much on the foot of a conquered country,' but he could not control his Dutch colleagues at Brussels as Marlborough could have done. The unhappy business of the offer and refusal of the Governorship made it impossible for the Duke to interfere directly with the administration of the *Condominium*. In judging the conduct of the Dutch, it is

* The Jacobite Earl of Ailesbury, who had lived among the Belgians for years and knew them well, thus described the regime of the *Condominium* : ' I cannot say their laws were violated, but their purse paid well, and great sums were laid upon pretence of giving safeguards, and contributions were exacted, and for three years the fields and meadows were as bare as the high road by continued foraging for to make the armies subsist. None got but the tradesmen and artificers in towns and the eating-houses, inns, taverns and ale-houses, and especially by the English, for the Dutch were great economists, and by rivers and canals lived greatly on what came from Holland. And to give them their due they [the Belgians] loved the English officers and soldiers, but not the hoarders up of money.' *Ailesbury Memoirs (Rox.)*, II, p. 602.

only fair to remember how deeply they had already mort-gaged their own resources. If the Allies would not make peace, many evils must follow, and among others the im-poverishment and alienation of the inhabitants of Belgium. [83]

During the autumn and winter of 1706 a first attempt was made by England and Holland to come to an agreement as to the extent of the Barrier that the Dutch were to obtain at the peace. The negotiation became involved in the question of the Hanoverian Succession in Britain. The Dutch wanted a good Barrier, and looked to English states-men and soldiers to help them to get it from Austria and from France. The English statesmen wanted security for the Protestant Succession, and looked to the large army of Holland to render aid against French invasion and Jacobite rebellion whenever the crisis should come. The Act of Settlement had made the Hanoverian Succession the law of the land, and the Regency Act passed by Parliament in the winter of 1705–6 had further strengthened the constitu-tional rights of Sophia and George. But in view of Anne's feeble health, the open Jacobitism of half Scotland and the anti-English feeling of the whole nation, the uncertainty as to the line the High Tories of England might take, and the perpetual threat of French invasion, the question of the Succession lay like a cloud of anxiety over Britain. The difficult negotiations between England and Scotland that year kept all men in momentary fear of civil war in the north of the island, which would assuredly break out if the Queen were to die before the Union had become law. In 1706 Marlborough and Godolphin were heartily at one with the Whigs in the matter of the Succession, and were for that reason working with Somers and Halifax to secure the Scottish Union. They also co-operated with them in an attempt to get a double treaty with Holland, by which Holland should guarantee the Protestant Succession in England, and England should guarantee a good Barrier to Holland.*

* The inter-connection of the questions of Barrier, Succession and Union is illustrated in the following words, written by Godolphin to Marlborough at the Hague in October 1706 : ' I hope you may soon conclude the Barrier Treaty and

The first part of such a treaty could be easily arranged, for the Dutch had every reason to regard the Protestant Succession as essential to their own safety. But it was more difficult to agree on the number of fortress cities to be included in the Dutch Barrier, and actually no such agreement was reached until the autumn of 1709.

The Dutch demands were extravagant, partly because they traded on the anxiety of the English statesmen to buy a guarantee for the Protestant Succession ; partly because the French, all through 1706, were making separate offers to Holland, attempting to shake her loyalty to the Alliance by the promise of a great Barrier. The English statesmen were kept in constant alarm lest the Dutch should take the initiative in making peace. Heinsius therefore was the better able to raise his demands in dealing with England. He claimed her support for a most formidable list of Barrier Fortresses : Thionville, Luxemburg, Namur, Charleroi, Mons, Maubeuge, Valenciennes, Condé, Tournai, Lille, Menin, Ypres, Furnes, Nieuport, Ostend and Dendermonde.* Some of these were in the Spanish Netherlands, others were in French territory.

To such demands the English statesmen could not be induced to agree. The Lords of the Whig Junto were not yet in the Cabinet, but the Queen's Ministers consulted with them on foreign affairs, and in particular made use of the diplomatic talents of Halifax. He strongly supported the Duke in refusing Dendermonde and Ostend to the Dutch. English cloth entered Belgium by Ostend, and Halifax, ' upon first hearing Ostend named,' told Heinsius that ' the Flemings might be apt to interpret the shutting them up on that side as if the design were to keep them in servitude as a conquered people.' The Dutch statesmen answered, with some show of reason, that if Holland was to protect the Netherlands in the future from French invasion,

the guaranty of the Succession, which will be of less importance to us every day if they go on as well as they have begun in Scotland. The letters to-day from thence give great hope of carrying the Union.' *Geikie*, p. 4, note. For the close communication between the Ministers and the Whig Junto on foreign policy this year, see *Hardwicke Papers*, II, pp. 467–472.

* The Dutch Barrier destroyed in 1701 consisted of Luxemburg, Namur, Charleroi, Mons, Ath, Oudenarde and Nieuport.

she must be able to prevent the enemy landing from the sea, and must therefore have both Ostend and Nieuport ; she must also be able to send reinforcements and supplies freely from her home territories to the distant Barrier Fortresses, and must therefore have Dendermonde to secure the line of communications. The events of February 1701 had proved how very inadequate, in the face of French attack, were the isolated fortresses that constituted the Dutch Barrier of that earlier day. This was true enough. But the real trouble lay deeper : the Barrier system, on which the Dutch had learnt to pin all their faith, was militarily unsound ; it was an artifice of diplomats rather than of soldiers. The events of 1745, when Marshal Saxe overran Belgium, gave fresh proof of it in a later age. It came to this, that unless the Dutch were effective masters of all the Spanish Netherlands they could be in no true military position to defend them against France.

Nothing therefore was agreed upon in the winter of 1706. The statesmen of the Hague were angry with Marlborough and Halifax for refusing them Dendermonde and Ostend. Harley, while denouncing the greed of Holland in his letters to Stepney, was secretly telling the Dutch Envoy in London that Halifax and the other Whigs betrayed the interests of the Republic over the Barrier in order to curry favour with the English nation. There is little wonder that, for all his merits, Harley was nicknamed 'Robin the trickster' by men of all parties, or that the Whigs next year determined to get rid of him from the Cabinet. [84]

While Marlborough had been engaged on the siege of Ath, the last military operation of his year of glory, he learnt that Eugene had triumphed at Turin, and that French dominion over Italy was at an end.

This crowning mercy, completing the list of the objects which the Grand Alliance had originally undertaken to secure, was due to the dogged courage of Victor Amadeus of Savoy, the great military qualities of Prince Eugene, and the use made of the German armies and English money which Marlborough and Godolphin had provided for several years past to make up the deficiencies of the Austrian effort.

Though not a single British unit was engaged under the walls of Turin, the victory was a triumph of our island policy. Though in the first years of the war Austria had made great efforts in Italy, she had done but little for two years past. The result of Blenheim followed by Ramillies should have been to set Austrian armies free to cross the Alps. But they were diverted to wage war on the Hungarian rebels, with whom the Emperor Joseph refused to come to terms in spite of the constant solicitations of Marlborough and the English Ministers. 'The hearts of these people,' Stepney wrote just before he left Vienna, 'are hardened by your victories ; the whole burden of the war against France lies on us.' In May 1706 Hessian troops on the way to Italy had been stopped in Bavaria by the Imperial orders. In July and August, while Turin was on the point of falling unless relieved, more Imperial troops were called from the Rhine to the Danube, where an army of 36,000 men was assembled to make war on the Hungarians. England was to pay for the reconquest of Italy for Austria's benefit, while Austria reconquered Hungary, in effect therefore at our expense.

Though bitterly incensed at such conduct, the English Ministers, inspired by Marlborough, continued their efforts to save Italy. At midsummer Harley writes : ' I sent the Duke of Marlborough 50,000 pounds to be sent to Prince Eugene, so that I hope he will be able to carve out his own revenge for the battle of Calcinato and at the same time relieve Savoy.' Scarcely half his force was Austrian ; the Prussian and other German troops whom he commanded had been procured by Marlborough's diplomacy and were in the pay of the Maritime Powers.[85]

The prospects in Italy, when the campaign of 1706 opened, were gloomy in the extreme. Louis had made every preparation for the siege and capture of Turin, which would dethrone Victor Amadeus of Savoy and bring the Italian war to an end. Vendôme scored the first success at Calcinato,* shutting up Eugene in the Alpine passes round Lake Garda, while the French general La Feuillade began the long siege of Turin. In May, Richard Hill, the English Envoy at the Court of Savoy, wrote :

* See p. 101, above.

The Imperialists are just now where they were this time five years and have not yet set their foot on the State of Milan. . . . I do not see how it is possible to keep the war on foot in Italy upon equal terms after this campaign, unless the Venetians can be brought into it. Whatever they can reasonably desire of the Queen will be less than what it will cost Her Majesty if the Duke of Savoy is quite driven out of his dominions.

Yet Hill admitted that Venice, if she ever abandoned her timorous neutrality, was just as likely to come out on the side of France. Meanwhile the French and Allied armies manœuvred and fought on her territories round Verona. English trade with the Adriatic ports of Austria passed through Venetian hands and paid heavily in the passage. Naples, Sicily and Milan, being in French occupation, were closed to English commerce. One result of the expulsion of the French from these places would be to open the trade of Italy, of the Adriatic and of Austria freely to English merchants. They would then be able to negotiate about tariffs on more equal terms with the Venetians, who so long as the French held the rest of the peninsula and infested the Adriatic, exacted what terms they liked from the embarrassed English merchants.[86]

In the darkest hour for the Allied cause in Italy, in July 1706, Eugene began his wonderful march from the foot of the Alps round Garda, up the long valley of the Po, to the relief of Turin, crossing river after river, passing through hostile territory, outmanœuvring hostile armies, week by week nearing his goal. He was aided by the recall of his able antagonist Vendôme to restore the situation in the Netherlands, and by the hopefulness infused into the Allies generally by the news of Ramillies, and of the progress of ' King Charles ' in Spain.

Meanwhile Victor Amadeus and Turin were in sore straits. In May the capital was besieged by La Feuillade, but the Duke escaped into the open field to get into touch with Eugene. La Feuillade pursued him with a flying column, and twice that summer chased him up into the Alpine valleys. On one occasion Victor Amadeus took refuge among the Vaudois Protestants, whom his family had so long and so terribly ill-used, latterly at the dictation of

France.   Now that he had thrown off the yoke of Louis, the persecuted remnant were his most loyal subjects, and the pursuers dared not follow the Duke up the Waldensian valleys in face of the mountaineer militia on the heights, burning to strike a blow at the French, whose victory would mean their extermination.

All this while the siege of Turin went forward, the Piedmontese army and inhabitants grimly resisting a fierce bombardment and repeated assaults.   Early in the year, the clergy had urged Victor Amadeus to make terms with France, but he stubbornly refused, and as the siege went on the patriotic enthusiasm of all classes of his subjects rose, with the news of Ramillies and the rumour of Eugene's approach.   But the fortifications of the citadel were breached, and Turin was at its last gasp, when in the first week of September took place the famous junction of the forces of Eugene with the small field army of Victor Amadeus. The situation was still dangerous in the extreme. The joint relieving force numbered less than 35,000 ; the besiegers were nearer to 60,000.   Going up to the summit of the Superga hill, that rises two thousand feet above the plain of the Po, Eugene and Victor Amadeus gazed down on the beleaguered city and the works of besiegers and besieged.   From their point of vantage the two Savoyards could see it all, through their telescopes, laid before them like a map :   they noted that the lines of circumvallation, made by the French to keep off a relieving force, were strong everywhere except between the Dora and Stura rivers that fall into the Po from the west.   The besiegers could not imagine that relief could come from that quarter. The Prince and the Duke decided to cross the Po, march right round and attack the enemy there.   The relieving force was small, but its courage was high, it was made up of some of the best German troops in Europe, and it believed that Eugene's presence meant victory.   Viewing from the Superga the irresolution and disorder of the enemy's dispositions in the plain below, the Prince turned to his cousin the Duke and said, ' Those men seem to me already half beaten.'

Indeed confused and timid counsels prevailed in the French camp.   The Duke of Orleans, a Prince of the Blood nominally in command, wished to march out against Eugene, leaving the town blockaded. The size of the French force fully justified that policy. But Marsin, the old and experienced general by whose advice Orleans was bound to be guided, declared for remaining behind their lines of circumvallation. Marsin was not the man he had been at Blenheim. He suffered from a strong presentiment of his own approaching death, which had the effect of breaking his nerve ; the letter he wrote to Chamillart while in this state, the day before the battle, is a curious document : ' This letter will be given you only after my death.' The French soldiers, ever sensitive to the changes of the moral barometer of the camp, had lost all faith in their own leaders, when they saw the German army, led by the redoubtable Prussian bluecoats, coming Sept. 7 at them at the weakest point of their lines, where 1706 only twenty-four hours' work had been done upon the trenches. After a short and fierce struggle, the unfinished line of circumvallation was carried ; Marsin was captured, mortally wounded as he had foreseen ; the garrison of Turin issued out to complete the victory ; and the French army fled across the Alps by way of Pignerol, leaving their garrisons in Milan, Naples and Sicily to be reduced by the victors. Italy had passed into the hands of the Allies. The balance of power had been restored in Europe. The hegemony of Louis XIV was no more.

As a result of this battle, not the French but the Austrians succeeded the Spaniards as the dominant nation in Italy, until their power was first shaken by Napoleon, and finally overthrown by Victor Emmanuel, successor to the throne and policy of Victor Amadeus of Savoy.

When Marlborough heard that the plans he had been so long laying for the relief of Savoy had been carried to success by Eugene, he wrote to Sarah :

It is impossible for me to express the joy it has given me ; for I do not only esteem, but I really love that Prince.

It does not appear that the least tinge of jealous competition ever clouded the friendship of Eugene for Marlborough, or of Marlborough for Eugene.[87]

CHAPTER VIII

The War in Spain Decided, 1706

' King Charles ' besieged in Barcelona. Its relief by Leake. Peterborough's
conduct. Galway occupies Madrid. ' King Charles ' delays and loses
his chance. Retreat of the Allies from Madrid to Valencia.

THE campaign of 1706, in its various, widely scattered seats
of war, determined the main outlines of the Peace of Utrecht.
For if, at Ramillies and Turin, the Spanish Netherlands and
Italy were lost to France, in the same year Spain itself was
lost to the Austrian claimant. Events in the field were dic-
tating to the statesmen of Europe the precise system of Partition that had been laid down in the Grand Alliance Treaty
by the prophetic wisdom of William III. Years might
elapse before they would accept the inevitable, but the
writing was already growing clear upon the wall.

In January 1706 Marshal Tessé * and his compatriots
found themselves on the southern borders of Aragon, beset
by the Carlist enthusiasm of the city populations, who
indulged in sporadic acts of hostility against the French
troops. Tessé, mistaking Aragon for all Spain, wrote to
Versailles that the whole country was ' discontented and
disposed to change its master,' that a separate French army
would be needed ' in every province,' and that Philip, without money, soldiers or policy, was on the road to ruin. Louis
being outside the trees saw more of the wood, and took a
less gloomy view than his Marshal. He ordered the
unwilling Tessé to undertake the siege of Barcelona. A
reinforcement was sent, that raised to 20,000 the French
force that sat down before the town in the first days of April.[88]

* For Tessé, see p. 43 above. *For this chapter see Map X (Europe) at end of
volume, and Map III (Barcelona), p. 69, above.*

Barcelona had been surprised, and was utterly unprepared to resist. Peterborough was away in Valencia. With great haste a few troops were collected and thrown into the town. At most the garrison did not number above four thousand regulars, of whom only a thousand were English. But the enthusiastic citizen militia undertook to make good what was wanting ; and in the country around, the Catalan rising assumed such proportions that the besiegers in their turn found themselves closely encircled by the guerilla bands of ' Miquelets.' Tessé's land communications were cut, and he depended for supply on the fleet sent to his aid from Toulon.

The rival kings of Spain were present. Philip was a nonentity in the French camp. But Charles, as King among the Catalans, showed, in the early months of this fateful year, an energy of spirit which deserted him in the summer. For a while he was infected by the fever of loyal enthusiasm raging among his subjects in Barcelona. The priests and monks fostered the excitement by sermons and alleged miracles. But it was openly said that, if the Prince who was the object of all this emotion were to slink away, the town would be surrendered, and the English massacred by the enraged and betrayed populace. Charles, however, took a manly resolution befitting his one-and-twenty years. He stayed to see it out. By this decision he actually saved Barcelona, but he ran a great risk of being made prisoner by his rival, and so bringing the Peninsular War to an ignominious end. Thirty years on, as the careworn Emperor Charles VI, hawking his Pragmatic Sanction round the courts of Europe, with what thoughts did he remember these glorious days of his youth, on the breach of the beleaguered city, at the head of his fierce Catalan adorers ?

Meanwhile, the weaker elements in Peterborough's complex character were in the ascendant. In winter quarters, at Valencia, he had played Don Juan with every advantage in his favour. But he had quarrelled with all his allies of the male sex.

There cannot be worse company than a beggarly German and a proud Spaniard [he wrote to Halifax], and were it not for the revenge we seek on the disagreeable men with the agreeable ladies, our

condition were intolerable, black eyes and wit in the wives being
what alone can make us endure the husbands ; the fair sex especially
never failing to put in practice the making use of all opportunities in
pleasures, the reverse of what our statesmen practise in business.

When he heard that ' King Charles ' was besieged in
Barcelona, and might easily be killed or captured there, his
first thought was to nominate a successor, reserving to
himself the post of Grand Vizier.   He wrote from Valencia
to Victor Amadeus, Duke of Savoy, that in case Charles
were killed, ' I will give Spain to him who ought to have it '
—that is to his correspondent.   ' I ask only 1,500 good
horsemen, with horses, harness and arms, and I will answer
for the rest.'   If, indeed, Charles were merely taken
prisoner, instead of being killed outright, it would, Peterborough confessed, be highly inconvenient.   But, even so,
though the position would be more delicate, he will do his
best for Victor Amadeus, ' for your interests, Monseigneur,
will always be at my heart.'   The impropriety and folly of
this letter are amazing, even in Peterborough.   How could
he suppose that, if Barcelona fell to Philip, Spain would then
be in a mood to accept yet another King, chosen by the
English general, and carried to Madrid by ' 1,500 good
horsemen ' ?   The best that can be said for the man who
wrote the letter, is that he had probably forgotten all about
it in two days.   And then, after two centuries, historians
have a way of finding these unlucky documents and reading
a man's character off the forgotten and fading ink.[89]

Tessé's army was a very much larger force than that
with which Peterborough had taken Barcelona.   The
French expected to carry the outworks of Monjuic at a rush,
as the English had done last September.   But this time
the redcoats were the other side of the wall, and the
assault was repulsed with heavy loss.   Monjuic had to be
approached and bombarded in form, and till it was taken
the attack on the town was not pressed.   This gave the
inhabitants time to repair the breaches, which had been left
in ruin since the late siege.   Barcelona was saved by Lord
Donegal and six hundred Englishmen, who held Monjuic
for nearly three weeks against the French army.   When,
at length, it was stormed on April 21, Lord Donegal

threw himself among the thickest of them, refusing quarter twice, upon which he was shot through the head, but he had killed four of the enemy with his own hand. He acted the part of a good grenadier.

After this long delay before the fort, the French turned against the town, but even now with a certain lack of energy characteristic of the charming diplomat who commanded them. It ought to have been an easy task. The defenders' cannon were unskilfully served. The breaches, made in last year's siege, had been filled up, but not rebuilt. The best troops of the garrison had been killed or captured in Monjuic, and an army was now besieging a mob. Nothing but the enthusiasm of the Catalans, kept hot by the continual appearance of 'King Charles' at the point of danger, enabled the defence to be protracted yet awhile. The citizens, Tessé reported, 'acted as regular troops' and made frequent and effective sorties into his trenches. In this hand-to-hand fighting the monks were conspicuous, and several were killed at the head of the Catalan militia. His own cannoneers, Tessé declared, were as bad as those of the besieged, and forty of his guns had burst. But at the end of the first week in May, two effective breaches had been reopened, in and near the Sant Antonio bastion. An assault was prepared and, if delivered, could hardly fail to be successful.

On the eve of the assault the French warships suddenly left the bay. Next morning the English fleet swept in, just May 8 too late to destroy the enemy squadron, but just in (N.S.) time to save Barcelona. Admiral Leake had had 1706 the good sense to bring with him the 5,000 troops on board his transports, having declined to obey Peterborough's orders to land them in Valencia on the way. They were now landed on the quay of Barcelona, and marched straight up to the breach. Another thousand infantry, under Peterborough's immediate command, also entered the town in a flotilla of boats which he had collected, and which now came in under cover of the fleet.

If these military reinforcements had not arrived, the French might have stormed the town under the eyes of the English seamen. Indeed, the assault might have been successfully made a few hours before their arrival, even after the departure of the French fleet, if Tessé had been a man to take risks. But he had no communications open except by sea, and he had, therefore, some reason to fear embarrassment even if he took Barcelona. It is, indeed, highly probable that if the town had once fallen, the Miquelets would have been so much discouraged that he could have opened his communications again by land. But, as his letters show, he was thoroughly alarmed by his position, and after the departure of the French fleet never thought of attempting to storm the town. A day or two later the besiegers decamped, leaving behind their cannon, ammunition and stores. They cut their way back to the French border through hordes of Catalan insurgents hanging on their flanks. Tessé lost, in the siege and retreat, a quarter of his total force.

On the very day the siege was raised, occurred an eclipse of the sun, so complete that English officers in Barcelona lit candles at midday. It seemed to the delighted Allies to portend the veiled fortunes of the Grand Monarch who, in his pride, had chosen the sun for his emblem. Medals and prints representing the symbolic eclipse filled the shops of London and Amsterdam that summer, for the news of Barcelona mingled with the news of Ramillies, and seemed the beginning of the end.

The relief of Barcelona had been due to Leake, and to Leake alone. Whether as a dashing young captain or as a sage, responsible admiral, John Leake had a remarkable way of relieving beleaguered cities with a margin of a few hours in hand. Londonderry, Gibraltar and Barcelona owed him their safety, and if the margin had always been dangerously small, the fault could never justly be laid at Leake's door. On this last occasion, he had, in making his preparations, overcome great difficulties at Lisbon, due to the recalcitrance of the Portuguese and Dutch. He had got the armament equipped and started. He had then very wisely waited till he was joined by a squadron under Byng, without which he would have appeared before Barcelona inferior to the enemy in numbers. But the necessity for haste had been kept before the seamen by General James Stanhope, sent out with the reinforcements as English Minister to the King of Spain. Stanhope was statesman enough to know that, before everything else, ' King Charles ' must be saved from capture, and he impressed this point upon Leake.

The Admiral had kept the troops on board in spite of Peterborough's reiterated orders to land them in Valencia, where they would have swelled My Lord's command, but not in sufficient numbers to enable him to cut his way through Tessé's army.*

Last of all, Leake had kept his temper under desperate provocation from the erratic Earl.   Peterborough on shore had instructed Stanhope on the fleet to warn him of its approach by sending a piece of paper cut to a particular pattern.   On receipt of the arranged signal Peterborough put to sea in a small boat, waylaid the English fleet as it hastened northwards along the coast, came on board, and hoisted his flag on Leake's flagship.   He bore the superior commission even at sea.†   But the salt-water Admiral kept his own flag flying as well as My Lord's, and said nothing. To discuss the situation would have precipitated a crisis that might have been fatal to their enterprise.   Peterborough, who had only a midshipman's experience of the sea, had no intention of taking over the real command, and left everything to Leake—except the reputation of having relieved Barcelona.   To that he intended to lay claim.   His partisans at home wrote up the story.   In those days, and for many years to come, the history of naval operations was written by landsmen.   The sailors' view of the affair was seldom heard, and seldom heeded in polite society.   In his claim to have saved Barcelona, the madcap Earl imposed on most of his countrymen for nearly two centuries, at the expense of the honest, unadvertising representative of the ' silent service.' [90]

The relief of Barcelona, the flight of a great French army headlong out of Spain, the news of Ramillies, the

---

* Peterborough's defence of these orders, which he came to see needed apology, was that, if Leake had transports with him, they would hamper him in his battle with the French fleet.   Later, he began to advise Leake to take with him ' a thousand ' troops for the town.   But would they have been enough ?   *B.M. Add. MSS.* 5438, pp. 70–72.

† He had repeatedly written home during the winter that ' without the command of the fleet and troops I desire to be called home and will not serve.'   *P. to St.*, pp. 3, 4, 6–7.

advance of Galway and the Portuguese on Madrid, caused, during the midsummer months, such depression on one side and such confidence on the other as to render not impossible a change in the allegiance of the Spanish people as a whole.   Carlist enthusiasm in the Eastern Provinces was beginning to solidify into a fixed loyalty.   Castilian pride was shaken by the proved incompetence of King Philip and his entourage, and now by the failure of the arms of France, on which the Spanish nation had confidently relied in making its choice of a King.   A door was open to the Allies if they had the sense and resolution to push in.   ' Wilt thou ? ' said the winged minute.   But Charles and Peter-borough would not.   Instead of marching straight on Madrid, when there was no one to oppose, they spent May, June and most of July in doing nothing at all.   The egoism, the irresolution and the quarrels of the allied chiefs in Spain reached the climax at the moment of their greatest opportunity.

On the other hand, Philip's affairs, so long and so disastrously mismanaged in every department, passed under strong and united control, just in time to save his throne. By the recent return of the Princess des Ursins to Spain harmony had been restored between Versailles and Madrid, and a courageous woman, schooled now by a little mis-fortune, again stood at the Queen's side to direct and inspire the royal couple.   By itself this would not have been enough.   But in February 1706 Berwick also returned to Spain.   The Queen had learnt wisdom from the dis-asters which had followed her insistence on his recall. Philip, indeed, was a cipher, but Berwick and des Ursins, acting together, might yet save Spain from Charles and Peterborough, acting one against the other.*

* During his retirement from the Spanish scene, Berwick had, in 1705, been coping with the rebellion of the persecuted Cevennois, or Camisards, in the heart of southern France ; it was the same employment that had been found for Villars in the year of Blenheim (*Blenheim*, pp. 321-322).   Villars had tried pacification and toleration, but the bigots at Versailles had thrown over that policy.   Berwick had, therefore, to fall back upon burnings alive and breakings on the wheel, retreading the circle of mutual atrocity in which that fearful war of religion revolved.   One of Berwick's opinions is worthy of notice in an English history : ' It is astonishing that the English and Dutch, who fomented this revolt underhand, never sent the Cevennois any capable leaders, or even gave them any better counsel.' *Berwick*, I, pp. 178-183, 196-197.

While the great French army, under Tessé's command, was unsuccessfully besieging Barcelona, it was Berwick's task, with a much less powerful force, to delay as best he could the advance of Ruvigny, Lord Galway, from Portugal into the heart of Spain. The Huguenot General of the English, though not a great soldier, was more competent than Charles and more steady and disinterested than Peterborough. It was due to his initiative that the Allies came so near to final victory that summer.

Seeing the bulk of the French forces deeply engaged in Catalonia, Galway insisted that the Anglo-Portuguese on the western frontier of Spain should march into the heart of the country. He carried them forward to the important frontier fortress of Alcantara, which he besieged and took, together with its garrison of 4,000 Spanish infantry.

April 14 (N.S.) 1706

The road to Madrid was now open. For the moment Berwick had not the troops to resist the Allies. In May they took Ciudad Rodrigo in less than a week. Salamanca made no resistance at all. But the Portuguese General, Das Minas, and his men cared for nothing but plundering Spain, and had no relish for a risky adventure to the capital. Galway called in the help of Methuen. The English Ambassador at Lisbon coerced King Peter by threatening to send away the English troops by sea, and to stop the pay of their half-hearted allies.* The King submitted, and ordered Das Minas to go forward. A few weeks later John Methuen died, but meanwhile Galway and his English had arrived in Madrid, dragging with them the Portuguese army, loaded with the plunder of Spain.

June 27 (N.S.) 1706

* 'I find myself obliged to represent to your Majesty in the name of the Queen my Mistress, that, since it appears now to be in your Majesty's power by marching immediately toward Madrid to make a revolution in Spain, if any other resolution than that be taken the Queen my Mistress will look on it as the loss of the greatest occasion that could be wished. If the army shall be otherwise employed this spring than in marching into Spain toward Madrid, I am commanded to retire the English forces in Portugal to be embarked on the fleet which I expect in the next month, and in that case I am likewise commanded not to continue the payment of the Subsidies for the pay of the troops of your Majesty according to the Treaty.' *Account of what was insisted on by Mr. Methuen at the Conference of the 9th, 19th and 21st of April and presented in writing to the King of Portugal on April 22, 1706. P.R.O., S.P., 89, 19.*

The first reception of the Allies in the capital was better than they could have hoped ' considering the unaccountable absence of the King of Spain.' Galway had, in vain, implored Charles to join him at Madrid. An army of invaders, consisting chiefly of Portuguese banditti ' committing the greatest disorders and robbing the people of what they could,' and a few disciplined regiments of heretics, the countrymen of Drake and Cromwell, could not hope to be popular in Spain except as the bodyguard of the King. And the Austrian King of Spain seemed to prefer to be King of Catalonia. Even so, many thought the Bourbon cause lost. Philip V had hastened round from the trenches of Barcelona by way of France and Navarre to Madrid, only to fly thence from the approach of the enemy. The rats began to leave the ship : four Grandees of the Kingdom came to pay their respects to Galway. Cardinal Porto Carrero, who had his personal grievances against the Bourbon whom he had set on the throne, sent letters of submission to the victors, and caused the city of Toledo to declare for King Charles. Opinion trembled in the balance.

But the precious weeks slipped by, and still Charles lingered in Catalonia. The partisans of France started a rumour in the streets of Madrid that he was absent because he was dead ; two priests took oath in public that they had seen him embalmed. Every day popular sentiment in Castile ebbed back to the side of Philip. Berwick had induced the King and Queen not to seek refuge on the frontier of France, but to remain at Burgos during the dangerous days, as a rallying point to the hopes of loyal Spaniards. Residing there in poverty, misery and squalor unspeakable, the exiled Court became the centre of a national revival that was soon to carry them irresistibly back to Madrid. The Princess des Ursins appealed to the Spanish people and clergy for money, and money began to flow into Burgos from all the provinces of Central and Western Spain. The peasants of Old Castile and Leon sprang to arms in guerilla bands and cut Galway's communications with Portugal. As in Napoleon's time, so in Marlborough's, Spain, that could raise no regular army of any value in the field, was the one land in Europe that no

regular army could hold down.   Meanwhile, Berwick was
being strongly reinforced from France and would soon be
more than a match for Galway.*   The opportunity of the
Allies was passing beyond recall, and Charles was not yet
at Madrid.[91]

Was the young man's fatal delay to come and pick up
his crown chiefly his own fault or chiefly that of Peterborough ?   That controversy raged in England as a question
of party politics during the remainder of the Queen's reign.
It was made the subject of prolonged enquiries in Parliament, with a voluminous production of documents ; it
became the subject of many books and pamphlets.   The
documents produced in those debates, and others that still
lie unprinted in the British Museum, help the modern
historian to form a judgment on this difficult question.

Stanhope and Richards,† two honest and unselfish
soldiers who strove in vain to keep the peace between
Charles in Catalonia and the English Commander-in-Chief
in Valencia, were both of opinion that Peterborough was right
in wishing that Charles should go to Madrid by the route
of Valencia, not of Aragon.   But Richards and Stanhope
were also of opinion that Peterborough threw obstacles in
the way of his own scheme by writing to Charles from
Valencia near the end of June, to complain that he had no
money to pay the troops, and no mules for transport—
' though I fear he never took any measures to get them,'
adds Richards.   Worst of all, at this moment, when he
should have been concentrating every man of his own
whom he could spare at Requena on the route to Madrid,
he sent off four regiments of foot to take Alicante in the
far South.   His mind could no more stay fixed on a point
than a bladder charged with gas.   Charles, on hearing these

* If the chief blame lay with Charles and Peterborough, Galway was charged
with having wasted his time in Madrid.   Berwick wrote in his memoirs that if,
instead of waiting in the capital, Galway had pursued him hard early in July,
' he would infallibly have driven me beyond the Ebro before the arrival of
reinforcements.'   Peterborough, on August 25, wrote to Leake that Galway ought
in July to have pursued Berwick, or else have formed a strong entrenched camp
near Madrid, but that he did neither.

† For Col. John Richards see p. 71, above.   It will be noted that he had no
personal prejudice against Peterborough, to whom he gave the full credit for the
taking of Monjuic in 1705.   And he acted as Peterborough's man of confidence.

reports, was only too ready to believe that Peterborough did
not really want him in Valencia—as may, indeed, have been
the case for a few days.   So the German Prince, in an evil
hour, returned to his own fatal policy of going by the much
more difficult way of Aragon.   He started for Madrid by
the wrong route exactly two months after the relief of
Barcelona, when, in the opinion of Richards, he ought to
have set out at once for the capital.

As soon as Peterborough found that his complaints on
the score of money and mules had stopped the King from
coming to Valencia at all, he bitterly repented of his letters,
or rather forgot that he had written them.   In Richards'
words, ' the wind carried away all the cobwebs which he had
been so long a spinning,' and ' seeing that the glory of
conducting a King of Spain to the throne would be given
to another,' he earnestly entreated Charles to come by
Valencia after all.   But the Austrian, having started for
Aragon, would no longer listen, being ' nettled to the quick
at this unhappy conduct of my Lord.'

The bitter hatred that had grown up between the
English Commander-in-Chief on one side and Charles and
his counsellor, Prince Lichtenstein, on the other, rendered
both parties unwilling to co-operate and anxious to
remain geographically apart.   Stanhope, Galway, Richards,
or any moderately tactful and disinterested English
officer, could, in Peterborough's place, have brought Charles
to Valencia and thence to Madrid.   But the mere fact
that the Earl chose the Valencian route made the German
Court wish to go by Aragon, though the military opinion
of the Council of War was almost unanimous on the
other side.   As to the want of mules and money, it may
have been a serious difficulty, and may have been in part
the fault of the authorities at home.*   But Peterborough
should have made the least of it to Charles instead of the
most.   The road from Valencia to Madrid being—as the

---

* Richards, who had direct knowledge of the matter, says that Peterborough
could never have squared his accounts with Government, for all his complaints.
' The public accounts were not rightly stated, for I knew that there had been very
considerable sums drawn upon the Treasury that never came into the hands of the
army's paymaster, for they were put into the hands (by my Lord's order) of private
officers and disbursed by them.'   *Stowe MSS.* 471, f. 36.

Earl himself said—as open as in time of peace, no great force would be needed to carry the King to his capital. There his arrival was eagerly expected by Galway and his army, and was awaited by the Spanish people with a curiosity that might have been coined betimes into approval and loyalty.

One cause of Peterborough's unwillingness to act at the critical moment in June was that Galway, as he averred, had not sent dispatches to him but had appealed only to Charles. If it were so, it was a fault in Galway, but not a reason why Peterborough should sulk like Achilles in his tent.   Where was the fiery energy of purpose to accomplish great things with small means which had enabled him to capture Monjuic ? There was in him a flame akin to genius, but it burnt inter-mittently ; it usually smouldered under ashes, and at the crisis of his life it was nothing but a dull glow of angry egoism.[92]

Galway was now at Guadalaxara awaiting the arrival of Charles by way of Saragossa and Molina, and of Peter-borough by way of Valencia and Requena.   As day after day passed by, his position became more and more uneasy. Behind him Madrid grew openly hostile.   Around him the peasants rose and cut off his supplies.   Opposite to him Berwick's army reached alarming proportions by constant reinforcements from France.   Berwick, combining caution with activity, declined to attack Galway, but sent round a detachment to re-occupy Madrid behind his back.   On August 4 they were enthusiastically received in the squalid streets of the old capital ; three hundred Carlist Spaniards shut themselves up in the Palace and held it for two days till they were starved into surrender and treated as traitors to the Crown, for Berwick had none of Marlborough's clemency.

Almost on the same day Charles joined Galway at Guadalaxara.   He only brought two or three thousand men. Peterborough arrived at much the same time with a handful of dragoons ; he had left the English infantry in Valencia. The Allies in Central Spain numbered about 15,000 in all. Berwick had, by that time, a much larger regular force, supported by the guerilla enthusiasts of every town and village in Castile.

The game was up, and Peterborough went back to Valencia, to take ship for Genoa, on some excuse of raising money for the Duke of Savoy. His real object was to get away from the unwelcome company of his rivals and critics, nor was a voice raised, in the language of any nation represented at the Council of War, to deprecate the withdrawal of the English Commander-in-Chief. ' I intend,' he wrote to Stanhope, with whom he had quarrelled less than with any other person of note in Spain, ' I intend to mortify you with the account of our happy days in Italy ;—of the nights we will say nothing.' Galway and Stanhope remained to do their unpleasant duty, to bear the burden of the defeat that was now the inevitable end of the Peninsular War. As the light-hearted Earl, all agog for his holiday, made his way down to the coast, his company had evidence of the cruel hatred of the peasant populations against English stragglers and sick.

By this time Marlborough had found out the mistake he had made in sending to Spain ' so ill a man ' as Peterborough. His long, brilliant letters ' full of extravagant flights and artificial turns,' and packed with abuse of his German and Spanish colleagues, had disgusted the patient Duke, who knew what was due to foolish allies. Although he agreed with Godolphin ' that the Germans with King Charles are good for nothing,' he added that ' the anger and aversion the King has for Lord Peterborough is the greatest cause of taking the resolution of going to Saragossa, which I am afraid will prove fatal.' Already, in September, the Duke wrote to Sarah, hitherto the Earl's friend and patron : ' I do not think much ceremony ought to be used in removing him from a place where he has hazarded the loss of the whole country.' Godolphin was of the same mind : ' He is both useless and grievous there, and is preparing to be as troublesome here, whenever he is called home.'

Trouble, indeed, was the element in which he moved and had his being. Henceforth, as the Government had no more use for him, he stood as a hero to be exploited by Opposition. The triumphs and the wrongs of the Whig nobleman became, for the rest of the reign, the special theme of the stern and unbending Tories. Swift, in his public pamphlets, praised him to the skies, and called shame on the betrayal of ' the only general who, by a course of conduct and fortune almost miraculous, had nearly put us into the possession of the Kingdom.' But it was observed that, when at length his new Tory friends came into power, they did not employ the man whose achievements they extolled above those of Marlborough.

Galway and the army soon followed Peterborough to Valencia. It was impossible to return by land to Portugal, for Galway's communications were cut. His new base must be the coast of Valencia and the English squadron in its ports. So, in September 1706, he arrived with his Portuguese and English on the east coast, having, as Berwick sarcastically said, ' made the tour of Spain.' The English fleet, meanwhile, had taken Carthagena and Alicante further down the coast, and the Balearic islands of Ivica and Majorca. In November Berwick recaptured Carthagena, and so ended the campaign of 1706.[93]

It is improbable that, at any time after this year, any combination of circumstances could have permanently established Charles on the throne of Spain. For Spanish opinion had now hardened against him. If, in that summer of decision, the Allies had kept their hold on Madrid and crowned him there, Carlist sympathies on the east coast might have solidified, and even the proud Castilians might have learnt to acquiesce in the accomplished fact. But after the vicissitudes of the actual campaign Charles lost men's confidence, and was regarded as one who could not seize occasion when it came ; while Philip, poor creature though he was, acquired the halo of a hero King, who had successfully weathered exile and defeat for the nation's cause in the struggle against foreign invaders. In the winter of 1706 the Bourbon party again became active even in Valencia, the new headquarters of the Allies. Murcia was strong for Philip, and so was every other province of Spain except divided Aragon and whole-hearted Catalonia. But the fact that the Catalans were for Charles was a reason why the Spaniards should be for Philip. The fact that the

Aragonese still hesitated was a reason why the Castilians should be doubly sure. Henceforth, in three quarters of Spain, the guerillas, the peasants and the priests devised destruction against the English soldiery, as against Napoleon's armies in days to come. The inhuman horrors of Spanish warfare, such as were depicted a hundred years later by the graphic art of Goya, were, in this earlier epoch, faced by our soldiers in a useless struggle continued long after the issue had been decided in 1706. Starved, when not sickened by strange food and drink ; unprepared and ill-equipped for a semi-African climate ; ill-paid, hated, ambushed, assassinated, massacred, the English carried on the horrid struggle, themselves miserable and inflicting misery, without any longer the remotest chance of success. The war in the Peninsula came to cost England almost as much per year as the war in Flanders.* That Marlborough for so many years insisted on the maintenance of the war in Spain, without seriously bending his mind to the local conditions of the problem, is the worst blot on his scutcheon as England's war-lord.

But if the events of 1706 should have taught the statesmen of the Alliance that they had lost Spain, they showed no less clearly that England had won the mastery of the Mediterranean Sea. Of the Toulon Grand Fleet that year it could be said :

> We never see them but we wish them to stay ;
> They never see us but they wish us away.

The Mediterranean policy that William had bequeathed to Marlborough was fast taking shape as a principal fact in the new Europe. In 1702 the inland sea had been a French lake ; by the end of 1706 it was more nearly English. The ports of Eastern Spain, of North Africa, and of Italy were

---

* ' The [English] expenditures in the Low Countries, for both British and foreign troops and subsidies, amounted to £1,366,076 in 1706. For that year, in Spain and Portugal, they were £1,093,071. The relatively heavy expense of the Peninsular campaign was due to the large subsidies paid to the Kings of Spain and Portugal, the distance from England, and the high cost of forage and subsistence.' Distant *side-shows* are always expensive on account of their distance. *Letters and accounts of James Brydges 1705–13*, by Léon Harvey (Huntington Library Bulletin No. 2, Nov. 1931). Brydges (later Lord Chandos) was Paymaster to the Forces Abroad, 1705–1713.

open to the Allies and closed to France. The Balearic islands, all save Minorca, had been seized. But another and a better harbour, in addition to Gibraltar Bay, was needed as a permanent base for the English fleet. Experts agreed that Minorca was the place indicated. Would Marlborough order its capture next year ? He would have done so, had he not cherished the still more ambitious design of taking Toulon and so bringing the war to a victorious close.

In December 1706 King Peter of Portugal followed John Methuen to the grave. These two men, in conjunction with Secretary Nottingham, had, contrary to many strong influences, secured Portugal's entry into the war on the English side. From that moment of decision in 1703 flowed an unbroken alliance of more than two centuries, for the Methuen Treaty was based on the real interests of both countries. If Portugal, unlike most European States, has retained her ancient colonial Empire, certainly not by reason of her own strength ; if England conquered and held the sea control of the Mediterranean from the Lisbon base, we must look for the causes of these things in the Methuen Treaty and the naval activities that it rendered possible.

CHAPTER IX

England's New Place in Europe

Parliamentary *versus* despotic Monarchy. The English Treasury as the key
to the working of the new constitution. Political crisis of autumn 1706.
The Whigs force Sunderland into the secretaryship against the Queen's
wish. Breach between Anne and Sarah begins. The Cabinet ceasing
to be royal and becoming parliamentary in its allegiance. The Session
of 1706–7. Height of Marlborough's popularity.

WITH the expulsion of the French from Italy and the Spanish
Netherlands, the war was won, as its objects had been defined by William in the Treaty of Grand Alliance. Moreover, the destruction of the naval strength, the military
prestige and the financial competence of France had secured
the underlying principle of that Treaty, the reduction of the
power of Louis to a measure compatible with the independence of the other States of Europe and the safety of its
Protestant churches.

England had been the chief agent in this great deliverance, and Great Britain would be the leading power in the
post-war world. England and Holland had borne up the
Alliance—its finances, its diplomacy, its military operations
by land and by sea. The contribution of the Dutch was
very large, alike in men and money, but it exhausted the
resources of a small state whose greatness depended not on
population, agriculture or industry, but on trade alone. The
further prolongation of the war for half a dozen unnecessary
years was to complete this process, and to render Holland
in the coming era no longer the rival, but the client of Great
Britain. The other chief beneficiary of the victorious war
was Austria, and she was even less likely to be a rival to
England, least of all at sea. The territories ruled from
Vienna did not constitute a modern state in spirit and
institutions. They were a collection of satrapies, the leavings

II.   M of the Turk and of the defunct Spanish Empire. In French hands Italy and Flanders would have been formidable to England, but in Austrian hands they relapsed to their proper place in the English scheme of things, as markets for the vent of the island cloth. The revival of trade with the great towns of Belgium, as they fell one after the other into Marlborough's hands, was much in the minds of the English public during the summer of 1706.* Our merchants regarded the Marlborough wars as a necessary expense ; and the money invested was returned a hundredfold to them and their descendants.

The causes of the British triumph over France were in part accidental. William and Marlborough had been the two great accidents. In an hour of desperate need William had painfully founded a system of policy at home and abroad, on which his successor in a happier hour had erected trophies that would endure.

But the victory of the English had not been due merely to the chance of good leadership. It was due also to their naval and economic strength, and to a system of free but efficient government, that the national genius had almost unconsciously evolved from the struggle of its sects and factions. The possibility that Parliamentary government might be superior to despotism, as a system of finance and national efficiency, had been demonstrated in the twenty years' contest which the events of 1706 decided. It was a result that contradicted the world's expectations and established theories. The surprising outcome of the war between the Parliamentary Monarchy of England and the Absolute Monarchy of France prevented the acceptance of despotism in Church and State as the rule of perfection in the New Europe. It raised other standards, which the Eighteenth Century admired in theory and the Nineteenth Century attempted to follow in practice.

If the *ancien régime* in France received its first shock on the fields of Blenheim and Ramillies, it was brought to the ground eighty years later by bad finance and national

* The *Postman* and other newspapers of the date show this. The export of English cloth abroad was said to have gone up 15 per cent. in 1706, largely owing to the opening of the Netherlands market. *Add. MSS.* 17677, BBB, f. 457.

bankruptcy. The Revolution settlement in England survived because it could pay its way. The symbol of the new
system of national government, the pulse of the machine of
the new England, was her Treasury administration. The
novel relations that the Treasury was now assuming to the
Crown, to Cabinet, to Parliament, to the taxpayer and to the
spending departments was the heart of the new Constitution.
In vain would lawyers, patriots, soldiers plead, rant and
fight, if their efforts were not fortified and controlled by
Godolphin and his Secretary of the Treasury, Mr. William
Lowndes, whose puppets, in a sense, they all were. The war
would not have been won, the famed Constitution would not
have worked, had English finance been as bad as French.
The complicated system of relationship between Treasury
experience, Cabinet policy and Parliamentary control was
the most original and the least advertised invention of the
English genius under the last Stuart reigns. If Montesquieu
had sought the secret of English liberty in those prosaic
arrangements, he would have been the less misled. He would
then have seen how the new Treasury system enabled the
Executive and Legislative to function harmoniously and even
to co-operate actively ; how the rival principles of popular
control and expert administration had been wisely reconciled
by this nation of squires and shop-keepers, at least in all that
appertained to the sacred cash-box.

In the Treasury of the first twenty years after the Revolution we see the emergence of the best modern traditions
of the permanent Civil Service ; we see the trained and
specialized servants of the Crown securing a new position
under a more popular system of government, and accepting
regular control of their work by the House of Commons as
the price of their undisturbed continuance in the royal
service.

There was a new danger in the new state of things. Since
Parliamentary government would mean Party government,
the security of tenure even of the lower grades of Crown
servants was imperilled at every political change in the
Cabinet ; ' the spoils for the victors ' threatened to become
the law of English politics. Such indeed had been the claim
and design of the High Tories in 1702. But the older

element in our happily ' mixed ' Constitution, the prerogative of the Crown, had saved the situation.   Anne's famous
' obstinacy ' and Godolphin's essentially ' civil service ' mind
had led them to defend the Treasury officials, irrespective of
their views on the Occasional Conformity Bill.*   The new
Lord Treasurer had left the personnel of the Treasury Commissioners almost unaltered, and that of the Clerks not
altered at all. The importance to the Crown of good finance,
especially in time of war, caused Anne and Godolphin to
save the nascent traditions of Treasury experience and skill
from being offered up as a sacrifice to party. Otherwise the
rage of faction, let loose on the civil servants at each successive triumph of Whig and of Tory, would have destroyed
the Treasury tradition in its early youth, and would have
swept away all those elements of permanence and impar-
tiality in the public service which it is the privilege of
constitutional monarchy to protect and represent.

On the other hand, the financial powers of the Crown
had been reduced to complete dependence on the legislative.
The control of Parliament over the levy of taxes and their
expenditure when raised, was no longer either disputed or
evaded. Since the Revolution it had become regularized by
custom, in which the Treasury officials played a well-defined
part. The taxes were not voted by the House of Commons
at the irresponsible motion of private members.   The
Treasury officials drew up a scheme for the year's taxation,
and Ministers of the Crown proposed it to the House.
These proposals were not, as in later times, collected in a
single all-inclusive Budget Bill ; but none the less each tax
proposed to the House fitted into the general plan drawn
up by the Treasury. The plan was often altered in detail by
the Commons, but always in a reasonable and practicable
manner. Several of the Treasury officials were members of
the House, and took an active part in the lobbying and
debates.† The result was that, even when the majority of

* *Blenheim*, pp. 206–208.
  † William Lowndes, the famous Secretary of the Treasury, was put in by the
government for Seaford, one of the Cinque Ports, throughout Anne's reign.
This is an example of the use, as distinct from the abuse, of pocket boroughs.
Lowndes is said to have originated the expression ' ways and means ' ; at any rate,
it was adopted as the motto of his family.

the Lower House was in no very gracious mood with the Ministers, as in the second and third winter of Anne's reign, there was singularly little trouble about finance, in itself the most difficult subject of all. Except for the attempt to ' tack ' the Occasional Conformity Bill, there had been no friction over the voting of great and complicated schemes of taxation.

So, too, with regard to the appropriation of supply, the Commons had control over the way in which the money was spent, no less complete than over the way in which it was raised. Nothing more than the sum specified by Parliament could be spent on any particular service, without grave irregularity for which Ministers would have to answer. Between the Revolution and the death of Anne, the system of appropriating supply to particular purposes of war and peace was perfected, and Committees of the House regularly audited the accounts. Here again the Ministers and the Treasury officials were brought into direct contact with the legislators, explaining, defending and modifying the policy they advocated as experts, to suit the criticisms of country squires. The squires on their side were trained by these conferences in the arts of statesmanship and finance, and learnt to appreciate the needs and methods of government. Under this peculiarly English system, the Crown, the Ministry and the Treasury were all attached by leading-strings to the Commons House—but whether the House was leading or being led it was often difficult to say. It was an altogether admirable arrangement, the basis of sound finance, honest administration and free government. The mutual confidence of legislative and executive, secured by this elaborate machinery of mutual control, rendered the Commons generous in their money votes for the war, in striking contrast to the niggardly supplies their fathers had dealt out to Charles II, in days when members had only a very irregular control over the purposes and policies for which the money they voted would be spent.

Under the new system, private members were ready to leave more and more to the initiative of Ministers and
June 11
1713 of the Treasury. At the end of Anne's reign, the House passed the famous Standing Order No. 66, which still prevents public money from being voted for

any purpose except on the motion of Ministers of the Crown.*

In the reign of Charles II the Treasury still served the King in person. This was more and more ceasing to be the case. William had depended on Parliament in matters of supply and appropriation, but he had studied and understood as a master the intricacies of State finance. Queen Anne was incapable of grasping its details. The Treasury officials had to explain their policies not to her, but to the Cabinet and to the House of Commons. The powers and the personnel of Cabinet, Treasury and Commons were so closely linked that they must move together if they moved at all. For this reason it was inevitable that the Lord Treasurer should be the real head of the Government, and should, as the reign went on, be increasingly recognized in common parlance as ' the Prime Minister.'

So, too, the debts of Government were ceasing to be personal debts of the sovereign and were becoming the nation's debts contracted through the action and on the credit of Parliament. By the end of the reign all loans were national loans made by the authority of Parliament on the advice of the Treasury.

But taxation is not merely a matter of voting and appropriating money ; it also involves the difficult business of raising it from the taxpayer. This difficulty had been too great for the French Government, which had fallen back on the miserable expedient of farming out the taxes to individuals, who paid a sum down to Government for the right to extort what they could from their fellow-subjects. Scotland before the Union similarly farmed out its excise to individuals who ' took a tack ' of it.[94] This ' farming of the taxes,' which has ruined so many societies and empires in the world's history, had threatened England in 1662, when the excise had been ' farmed out.' But in the course of Charles II's reign the Treasury had gradually reasserted its control, and in Anne's reign all the taxes raised were

---

* So, too, on March 29, 1707, Standing Order No. 67 was first passed : ' This House will not proceed upon any petition, motion, or bill, for granting any money, or for releasing or compounding any sum of money owing to the Crown, but in a Committee of the whole house.'

accounted for to the Treasury. The Commissioners of Customs and the Commissioners of Excise worked as separate bodies, but under Treasury control ; every important post in the two Commissions was a Treasury appointment. But although England was ahead of other countries in the machinery for the raising of taxes, the machine had by no means attained the terrible efficiency of the modern Inland Revenue Service. It has already been pointed out that in the first year of the Queen's reign the attempt to assess the taxpayers for income-tax had broken down before the passive resistance of the subjects of the land.*

During the autumn and early winter of 1706 the Queen lost the decisive battle in the war that she waged all through her reign for the independence of the Crown in the choice of its Ministers. The Whigs, like the High Tories, considered that when they controlled the majority of the House of Commons they ought to control the Cabinet also. A great issue was at stake as to the future form of government in England—were Ministries to be servants of the Crown in reality as well as in name, or were they to be in effect the servants of Parliament and therefore of Party ? Within the limits of the constitution as defined in 1689 there was room for either interpretation, and the matter had not yet been decided. For this reason the forcing of Sunderland into the Secretaryship of State against the Queen's wishes in December 1706 was a memorable step in constitutional practice ; it was also the first act in the high political comedy of the quarrel between the ' faithful Mrs. Freeman ' and ' her poor unfortunate Morley.'

The Lords of the Whig Junto † had made up their minds to have one of their number in the Cabinet as Secretary of State. They were politically so like-minded and personally so loyal to one another that it scarcely mattered which of them was chosen. The Queen's prejudice would not allow her to take Somers, nor her decency to take Wharton.

---

* See *Blenheim*, p. 293. I am much indebted to Miss D. M. Gill's article on the Treasury from the years 1660–1714, in the *English Historical Review* for October 1931, which she kindly allowed me to peruse while it was still in MS. It is most important.

† For the five Lords of the Whig Junto, see *Blenheim*, pp. 194–200. They were Somers, Wharton, Halifax, Sunderland and Orford.

Sunderland was the Marlboroughs' son-in-law, and as such it was hoped he would be more acceptable. So the Junto pitched upon him ; as they told their confidante Sarah, ' it was driving the nail that would go.' But in fact the Queen disliked Sunderland, who, though honest and able, was un-conciliatory and hot-tempered, very little accustomed to conceal his opinions, or to wrap them up in fine words when they had the misfortune to differ from those of Royalty. Moreover, she realized that, if any one of the Junto were Secretary of State, the Cabinet would soon be a Whig Cabinet rather than a Cabinet of servants truly her own.

Marlborough and Godolphin would much rather have left things as they were. They had no wish to share supreme power with the Whigs or with anyone else. But throughout the autumn of 1706 the Treasurer grew every week more aware that the Whigs must be paid the price of their Parliamentary support, or the Government would be put in a minority when the Houses reassembled that winter. Marlborough, being absent abroad until the middle of November, was longer in coming to the same conclusion. In spite of his close family relationship to Sunderland, he regretted the proposed change more than Godolphin, and very much more than the fiery Whig, Sarah. But before he returned to England he had been converted to its necessity by a long series of letters from his friend and from his wife.*

Harley alone held out against the change, and against the system of government by party to which it opened the way. Already in August the Whigs were warning one another that Harley was their enemy. In September and October he was writing to Godolphin against the admission of the Whig leaders, urging that the Government could still rely on the support of the ' moderates ' of both parties, that Tory feeling ought not to be further alienated, that the unofficial Whigs would still support the

1706

* Sarah's friendship and political alliance with Godolphin was very close and always remained so. She came in later years to speak ill, not only of all the Tory chiefs, but of all the Whig chiefs except Cowper. But for Godolphin she retained a real affection. In her Bible, now at Althorp, she has written in the fly-leaf : ' The 15th of September 1712 at two in the morning the Earl of Godolphin dyed at the Duke of Marlborough's hous in St. Albans, who was the best man that ever lived.'

Ministry, whatever the Junto bade them do. To judge by what we know of Whig Parliamentary discipline in this reign, he was wrong on the last all-important point. Godolphin at least thought so, and surrendered when the Junto sent in its ultimatum. It came, towards the end of September, in the form of a letter of Sunderland to his mother-in-law Sarah :

Lord Somers, Lord Halifax and I have talked fully over all this matter, and we are come to our last resolution in it, that this and what other things have been promised must be done, or we and the lord treasurer must have nothing more to do together about business ; and that we must let our friends know just how the matter stands between us and the lord treasurer, whatever is the consequence of it.

This was plain speaking. Yet even then another two months and more passed before Godolphin and Sarah, backed as they soon were by the Duke himself, could wear down the stubborn resistance of the Queen.

Her view was one with which it is impossible not to have some sympathy, both personal and political.

You press [she wrote to Godolphin] the bringing Lord Sunderland into business, that there may be one of that party in a place of trust, to help carry on the business this winter. And you think if this not complied with, they will not be hearty in pursuing my service in Parliament. But is it not very hard that men of sense and honour will not promote the good of their country, because everything in the world is not done that they desire !

Alas for human nature ! But the inexorable facts, the dynamics of party politics, were carrying into the limbo of fine impossible ideals her vision and Harley's of the non-party Cabinet chosen for its merits by a Patriot Queen. Marlborough tried to make the situation clear to her intelligence :

Madam [he wrote], the truth is that the heads of one party [the Tories] have declared against you and your government. . . . Now should your Majesty disoblige the others, how is it possible to obtain five millions for carrying on the war with vigour, without which all is undone ?

And how else was the Union with Scotland to be carried ?

In vain, therefore, she stated her own excellent constitutional doctrine :

> All I desire is my liberty in encouraging and employing all those that concur faithfully in my service, whether they are called Whigs or Tories, not to be tied to one nor the other.

In vain she declared her dislike of ' those violent persons ' the High Tories, ' that have behaved themselves so ill towards me.' Nothing would satisfy the Whigs, nothing therefore could save the Ministry when Parliament met, except the admission of Sunderland to the Secretaryship. The wearying contest between the Queen and her best friends went on until December, and left them, when at last she yielded, less good friends than before. The long intimacy between Anne and the Churchills received now its first serious shock. Sarah, at the height of the dispute, had written to the Queen :

> I must take the liberty to say it looks like infatuation that one who has sense in all other things should be so blinded by the word Tory . . . ; and that you will believe any villain or any known Jacobite, if to serve their own ends they do but call themselves Tories and other men Whigs.

And again :

> I beg of God Almighty, as sincerely as I shall do for His pardon at my last hour, that Mr. and Mrs. Morley may see their errors as to this *notion* before it is too late.

Sarah's handwriting, when she was angry, was none too clear, and Anne read the word *notion* as *nation*, a difference which made the sentiment appear more general in its censure and therefore much more impertinent as coming from a subject to a monarch. A breach ensued which was only repaired by the personal intervention of Godolphin and by explanations of the word misread. But a friendship that is endangered by the misreading of a vowel may be held to have passed its prime.

Finally Marlborough came home from his military triumphs and diplomatic failures abroad, and on December 3, the very day of the meeting of Parliament, the Queen gave way. Sunderland became Secretary of State for the

Southern Department in place of Sir Charles Hedges. Harley still retained the Northern Secretaryship, but with diminished authority in the Cabinet ; he had ceased, in fact, to be the leading Secretary of State. A brother of Lord Halifax became Solicitor-General, and other minor offices and promotions in the Peerage were given to Whig partisans. In these rearrangements the poet Matthew Prior lost his place as Commissioner of Trade ; Marlborough was still his friend, but Sarah and Godolphin had turned against him, and even ' Mæcenas ' Halifax refused to listen to his appeal. His ill-treatment and consequent poverty drove this essentially moderate politician over to the Tories, to whom he was ere long to render famous services in the diplomatic field.

The party character of the Queen's Ministry was not complete until November 1708, but by Christmas 1706 the Whig element was already beginning to prevail.[95]

The Queen's tardy surrender came just in time to have its full effect at the opening of Parliament. The Whigs were in high good humour and performed their part of the bargain. Indeed there were other reasons for rejoicing beside the triumphs of party. Belgium and Italy had been won since last the Houses met, and nothing was too much for the Queen's servants to ask and for her faithful Commons to grant. The money votes for next year, Land Tax, Malt Tax and all, were rushed through before Christmas, to demonstrate to Europe England's will to war.* When the High Tories tried to call Ministers to account for undertaking certain military expenditures on behalf of the Duke of Savoy, which had not been previously sanctioned by Parliament, the irregularity, which in other circumstances might have figured as an item in an impeachment, was indemnified by the majority of the House as a wise exercise of discretion sanctioned by the necessities of war.

Dec. 3 1706

* The Speaker, in presenting the money bills to the Queen, said : ' As the glorious victory obtained by the Duke of Marlborough at Ramillies was fought before the enemy was apprised that the confederates had taken the field, so your faithful Commons have granted subsidies before the enemy were apprised that Parliament had assembled.'

No small part of the business of Parliament and of the whole nation that Christmas was to honour the Duke. The thanks of both Houses were conveyed to him, and faction itself dared not this time compare his achievements with those of any other British commander by land or sea. He stood without rival, the hero of the nation he had saved and exalted. The desire of the Queen to settle £5,000 a year from the Post Office on his posterity after him for ever, which four years back had been vetoed by the opposition of the High Tories, was now carried with acclamation.* The Dukedom, Woodstock Manor and Blenheim House therein were made heritable by his daughters and their heirs male in succession, since the death of poor Lord Blandford had cut off the hope that a son of his own would follow him.

Pageants of victory delighted London that winter. The flags taken at Ramillies could not be hung in Westminster Hall, for it was already filled with the flags of Blenheim. They were therefore borne with military pomp from Whitehall, passing under the Queen's window at St. James's Palace, and on through the shouting streets to Guildhall to hang there. On the way, the Duke, in one of the Queen's coaches, was met at Temple Bar by the City Fathers with the honours usually accorded to Royalty. Anne had already in June been once to St. Paul's to give thanks for Ramillies ; on the last day of December 1706 she went again, to give thanks for all the triumphs of that wonderful year. The two Houses of Parliament came in her train, and the sword of state was borne before her by the Duke of Marlborough. It was the crowning moment of their two lives. He seemed still in the prime of manly beauty, despite his fifty-six years. But the poor woman at his side could with difficulty support the fatigue and pain it cost her to appear thus before her people as the successor in fame and fortune of Elizabeth in all her glory.

The Queen's Speech, the replies of the two Houses and the debates of the session that followed showed no sign of any desire for peace. The Lords voted for the restoration ' of the whole monarchy of Spain to King Charles the Third.' The Lower House assured Her Majesty that

* *Blenheim*, p. 274.

the Commons of England are determined that no specious pretences of peace shall divert them from their steady resolutions of enabling your majesty to improve in all places the advantages of this successful campaign.

In all this there was a high national spirit and readiness to spend and be spent in the public cause ; whether there was an equal amount of wisdom and humanity in the attitude to the terms of peace, is perhaps more doubtful. In any case the true wisdom of Parliament this session, and the best vindication to posterity of the Godolphin-Whig alliance, appeared in the passing of the Treaty of Union with Scotland.[96]

CHAPTER X

The State of Scotland in the Reign of Queen Anne

The place of the Union Treaty in British history. Mutual antagonism of Scots and English. Travelling in Scotland. The Edinburgh Parliament. Nobles. Lairds and their houses. Presbyterian and Episcopalian. Education. Universities. The peasants. Agriculture. Poor Law. Bondsmen.

'Whatever we get by treaty will be firm and durable ; it will be conveyed to posterity. That which you have by force, I look upon it as nothing.' So said Oliver Cromwell, and so saying prophesied the fate that befell most of his own constructive work in the British islands. His far-sighted policy of uniting England and Scotland on terms advantageous to the inhabitants of both countries perished at the Restoration, because it had rested upon ' force ' alone. Forty years had passed since then, and now the time had come when a similar Union was to be sought ' by treaty,' so that it should be ' durable ' and ' conveyed to posterity.'

It would be an error to suppose that the Union was passed in the reign of Anne because English and Scots were in a friendly mood. The opposite was the case. The badness of the terms on which the two nations were living was the motive of the Union. Statesmen on both sides of the Border saw the necessity of a union of the two Parliaments in one, as the only alternative to war, and as the only political machine strong enough to stand the shocks of the perpetually recurring antagonism of North and South Britain.

Fortunately, the English were in no position at that moment to coerce the Scots into a Union, as they had done in the days of Cromwell. In Anne's reign Union could

only be obtained by consent, and consent had to be purchased by sacrifices made on both sides.   The Scots were
called on to sacrifice their independent Parliament ;   the
English to admit them to the jealously guarded trade with
the Colonies.

The attitude of the two British peoples towards one
another was very different then from anything that it has
been for the last century and a half.   Ever since the days
of Burns and Walter Scott the English have delighted in
Scottish tradition and romance, highland and lowland alike,
sometimes to the point of sentimentality.   They go to
Scotland in crowds to admire her scenery, and in their
own country and throughout their world-wide Empire they
have acknowledged, not without envy, the sterling qualities
of her sons.

But when Anne ascended the throne ignorance was
still the fruitful parent of hostility and contempt.   Contact
between the two peoples was slight, and for the most part
unfortunate.   Wandering Scots still sought their fortunes
less often in England than on the Continent of Europe,—
Jacobite exiles in Italy and France, Presbyterian traders
and soldiers in Scandinavia, Germany and Holland.   Edinburgh lawyers went to Leyden University for the finish of
their legal education at the fountain-heads of Roman law.[97]
Scottish traders were excluded from the English colonies,
and they had none of their own.   The English who crossed
the Cheviots on business were very few, except the Borderers
who nursed a traditional hostility to everything Scottish ;
the jealous Northumbrians used to warn travellers from
the South that Scotland was ' the most barbarous country
in the world.' [98]   Perhaps not more than a dozen people in
the year visited Scotland for pleasure.   And of these few
the weaker sort were speedily driven back across the Border
by the badness of accommodation in the slovenly inns,
where good French wine and fresh salmon could not alone
compensate for the want of other palatable victuals, and
for the utter filth of the lodging.*   And while the English

* It is observable that Miss Fiennes (William III or Anne) and Sir John Perceval
(1701), both of whom turned back in disgust, had tried to enter Scotland on the

traveller complained of his own treatment, he was no less bitter on the stabling of his horse in a place ' hardly fit for a hog-house,' where the poor beast was offered straw to eat in place of hay.[99]   If indeed these tourists had come provided with introductions and could have enjoyed Scottish hospitality in gentlemen's houses, as the native gentry did upon their journeys, they would have fared less ill.

Nor was there in Scotland anything specially to attract the seeker after the beautiful as it was understood in those days.   No Southerner then admired wild moorland scenery; the Scots doubtless loved, in their innermost hearts, the

land of brown heath and shaggy wood,

but they had not yet, through the medium of literature, expressed that still unconscious passion even to themselves, still less to their unfriendly neighbours.   The Englishman who rode from Berwick to Edinburgh despised the Lowland scenery as divided between melancholy wastes and ill-managed fields of oats.   It was unenclosed ; almost treeless ; devoid, except in the immediate neighbourhood of Edinburgh, of the fine mansions and parks, well-built farms and stately parish churches which the traveller had left behind him in his own country.   As to the Highland mountains, the very few Englishmen who ever penetrated into their recesses pronounced them ' horrid,' ' frightful,' and ' most of all disagreeable when the heath is in bloom.' [100]

The coarse brutality of many English writers on Scotland,* and the want of understanding and sympathy in nearly all, with the signal exception of Defoe, embittered

---

west from Cumberland. If they had entered the other side by Berwick and the richer Lothians, they might have succeeded in riding as far as Edinburgh, as did Taylor in 1705, though even he complains of the ' sad entertainment ' and the ' nastiness and ill manners of the inhabitants.' *Fiennes*, pp. 170–172 ; *H.M.C. Egmont*, II (1909), p. 206 ; *Taylor, Jos.*, pp. 94–99. See also *Macky's Scotland*, p. 3.

* Lest I be thought to exaggerate, I will give two typical examples. E. B., in his *Description of Scotland* (1705), says ' The most sacred tyes, as oaths and the like, are snapt asunder by them [the Scots].   There is nothing among them to their Kings that is not vendible. . . . proverbially clownish people . . . their women ugly, stupid, immodest, etc.' And *Observator's Trip to Scotland* (1708) says : ' The people are proud, arrogant, vainglorious, boasters, bloody, barbarous and inhuman butchers. Couzenance and theft is in perfection among them.' Their Church services are ' blasphemy as I blush to mention.'

MAP V

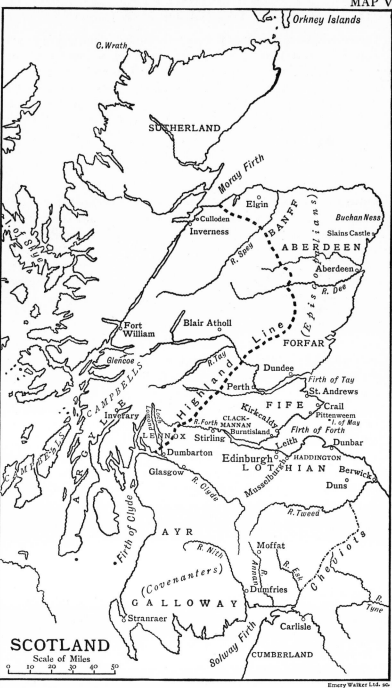

Orkney Islands

C. Wrath

SUTHERLAND

Moray Firth

Elgin

Culloden
Inverness

BANFF

Buchan Ness

Slains Castle

ABERDEEN

Aberdeen

R. Spey

R. Dee

(Episcopalians)

Fort
William

Blair Atholl

Highland Line

FORFAR

Glencoe

R. Tay

Dundee

Perth

Firth of Tay

St. Andrews

Inverary

CAMPBELLS

ARGYLE

Loch Lomond

FIFE

Crail

Kirkcaldy

Pittenweem

I. of May

CLACK-
MANNAN

Burntisland

Firth of Forth

LENNOX

R. Forth

Stirling

Leith

Dunbar

Dumbarton

Edinburgh

Musselburgh

HADDINGTON

LOTHIAN

Berwick

CAMPBELLS

Glasgow

R. Clyde

Duns

R. Tweed

Firth of Clyde

AYR

R. Nith

Moffat

Cheviots

(Covenanters)

GALLOWAY

R. Annan

R. Esk

Dumfries

R.
Tyne

Stranraer

Carlisle

SCOTLAND

Solway Firth

CUMBERLAND

Scale of Miles

0   10   20   30   40   50

Emery Walker Ltd. sc.

II.

N

the relations of the two peoples throughout the crisis that
ended in the Union.   The Scots gave back as good as they
got :   *A Pill for Pork-eaters, or a Scots lancet for an English
swelling*, published at Edinburgh in 1705, advises that

> For England, insolent and proud like hell,
> Whose saucie boldness nought but blows can quell,
> . . . let another Bannockburn redress
> Too long endured affront and grievances.

Among the English champions in this duel of international
mud-slinging the High Tories were the foremost, for they
wished to keep the two countries and Parliaments separate ;
they regarded Scotland with peculiar aversion, as the land
where Jack Presbyter rudely triumphed over ' rabbled
curates ' and persecuted the Episcopalian remnant.   But
even Whigs and Moderate Tories looked askance on Scotland as the home and harbour of Jacobitism and of anti-
English policies in the island.

The Scot was either a Jacobite or a Presbyterian, and in
either capacity he alienated four-fifths of English sympathy.
And the English of all religions or none were shocked or
amused at the rigour of the social discipline of the Kirk.
Cromwell's troopers, in their day of power in Scotland, used
to seat themselves in derision on the ' stool of repentance '
in the parish churches ;   and in Anne's time that instrument
of moral reformation was as alien to the free spirit of the
English Dissenting sects as it was to the mild authority of
the village parson.   Calamy, the leader of the English Nonconformists, in his tour of fraternization among the Scottish
Presbyterians in 1709, gave offence by calling some proceedings of the Kirk Assembly 'the Inquisition revived.'[101]
And apart from all questions of politics and religion, the
national and personal pride of the Scot appeared to the
unimaginative Englishman ridiculous when associated with
poverty.   That a ' gentleman ' should be proud though
out-at-elbows seemed absurd to the English merchant in
his broadcloth.   And the Scot, when at every turn he en-
countered this vulgar scorn, only became more proud and
more dour.[102]

The Scots, indeed, regarded the English with sour

aversion, as purse-proud and overbearing neighbours. Popular poetry, tradition, history—strong influences on an imaginative and emotional race—all pointed to England as the ancient enemy. Four centuries of intermittent warfare with the Southerner formed the subject of Scottish legend and ballad. Hardly a place in the Ancient Kingdom but its inhabitants told how the English had burnt it. And Flodden, still unavenged, was the lyric theme vibrating in every Scottish heart. Even the Union of the Crowns had been used to impose England's will on Kirk and State. Charles and Laud had invaded the religion of the Scots till they had asserted their independence in arms ; Cromwell had triumphed over them at Dunbar and held Episcopalian and Covenanter in a common vassalage to English Sectarian troopers ; Charles and James II had misgoverned the land, and filled it with the blood of those fanatics whom persecution fairly made martyrs, and whom two Scots out of three were brought up to regard as Saints. William had massacred Highlanders at Glencoe, and had been compelled by his English subjects to oppose the interest of all Scotland in the affair of Darien.

Jacobite and Presbyterian were agreed on but one thing, that this ignominious subordination of their common country to her great neighbour must cease. And the Edinburgh Parliament, acting ever since the Revolution with a vigour and independence which it had never shown before in all its long and not very splendid history, had become the mouthpiece of this national resolve.

But there were two alternative ways of effecting deliverance. Either the Union of the Crowns could be abolished and Scotland become once more a country under a King of her own. This was the desire of most of the Scottish Jacobites and of many Presbyterians. But as everyone knew, this would mean, at best, the renewal of the age of periodic wars with England, even if Marlborough's army did not at once succeed in doing what Cromwell's army had so recently done, and conquer Scotland outright. The other method was, by peaceable means, to induce the English to admit the Scots to all the commercial and other privileges of the Empire. The advantage of that, as everyone knew, was that Scotland would become far richer than she could ever be as a separate State ; the disadvantage was that such privileges could be purchased only by sacrificing the separate existence of the Edinburgh Parliament.

That assembly held its sessions, so important in the story we have now to relate, in the great hall off the High Street, known as the Parliament House, which after the Union was assigned to the lawyers of the capital, and has remained the most famous room in Scotland.   There, under its high, open-timbered roof, Nobles, Barons and Burgesses sat together ; they were reckoned as three separate Estates, but they debated and voted in a single Chamber.

The Barons, or County members, unlike the corresponding class in the English House of Commons, were not elected on a popular franchise of forty-shilling freeholders, but were each chosen by a few score gentlemen who happened to be, in the eye of the old Scottish law, tenants-in-chief of the Crown.   The Burghs, too, were all of them as ' rotten ' as the rottener part of the English Boroughs. The representative element was therefore weaker in the Scottish than in the English Parliament ; such representation of the people as there actually was, could only be called ' virtual.'   Partly for this reason, partly because the social structure of Scotland was still essentially feudal and aristocratic, the Nobles were the most powerful element in the Chamber.   It was chiefly they who led its debates, headed its factions and formulated its acts and policies.[103]

The predominance of the aristocracy was not confined to Parliament.   In each district of the countryside the common people were attached by custom, pride, awe and hope of protection to some great House that represented their region in the eyes of Scotland.   The lairds, as the Lowland gentry were called, were trained to use the arms with which they commonly rode abroad ; the local nobleman entertained them royally at banquets in his mansion, espoused their quarrels, pushed their interests, and confidently expected them in return to follow his standard, if he raised it for the Government that had given him office, or against the Government that had neglected his claims.[104]

If Whig and Jacobite came to blows, as they nearly did

on several occasions under Anne, and as they actually did in
1715, it would be to the banners of Argyle, Atholl, Mar or
some other grandee that each region would rally, in the
Lowlands only to a less degree than in the Highlands. If all
the nobility had been united against Government, the little
Scottish army would not long have availed to hold them
down. But the most important element in the Government and Privy Council at Edinburgh consisted of Nobles,
chosen, indeed, by the Queen in London on Godolphin's
advice, but chosen with a very careful consideration of their
weight and influence in the political and military dynamics
of Scotland. Some were convinced Jacobites, like the
Roman Catholic Duke of Gordon, or semi-Jacobites like
Hamilton and Atholl, and for that reason it was not easy for
Anne to employ them as her Ministers. More, like
Queensberry, Argyle, Tweeddale, Stair and Marchmont,
stood ' on a Revolution foot,' as the phrase was, and were
staunch for the Kirk and the Hanoverian succession.
Others, like Mar, cared chiefly for what they could get out
of politics and trimmed their sails accordingly.

Nearly all, indeed, who engaged in politics, were greedy
of office, for nearly all were embarrassed by the need of
keeping up feudal state on the meagre rentals and payments
in kind of a countryside desperately poor ; and they had all
been taught to regard office as the natural remedy of a great
nobleman's finances.* But many, both in the Jacobite and
in the Whig camp, were patriots as well as self-seekers, and
some were, besides, shrewd and politic statesmen, who knew
how to pursue their country's true interest, and whose
aristocratic position and upbringing set them above the
necessity of courting popularity with the mob. Such were
the men who passed the Union.

---

* In 1703 the Earl of Seafield wrote a memorial for Government, advising what
we should now call a ' cut in salaries ' of Ministers and officials, which will
'exceedingly oblige the generality of the people, both because the less subsidy will
be required, and likewise because nothing is more disobliging to the generality
of an unmonied nation than to see new men become rich by sucking in the public
money, as they have done since the Revolution ; most of those employed since
having doubled or tripled their estates.' *H.M.C. Laing,* II (1925), p. 43. For
a not very edifying scene in the Scottish Privy Council of this period as imagined
by Scott, see *Bride of Lammermoor,* end of chap. v.

After the Nobles came the lairds or country gentlemen. Their tall, stone mansions, each with its corbel-stepped gable roof, stood up gaunt and fortresslike in the treeless and hedgeless landscape. Architecture did not flourish as in England. Many of these country houses had grown up by clumsy additions to the war-towers of former days. There was seldom any window on the exposed north side, even when it commanded the best or the only view of the landscape. But of recent years proprietors, especially in the rich Lothian district, had begun to plant groves of trees round their houses, to shelter them from the wind and to give the meagre orchards a chance. But the day of lawns, avenues and walled gardens was yet to come. The farm-buildings, with their homely smells and litter, abutted on the mansion ; the cornfields came up to its walls on one side, and on another an ill-kept garden of physic-herbs and native flowers.[105]

The interior was equally devoid of luxuries common in the south of the island. The furniture was of the simplest, the floors had no carpets, the walls were usually devoid of paper, panelling, arras or pictures. The bed-chambers had no fire-places, except in the envied ' fire-room.' The drawing-room held a closed bed ready for guests, since it was not always safe for a convivial laird to ride home o' nights, any more than for Tam o' Shanter from his humbler rouse. Hospitality took the form of plentiful plain meats served in one course, washed down by Scottish ale and French brandy and claret—and, in the Highlands, by whisky. Tea was only known to the Scottish subjects of Queen Anne as an expensive medicine. Thrift was a dire necessity, but hospitality was a national instinct. Neighbours would arrive on horseback on surprise visits of half the day in length ; they were heartily welcome, for the means of passing the time in a country house were fewer even than in contemporary England.[106]

Near Edinburgh and other towns golf was a time-honoured institution. And all over Scotland hares, grouse, blackgame or partridges were pursued with dogs, hawks, and snares, and less often with the long gun. But the red deer, once common, were already withdrawing into the

Highland glens.[107] The extraordinary abundance of salmon and trout afforded not only good sport, but a cheap food for the people. In some parts the gentry despised salmon as a dish that cloyed, and farm-hands struck if they were fed upon it every day.[108]

The gentry of the Lowlands were divided not unevenly into Presbyterian and Episcopalian, a division scarcely distinguishable from the political division of Whig and Jacobite. Tories there were none, in the English sense of the word, for the Tory was an Episcopalian who had accepted the Revolution Settlement because it left his Church established and privileged, whereas in Scotland the Revolution left the Episcopal Church disestablished, and not even tolerated according to law ; Scottish Episcopalians, therefore, were necessarily Jacobites, looking to a counter-revolution for their relief. This was the essential difference between English and Scottish politics.

Family and religious discipline tended to be more strict in Presbyterian than in Episcopalian families. There was usually more pleasure and freedom in a Jacobite household. But deep Presbyterian piety and a strict sense of public duty did not prevent Forbes of Culloden from indulgence in hard drinking, convivial hospitality, profound learning and liberal culture. And when in 1702 a Presbyterian minister of Elgin searched houses to smell out and seize that ' superstitious bird,' the Christmas goose, a laird who shared his religion but not his bigotry wrote to an Episcopalian friend :

Dear Archie, I am not so great a presbyterian but I can eat a leg of a goose and play at Umber on Yule-day. If you will come out here on Thursday's night, the doctor and you and I shall be as merry as we can, and if you bring Mess John [in this case the Episcopal clergyman] to be fool in the family, and make us laugh, you shall have a revenge off your lost fifteen shillings.[109]

' Mess John ' seems to have been a more sociable being than his goose-hunting rival.

It must be remembered that, when Anne came to the throne, the services of psalmody, preaching and extempore

prayer were very much the same in the Episcopal Meeting
Houses as in the Presbyterian Parish Churches. The Prayer-
book only began to find its way into some of the Meeting
Houses in the last half of her reign. The doctrines professed
by the rival denominations differed little except on Church
government, and not much even on that, seeing that the Episcopalians too had their Presbyteries and Kirk Sessions with
their inquisition and discipline over morals. The division
therefore was deep only on its political side ; it did not
touch the basis of a common Scottish mentality and civilization. Free thought had not yet spread from the land of
Shaftesbury and Bolingbroke to the land of Hume. Nearly
all families, especially those of the gentry, regularly attended
either the Parish Church or the Episcopal Meeting House,
where they received much the same spiritual medicine, only
diluted with different quantities of water. Poverty and
religious instruction and controversy combined to form a
national Scottish character, overriding the acute political
divisions, and uniting all Scots in a mental and moral
antagonism to the wealthier, more libertine civilization on
the south of the Cheviots. The popularity of Addison's and
Steele's *Spectators* among Scottish ladies and gentlemen at
the end of Anne's reign was one of the first instances of
a real intellectual invasion of North by South Britain.
As a consequence of the Union such influences began to
multiply.[110]

The unity of the nation and the good understanding of
its component classes were all the greater because Scottish
lairds in those days sent their own bairns to the village
school. The odd idea of sending a Scottish gentleman's
son to an English public school was rendered unthinkable
alike by thrift and by patriotism. Education in the village
school strengthened the young laird's love of his native
land and landscape, and inclined him when he came to man's
estate to sympathy with his tenants who had once been his
schoolfellows. The broad Scots tongue, of which the
highest were not ashamed, the traditions and ballads of each
countryside, were the common heritage of all. That was
why, two generations later, in the days of Burns and Scott,

the poetry and traditions of Scotland went forth to conquer the imagination of men bred in less fortunate countries, where rich and poor had no culture in common. Scotland was at once more feudal and more democratic than England. An amazing freedom of speech, between classes that were yet perfectly distinct in a strict social hierarchy, characterized the relation of men who had sat on the same bench at school, and whose fathers had ridden shoulder to shoulder to fray and foray.

But in the age of Anne no literary or intellectual palms were won by Scotland in the world's arena. Her poverty was still too bitter and her religion still too narrow. But the seeds of greatness were there ; that very poverty and that very religion were forming the national mind and character. Already Swift, who hated the Scots as Presbyterians, confessed that their youth were better educated than the English ; while Defoe wrote, though with some exaggeration :

You find very few gentry either ignorant or unlearned. Nay, you cannot ordinarily find a servant in Scotland but he can read or write.

When Forbes of Culloden, in 1705, went to finish his legal education at Leyden University, he was led to contrast the grave and studious habits of his own countrymen abroad, with the 'riot and debauchery' of the young English spendthrifts making the grand tour, 'who repaid the forbearance and politeness of the inhabitants with contempt and ignorance.' [111]

Scottish school education would, however, by modern standards, be judged miserably inadequate. The excellent laws of 1633 and 1696 had ordained that a well-appointed school should be set up in every parish and maintained by local rates. But the reality was very different. In Anne's reign many parishes had no school at all, and where a school was to be found it was too often a dark, draughty, dirty hovel, and the master or mistress usually lived on starvation wages. In Fife, at the end of the Queen's reign, only two men out of three could sign their names, and one woman out of twelve, while in Galloway few of the people could read.

On the other hand in many, if not most, of these schools Latin was taught after a fashion ; * and it was often very well taught in the Burgh schools maintained by the towns. The village and the Burgh schools were not merely primary schools ; some of the older and better scholars were being prepared for the University by masters who were very often themselves College men. Many, indeed, of the half-starved dominies, though they could not afford to buy books, had the root of the matter in them ; and though they taught only a part of the population, that part was the pick of the Scottish democracy, lads taught to make sacrifices to obtain education, who used the slender equipment of learning available to them as no other nation in Europe could do, and so in the end raised themselves and their country to higher ranges of civilized life.[112]

The Universities of Scotland were in a dull condition at sunrise of that century which was to set in the golden glow of Principal Robertson, Adam Smith and the Edinburgh philosophers. An age of violent civic commotion is seldom favourable to academic institutions controlled by the State. The Episcopal regime of Charles and James II had excluded half the Scottish men of learning from academic life, and the Revolution had extruded most of the other half, replacing them by men who had learnt more fanaticism than scholarship in moorside conventicles liable to be attended by dragoons. It is true that in Aberdeen the politic clemency of William allowed most of the Jacobite dons to continue in a University which served a Jacobite countryside. But in Glasgow, St. Andrews and Edinburgh the change had been fairly complete, and the new teachers were raw men.

Fortunately a great leader took Scotland's academic life in hand. William Carstares, the wisest and noblest of the Presbyterian divines, had been King William's private adviser on Scottish affairs. In the new Queen's reign, when he could no longer hope for such a place behind the throne, he returned to Scotland, to lead the counsels of her

---

* ' There are in the Kingdom near 1,000 parishes and in most of them Latin is pretended to be taught, though not one in fifty of the schoolmasters is capable to teach it. And no wonder for not one in fifty was tolerably taught it, and not one in a hundred has books to enable him to acquire it by his after industry.' *Proposals for the reformation of schools and universities.* 1704.

Church into the paths of moderation, and to order and inspire her academic life. As Principal of Edinburgh University * he had many difficulties to face : the pedantry and superficiality of the innumerable courses in abstruse subjects ; the monopolistic spirit of the College teachers who strove to enforce the prohibition of Greek teaching at schools lest they should compete with the function of the Universities ; the general want of liberality and learning. But Carstares himself was not only learned but liberal, in spite of all that he had suffered in the dreadful past in the torture chamber of the Edinburgh Privy Council. He won the hearts of the difficult men he now had to lead, and gave a new and larger vision not only to the Established Church and its Assembly, but to the Universities that supplied that Church with ministers.

The students were of all classes, sons of nobles, lairds, ministers, farmers and mechanics. The most part were seeking to be beneficed clergymen, and there were far too many candidates. The number of small bursaries and the Scottish peasant's zeal for knowledge overcrowded the sacred profession in days when there were few other openings for an educated man. The lot of the ' stickit minister,' the laird's tutor and the underpaid schoolmaster was hard. But those who were able to obtain charge of a parish were not so ill off by the modest standards of that day. Calamy, the English Nonconformist leader, wrote after his visit to the Presbyterians of North Britain in 1709 :

As for the settled ministers of the Church of Scotland, though they are not so plentifully or profusely provided for as many of the Established Church in England, yet are there none but what have a competency, whereupon to live easily and conveniently and above contempt.

The Scottish lad, in his hard struggle to reach this harbour, supported life at the University from the sack of oatmeal

---

* He was chosen to the post in 1703, and the Town Council raised the Principal's pay from £41 13s. to £92 sterling. That was a higher salary than was enjoyed by the heads of other Scottish Universities. *Calamy* (II, p. 186) bears witness in 1709 to ' the entire freedom and harmony between the Principal [Carstares] and the Masters of the College, they expressing a veneration for him as a common father, and he a tenderness for them, as if they had been his children.'

leaning against the wall of the garret where he lodged in the town. On holidays fixed for the purpose, the rustic student tramped home with the empty sack, and returned with it refilled from the harvest of his father's ' infield.'[113]

The peasants on a Scottish estate lived on terms of traditionally familiar intercourse with the laird, who on his daily ride across his lands had to listen to the sharp tongues of an outspoken race. None the less they were living under him in a position of servitude at once feudal and economic. This kind of relationship was remarked on by English travellers as something new in their experience.* Private jurisdictions over tenants, civil in some cases, civil and criminal in others, were common all over Scotland, though such feudal courts had long ago ceased in England. Statesmen in London held that the Protestant succession was in imminent danger from these *superiorities*, which removed the Scottish vassal from the protection of the royal courts and subjected his person and property to Jacobite overlords.[114]

The peasantry held their small farms on annually terminable leases which left them at the mercy of the laird or his factor, and fatally discouraged any attempt on their part at improving the land they tilled. And the laird on his side seldom put capital into the improvement of his tenants' farms. Had he wished so to do, he lacked the means. A rent-roll of £500 sterling was considered great wealth in Scotland, £50 was common, and many ' bonnet lairds ' supported their families on £20 of rent and the produce of their own ' infield.' Moreover rents were paid more than half in kind : sheep, poultry, oatmeal, barley and peat were brought to the door of the manor house by the tenantry—not in carts, for they had none, but balanced on the backs of half-starved horses. Another source of supply for the laird's

* ' The noblemen and gentlemen keep the common people in mighty subjection ' (*North Eng. and Scot. in 1704*, p. 52). ' The commonalty are used to worship and adore their lairds ' (*Kirke*, p. 16). ' Without those long and kind leases the tenants of England have, they are not encouraged by their lords in improvements ' (*Morer*, p. 4). In the year 1700 the Scottish author of *The Interest of Scotland*, pp. 77–78, admits these English strictures and adds : ' I believe we have learned that method of oppressing our peasants from the French.'

modest household was the cloud of pigeons from his dove-cot, which preyed on the surrounding fields, transforming a large proportion of the tenants' meagre crops into flesh for the landlord's table.   For the rest, the Scottish farmer, like the villein of medieval England, had to manure, sow and reap the ' infield ' of the laird, often on days between two spells of bad weather, when he might otherwise have saved his own precarious harvest and secured his family against starvation during the coming year.

A nobleman or laird was usually inclined to be a good landlord, so far as custom demanded and necessity allowed, and to reciprocate the affection of the men whose ancestors had bled in the feuds and forays of his family.   But many of the hard-pressed ' bonnet lairds,' and factors acting for great men and absentees, were hard as flint.   A dozen and more years after Queen Anne's death the wisest observers in Scotland were still raising the same complaint.   In 1729 the author of the *Ways and Means of Enclosing* addressed the nobles and gentry as follows :

To the great misfortune of most of these poor people, they are the property of bailiffs and chamberlains that manage your estates, very often for themselves rather than for your lordships ; and by grinding the face of your poor tenants with double the service your noble souls would allow you to take of them, and by bribes to keep the highest bidder in his old hereditary possession or turn him out if another bid yet higher, become soon rich enough to buy their chamberlainries.

And as late as 1733 Patrick Lindesay wrote : ' So long as our farmers are kept low by a precarious possession upon short leases, no improvement can be expected.'   It was only as the century advanced that the change towards long leases and the investment of capital in the improvement of the land began to make the rapid headway which, by the time Sir Walter Scott started on his tours of observation, had already transformed the Lowland landscape with walls, hedges, plantations and well-built farmhouses, and made the prosperity of the Scottish people.[115]

Under these conditions it is no wonder that in Queen Anne's reign nine-tenths of the fields of Scotland were un-enclosed by wall or hedge.   The cattle had to be tethered or watched all day and shut up all night. Only in the Lothians the wealthier landlords had begun the process of enclosing by stone walls. Quick-set hedges were hardly anywhere to be seen, and the want of them was not regretted, for it was believed that they harboured birds which would eat the corn. There was a similar suspicion attaching to trees. Saplings were often injured by the peasants and oftener by their cattle, in spite of proclaimed penalties. But there were few trees for them to injure except close round the manor house and the kirk. The ancient forests, where, according to the instructions of Robert Bruce's 'testament,' the population used to shelter in time of English invasion, had now almost everywhere disappeared. And the modern movement for plantations to keep the wind off the land and supply the market with timber was only in its infancy.* The general aspect of Scotland was then more treeless than ever before or since. Here and there, particularly in Clydeside, could be seen woods of some size and pretension, and, in the distant and unvisited North, old forests still rustled their branches to the Highland winds. Even in the Lowlands the denes and steep banks of the burns sheltered in their dank recesses the sparse remains of the blanket of birch, alder and dwarf oak that had once been spread over the land.[116]

The houses of the peasantry were in keeping with the starved aspect of the landscape and the want of any proper system of agricultural improvement. Rightly to imagine the home of a Scots farmer in Queen Anne's reign, we must forget the fine stone farms of a later date, and think of something more like the cabins of Western Ireland. It consisted almost always of one storey and often of one room. The style and material of building and the degree of poverty varied in different regions, but walls of turf or of unmortared stone, stopped with grass or straw, were very common ; chimneys and glass windows were rare ; the floor was the

---

* John Clerk of Penicuick, one of the most estimable of the statesmen of the Union, notes under March 1703 : ' I fell exceedingly into the humour of planting and making nurseries. My father observing this devolved upon me all his concerns this way, and I began my first plantations on the south side of the House, near the Water of Esk, at an old coal hole on the brae, to which, from Quixote's cave, we gave the name of Montesina's Cave.' *Clerk* (*Rox.*), p. 45.

bare ground ; in many places the cattle lived at one end of
the room, the people at the other, with no partition between.
The family often sat on stones or heaps of turf round the
fire of peat, whence the smoke made partial escape through
a hole in the thatch overhead.   ' Yet foul, dark and fetid
as they were, the people liked these hovels for their warmth,'
writes Mr. Graham.   Sayings like ' the clartier the cosier,'
' the mair dirt the less hurt,' and ' muck makes luck ' consoled people for the circumstances of their lot.   But English
travellers observed that they suffered terribly from the itch.
Since also they worked on an undrained soil, half of it
unreclaimed from marsh and rushes, and came back to a
damp home in wet clothes for which they too seldom had
any change, it followed that rheumatism and ague plagued
and shortened their lives.

Men and women wore clothes made up in the immediate
neighbourhood by local weavers and tailors, and often spun
and dyed in the wearer's own cottage.   Children always
and grown-ups often went bare-foot.   The men wore the
broad, flat, round, blue bonnets of wool, the distinctive head-
gear of Scotland in the eyes of the world.   The laird and
minister alone sported a felt hat of the English type ; but
they too wore home-spun clothes made up by a country
tailor.   To the surprise of even Dissenters from South
Britain, the minister wore no black or clerical garments,
either in or out of church, but made his rounds and preached
his sermon in lay neck-cloth, and in coloured cloak and
waistcoat of homely wool.[117]

In Scotland yet, as in the England of pre-Saxon times,
much of the land that was potentially the best for agriculture
was still undrained marsh cumbering the valley bottoms,
while the peasants painfully drove their teams on the barren
hillsides above.   The enormous ploughs of primitive
design were all of wood except the share and coulter, and
were usually made by the farmers themselves ; they were
dragged along the slope by eight or ten small and meagre
oxen, urged on by the blows and shrill cries of half-a-dozen
excited farmers.   The cortège, with the united efforts of
beasts and men, scratched half-an-acre a day.

A group of farmers usually tilled their lands together,

and shared the profits on the ' run-rig ' system, each farmer
claiming the produce of a ' rig ' or ' ridge,'—a different
' rig ' each harvest.   A farm paying £50 sterling rent might
have a dozen or a score of tenants, among whom the land
was every year re-divided by lot.   This system, and the
precarious annual leases granted by the laird, rendered
agricultural improvement impossible.   The quarrels inside
the group of co-operating farmers—some of them of that
dour type that bred Cameronians and Kirk seceders—too
often held up the common cultivation for weeks at a time.

The farm was further divided into an ' infield ' and an
' outfield.' On the ' infield,' near the houses of the clachan,
was lavished all the manure that could be locally collected,
including sometimes the thatch covering the turf on the
goodman's cottage roof.* But the ' outfield,' perhaps three-
quarters of the total acreage, was left unmanured, used as
rough pasture for eight or ten years on end, and then cropped
for a year or two before relapsing into something scarcely
distinct from moor.

The crops consisted of oats for the staple food, and
barley to make either scones or the Scots ale, which was still
the wholesome national drink of the Lowlander before the
ill-omened invasion of whisky from the Highlands. Pease
and beans also were grown for the cottage kitchen. But
turnips and artificial grasses for cattle were unknown, and
potatoes were grown only by a few gardeners to season the
laird's dish of meat, not by farmers as part of the people's
food.[118]

The tyranny of these primitive customs of cultivation,
approved by the people themselves, kept them always near
the verge of famine. Their grain, but little multiplied by
such methods of agriculture, went in the three shares celebrated in the old saying :

Ane to gnaw, and ane to saw, and ane to pay the laird witha'.

The lairds were bound fast by their own poverty, unable to
help themselves or their tenants. Yet it was the lairds who,

---

* The use of lime for manure was only just beginning on a few progressive
estates in the reigns of William and Anne. *Scot. and Scot.* II, p. 205 ; *Agnew*, II,
pp. 203–204.

in the century now dawning, were able so to make use of the
commercial conditions introduced by the Union as to revo-
lutionize the system of agriculture and create a new
prosperity for all classes.

The first years of Anne witnessed a slow recovery, not
due to any large changes or improvements, but to the chance
of better harvests. The last half-dozen years of William's
reign had been the ' dear years ' of Scottish memory, six
consecutive seasons of disastrous weather when the harvests
would not ripen. The country had not the means to buy
food from abroad, so the people had laid themselves down
and died. Many parishes had been reduced to a half or a
third of their inhabitants. This sombre experience, from
which the nation was slowly emerging during the years
when the Treaty of Union was under debate, coloured the
North Briton's outlook, deepened his superstitions and
darkened his political passions, especially in relation to the
hated English who had watched the kindly Scots die of
hunger, and had moved no finger save to make their lot
worse by opposition to the Darien scheme. Fortunately a
cycle of fat years under Queen Anne followed the lean years
under King William. Then, in 1709, after the Union was
safely passed, the failure of the harvest again produced
famine, unpeopling farms and hamlets and filling the villages
with beggars. Until the methods of agriculture had been
completely changed, such might always be the result of a
single season of bad weather.[119]

In these circumstances, the principal source of agricultural wealth, as distinct from mere subsistence, was sheep
and cattle. The sheep's wool supported the home cloth
manufacture, and both sheep and cattle were sold into
England in great numbers. Stock-breeding flourished most
in Galloway, but even Galloway had hardly recovered the
depredations on her livestock made by the Highlanders and
other emissaries of a paternal government in the ' killing
times ' of the persecution. It was reckoned that in 1705
Scotland sold 30,000 cattle into England ; the usual price
was something between one and two pounds sterling a head.
This marketing of ' black cattle ' was one of the most important of a Scottish laird's few sources of wealth. The sheep

and cattle were small, even as compared to the small English beasts of that period. Their pasture was for the most part unimproved moorland. The cattle were shut up all night for want of fences. Of the remnant that had not been sold south to the English pastures, many had to be slaughtered at Martinmas on the approach of winter, for there was little hay and no root-crop on which to feed them. During the next six months salted meat supplied the tables of the gentry, and meat seldom graced the peasant's board at any time of year. On the return of the tardy Scottish spring, the poor beasts, mere skeletons after their winter-long imprisonment in the dark on rations of straw or boiled chaff, were led back from the byre to the pasture, a pitiful procession, half supported, half carried by the farmers. This annual ceremony was only too well named the ' Lifting.' [120]

The standard of life in Scotland was very low in almost every material respect, but hardships had not crushed the spirit of the people, not even after the ' dear years ' of William. To avoid the receipt of alms was a passion with common folk more decidedly than in wealthier England. The poor law system was totally different in the two countries. In England the poor had been, ever since Elizabeth's reign, a charge on the State ; they were maintained by compulsory parish rates that amounted at the end of Anne's reign to a million pounds a year, then regarded as a heavy national burden, over and above private endowment and religious and private charity. In Scotland there was no compulsory rate, and poor-relief was an obligation not on the State but on the Church. Endowments of the poor were made by private persons, announced in the kirk, and sometimes commemorated on boards hung upon its walls. In the kirk also stood the poor's box, which the thrifty Scots constantly replenished with most of the bad copper of the neighbourhood, besides a useful minority of good coins. The deacon was a lay officer of the Church, found in many parishes, though not in all ; it was the deacon's business to distribute these alms among the necessitous, who were for the most part creditably unwilling to receive it. The duty of keeping their relations independent of such relief was keenly felt and nobly undertaken by persons themselves desperately poor.

Licences to beg from door to door in a given area were also issued by the Kirk Session to privileged ' gaberlunzies,' or ' blue gowns.' Many of them, like Edie Ochiltree, acted as welcome carriers of news to lonely farms, repositories of regional lore and legend,—popular, respectable figures with a place of their own in rural society.

But unhappily there was a much larger number of unlicensed and less desirable vagabonds. The ' sorners ' of Queen Anne's Scotland answered to the ' sturdy beggars ' of Tudor England. The ' dear years ' had swelled this army of broken and masterless men, though there is no support to Fletcher of Saltoun's wild guess that they numbered 200,000, which would have made them between a fifth and sixth of the whole population. But the ' sorners ' were numerous enough to terrorize a countryside of lonely farms and clachans of two or three houses apiece ; a company of ' ill men ' could rob in the face of day, taking the last crust from the cottage, the cow from the byre, and often wresting the child from its unhappy parents. The number and power of the ' sorners ' was the penalty paid by Scotland for the want of a regular poor law like the English. And in neither country was there any attempt at a proper police.[121]

Fletcher of Saltoun, the grim republican patriot who lent a flavour of his own to the Scottish politics of the age, proposed as a remedy that the ' sorners ' should be put into compulsory servitude ; his idea was only the extension of existing practice in Scotland. Coal mines and salt mines were worked very largely by ' bondsmen,' veritable serfs, who could be caught and punished for running away. Even in modern establishments based on free contract, like the New Mills cloth factory in Haddingtonshire, there was a ' prison att the manufactory,' and hands who ran away or broke their contracts could be dealt with by summary methods. But the condition of the employees of the New Mills was not bad by the standard of those days, whereas the hereditary bondsmen in the mines were treated by their masters as chattels, and were spoken of by the rest of the population with a kind of pitying terror, as ' the brown yins ' or ' the black folk.'[122]

CHAPTER XI

THE STATE OF SCOTLAND IN THE REIGN OF QUEEN ANNE (*concluded*)

Trade and industry. Glasgow. Edinburgh. The Church and religion. Kirk sessions discipline. The Episcopalians. The Toleration question. The Cameronians. The General Assembly. Witches. Superstition and imagination. The Highlands.

IF Scotland lagged behind England in agricultural methods, her industry and commerce were in no better way. Almost all her articles of export were food or raw materials—cattle and salmon for England, coal and salmon for Holland, salt and lead for Norway, herrings for the Iberian Peninsula. The Scots themselves wore cloth woven by village wabsters for local consumption ; but only a very little linen or woollen cloth was sold abroad. The Haddington New Mills were famous, but they were not flourishing. There were, besides, other woollen factories, as at Musselburgh and Aberdeen, all clamouring to the Scots Parliament to support them with money and monopolies, and being only in part satisfied. The wool-growing landlords, on their side, compelled the legislature to allow them to export raw wool to Sweden and Holland, to the detriment of the market for Scottish cloth in those countries, and of course clean contrary to the established policy of England. The herring trade was a chief source of the nation's wealth, but even so the Dutch fishermen took many more herrings off the Scottish coast than did the Scots themselves. A great part of the business of the Edinburgh Parliament consisted of regulations to encourage and direct the meagre manufacturing and trading efforts of the country.[123]

Though Scottish officers and regiments were winning

honour for the land of their birth in the ranks of the Allies, the war with France meant little to the Scots at home. There was no such national enthusiasm as was shown in the Napoleonic and later wars. The Edinburgh Parliament, therefore, passed in 1703 a Wine Act, to legalize the most popular part of trade with the enemy. The English were scandalized at this bold defiance of propriety, for they themselves were content with illegal smuggling to the French ports. But they dared do nothing, for if one of their cruisers had seized a ship freighted with brandy, claret and Jacobite agents, they might have woken up one morning to find themselves at war with Scotland.[124]

Since the Restoration, Glasgow had been reckoned as the second city in the kingdom, and the first for trade and manufacture. Probably on account of the famine and distress in William's reign, the population had recently declined : when the Union of 1707 was passed, it numbered only 12,500 souls out of a total of a million or more for all Scotland. The Glasgow merchants owned between them fifteen trading ships, with an aggregate tonnage of 1,182 tons, and even these small vessels had to unload more than a dozen miles below the town, as the Clyde was still unnavigable to anything larger than a boat. Since no Scottish firm was permitted to trade with an English dependency, their commerce was confined to Europe, until the Union Treaty opened the tobacco trade with the English colonies to Bailie Nicol Jarvie and his fellow-citizens. In Anne's reign Glasgow was still a pretty little country town, with colonnades at the cross roads in the centre, where the merchants met to transact their modest affairs.* It was, moreover, one of the four University towns of Scotland : 'there are only forty scholars that lodge in the College,' an English traveller noted in the year of Blenheim, ' but there are two or three hundred that belong to it, and all wear red gowns, as do likewise those at Aberdeen and St. Andrews.'[125]

The fourth university town was Edinburgh herself—

* In 1704 we read : ' the town consists of two open, long straite streets, which cross one another in the middle and the streets are well paved.' The crossing-place of these two streets ' serves as a change,' and ' on every side are piazzas or small arches under the houses, where the merchants walk and screen themselves in the bad weather.' *North of England and Scotland in 1704*, ed. 1818, p. 47.

the headquarters of Scotland's law and law courts, the meeting place of the Parliament of the three Estates, and of that other Parliament which proved more enduring—the General Assembly of the Church. There, too, was Holyrood Palace, the empty nest whence Scotland's Kings had flown. At the other end of the mile-long Canongate and High Street—'the stateliest street in the world,' as a traveller of the period called it [126]—rose the Castle on its rock, where the absent Queen Anne was represented by the red coats of her small Scottish army. The idle soldiers looked down upon the reek and roofs of Edinburgh, in perpetual wonder what was brewing below in the most turbulent spot in Britain, and what riot, religious, political or economic, it would be their next duty to quell.

Although the antique City Guard of Edinburgh, with their Lochaber axes, were the laughing-stock of Scotland, yet housebreaking and robbery were almost unknown in the chief city of the kingdom, where men left their house doors unlocked all night. The fact speaks well for the honesty of the Scots, and perhaps speaks well for the religion in which they were bred. It ruled the town effectually, preventing, in Scotland's very capital and centre of fashion, all theatrical shows and all dances, and on the Sabbath all 'idle gazing from windows,' all loitering and all walking fast in the streets. No wonder Dr. Pitcairn wrote his witty rhymes lampooning the clergy, and no wonder 'Hell-fire Clubs' and 'Sulphur Clubs' met surreptitiously to flout the Kirk in ways more questionable than the drama and the dance.*

The more respectable portion of Scotland's upper class found one consolation on an Edinburgh Sabbath : the fashionable world went to the Tron Kirk in High Street to gaze upon itself there and to meditate matches : the Tron Kirk was commonly called 'the maiden market,' and the Church Assembly in 1709 vainly voted 'an act against bowing or conversing together in time of worship.' [127]

* In 1710 the first Assembly for dancing was held, in spite of clerical censure. But the theatre was unknown in Edinburgh till some years later. *Wodrow. Anal.*, III, p. 476. *Graham*, I, pp. 92–97, also p. 123 on Edinburgh police and rarity of crime.

But not even the Kirk attempted on week-days to stop horse-racing on Leith sands, golf, cock-fighting or heavy drinking. On six evenings of the week the taverns were filled with men of all classes at their ale and claret, till the ten o'clock drum, beaten at the order of the magistrates, warned every man that he must be off home. Then were the High Street and Canongate filled with parties of every description, hurrying unsteadily along, High Court Judges striving to walk straight as became their dignity, rough Highland porters swearing in Gaelic as they forced a passage for their sedan-chairs, while far overhead the windows opened, five, six or ten storeys in the air, and the close stools of Edinburgh discharged the collected filth of the last twenty-four hours into the street. It was good manners for those above to cry ' Gardy-loo ' (*gardez l'eau*) before throwing. The returning roysterer cried back ' Haud yer han',' and ran with humped shoulders, lucky if his vast and expensive full-bottomed wig was not put out of action by a cataract of filth. The ordure thus sent down lay in the broad High Street and in the deep, well-like closes and wynds around it, making the night air horrible, until early in the morning it was perfunctorily cleared away by the City Guard. Only on Sabbath morn it might not be touched, but lay there all day long, filling Scotland's capital with the savour of a mistaken piety.

This famous sanitary system of Edinburgh aroused much comment among English travellers and made the Scots ' traduced and taxed of other nations,' as being, in Defoe's words, ' unwilling to live sweet and clean.' But it is only fair to quote his defence of them in the matter :

Were any other people to live under the same unhappiness, I mean as well of a rocky and mountainous situation, thronged buildings from seven to ten or twelve story high, a scarcity of water, and that little they have difficult to be had, and to the uppermost lodgings far to fetch, we should have a London or Bristol as dirty as Edinburgh ; for though many cities have more people in them, yet I believe that in no city in the world so many people live in so little room.

Edinburgh indeed was an extreme example of the French type of town, kept within its ancient limits for reasons of

safety and defence, and therefore forced to find room for
growth by pushing its tenement flats high in air—in contrast to the ground plan of the easy-going peaceful towns of
England, that sprawled out over suburbs ever expanding,
to give each family its own house and if possible its own
garden. French influence and the disturbed condition of
Scotland in the past had confined the capital within its walls
and diverted its growth up aloft. It was not, indeed, so long
since it had been a matter of great peril for a gentleman to
pass the night in a house without the walls, like Darnley in
Kirk o' Fields. And so the Scottish grandees had no fine
Edinburgh mansions like those of the English nobles in
Bloomsbury and the Strand, but were fain, during the
session of Parliament, to live each in a flat over the
High Street.

Canongate and High Street kept the crest of the ridge
that runs up from Holyrood to the Castle, while the steep
slope fell away on either side towards Cowgate to the south
and the Loch to the north. On these slopes were crowded
the tall wynds and closes into which the population of Edinburgh was packed. But Cowgate, parallel to High Street
on its south side, was also included in the city walls. On the
north there was then no parallel street, for the future site of
Princes Street and the Waverley Station was occupied by the
waters of the Nor' Loch. Defoe's shrewd criticism reads
like a prophecy of the future :

Were the loch filled up, as it might easily be, the City might
have extended upon the plain below, and fine beautiful streets would,
no doubt, have been built there. Nay, I question much whether, in
time, the high streets would not have been forsaken, and the City, as
we might say, run all out of its gates to the North.

The stone houses made up in solidity for what they lacked
in convenience. The tempests of the northern climate beat
in vain on those gaunt, fortress-like 'Babels.' 'No blowing
of tiles about the streets,' writes Defoe, 'to knock people
on the head as they pass ; no stacks of chimneys and gables'
ends falling in to bury the inhabitants in their ruins, as we
often find it in England,' as in the brick-built London that
had suffered so severely in the Great Storm of 1703. The

older houses of Edinburgh had outside stairs, unfenced and giddy to ascend, that led from the street to each storey in turn, where a separate family kept house. Contrary to the custom in English lodging-houses, the higher storeys were the more fashionable and commanded the higher rents. The newer houses usually had the staircase inside the building and had glazed windows instead of wooden shutters.

In such a town, where every flat was accounted as a separate ' house,' and no houses were numbered, it may well be imagined that it was difficult for letters to reach their destination, or for strangers to find their way.* Indeed, without the services of the self-disciplined regiment of keen-eyed, quick-witted, dependable ' caddies,' business could scarcely have been carried on in old Edinburgh.[128]

Scottish literature was centred in the capital, but it gave no sign as yet of the great awakening that lay before it in the latter half of the new century, when the high imaginative and reasoning faculties of the race and the historical and ballad lore of Scotland should be kindled by Burns and Scott, Hume and Adam Smith into a blaze to light all Europe. The material was there in the heart and mental habits of the nation, but the Promethean fire had not yet descended. The mind of the people throve on the ballads sung, the stories told, the doctrines debated round the peat-fire in the peasant's cottage. Printed books, other than the Bible, consisted chiefly of theology or political pamphlets.

There was no native journalism. The two papers, issued three times a week at Edinburgh, were the old-established *Gazette* and its rival the *Courant*, started in 1705; both existed by special permission of the Privy Council ; they were tame organs of officialdom, in form mere imitations of the London papers, full of continental and English news but telling the Scots nothing about their own affairs. With the disappearance of the Scottish Privy Council after the Union, the

---

* Here is a typical Edinburgh address of the year 1702 : ' ffor Mr. Archbald Dumbarr of Thundertoune to be left at Capt. Dumbar's writing Chamber at the Iron revell third storie below the Cross north end of the close at Edin^r.' *Dunbar*, I, p. 33.

Edinburgh press acquired a certain freedom, and in the last years of the reign began to have a life of its own, with a somewhat larger variety of newspapers.[129]

The Scottish peasant, cramped in feudal bonds and medieval poverty, had one method of escape from his material lot—religion.   Other intellectual food he had none offered him.   Bible on knee, in harsh, delightful argument with his minister or his cronies, he inhabited a realm of thought and imagination, deep, narrow, intense—for good and for evil utterly unlike the merry-go-round of disconnected information and ideas in which the popular mind of our own day gyrates.   Never consulted by his betters about politics, and without representation in the Estates of Parliament, he took all the keener interest in the proceedings of the assemblies where his influence was felt, the hierarchy of Church courts,—the Kirk Session of the parish, the Presbytery of a dozen parishes, the Provincial Synod, and the national General Assembly annually held at Edinburgh. In all of these the laity were represented, as they were not in the purely clerical convocations of York and Canterbury. It has often been said that the Church Assembly was Scotland's Parliament more truly than the three Estates. And in the absence of any representative local government, the Kirk Session, where the lay elders kept the minister in awe, was the nearest approach to a parish council.

The parish church, with its roof of turf or thatch, was a small and tumble-down building ; it had no medieval splendours or amenities, and would in England have been deemed more fitted for a barn.   In the country churches there were seldom pews, except for the elders and a few privileged families.*   Most men and women stood during the service, or else sat on ' creepies,' stools such as that with which Jennie Geddes had marked her disapproval of the Prayer Book.   Yet the hard place was crowded every Sabbath for two services of three hours each by a congregation

---

* In a church near Edinburgh, in the reign of Anne or George I, an English Colonel's wife wished to have her pew lined, as her clothes were dirtied on the ill-washed boards. ' Line the pew ! ' cried the minister's wife in alarm, ' my husband would think it *rank papery.*' *Burt,* I, pp. 51–52.

of whom many had come on foot long miles across the moor. So small was the room inside the church that an overflow of the pious was often crowded out into the churchyard, where the Bible was read to them by a lad put up upon a tombstone.

The most solemn and impressive of popular religious rites were the Communions, held out of doors at long tables, gatherings under the eye of summer heaven that reminded everyone present of more dangerous meetings held on the moorside in the killing times. Eight or ten parishes combined to hold a communion each in turn, from June to August, and many persons attended them one after the other, thinking nothing of walking forty miles over the hills to get there. In 1710 Robert Wodrow, the historian of the Covenanters, wrote: ' I have been throng with communions in this neighbourhood,' ' a mighty indrink of communicants.' Yet even so he denounced the ' sin of fondness upon trade ' and the ' worldly spirit ' it was beginning to breed in the reign of Anne, dimming a little that ' hunger and edge upon people's spirits ' that he had noticed in the ' golden tide there was for a year or two after the Revolution.' * The competition of secular interests had hardly begun, except to the keen sight of one so jealous for the Lord as Wodrow, but a little material prosperity might soon set it fairly going, in a nation that had already gone mad to so little purpose over the Darien scheme.[130]

The older Presbyterian clergy in Queen Anne's reign were men whose education had been interrupted and whose spirits had been disturbed and embittered by persecution. One who knew them in their later years described them as—

weak, half-educated men, their lives irreproachable, and their manners austere and rustic. Their prejudices coincided perfectly with their congregations who in respect of their sound fundamentals made great allowances for their foibles and weaknesses.

' Presbyterian eloquence ' was a byword with English

* In 1696 Gabriel Semple testified in the Church Assembly : ' I was witness to the old times before the Restoration, and to the times under the persecution, and I never saw so much of the spirit poured out as I have since the Revolution.'

hearers for its uncouth treatment of religious mysteries, its familiar apostrophes of the Almighty, its denunciation of such harmless acts as wearing smart clothes in church or taking in the London *Spectator*. But it was an Englishman who wrote :

> Were the ministerial office in England discharged as it is in Scotland, in that laborious and self-denying manner, and under such small encouragements, thousands of the clergy I daresay would wish to have been brought up mechanics rather than parsons. Here are no drones, no idle parsons, no pampered priests, no dignities or preferments to excite ambition.

Indeed the ambition of a peasant's son, such as most of the ministers were in origin, was honourably satisfied with the leadership of a parish and the confidence of his people. Meanwhile there was growing up a younger generation, better educated in less troublous times, with more sense of proportion in thought and refinement in language, who were soon, as ' Moderates,' to be openly at odds with those whom Claverhouse had dragooned into bigotry.[131]

The Kirk Session of self-important lay elders, acting conjointly with the minister, interfered in ordinary life to an excessive degree. Week in, week out, the Kirk Session and the superior court of the Presbytery were trying cases of alleged swearing, slander, quarrelling, breach of Sabbath, witchcraft and sexual offences. Some of these enquiries and judgments were properly conducted and useful, being such as were dealt with by ordinary magistrates in England. Others were intolerably vexatious, as when a woman was arraigned for carrying a pail on a Fast Day, and a crowder for fiddling at a christening feast. The adulterer or fornicator of either sex was exposed on the stool of repentance in church, to the merriment of the junior half of the congregation—including sometimes Jacobite lairds who came to see the fun—to the grave reprobation of the more respectable, and to the unblushing denunciations of the minister, renewed sometimes for six, ten or twenty Sabbaths on end. There was often a long row of penitents, and the ' gowns ' in which they were clad were in such constant use that they had frequently to be renewed. To avoid this

intolerable humiliation, poor girls often resorted to concealment of pregnancy and sometimes to child murder. The
Privy Council in Anne's reign was constantly dealing with
the question of the remitting or enforcing of the extreme
penalty in such cases.

These activities of the Kirk Session and Presbytery had
much support in public opinion or they could not have so
long survived the disuse of similar Church jurisdiction in
England. But they aroused deep resentment in many, not
least among the upper classes. It is true that commuta-
tion of penance for fines was often allowed in the case of the
gentry, a worldly compromise that recalls to ill-thinking
minds the policy of Church courts in the blinded days of
Popery ! But, even with these mitigations, the jurisdiction
over conduct claimed by low-born elders and clergymen
was an offence to the proud families of lairds and nobles ;
it was an underlying cause of Episcopal religion and
Jacobite politics in many who had otherwise no quarrel with
the services and doctrines of the Presbyterian Church.
Anti-clericalism strengthened the Jacobites in Scotland, as
it strengthened the Whigs in England. Yet it must be
remembered that the stool of repentance and the jurisdiction
of Kirk sessions had gone on even in the Episcopal days of
Charles II, and had not yet ceased in those numerous
parishes still ruled by Episcopal ministers.[132]

On the whole, the Episcopalian or Jacobite party
depended on upper class support even more than the
Presbyterian or Whig. The more rigorous the disciple-
ship of Knox, the more democratic was doctrine and practice
likely to be. The clash came in the appointment of
ministers, which the true-blue Presbyterian claimed for the
people of the parish, both on grounds of religious doctrine
as to the call of pastors, and because the private patrons
who claimed to appoint were often very doubtful in their
Presbyterianism. At the Revolution, private patronage had
been abolished : the right of individual nobles and lairds
to appoint ministers had been taken away by the Act of 1690,
and had been vested in the Elders and Protestant Heritors
of the parish, while the congregation was given a negative
voice. The power of the patron to name the minister was

restored by the Tory Parliament at Westminster in 1712 as
one of the first-fruits of the Union. But even before that
decision, which was very far from being a final settlement of
the most vexed question in Scottish ecclesiastical history, the
earlier years of Queen Anne had been full of the sound and
fury of this debate, whenever the Presbyterian democracy of
a parish had tried to induct a minister not agreeable to the
local grandee.

Episcopalian pamphleteers twitted the Presbyterians
with their want of policy in ' constant taking part with the
mob in all the disputes that happen betwixt them and the
Nobility and Gentry in the choice of ministers, as if you
relied upon them for the security of your establishment.
. . . The Nobility and Gentry in Scotland have the commons
so much under, that it argues no small stupidity in you to
have blundered in so plain a case.' Even English Nonconformist visitors to Scotland were astonished and alarmed
at the boldness of the Church in its dealings with ' the
Great.' Whatever its other faults, the Church of John
Knox raised the downtrodden people of Scotland to look
its feudal masters in the face.[133]

The position of the Episcopalians in Scotland when
Anne began her reign was most anomalous. Their services, doctrines, organization and discipline—except for the
presence of Bishops who in fact exercised small authority
—differed little save in emphasis from those of the Presbyterian Establishment. Yet the greatest bitterness prevailed
between the two communions, because the difference of the
Churches answered to the political difference of Whig and
Jacobite, behind which lay two generations of feuds and
wrongs inflicted and remembered on both sides.

The Episcopalians of Scotland were at once better and
worse off than the Nonconformists of England. On the
one hand there was not, until 1712, any Act of Toleration
to legalize their services. On the other hand, more than
a sixth of the parish churches were still occupied by their
ministers. In Aberdeenshire, in the Highlands and along
their whole eastern border, Presbyterian clergymen who
showed themselves were liable to be attacked by mobs as

savage as those who had ' rabbled ' the Episcopal ' curates ' of the South-West in the winter of the Revolution. When in 1704 the Presbyterian minister was to be inducted at Dingwall, he was stoned, beaten and driven away by a mob of men and women crying ' King Willie is dead and our King is alive.'

The popular feeling that thus found expression in the North-East arose less from religious differences than from political feuds, regional hatred of the Whiggamores of the South-West, and personal loyalty to old and tried pastors. In 1707 there were still 165 out of some 900 parishes in Scotland where the minister adhered to the Episcopal Church. In some cases he had taken the oaths to Government, in others his Jacobite principles had been too strong to admit of such compliance. These ' incumbents,' as the survivors of the Revolution deluge were called, were tolerated in view of the support they received from their parishioners ; but Church Assembly and Privy Council co-operated to prevent the ' intrusion ' of successors of the same breed. The Episcopalian foothold inside the Establishment would therefore not outlast another generation. After that, the Episcopalians would all be, what most of them already were, dissenters from the national worship, and, since most of them also remained opponents of the reigning dynasty, their position was likely to become worse rather than better.[134]

But the great majority of the Episcopalian clergy had been deprived at the Revolution. In Anne's reign they were living miserably enough, the more fortunate as chaplains in some great house, too many on alms collected from their co-religionists in Scotland, or from English churchmen who regarded them as martyrs in a common cause. Not only did the English Tories take up collections, but the warm-hearted Burnet of Salisbury, who, though an English Whig by adoption, was by origin a Scottish moderate, gave £200 sterling towards the needs of these unfortunate men. In 1707 some of them were driven by sheer want to appeal to the ' bowels of compassion ' of the Corporation of ' baxters ' in Edinburgh, and received from that source exactly a hundredth part of what had been given by the much-abused Whig bishop.* The Episcopal 'Meeting Houses' had no legal claim to protection, but were often undisturbed, especially when, as sometimes happened, the officiating clergyman had taken the oaths to Government. In Edinburgh fourteen Meeting Houses were said to be ' as open as the Churches and as freely resorted to.' [135]

The Privy Council at Edinburgh was constantly being called upon to take action either for or against the Episcopalians, whose position in the country was so equivocal, who were at once so strong and so weak, many of whom refused to pray for Queen Anne and all of whom were opposed to the Hanoverian succession. In Glasgow, Dumfries and the South-West generally, mobs sometimes broke up their services. At other times popular zeal demonstrated with even more vigour and impunity against the Roman Catholics. The Privy Council itself was constantly issuing proclamations to enforce the laws against ' Jesuits, trafficking Papists and their resetters.' † But in parts of the Highlands and of Aberdeen and Banff shires the Roman Catholics had churches to which they resorted ' almost avowedly, as Protestants go to their paroch churches '—and Episcopalians and Catholics made common cause in the interest of the Pretender.

Such, when Anne began her reign, was the mutual relation of religious parties in Scotland. The accession of a Tory Queen, the High Church revival in England and the Bill against Occasional Conformity in the Westminster Parliament caused a panic among the Scottish Presbyterians. They expected that an attack on their Church

---

* Carstares also impoverished himself to keep the poor Episcopalian clergy from want. At his graveside two men burst into tears ; they were two non-jurant Episcopal clergymen who had long been supported by their friendly foe. Story's *Carstares*, p. 366 ; John Watson, *Scotland of the Eighteenth Century*, p. 150.

† *Popery Reviving*, 1714 ; *Privy Council Register, Edinburgh, passim ; e.g.* January 17, 1704, mobs in Nithsdale have broken into houses of noblemen and gentlemen under pretence of searching for priests and Jesuits ; February 7, 1704. A ' convocation of lieges in a warlike manner upon 2nd of Feb. inst. marched into the town of Dumfries,' where they burnt at the cross a considerable number of Popish books and images. The Privy Council proposes to examine these riots, but also to carry out laws for the arrest of priests. For the Glasgow riot against the Episcopal meeting-house see *P.C. Registers*, March 8, 1702/3.

Establishment would at once be made by the Queen's government. 'The Lord prepare me for suffering and whatever is before me,' wrote Wodrow, the historian of the 'sufferings' of the former generation, when he heard that King William was no more. The form of argument into which these Presbyterian fears translated themselves was a warfare of pamphlets against the claim now advanced for a legalized Toleration of Episcopalians. In the first two years of Anne the number and the warmth of the pamphlets appearing in Scotland for and against Toleration * was much greater than of those dealing with the European war, into which the country was supposed to be entering. But as soon as it became clear that the English Tory Queen could not ally herself with the Scottish Jacobites, the fears of the Presbyterians and the hopes of the Episcopalians declined, and the question of the Union swallowed up all other issues.[136]

During the early months of Anne's reign, while the first alarm of the Presbyterians was at its height, a dangerous tendency showed itself among the less wise of their clergy to seek security for the Church by asserting its *intrinsic* or *jure divino* power, reviving the old covenanting claim to independence of or superiority over the State. Carstares, who knew that that way led to ruin, was diligent in damping down the rash ardour of his co-religionists.[137]

The failure of the Church, when restored at the Revolution, to reassert her *intrinsic* power according to the older Covenants, had led to the secession of the Cameronians. They may be called the Non-jurors of Presbyterianism, for they, like their English opposites, refused to take the oath to the governments born of the Revolution. An 'uncovenanted' King or Queen had no claim on their allegiance. The Cameronians of Queen Anne's reign, strongest in the South-West, formed a body of zealots, many thousands strong, with famous fighting traditions. The Jacobite agents were busy among them at every crisis of the reign,

* The tone of much of this controversy may be exemplified by a sentence from *A stone returning upon him that rolled it*, 1703 : ' I am now by these presents sending my opponent another dose ; and what corrupt stuff and venom it may draw from his brains and bowells, his countrymen will understand by his next.' Sage on the Episcopal side and Carstares for the Establishment held a higher flight.

inviting them to unite with their former persecutors to rise and overthrow the government.   From the other side advances were made to them by the established ministers, seeking to heal the schism among Presbyterian brethren. But the Cameronians continued to plough their lonely furrow, denouncing the ' Erastian Church,' and accusing it, surely by a rather harsh construction, of ' tolerating Popery and Prelacy,' of joining in war in alliance with Popish princes, and of other national sins.[138]

If the charge of abetting resistance to the Crown always made the English High Church conscience uneasy, the Scottish Presbyterian conscience was equally sensitive to the very different accusation of Erastianism.   For the Scottish Church was not, like the Anglican, a client of Tudor and Stuart Kings.   It had been fashioned by the rough hands of John Knox and the Congregation of the Lord, a self-appointed body of men who had carried through the work of Reformation in the teeth of the Crown.   And so the high churchmen of Scotland claimed divine right not for the King but for the Church.   In the Seventeenth Century King and Kirk had fought out their quarrel, trampling Scotland's welfare beneath the hoofs of that fierce scuffle.   At length the Revolution Settlement prescribed definite limits to the power both of Kirk and King.   Consequently the Parliament of Edinburgh had more independent power in the shaping of Scotland during the last eighteen years of its existence than Crown and Church had ever allowed it before.

1689–
1707

The Presbyterian Church, in return for her re-establishment in 1689, agreed to leave her ancient Covenants on the shelf, and to acknowledge, since needs she must, the secular power supreme.   But she agreed with many misgivings and reservations.   The nice line of demarcation between spiritual and temporal authority had still to be very carefully observed by both parties, particularly at the meetings of the General Assembly of the Church.   That national gathering of the representatives of clergy and laity met at Edinburgh every spring.   It was presided over by Queen Anne's Commissioner, some great Scottish noble, sitting throned aloft.   But its business was conducted by the

clergyman who acted as Moderator for the year. Since
the Royal Assent was not required to give legal sanction to
the Acts of the General Assembly, there was no check on its
proceedings except the royal power of dissolution. Lord
Seafield as Commissioner exercised that power in 1703,
though usually it was held in reserve. The knowledge that
it existed prevented much wild work.

Yet the Assembly would never quite admit in theory
that the Crown had the power to dissolve it.* After the
dispute of 1703, a curious compromise was agreed upon to
symbolize the dual control. Henceforth, at the end of
every General Assembly, the Moderator from the chair
declared it to be dissolved in the name of the Lord Jesus
Christ, the Head of the Church, and by the same spiritual
authority named a day for its meeting in the ensuing year.
Then up would rise the Royal Commissioner from his
throne, and by the authority of the Queen would dissolve
the Assembly and fix the next meeting for the same day as
that which the Moderator had just named. And so all the
canny Scots could go away content.[139]

In an earlier volume † I have explained how the belief
in witchcraft had already so far declined in the upper strata
of English society that the persecution of witches in
accordance with the law and with the dictates of popular
superstition was ceasing to be permitted, in a country that
was then ruled according to the ideas of its educated class.
In Scotland the same phenomena were just beginning to be
observable. Part of the upper class was already weakening
as to the frequency of diabolic agency, but popular and
clerical fanaticism was still very strong. Several supposed
witches were put to death in Queen Anne's Scotland, and
several more were banished forth of the realm. In the reign of
George I capital punishment was inflicted on witches for the
last time in this island, in the recesses of far Sutherlandshire.
In 1736 the law punishing witchcraft with death was

---

* It is characteristic that in Anne's reign the high churchmen of England were
trying to have the right of dissolving Convocation taken from the Archbishop and
given to the Crown, while the high churchmen of Scotland were trying to have the
right of dissolving the Assembly taken from the Crown and given to the Moderator.

† *Blenheim*, pp. 59–60.

repealed for Great Britain by the Westminster Parliament. After yet another generation had passed, witches and ' the muckle black deil ' were a subject of jest rather than of dread to Bobbie Burns and his farmer friends.

In the England of Queen Anne, as I have already described, the case of Jane Wenham caused a pamphlet controversy which attracted public attention to the question of the reality of witchcraft, and tended to diminish the belief. A similar but more tragic case occurred in Scotland in 1704–5, and became famous as that of ' the Pittenweem witches.' But whereas English Jane Wenham escaped, Scottish Janet Corphat perished miserably as a result of three hours' ' rabbling ' by the people of Pittenweem. Thomas Brown, who had been accused with her of witchcraft, died in prison ' after a great deal of hunger and hardship.' In the long course of the proceedings the Edinburgh Privy Council interfered several times, not very effectively, but always on the side of reason. It caused the survivors among the accused women to be liberated, but Janet's murderers were not brought to justice.

Fortunately, however, this test case was brought to the bar of public opinion by the Jacobite lairds of the neighbourhood. They held more sensible views about diabolic agency than their enemy, Patrick Cowper the minister of Pittenweem ; as a young man he had ' suffered ' in the days of the persecution, and the neighbouring lairds had, probably for that reason, opposed his original entry into manse and kirk. They now took up the cudgels against him, and accused him of inciting the mob to the murder of Janet Corphat. Opposite statements of fact were made in the war of pamphlets that followed.* But whether or not he had himself tortured the women in prison, whether or not he failed to rebuke the murder from the pulpit, he had undoubtedly encouraged the belief in the reality of the

---

* It has been usual to quote only the pieces attacking Cowper, *A Letter from a gentleman in Fife* and *A Letter from a gentleman in Fife to a Nobleman*. But the answer to these pamphlets, *A just reproof to the false reports*, ought to be collated with them. For Cowper's previous relation with the neighbouring lairds see *Fasti. Ecc. Scot.*, 1925, *sub*. Pittenweem. The ' rabbling ' of Janet Corphat probably gave Stevenson hints for the masterpiece of horror, *Thrawn Janet*, although the rest of the story is quite different.

crimes of which they were accused. Indeed he and most
of his fellow-labourers regarded disbelief in witchcraft as
' atheism ' and flying in the face of God's word.[140]

The Presbyterian Church was not the fount and origin
of popular superstitions. It fostered some kinds and discouraged others. But all had their roots far back in Popish,
in pagan, in primeval instincts and customs still strong in
a land of mountains, moors and yet unconquered nature,
amid a population which even in the Lowlands was largely
Celtic in origin and which lived under conditions in many
respects little changed since the remote past. Still, when
the goodman came splashing home across the ford at midnight, he heard the water kelpie roaring in the spate.
Fairies still lurked in the thorn trees of the dene, known
visitants to be propitiated by rites lest they should slay the
cattle in the byre or take the child from the cradle. North
of Tay, men lit Beltan fires and danced round them, on
traditional heights, upon the first of May. Crops and cattle
were defended by a number and variety of local formulas of
propitiation, some dating back to the earliest times of
agricultural and pastoral man,

> When holy were the haunted forest boughs,
> Holy the air, the water and the fire.

Magic wells were visited, and trees and bushes were decked
with rags of tartan and offerings of the fearful and grateful.
In parts of the Highlands such rites were the main religion
of the people ; in the Lowlands they were a subordinate
but still a real part of life and belief among a nation of
kirk-goers.

In the absence of proper doctors for the countryside,
popular medicine was traditional, and it was sometimes
hard to distinguish it from a popular form of witchcraft.
There were wise men and women who helped human happiness, as well as warlocks and witches who hampered it.
The Church encouraged the people to destroy the latter, but
could not prevent them from seeking the aid of the former.
The minister was not all-powerful. How could he be, since
he forbade harmless pleasures ? Lads and lassies ' danced
promisky ' to fiddle or pipes at every festal meeting, in spite

of the Church's ban ; and neither old nor young could be
held back from rites older than Presbyter or Pope.   There
were a hundred different charms and customs to avert ill-
luck, suited to every event in life—birth, marriage, death,
the churning of milk, the setting forth on a journey, the
sowing of a field.

Miracle was looked upon as an everyday occurrence far
more than in contemporary England, where scepticism was
already strong.   Ghosts, omens, apparitions were of the
ordinary pattern of Scottish life ; tales of living corpses
taking part in the common affairs of men were told with
circumstance and believed ; like the Greek of Homer's
time, the Scot who met a stranger on the moor might well
be uncertain whether he was what he seemed to be, or was
' no that canny.'   The ' muckle black de'il ' was often seen
waiting in the shadow at evening outside the cottage door,
or slipping away over the north side of the kirkyard wall.
The men who had been hunted on the moors by the
dragoons, like Wodrow, their historiographer, were always
agape for the wonderful, moving in an element of divine and
diabolic manifestations of power.   Ministers encouraged
such beliefs in their congregations.   Shepherd lads, out
alone long hours upon the hills, had strange and sometimes
beautiful fancies : Wodrow tells us in 1704 of one who
declared that ' when herding in such a lee, there was a bonny
man came to him, and bade him pray much and learn to
read ; and he supposed it was Christ.'   Next year he tells
us of another lad who was once drowning in a well, but
' a bonny young man pulled him out by the hand.   There
was nobody near by at the time, so they concluded it was
no doubt ane angel.'   This is an older Scotland, not the
Scotland of David Hume, Adam Smith or the Edinburgh
Reviewers, not even the Scotland of Burns and Sir Walter,
though it supplied them with matter for their argument.[141]

If even in the Lowlands primitive and natural conditions
bred primitive beliefs and natural fancies, it was even more
so in the Highlands, the very home of the fairies and spirits
of the mountain, of the formless monster that brooded
unseen in the deep water beneath the boat, of second-sight,

of omens and prophecy with which the little life of man was girt round.   Beyond the Highland line, seldom passed by the Lowlander, and never without those qualms which beset Bailie Nicol Jarvie on his famous expedition, lay the grim, unmapped, roadless mountains, the abode of the Celtic tribes, speaking another language ; wearing another dress ; living under a system of law and society a thousand years older than that of Southern Scotland ; obedient neither to Kirk nor Queen, but to their own chiefs, clans, customs and superstitions.   Till General Wade's work a generation later, there was no driving road through the Highlands.   Nature reigned, gloomy, splendid, unchallenged—as yet un-admired—and man squatted in corners of her domain.

Far less accurate knowledge was available in London or even in Edinburgh about the state of the Highlands than can now be bought across the counter of a bookshop con-cerning the remotest parts of Africa.   There was no tolerable book on the Highlands until Mr. Burt's letters of the following generation.*   A few pages at the beginning of Morer's account of Scotland told the English of Queen Anne's time almost all they cared to know about the unreclaimed northern end of the strange island they inhabited.   But those few paragraphs told much in little :

The Highlanders are not without considerable quantities of corn, yet have not enough to satisfie their numbers, and therefore yearly come down with their cattle, of which they have great plenty, and so traffick with the Low Landers for such proportions of oats and barly as their families or necessities call for. . . . Once or tweice a year great numbers of 'em get together and make a descent into the Low-Lands, where they plunder the inhabitants and so return back and dis-perse themselves.   And this they are apt to do in the profoundest peace, it being natural to 'em to delight in rapine.

Pladds are most in use with 'em.   They not only serve for cloaths by day, but as pallats or beds in the night, and for that reason in cam-paigns are not unuseful.   The Low-Landers add that being too often men of prey, by this means they cover their booty the better, and carry it off without the owner's knowledge.   These pladds are about seven

* Oddly enough there was a good book about the Islands (Lewis, etc.)—*Descrip-tion of Western Islands of Scotland*, by M. Martin, gent., 1703, London.   It was still the best book about the Islands in Dr. Johnson's day.

or eight yards long. They cover the whole body with 'em from the neck to the knees, excepting the right arm. Many of 'em have nothing under these garments besides wastcoats and shirts, which descend no lower than the knees, and they so gird the pladds about the middle as to give 'em the same length as the linen under 'em, and thereby supply the defect of drawers and breeches.

You shall seldom see 'em, though only taking the air, without sword and dirk, which is a short dagger. They carry muskets and other fire-arms ; and when they are on the defensive part, they depend much on the targes or targets, which are shields of that form which the Latines called by the name of *clypeus*, round and aequidistant from the center, and are made of the toughest wood they can get, lined within and covered without with skins, fenced with brass nails, and made so serviceable that no ordinary bullet, much less a sword can penetrate.*

What manner of life did the tribesman lead, unobserved at home, when he was not trading with the Lowlander or driving off his cattle ? It is a pathetic fallacy to suppose that the tribal land was the people's, and that they lived on it in rustic felicity, until the chiefs, in a sudden access of wickedness, took it from them after the 'forty-five. In fact, the crofter of Queen Anne's reign was fain to hire a patch of ground from the ' tacksman ' or leaseholder of the chief, who sublet it on rack-rent terms that were usually most oppressive. The soil on the mountain-side was thin and stony, denuded by torrents, unimproved by manure ; the agricultural implements and methods were more primitive than even in Southern Scotland ; the crofts were the merest hovels. It could not be otherwise, for the scanty population was yet too large for the glens to support. As the clansmen multiplied, the little farms were divided and subdivided with disastrous results. It might easily have

---

* *Morer*, pp. 5–11. I have left out sentences and words here and there, without altering the meaning. It will be noted that the kilt was sometimes of one piece with the plaid.

Defoe, writing to Harley from Edinburgh in November 1706 (*H.M.C. Portland* IV, p. 349) gives his Englishman's impression of the Highlanders : ' They are formidable fellows and I only wish Her Majesty had 25,000 of them in Spain, as a nation equally proud and barbarous like themselves. They are all gentlemen, will take affront from no man, and insolent to the last degree. But certainly the absurdity is ridiculous to see a man in his mountain habit, armed with a broadsword, target, pistol, at his girdle a dagger, and staff, walking down the High Street as upright and haughty as if he were a lord, and withal driving a cow ! '

been prophesied that if ever the Highlands were brought
into connection with the outer world by roads, or by military
and political conquest, a great emigration would result as
soon as the clansmen had grasped the idea that change
was possible in their mode of life. In Anne's reign there
was only a trickle of emigration into the Lowlands for the
rougher types of service, and to the Continent to join the
' Irish ' regiments in French pay, which owed much to
the Highland element in their ranks.

The chiefs had the power of life and death, and exercised
it to the full, keeping their clan in awe, that was always
strengthened by traditional loyalty and often by affection.
But it depended on the uncertain personal factor whether
a chief was a tyrant or a father, or something between the
two. Just as Louis XIV taxed his peasants to keep up his
army, so the chief moved about with a train of armed relations and attendants, whom he supported in idleness at the
expense of the rest of the clan ; but any more economical
and peaceful habit of life would not have been appreciated
by a race in whom personal and family pride was the
dominant passion.

Many of the chiefs, besides the great Argyle, were also
noblemen with a place in Scottish politics, and with something of the culture of France or of England. But always
the civilized chief and his uncivilized followers had much
in common—the pride of clan, the love of the harp and of
the pipes, the stories and songs, in which old feuds and
fancies were still being woven by tribal poets into a living
Gaelic literature. If in the shadow of the glen and beside
the hill-girt arms of the sea there was more of poverty and
savagery than in other parts of the island, there was also
more of poetry and wild imagination.[142]

It was for the chief to decide whether the clan should
be Jacobite or ' on a Revolution foot.' But history and
tradition had already settled that point in most cases. The
Campbells, under the House of Argyle, had been Presbyterian and Whig since the quarrel first began, and for that
reason many smaller tribes at feud with the predominant
Campbells had followed Montrose and Dundee, and would
take the Jacobite side in any future war. But there were

other tribes not definitely committed, who took very little interest in the politics of London or of Edinburgh. The Scottish Privy Council stationed a few troops in isolated posts like Fort William, and kept many of the chiefs in receipt of allowances from government. Otherwise Queen Anne relied in case of need on the loyalty of Argyle. Her writ did not run in the Highlands, where she was the suzerain, but not the direct ruler, of the clans.

Politics, religion and cattle-raiding were all connected with one another. A report to Harley, made in 1705, by a zealous Presbyterian, instructed him as follows about 'the Lennox,' 'contiguous to the Highlanders' :

> The most part of the gentry, being nullifidians, take up with any impression. The commonalty, being zealous Protestants, are obliged, especially in the winter season, to defend themselves against the ravaging of the Highlanders committing hardships, that's robbing all their cattle. Though they are not able to reduce the Highlanders, yet do they oppose any small body or party, our fraternity having planted Christian societies whereby Christianity flourishes in the very borders of these savages. . . . The West Highlands [Argyle's country] be generally civilized and tolerable, and much hated by the others for their respect to the gospel. It may be said of the Highlands and Islands as Eusebius of the Romans, 'God Almighty suffered the Goths and Vandals to ransack the Romans, because they were not more zealous in their conversion.'

This state of things aroused the zeal of the Church Assembly and of the Society for Promoting Christian Knowledge; from 1704 onwards many thousands of pounds were raised to initiate libraries, schools and Presbyterian missions in the Highlands, where religion was divided between Presbyterian, Roman Catholic, Episcopalian and primitive Pagan, in proportions which it would be difficult to determine. Some success was achieved at once, but in some places the mission was suppressed by violence at the orders of the chief, and in others it lapsed in the course of years. It was after the 'forty-five, when tribalism had been effectively put down by military and political invasion from the south, that the Presbyterian missionary had his chance, and the real evangelization of the Highlands took place.[143]

Such, in some sort, was Scotland, when the circumstances of the passing hour brought to a final issue the ever-recurring problem of the closer union of the whole island. In that design stark King Edward had failed, and Cromwell's arm had laxed its hold in death ; where force had been tried in vain, Queen Anne was to succeed by means more befitting her womanhood.

CHAPTER XII

Scottish Events leading towards the Union Treaty
1702–1705

Reign of William in Scotland. Darien and the Union. The 'Rump'
    Parliament of 1702. The first Union Commission, winter 1702–1703.
    New Parliament, 1703. The Act of Security. 'The Scotch Plot.'
    Fall of the Queensberry Ministry, March 1704. The '*Squadrone
    Volante*' Ministry and its failure. Act of Security receives royal assent,
    August 1704.

The reign of King William had been an era of economic
disaster and political strife for Scotland, but it had settled
her ecclesiastical policy on lines that proved permanent, and,
equally by its achievements and by its failures, it had revealed to thinking minds that political and economic advance
towards a happier future must lie through a closer Union
with England.

As a result of the Revolution, the General Assembly had
been restored, along with the Presbyterian system, of which
it was the coping-stone. But it had not been permitted to
reclaim those extravagant powers over the State which it had
usurped in the Covenanting days. Beside it now, at once as
friend and as rival, stood the Parliament of Three Estates,
for the first time really free from royal control, and able to
speak as the mouthpiece of the nation. In 1690 the Convention Parliament abolished the Lords of the Articles, the
Committee which had held previous Parliaments in bondage
to the Court and to the Privy Council. In the reigns of
William and of Anne the Edinburgh Parliament was, for
the first time in Scottish history, a body debating freely, introducing what measures it would, however unpleasant to
the Court of England or to the Privy Council of Edinburgh.
It closely imitated the precedents of the Westminster Parlia-

ment in its struggle with the Crown, adopting such English devices as the refusal of supply till grievances were redressed; yet the motive force behind all its proceedings was the championship of the country's cause against England.

This novel freedom of debate was exercised harshly and riotously but most effectively by men who, for all their differences on dynastic and religious issues, were agreed in a common devotion to the interest of Scotland. Parliament became, for the first time, the voice by which the country spoke with England on equal terms. In the bargaining that led to the Union Treaty, the Edinburgh Parliament sold its life dearly, obtaining in exchange the material welfare of the nation which it had, in the last eighteen years of its own existence, so strongly and not unworthily represented. Yet because it had so seldom, before the Revolution, stood out as the historic champion of Scotland, it was not, like its rival at Westminster, the object of affection enough to make the sacrifice of its independent existence utterly intolerable to the nation. If, down the ages, the Scots had loved their Parliament as the English loved theirs, the Union could never have been made.*

1689–
1707

But if in matters political and ecclesiastical William's reign had done great things for Scotland, on the economic side it had been one long disaster. On the top of an unprecedented succession of famine years had come the Darien catastrophe. Almost every man in the kingdom who had a few pounds Scots to invest had put them into the ' Company for trading with Africa and the Indies,' equally in the hope of gain and in the spirit of patriotism. The wild project, which the Company had fathered and which had become the passion of the whole people, was to plant a Scots colony on a spot that should command the trade of Atlantic and Pacific. The site chosen was on the Isthmus of Darien, in a pestiferous climate and in Spanish territory ! The merchants of England, jealous of any rival to their commerce, and her statesmen then in friendship

1698–
1700

* On the more general aspects of Scotland and the Union Treaty I would recommend the reader to three fascinating and authoritative books : *Thoughts on the Scottish Union,* by Dicey and Rait ; *The Union of England and Scotland,* by Hume Brown ; and *Scotland and the Union,* by William Law Mathieson.

with Spain, had resented and opposed the scheme. And
William had no choice but to follow the suit of his English
subjects and of his continental policies. The Scots, for all
their anger against England, did William the justice to
realize that he had been no free agent. But that perception
made them all the more hotly demand either a King who
should be wholly their own, or else a Union which should
identify Scotland's interest with that of England. The
accredited apologist of the Darien Company * wrote :

> To be so treated by such a Prince hath some thing cutting beyond
> expression, and proves our disasters are no way to be remedied, but
> either by a total separation or a total union of the two Kingdoms.

From this time forward a number of pamphlets in favour of
Union with England began to appear from the Edinburgh
press, some of them displaying a remarkable grasp of the
real points in the situation. If there was heat in Scotland in
those days, there was also beginning to be light.

William himself had learned, by harsh experience, how
impossible was the position of an unhappy mortal striving
to be the common King of two countries with rival Parliaments and opposed commercial policies. His predecessors
had kept the Scottish Parliament as antechamber to their
Privy Council. But he and his successors had to deal with
two independent Parliaments in deadly opposition to one
another. The situation could only be relieved by uniting
them in one. Such was his dying advice, and Queen Anne,
since she inherited his difficulties, was heir to his policy.
In the matter of the Union, as in the matter of the war with
France, her position as Queen aligned her with the Whigs
and moderate Tories, and divided her from her old friends
the High Churchmen, who disliked a Union which should
force England to guarantee the Presbyterian Establishment
in the north of the island. In the debates that took place on

---

* For brevity's sake I use the common term ' Darien Company ' to describe
the ' Company for trading with Africa and the Indies.' The ' Indies ' could be
either East or West ; in fact, the Company's trade, such as it was, both before and
after the great Darien aberration, was directed to the African coast and the East
Indian Ocean. See *Darien Shipping Papers*, 1696–1707 (*Scot. Hist. Soc.*, 1924),
and a narrative of the events, *The Company of Scotland* (Scribner, 1930), also by
Mr. G. P. Insh.

the subject in the two Houses at Westminster, while William lay dying, the Lords tentatively favoured the idea of a Union: even Nottingham declared that Scotland was ' a large gap for the Prince of Wales to enter at,' which might be stopped by a merger of the two Parliaments. ' The opposition,' wrote Marchmont, ' will come from the High Church party in the House of Commons.'

A few days later William died. ' Pity the Reformed Churches, whose bulwark is taken away,' wrote Wodrow, ' so excellent a Prince as he has been living and dying.' In spite of the disasters of his reign, he was deeply regretted by the great body of Presbyterians, the majority of the Scottish people. His memory was odious only to the Cameronian zealots for the broken Covenant, and to the formidable body of Episcopal and Jacobite opinion. Even such fierce patriotic orators as Lord Belhaven, in their railings against England and denunciations of William's policy of Union, spoke of him with affection as ' our Deliverer and Benefactor.' [144]

The accession of Queen Anne not only spread consternation among Presbyterians and Whigs, but aroused the eager hopes of Episcopalians and Jacobites. Surely so good a High Churchwoman would destroy William's new-fangled Presbyterian Establishment, which had only a dozen years of prescription behind it : surely this stricken mother, already rumoured to be repentant of her unnatural conduct at the Revolution, would pave the way for her brother's accession upon her own death. Was she not, moreover, under the influence of Marlborough and Godolphin, who never ceased to maintain sympathetic relations with various Jacobite agents ? Some of these ingenious gentlemen proposed in 1703 that one of Marlborough's daughters should marry the Pretender.

But Godolphin's real sentiments and Anne's real position, at least so long as the war with France should last, were expressed in a letter written by the Lord Treasurer of England to the Scottish Chancellor :

The Queen is Queen of Scotland upon the foot of the Revolution, and if that cannot be maintained for her, I doubt nothing will be

maintained by her there.   We are now in so critical a conjuncture
with respect to other nations that all Europe must in some measure be
affected by the good or ill ending of the Parliament of Scotland.

In time of war, the Pretender's Court was a pawn in the play
of the national enemy ; Versailles and St. Germains were
constantly plotting a Jacobite-French invasion of Scotland
to dethrone Anne in favour of her brother, at least in her
northern kingdom. If, therefore, she wished to wage war
in Europe undisturbed, she could not afford to break with
the Whigs and Presbyterians of Scotland, for they alone
could be trusted to take her side if the flag of rebellion were
raised in earnest. Jacobites would sometimes flatter her,
but they would never fight for her.[145]

And so, within three days of her accession, in her first
speech to the English Parliament, she expressed the desire
for a closer Union of her two kingdoms.* Such a Union
could not fail to guarantee the Presbyterian Establishment
in Scotland, ensure the accession of the House of Hanover
in the united island, and shatter all Jacobite hopes.

While the new Queen was making this significant utter-
ance in London, the nobles of the Scottish Opposition were
riding post to Court, to pay her their respects and to beg
her to dismiss William's Scottish Ministers and dissolve his
Whig Parliament. But when they reached London, they
found that their welcome had been forestalled by weightier
influence, although there had come at their head no less a
person than James Douglas, fourth Duke of Hamilton.[146]

Hamilton, best known to English readers from the im-
aginary figure that stands for him in Thackeray's *Esmond*,
carried the most important single weight in the nicely
balanced scales of Scottish politics. How he would shift it
from moment to moment was of great concern to all.
His equivocal policies and uncertain character, joined
to an immense hereditary position, made him, as the
leading opponent of the Union Treaty, the instrument,
under Heaven, of its almost miraculous passage. His fine
presence, proud demeanour and vigorous debating power
well qualified him to lead a party, if only he could have led

* *Blenheim*, pp. 202–203.

it straight. So noble was his almost royal person, so high was his prestige, that his followers, though they murmured at each fresh betrayal of their cause, had never the heart to renounce him in earnest.

In William's reign Hamilton had ably led the 'Country' party in opposition to the Whig Government. The Country party consisted for the most part of Presbyterians angry at being left out of office, and therefore the more free to resent the subjection of Scottish policy to English needs. It contained a few Jacobites also ; but not many avowed adherents of the exiled House retained their seats in the Convention Parliament that had carried through the Revolution and was still sitting in 1702.[147] The great body of the Jacobites regarded themselves as a separate party.

Was Hamilton himself in the interest of the Pretender ? The agents of that Prince thought so, for he was constantly conspiring with them to rebel, though never rebelling. He passed as a Jacobite of the first water with the Court of St. Germains. And the Court of Versailles supplied him with their own and the Pope's money to distribute among the members of the Scottish Parliament and confound the policies of the governments of William and of Anne.* Yet he was also the leader of the Country party—the national anti-English party it might have been called—which was chiefly Presbyterian. He formed the only strong link between the Country party and the Jacobites, yet, as will be seen, he failed them both over the matter of the Union, on one occasion after another.

What other motives, then, besides Jacobitism and patriotic jealousy of England were contending in his breast, behind the magnificent façade of his grand seigneurship ? First, the consideration of his large English estates, which

* There has been so much said about the government bribing members to vote for the Union that it is interesting to note that there was also bribery in the anti-government interest done by Hamilton with French and Papal money. I do not think that in either case bribery changed people's votes to any extent : it was common form at that period to do a certain amount of it to encourage a party. *Legrelle*, IV, p. 299, note (Louis XIV's letter to Tallard, March 24, 1701) ; *Macpherson*, I, p. 666 : 'large sums of money which he (Hamilton) laid out during the sitting of the last Parliament of Scotland' (1703) ; Head, *The Fallen Stuarts*, pp. 130–134, 339 ; *B.M. Add. MSS.* 20242, f. 23, 27 ; *C.S.P. Dom. Anne*, II, pp. vi, 54, confirms Hamilton's receipt of enemy money in July 1703.

might well be forfeited if, with his connivance, Scotland proclaimed a different King from England ; it was the same handicap which had cramped the patriotic style of Bruces and Balliols four centuries back. On the other hand, it was whispered that, if both Hanover and James Stuart were excluded, Hamilton might himself sit on the throne of Scotland, as the Protestant nearest akin to the Royal Line. When Jacobite agents grew weary of his hesitation to draw sword for their master, they suspected him of such thoughts. And the Court of Versailles had dealings with him which were on this account kept secret from the Court of St. Germains. He and others were cautious not to breathe aloud these dangerous ambitions, equally offensive to the partisans of the Houses of Hanover and Stuart. But the thought that he might some day reign at Holyrood could seldom have been far from his mind, confusing his more avowable motives of action, and blending with the natural weakness of his character to produce the paralysis that always seemed to beset him whenever the moment came to strike for the King over the Water.[148]

Hamilton's chief rival, not for the crown but for the government of Scotland, was the Duke of Queensberry, another James Douglas, more courteous and ingratiating,* but of far stronger character and more defined political purposes. He had always stood staunchly ' on the Revolution foot.' If no very pronounced Presbyterian, he was a decided Whig. Jacobites called him the ' proto-rebel.' But he was a man of moderation, of ways and means, ready to make alliances where he could find them, provided he never lost sight of his ultimate goal. He was ready to consider toleration for the Episcopalians, but not as a step towards the overthrow of the Presbyterian Establishment. On occasions when the Presbyterians opposed him, he was capable of walking a few Parliamentary yards arm in arm with the moderate Jacobites, so long as they did not lead him out of his path. But, for all that, he was the strongest statesman in Scotland, and had saved the country as King William's Commissioner during the Darien crisis. Though he made more

---

* At the end of William's reign it was said that ' the Duke of Queensberry had never injured or offended any man in his administration.' *Carstares Letters*, p. 515.

than one serious mistake in the first years of Anne, Queens-berry's qualities enabled him in the end to be the chief architect of the Union. He had a reputation for avarice, and, as the world then went, for honesty. In the perpetual motion of Scottish intrigue, plot and counterplot, with parties per-petually shifting their ground and merging their existence in one another like pieces in a kaleidoscope, a less supple trader would have been a less effective statesman.

John Campbell, second Duke of Argyle, was not supple, yet his downright force had its uses, when allied with Queensberry's art. Argyle was the head of the less com-promising of the Whigs and Presbyterians ; he was as out-spoken in his words to Queen and colleagues as befitted the great Chief and the gallant soldier that he was.*

The third of the Triumvirate of Scottish nobles who in the end carried the Union through the Edinburgh Parlia-ment was the Earl of Seafield. He frankly offered himself to each successive government as the useful man, serving the public faithfully with his best abilities, but without party prejudice or allegiance. Always unaffected by the waves of other men's passion, he was unpopular be-cause he had not been the dupe of the patriotic infatuation over Darien. So cool a head was a useful ally for any government.

In the first weeks of the reign Anne and Godolphin were as yet too busy with England and Europe to attend much

March
1702

to Scotland. Partly for that reason they rejected the advances of Hamilton's deputation, continued William's Ministers in office, and took the advice of Queensberry. His first advice to them, not to dissolve the existing Parliament, was his first mistake.

There was no Triennial Act for Scotland. The Convention Parliament, which had bestowed the crown on William and Mary, was still in being when the King died. The circumstances of its origin and the lapse of years rendered it unrepresentative of actual opinion. The Jacobites had from the first denied that it was a legal assembly ; and even the Presbyterians held that, with a new

* See pp. 113–114, 127–128, above.

reign, a new Parliament was due, probably in law, certainly in justice. At best the old Parliament would have no moral authority to pass the Union. If it met again, it could do nothing but make itself more unpopular. A General Election was inevitable in the near future, yet Queensberry shrank from it as likely to give the Country Party, if not the Jacobites themselves, the power to overturn his government. He weakly tried to postpone the Election, and to make an unfair use of the existing Parliament, thereby enraging opinion against himself, and for the time drawing closer the union of the Country Party with the Jacobites, under the joint leadership of his enemy Hamilton.

As the law stood, framed in 1696 after the assassination plot against William, the old Parliament might be summoned within twenty days of his death, but it should then sit for no more than six months and should transact only such business as was necessary to secure the succession of Anne. In actuality it was found inconvenient, owing to the long distances, to bring together the notables of all Scotland within twenty days of the Queen's accession, nor was there any need to do so because the Privy Council sitting at Edinburgh took the necessary measures to secure her unchallenged authority.

March
1702

Was it, then, either lawful or expedient to summon this moribund Parliament after the twenty days had elapsed, to transact ordinary business ? Anne asked the opinion of the Privy Councillors at Edinburgh ; they took a division, and replied by a majority in the affirmative.

So the old Parliament met again on June 9, 1702, ninety instead of twenty days after the King's death. It was regarded as an illegal assembly by all Jacobites, and by all those Presbyterians who were not connected with the government of the hour. It seemed to patriots a further insult that Scotland's war with France had been proclaimed by the Privy Council on orders sent down from London, just ten days before the belated meeting of Parliament. The question of peace and war was not, it seemed, to be discussed by Scots tongues, but was to be settled at St. James's by Queensberry and Godolphin.[149]

As soon as the Nobles, Barons and Burgesses had taken

their seats in the hall, before the Parliament was constituted,
Hamilton rose in his place, and, putting down the
attempted interruption of the Chancellor, read a
formal protest against the meeting as illegal, 'with
a slow determined voice and high air, and immediately left
the house, attended by eighty peers and commoners.'
They marched out of the hall in a body 'with a solemn pace'
in the order of their rank, the magnificent Duke at their
head. Outside in High Street half Edinburgh was
waiting to cheer them. So accompanied they marched
on to the Cross Keys tavern, and swore themselves in at
a banquet as a band of brothers united against unlawful
tyranny. Queen Anne's government had made a bad start
in Scotland.[150]

June 9 1702

Some hundred and twenty members, inevitably nicknamed 'the Rump,' remained to conduct the business of
Parliament. They were said to be 'all one man's bairns,'
that is all governmental Whigs. They passed a number of
partisan resolutions of no great consequence, and voted
taxes of which only a fraction could be levied, and that by
constraint, in face of very common refusal to regard the
Rump as a legal Parliament. Yet, however much challenged
and despised, this assembly laid down the line of high
national policy which its legitimate successor was fain in
the end to follow. An Act was passed enabling Queen
Anne to appoint Commissioners to treat with England for
a Union, on the condition that Presbyterian government
of the Scottish Church was regarded as axiomatic, and that
the terms agreed on by the Commissioners should be
referred back for approval or rejection by the Parliaments of
the two Kingdoms.[151]

It was natural for a Parliament of Whigs to vote for the
Union. It is more remarkable that the same assembly
refused, until England had come to terms with Scotland, to
do anything to gratify the English by settling the Protestant succession. All true Scots, Presbyterian no less
than Jacobite, knew that the only method by which they
could bring pressure on their purse-proud neighbours and
extort leave to trade with England's colonies, was to keep the
succession to the Scottish Crown an open question. Both

Unionists and Separatists were agreed upon that. Moreover they deeply resented the fact that the Act of Settlement
of 1701, which had named the House of Hanover as heir
to the throne of England, had been passed without any
pretence of considering or consulting Scottish opinion.   It
was at once the instinct and the interest of outraged Scotland
to refuse to follow the suit of the Act of Settlement until her
grievances and claims had received fair dealing from the
predominant partner.*

And so, when the Chancellor, Lord Marchmont, rashly
introduced in the Rump Parliament an Act for Abjuration of
the Pretender like that recently passed in England,†
June 27 he obtained for its first reading only a bare majority
1702   of 57 votes to 53, even in that select assemblage of
governmental Whigs.   His ministerial colleagues compelled
him to let the measure drop, and Queensberry publicly
rebuked him in the speech he made a few days later ad-
journing the session.

Thus the last act of the famous Convention Parliament,
which had made the Revolution Settlement, was to initiate
negotiations for a Union, and meanwhile to refuse to do
anything to relieve the wholesome fears of the Englishry
anent the succession to the Crown.   For all their rage and
faction, the Scots politicians of that era were not wanting
either in shrewdness or in patriotism.[152]

In the winter months of 1702–3 the Commissioners,
appointed by Queen Anne for England and Scotland
respectively in accordance with the powers accorded to her
by her two Parliaments, duly met at the Cockpit in Whitehall to draw up a scheme of Union.   They sat repeatedly
through November, December and January, and the extent
and character of their agreement was remarkable.   The

---

* Wodrow, the most sturdy of Presbyterians, wrote when he heard of the
English Act of Settlement : ' It seems now to be the time to secure our religion and
liberties, before we declare also.   We never had such a nick since the Revolution.
The Lord put it in the hearts of our representatives to see to this, and our trade and
personal security, and the continuance of our Church Government, if a Prince of
such loose principles as the German Protestants are, come to succeed to our Crown.'
Wodrow Anal., I, p. 5.

† *Blenheim*, pp. 158–161.

Scots Commissioners at once accepted the Hanoverian Succession and the merger of the two Parliaments.   But the condition on which they insisted—complete Free Trade for Scotland not only with England but with her Colonies— was resisted by the English Commissioners over a number of sittings.   Then suddenly, at the turn of the year, they capitulated on this all-important point, since the Scots would proceed no further on any less terms.

But in making this surrender the English negotiators outran the opinion of the jealous mercantile interest. Moreover the trend of Anne's policy was becoming more Tory than it had been in the first months of her reign, and a strong Church reaction was blowing up in England. The enemies of the occasional Conformists were not willing to guarantee the Presbyterian Church in Scotland.*   In the winter of 1702 a new English Parliament was sitting, very much more Tory than that which had sat in the spring, and which would probably have passed the Union outright. Without any explicit repudiation of the concessions to which they had agreed, the English Commissioners gave sign of their growing embarrassment and waning enthusiasm, by their failure, again and again repeated, to appear in numbers sufficient to form a quorum.   Finally the Queen adjourned the meetings of the Commission till October—that is till the Greek Calends.   In her speech of adjournment she commented truly enough on 'the great progress you have already made, beyond what has been done in any former treaties.'

Feb. 3
1703

The work of the Commission had been cut short by forces outside itself—the Tory reaction in England and the anti-English reaction in Scotland, both of which found expression in elections to new Parliaments.   A treaty of Union, that seemed so near in the first months of the reign, was rendered impossible until three more years of evergrowing discord between the two countries showed them both that they must either come to blows at once, or else

---

* At the private meetings of the English Commissioners, the Archbishop of York argued that Episcopacy ought to be restored in Scotland under the Union, though Nottingham hesitated and Rochester said it was impossible to suggest it in the negotiations. *Jerviswood*, p. 11.

unite on the terms adumbrated by the abortive but by no means useless negotiation of 1702.[153]

While the Commissioners were winding up their unfinished work, the General Election in Scotland produced her new Parliament, destined to be the last that ever sat. Yet the Election itself seemed at the time to be the death-blow to the Union policy. The spirit of the nation had been roused against Ministers who had truckled to England and flouted Scottish opinion by holding the illegal session of the Rump Parliament. Government made the usual efforts, by the proffer of places and patronage, to influence the small body of gentlemen and burghers who formed the electorate, but on this occasion to very little purpose. The supporters of the government were placed in a decided minority. There was an element that had been absent from the later sessions of William's Parliament— a small body of avowed Jacobites, rechristened ' Cavaliers ' to denote their conditional loyalty to Queen Anne, side by side with their less doubtful devotion to her brother.

But the strongest section was the Country Party, sent back to champion the wrongs of Scotland against the pride of England, but not less emphatically commissioned to defend the Presbyterian Establishment against either Jacobite or English encroachment. The rumour that such an attack would be made on the Kirk by the new Tory governors of England had helped to make the Scottish Ministry unpopular and had caused the Presbyterians to put out their best effort for the Country ¶Party at the elections.

The government, therefore, had no majority to gratify the desires of English statesmen, either on the one hand to help the Episcopalians, or on the other hand to settle the Hanoverian Succession. England was too Whig in politics and too Tory in religion to suit Scottish popular sentiment. The Union seemed further off than ever in the anti-English atmosphere of the newly-elected chamber. Yet if in the course of events it should appear that the ' Protestant interest ' could only be secured by Union with England, it was by no means certain that this same Parliament

Spring 1703

might not, however reluctantly, sacrifice some of its national pride to its Protestant principles.

The position of the Scottish government, in face of this new and more nationalist Parliament, was most unpleasant. Before the Revolution, the Edinburgh Privy Council had simply taken its orders from England, while Parliament was dumb in obedience. Since the Revolution, Parliament was suspicious, enquiring, hostile to English interference, and in 1703 it promised to be more recalcitrant than ever. Yet even now any Scottish government would have to keep in close touch with English Ministers, because in the last resort it must rely on the English power to keep down Highland tribes and Lowland Jacobites. Scotland was so torn by faction that true self-government was impossible for her. Yet the nation, Presbyterian and Jacobite alike, ardently aspired after self-government, and writhed under the sense of English dictation.

Between the elections and the meeting of the new Parliament in May, the Queen completed the process she had begun before Christmas, of reconstructing her Scottish Ministry, infusing into it an element of the Tory, which in North Britain meant Jacobite. The stricter Whigs were turned out, including Marchmont, the tactless champion of the Abjuration Act. His place as Chancellor was taken by the adaptable Seafield. Atholl also took office as Privy Seal. He and Seafield helped Queensberry, the Queen's Commissioner in Scotland, in the delicate business of negotiating for ' Cavalier ' support in the new Parliament. The Queen issued a proclamation allowing Jacobite exiles to return to Scotland, and back they came from the countries at war with England, with plots enough in their pockets. There was even talk of a Toleration Act for Episcopalians, which caused the Edinburgh mob to riot, and the Presbyterians of the Country Party to denounce the Government for seeking ' to establish iniquity by a law.' 154

March 1703

Such was the strange confusion of parties and purposes when the last Parliament of Scotland met, ushered in by the time-honoured ceremony of the ' riding ' of a new Parliament. First each nobleman in his robes, then the Barons

and the Burgesses, each member escorted by a troop of
retainers proportioned to his dignity, rode in
May   solemn order from Holyrood to the Parliament
1703   House ' through a lane of citizens in arms,' a sight
often seen by wondering Edinburgh in ages gone by, but
never to be seen again.

The bargain between the Queen's Ministers and the
Jacobites facilitated the dispatch of the first business, and
the question of the illegality of the Rump was not pressed
by the Duke of Hamilton.   But such was the strength of
Presbyterian feeling in the new Parliament and in the
country that the promised Toleration Act had very soon to
be abandoned.   The alliance between Government and the
' Cavaliers ' proved powerless and came to an end.   The
men of the Country Party dominated the session and the
Jacobites passed over into alliance with them, under
Hamilton as the common chief of all the Opposition
groups.

Queensberry's Ministry, rent by political and personal
divisions within its own body, was left without a majority in
the Estates.   The victorious Opposition took the legislative
lead, and proceeded to vindicate the independence of
Scotland by compelling Ministers and their Mistress in
London to accept legislation they had not desired.   Instead
of the Toleration Act for Episcopalians which Ministers
had contemplated, an Act for securing the true Protestant
Religion and Presbyterian Government was placed on the
Statute Book.   Anne was also compelled to sanction an
Act anent Peace and War, which took away from her
successors, whoever they might be, the power of declaring
war without consent of Parliament.   Godolphin was horri-
fied at the passage of the measure, indicating as it did that
the Scots contemplated the possibility of being at peace
with England's enemies : he wrote to Atholl and Seafield
that it was another strong argument for the necessity of a
Union of the Parliaments.   Godolphin, who was in fact
Anne's Minister for Great Britain, was being driven by
experience to realize the utter necessity of a Union.[155]

This astonishing Parliament of 1703–1707, which
began by defying England and ended by passing the Union,

was no packed assembly sitting in awe of Ministers like the
Parliaments before the Revolution.   It was, from first to
last, singularly free and even licentious in debate.   ' The
factions rubbed upon one another with great severity,'
wrote Clerk of Penicuik, ' so that we were often in form of
a Polish Diet, with our swords in our hands, or at least our
hands at our swords.'   However strangely it had been
chosen according to our modern notions of mathematical
representation, it did, unlike its predecessor, represent all
the parties and interests in Scotland.   The governmental
Whigs were held in awe by the jealous patriotism of the
Presbyterian phalanx.   And there, too, observed and
courted by all, sat Scotland's Cato, the Republican Fletcher
of Saltoun, side by side with Jacobite Lords who received
letters from the Court of Versailles giving advices for their
conduct in Parliament, and promising military aid as soon
as the success of the French in Bavaria ' will put them into
condition of bringing the Dutch to terms and of assisting
Scotland.' [156]

In this heated atmosphere of intrigue and very free
debate, the famous Act of Security,* to preserve the country's
liberties from English aggression, was built up clause by
clause in the summer months of 1703.   It was the work,
not of the Ministers who wished to stand well with England,
but of the Opposition who wished to defy her.

The object of English statesmen, Tory as well as Whig,
and especially of Godolphin, was to induce the Scots to
accept the Hanoverian Succession.   Queen Anne's health
was bad ; she might die before the war was won, and a disputed succession in Scotland might lay all Europe and
England at the feet of Louis.   Before Ramillies, still more
before Blenheim, this fear amounted to an agony in England.
But England's necessity was Scotland's opportunity.   So
the Act of Security calmly provided that when Queen Anne
should die, the Scots Parliament should meet to choose her
successor, who was to be of the Royal Line and a Protestant,
but who should not be the same person as the English successor, unless England had previously satisfied Scotland as

* In the Scots Parliament a measure while still before Parliament was called an
Act, not a Bill, as in England.

to her conditions of government, and conceded ' a free communication of trade, freedom of navigation and the liberty
of the plantations.' *   The Jacobites rejoiced in the Act as
a nail driven into the coffin of the Hanoverian Succession.
The 'different successor' would assuredly be James Stuart if
the lad would turn Protestant, and might well be he in any
case if confusion enough were caused by the fact of a vacant
throne.   Hamilton, indeed, must have envisaged another
possible interpretation of the 'different successor' who should
be a Protestant and of the Royal Line.   The Act seemed
to open a path towards that veiled summit of his own ambition.

But to Fletcher of Saltoun, the austere and single-minded
bigot of patriotism, even the Act of Security seemed insufficient to vindicate the liberties of Scotland from English
thraldom.   He urged the Estates to seize their opportunity
and extort from the Queen a Parliamentary Constitution of
an almost republican type.   Such was his famous scheme of
' Limitations ' of the power of the Crown.   It could be
added to the Act of Security, or substituted for it, he scarcely
cared which.   Fletcher's Limitations would have taken
from the Crown and given to Parliament, after Anne's death,
the power of distributing ' all places and offices, both civil
and military, and all pensions formerly conferred by our
Kings, . . . so long as we shall have the same King with
England.'   The Prerogative was to be annihilated, because
it was the instrument of English domination.   If the Queen
refused to sanction this change, then indeed Fletcher saw
no alternative but to pass the Act of Security, and ' separate
our Crown from England.'

Fletcher's scheme of Limitations was fully debated by
Parliament, but was rejected by a majority of thirty-two.
Ministerialists were of course against it.   Jacobites
had no wish to pare down the Royal Prerogative for
the benefit of the Estates, especially as there might
in the near future be a Parliament as Presbyterian as the
present one, and a King—not so Presbyterian !   Moreover the average member, though neither Ministerialist nor

July 7
1703

---

* The words in inverted commas are in the Act as passed by the Scots Parliament
in 1703, but not in the Act as it received the Royal Assent in 1704.   *Acts Parl.
Scot.*, pp. 70, 137.

Jacobite, was uneasily aware that the assembly in which he sat was too like a ' Polish Diet ' to be safely entrusted with the executive power. Who, save one so ardent as Fletcher, could expect such a body to preserve peace and order in the distracted land, of whose distractions Parliament was itself the epitome ?

The first session therefore ended, in September 1703, with Fletcher's Limitations rejected and with the Act of Security passed through the Estates, but not yet given effect as law by the touch of the reluctant sceptre. Queensberry was so much afraid of his countrymen's humour as to advise Queen Anne to pass the Act of Security, for which a remedy could be found before it came into operation on her death : but Godolphin and Nottingham dared not yet, as English statesmen, permit her to take that course.[157]

Between the first and second sessions of the new Parliament, a sensational incident, known in England as ' the Scotch Plot ' and in Scotland as ' the Queensberry Plot,' broke up the Ministry, recast the combinations of groups and parties in the Edinburgh Parliament, and increased the anger against England.

The indemnity issued by Government in the spring of 1703, permitting Jacobite exiles to return to Scotland, had swelled to a flood the usual flow of conspirators from France.[158] Besides others of more honestly treasonable purpose, came a Highland Chief named Simon Fraser, Lord Lovat. He had suffered confiscation and outlawry for his rape of Atholl's sister, and he was prepared to do anything, however base, to obtain restitution of his estates, or even cash in hand. He was ready to be in the pay of the Government or of the Jacobites or of both at once, and he had small scruple about fabricating evidence. Moreover not much fabrication was necessary in order to accuse half the statesmen of Scotland, with too much truth, of dealings with the exiled Court. Early in 1702 Fraser had offered his services to Anne's government in vain.[159] He had then gone to France, turned Roman Catholic, and insinuated himself into the counsels of St. Germains and Versailles by his plausible manners and by his promise to produce 16,000 Highlanders in arms.* The Duke of Berwick, the best man in the Pretender's circle and the best Englishman in the French service, disliked the smell of Fraser from the first, and moreover as a soldier doubted the value of a Highland rising. Remembering the stories of Montrose and Dundee, he asked Fraser a number of leading questions, among others :

> If the men furnished will remain constantly with the King's general so that he need not apprehend having one day an army and the next day none.[160]

But the French were in a hopeful mood, for Blenheim had not yet been fought, and Marlborough was ensuring his head with high-sounding promises to the Jacobite agents, which he could never be compelled to perform.[161] Fraser was sent to Scotland with strong credentials. Among other documents he carried a letter from James II's widow, Mary of Modena, written to a Scottish nobleman unnamed ; on this missive Fraser took upon himself to write the address of John Murray, first Duke of Atholl, his own private foe and Queensberry's rival in the Ministry. The note, thus essentially falsified, he carried to Queensberry. It proved an apple of discord indeed.

The Queen's Commissioner fell straight into the trap, the more readily as Fraser was prepared to bring evidence, some of which was true enough, against Hamilton and other of Queensberry's rivals within the Ministry and without. He took the informer into his pay and protection, and sent him on to the Highlands to collect further evidence, still in the disguise of a Jacobite agent. Meanwhile the accusations against Atholl were placed before the Queen.

This step effectively broke up the Scottish Ministry and isolated Queensberry for a while from almost every politician in Scotland. In particular it drove Atholl into the arms of the Jacobites and made him a chief leader of resistance to the Union in the coming years. Though the head of a clan and family with strong Jacobite leanings, Atholl had done William good service ; being a prudent man, he

---

* The numbers of Highlanders (in buckram) vary from document to document, generally in proportion to the desperation of the writer's circumstances.

had his correspondence with St. Germains like any other nobleman, but hitherto it had been only of the nature of insurance against possible events. In the summer of 1703 Atholl was a loyal subject of Anne, in close alliance with her minister, Godolphin, and was hoping, through that influence, to marry his son Tullibardine to one of Marlborough's younger daughters, especially, so he declared, because 'their other daughters prove such good wives.' But by Christmas all was changed ; under the spur of the accusations of Queensberry and Fraser, Atholl flew into violent Jacobite opposition to Queen Anne's government. Yet it is to be noted that in the civil war of 1715 he took the side of the House of Hanover.[162]

Fraser's little game had been revealed too soon for success. That veteran of the political underworld, Ferguson the Plotter, discovered his connection with Queensberry and gave timely warning to Atholl, Hamilton, and the other accused. Their outcries of injured innocence filled the political world during the winter and spring that preceded Blenheim. England and Scotland were both agitated, but by very different feelings. The Scots were furious with Queensberry for conspiring with Fraser to destroy his colleagues and rivals. The English were incensed to hear that, at the most dangerous moment of the European war, a Jacobite plot had been discovered in Scotland and treated there with culpable indifference. As the Whigs suspected Nottingham of stifling the plot in order to save Atholl,* the House of Lords determined to probe the matter to the bottom and instituted an enquiry of their own, concurrent with the enquiry held by Her Majesty's servants. The Tory House of Commons protested against this procedure as an insult to the throne ; but instead of asking for a conference with the Upper House on the constitutional point, they addressed the Queen directly against the Peers. The question became yet another bone of contention between the two Houses.

---

* It is quite possible there was hushing up. William III used constantly to hush up these periodic revelations against his servants, a recurrent nuisance in the political world, because they were so often true. One of the witnesses in the Scottish Plot, Maclean, is said to have revealed the open secret that Marlborough and Godolphin had their Jacobite correspondents. *Leadam*, pp. 39-40.

The Lords, who had English popular feeling with them against the Jacobites, appealed to the man in the street by the publication of their case, ably stated by Somers. They also passed a resolution

that there had been dangerous plots between some in Scotland and the Courts of France and St. Germains, and that the encouragement of this plotting came from the not settling the succession of the Crown of Scotland in the House of Hanover.

The whole procedure of the Lords, and these words in particular, aroused hot indignation north of the Tweed, as displaying the intention of the English Parliament to manage the affairs of Scotland.[163]

Meanwhile Fraser, leaving Britain in the uproar he had aroused, had the effrontery to return to France, and report to Louis XIV that he had prepared a rising of 20,000 Highlanders under Breadalbane, and had refused great rewards offered him if he had consented to enter the service of Queensberry and Queen Anne. But he had trod on too many Jacobite toes, and found himself, for too short a while, in the French prison he so richly deserved.[164]

In the early months of 1704, as a result of Fraser's plot, Queensberry had become so unpopular with his countrymen and his colleagues that he could no longer govern Scotland. Anne and Godolphin, therefore, dismissed him and

March 1704

his party from office, and put in their place the chiefs of the Presbyterian Opposition, or Country Party—the Marquess of Tweeddale, the Earls of Rothes and Roxburgh, and James Johnstone. They brought with them their group of some two dozen members of Parliament, most of them Nobles, who acted together as independent Whigs, and became known about this time as the New Party, or *Squadrone Volante* (Flying Squadron). They now, for a while, undertook the heavy burden of government. Their chief, Tweeddale, was described by the Jacobites as 'a well meaning but simple man,' and by the Whigs as 'a very good man, but not perfectly qualified for Court intrigues,' at which indeed he proved no match for Queensberry.[165]

The *Squadrone* had, in the first instance, come up to London to represent the Country Party and the Jacobites against the Queensberry interest. But finding the Queensberry Ministry tottering to its fall, they had thrown over the Jacobite alliance to qualify themselves for office. They lightly promised Godolphin that they would pass through the Edinburgh Parliament, at its next session, the much desired settlement of the Scottish Crown on the House of Hanover, provided the Queen would agree to certain limitations on the powers of her successors. On these terms they obtained office. Thus were Scottish Ministries, as Fletcher bitterly complained, made and unmade by bargains struck with English statesmen in London.[166]

But the *Squadrone Volante* had promised Godolphin more than they could perform. They had not reckoned with the depth of Scottish popular feeling against England, which they had themselves been so recently exploiting. They underrated the resentment of the deceived Jacobites. And above all they forgot Queensberry. It was in his power to revenge himself on those who had supplanted him, provided he was willing to shift his political principles as readily as they had shifted theirs. To that he had no objection, for he knew how to tack in order to hold his course. Since the chiefs of the Country Party had turned ' English ' to reach office, Queensberry would turn ' patriot ' to lead the opposition. Again he struck a bargain with the Jacobites. It was agreed that if in the next session Hamilton and Atholl would not raise the question of his recent conduct over the Plot, he would join them in preventing the settlement of the Crown on the House of Hanover. And so, when Parliament met in the summer of 1704, the rather inexperienced noblemen who had undertaken to govern Scotland for Godolphin, found themselves in a minority and as much embarrassed as their predecessors last year.* Indeed the

---

* At the end of the session James Johnstone, perhaps the ablest man in that not very able Ministry, wrote to Godolphin : ' I told my Lord Marlborough that I would rather go and attack the lines with him than do what I have done, and yet I knew not half of my work.' Hume Brown, *Union*, p. 182.

session of 1704 was even worse for government than the session of 1703. The Jacobites put it about that the Queen did not really wish the succession to be settled on Hanover, whatever her Ministers might pretend. Hamilton and Queensberry combined their forces, and the Act of Security was again sent up for the royal assent ; and on this occasion, till it was passed, supply was positively refused.

In the first week of August 1704 Godolphin and his royal mistress were in deep waters. Ministers had no majority of their own either in the English or the Scottish Parliament. Marlborough's campaign on the Danube, after the initial success at the Schellenberg, had failed to bring the Elector of Bavaria to his knees, and the evacuation of his territories seemed to be imposed upon the Allies by the superior forces of Tallard.* While Europe appeared the destined prey of French ambition, Scotland was fast drifting out of English control. Faced with the heavy tasks of government, the politicians of the *Squadrone Volante* had proved as light weights as their name implied. Tweeddale had failed to deliver the goods. And Queensberry, ranging for revenge, was bent on recovering his lost popularity in Scotland by forcing down the throat of England the un-palatable Act of Security. If the Queen still withheld her consent to that measure, no taxes would be voted, the little Scottish army of 3,000 men would disband for want of pay, and the north of the island would become the scene of anarchy and rebellion, at the very moment that Marl-borough's failure in Germany became disastrously patent to the world. Seafield, who was still in the Ministry, warned Godolphin that invasion and insurrection were expected that autumn and that Government had not means to resist.

For these reasons, Godolphin, frightened by the dark-ness before the dawn, advised the Queen to yield to the pressure of her Scottish subjects. On his advice she gave her consent to the Act of Security upon August 5 Aug. $\frac{5}{16}$ (Old Style). She did not know that, three days 1704 before, her troops had conquered at Blenheim. While she was signing the Act with a heavy heart, Colonel Parke was already half way home with the good news.

* *Blenheim*, pp. 371–372.

When he arrived he was too late to affect the issue. If, on August 5, the Queen had known of the battle, she would never have signed the Act of Security, and the whole course of Scottish history would have been different.

Chance had so directed that a great step had been taken. To what end that step would ultimately lead was still uncertain. The Act of Security purported to provide for the Separation of the Crowns. But, it might lead instead to the Union of the Parliaments, since Godolphin's surrender tended towards the solacing of Scotland's pride and the softening of her opinion towards England. Moreover the presence of the Act of Security in the Statute Book forced the English to take Scotland's wishes seriously. England must now choose, once for all, between the perpetual hostility of a revived Northern Kingdom, or such full reciprocity of trade as would render the complete Union of the two countries possible. Would England choose foolishly or well ? [167]

CHAPTER XIII

The Framing of the Union Treaty, 1705–1706

Consequences of the Act of Security in England.   The Alien Act.   Scotland
  in arms.   Captain Green's tragedy.   The Argyle-Queensberry Ministry.
  The Scottish Parliament consents to treat.   The Commissioners at work.
  The Treaty of Union framed.

The problem presented to England by the passage of the
Scottish Act of Security into law was the other great issue
of the winter session of 1704–1705 at Westminster, besides
the famous 'tack' of the Occasional Conformity Bill.*
Both issues were treated by the High Tories as means of
revenging themselves on Marlborough and Godolphin, and
overthrowing the Ministry, regardless of the consequences
to Britain and Europe.   And on both issues the Whigs
saved the Moderate Tory Ministry, on the understanding
that they should presently have their reward by admission
into the circles of government.

It was during this winter session following Blenheim,
the last of the old Parliament, that Godolphin and Harley
combined with Somers, Halifax and Wharton to prescribe
a wise and careful treatment for the fever of Scottish
nationalism, in the hope of reaching a solution of the British
question by consent of the two nations.   Meanwhile the
High Tories under Nottingham, Rochester and Haversham
embraced the opportunity of inflaming English opinion
against the recalcitrant Scots.   Fortunately the drift of
English politics in these middle years of Anne's reign was
against the High Tory party, and the Queen herself was
opposed to the rash counsels of her former friends.   The
years 1705–1706 were therefore more favourable, as far as

* See p. 14 above.

England was concerned, to the difficult negotiation of a Treaty of Union, than either the beginning or the end of her reign.

Early in December, the High Tory attack was opened against Godolphin as the evil counsellor who had advised the Queen to sign the Act of Security.   Since it was confidently expected that the Whigs would join in the denunciation of a measure adverse to the Hanoverian Succession in Scotland, the Ministry was in grave peril.   As was usual in those days, the chief debate took place in the Lords, where sat the great political chiefs whose decisions on party tactics gave the cue to their underlings in the faithful Commons.   The Queen, knowing that her servant Godolphin was in danger, came down to the Lords to give him countenance, sitting ' at first on the throne, and after (it being cold) on a bench by the fire.' [168]

Dec.
1704

Lord Haversham led off the debate with an attack on Ministers for betraying the interests of England and the Hanoverian Succession.   No one ventured to defend the Act of Security, not even Godolphin himself, who pleaded that he had advised its acceptance only to prevent the worse evil of an immediate revolt in Scotland.   Since Blenheim had created a new atmosphere of confidence in England, such excuses appeared more timorous and foolish than they actually were.   Godolphin was clearly embarrassed and spoke badly.   But he spoke sense, pointing out that ' the hurt the Act could do was contingent and might be prevented.'   Bishop Burnet, by birth and upbringing a Scot, uttered healing words.   But what line would be taken by the Lords of the Whig Junto, in whose hands the fate of the Ministry lay ?   Halifax, who spoke for them first, made a damaging attack on Godolphin.   If such was to be the final attitude of the Whigs, the Government was lost, and with it all hope of reconciliation between Scotland and England.   But while Halifax was still on his feet, Wharton crossed over to the Government bench and was seen to ' discourse very seriously ' with Godolphin.   Those who watched the scene presumed that he was offering the Whig alliance to the distressed Minister upon terms.   At least, after that whispered colloquy, the Whigs 'diverted the whole debate.' In the latter part of the discussion, which lasted for several days, the line taken by Somers and Wharton was eminently prudent. They recommended that the defiance flung down by the Scots should be taken up, but not in a spirit of exasperation. An offer to negotiate should be held out together with measures of provisional retaliation on Scotland's commerce, to remind her feelingly that if she chose to become a separate kingdom she would have to face the very unpleasant consequences of such isolation.

This shrewd policy, emanating in the first instance from the Whig leaders, was accepted by Government and embodied in a measure known as the Alien Act. Though very ill received by the Scots, it eventually led them towards the Union Treaty, whereas a different and more passionate procedure on the part of England might have had results as eternally disastrous as those which unwisdom procured in America and in Ireland.[169]

The Alien Act, after long debates in both Houses, became law on the last day of the old Parliament. At once firm and conciliatory, it offered to Scotland the free choice between a Union Treaty, to be negotiated on equal terms between the two countries, or the acceptance of the Hanoverian Succession without any change in the existing international relation. Only if Scotland persisted in the design which she had announced to break the Union of the Crowns and to choose a King other than the King of England, then certain consequences were to follow. Every native of Scotland, with a few exceptions, was to be treated as an alien born out of the allegiance of the Crown of England ; and the principal Scottish exports—cattle, linen and coal—were no longer to be imported either into England or Ireland. These penalties were to begin on Christmas Day 1705, if the Scots had not by that time remedied the situation created by the Act of Security in either of the ways open to her.*

Mar. 14
1705

---

* An excellent synopsis of the Alien Act and a commentary upon its fairness and wisdom will be found in Dicey and Rait's *Thoughts on the Scottish Union*, pp. 170–173. At the first rumour of the English intention to prohibit the importation of cattle and linen, Roxburgh wrote : ' If that's done, we are ruined.' *Jerviswood*, p. 13.

Although the Alien Act caused as much wrath in Scotland as the Act of Security had caused in England, both measures may be defended because, in the event, each had the happy effect of opening the eyes of the opposing party to the realities of the situation. The Act of Security taught the English that Scotland must be treated with on terms of equality or else she would secede. The Alien Act taught the Scots that if they chose to secede they must submit to see their poor commerce still further reduced—whereas if they took the opposite course and formed a closer Union, the whole Empire would become an open field for the trade and activity of their sons.

During the early months of 1705, while the Alien Act was on its way through Parliament, the two countries seemed to be on the point of war. The last sections of the Act of Security had provided for the arming and organization of the Scottish militia on a national scale. The spirit of their fathers, when they defied Charles I and his English bishops from Dunse Law, was abroad in the land. The local militia met twice a week at the door of every parish church. In Ayrshire alone 7,000 armed men were reported to be drilling, many of them the redoubtable Cameronian fanatics. And while Southern Scotland sprang to arms, the Highlanders sharpened their claymores and awaited the word in the glens. Presbyterian and Jacobite would march shoulder to shoulder. The Scots were still a fighting race, apt and trained to war, feared as such by those who mocked their poverty :

*Nemo me impune lacessit.**

Meanwhile the English border counties were defenceless. Northumberland and Durham could again be occupied

* The English were justly alarmed at the arming of Scotland, but the strong Scottish Whig, Marchmont, wrote to Somers pointing out a less alarming aspect of the organisation of the militia. The Jacobites, he said, were always secretly armed and ready for war ; now the Presbyterians would be ready also. *Marchmont*, III, p. 282. See also Defoe, *Union*, p. 84.

In April 1705 Englishmen returning from Scotland report : 'That nation is very uppish, and the town of Dumprooz [Dumfries] are all in arms and exercise their men once every month, and that there are a considerable number of gunsmiths and sword cutters come lately from France, so they are equipping themselves might and main to force a trade with England if the Union does not succeed. This town has 700 fencible men in it.' *H.M.C. Portland* VIII, p. 177.

by the invader, as easily as when Leslie's blue-bonnets had
crossed Tweed and Tyne in 1640.   The coalfields could be
seized and London's fuel cut off.   A north-country squire
wrote to his Parliamentary friend Thomas Coke :

> It's not the first time the Scots have invaded this nation with
> success :   there's some alive that don't forget Leslie's coming into
> England, which gave so much encouragement to the late unhappy
> Civil War.   The French King, I suppose, won't let them want
> money to go through with it.[170]

England was both angry and alarmed, but fortunately
refrained from measures of panic.   The Alien Act was
steadily pushed through its stages till it received the royal
assent. Pamphlets appeared, arguing that a Treaty of Union,
even if it conceded freedom of colonial trade to the Scots,
would be preferable to border fortresses, armies in time of
peace and periodic war.   The anti-militarist prepossessions
of the English came to the rescue of their good sense in
this controversy. At the end of January the House
1705   of Commons rejected the proposal that the six
northern counties should arm themselves against invasion,
both for fear of provoking that catastrophe in seeking to
meet it, and for fear of unforeseeable trouble of all sorts :
it was remembered that a very large proportion of the
Northumbrian squires were Papists and Jacobites.   Parliament decided instead to rely on the regular army in case of
invasion, though it might mean the recall of some of Marlborough's regiments from Flanders.   Godolphin was determined not to be bullied by the Scots' threat of civil war
and wrote to warn Seafield :

> England is not now in the condition it was when Scotland used
> to make inroads upon us.   We have the power, and you may give us
> the will to return those visits.   And supposing the French are more
> able to assist the Scots than I hope they are, the French have the
> character of being very good servants but the worst masters upon
> earth.

Indeed it is noticeable that although the Jacobite agents
reported to France that now was the moment to strike, that
all creeds and parties north of Tweed were united against
England, and that even Hamilton was agog for action,

King Louis had also been informed that ' the Scots would not be pleased at the sight of French troops landing in their country.'[171]

At this critical stage of the relations between England and Scotland occurred the tragedy of Captain Green. It might well have precipitated war, but by a fortunate turn of events it acted as a purge to the ill-temper of the Scots, who felt better after they had been permitted to take the blood of an Englishman with all the formalities of an act of public vengeance. At this distance of time the story of the judicial murder of Captain Green can be read in pity rather than in anger, especially if we bear in mind that the conception of the nature of evidence was in those days most unscientific; and that thirty years had not passed since Titus Oates had been the most popular man in England.

On no point was Scottish opinion more sore and sensitive than on the failure of the Darien adventure,* and the continued hostility of the English East India Company to the few small Scottish ships that occasionally ventured a voyage round the Cape. Early in 1704 the *Annandale*, a vessel acting for the Darien Company, had been seized in the Downs at the instance of the East India Company, on the ground that, although a foreign ship, its Captain had enlisted seamen in England for an Indian voyage contrary to the Company's privileges. In fact the Welsh skipper had betrayed his Scottish employers and was in league with the English Company. The *Annandale* was condemned and impounded by process of law.

At the end of July 1704 the news of this piece of unneighbourly English insolence had set all Scotland aflame, when, at that ill-chosen hour, there put into the harbour of Leith an English trading vessel, the *Worcester*. Her Captain, Thomas Green, a simple young fellow of twenty-six, thought life sweet, bringing home his ship after a successful voyage to Calcutta. Fear of the French privateers from Dunkirk had caused him to make the wide circuit of Ireland and Cape Wrath, rather than take, without an escort, the direct route to London by the Channel and the Straits of Dover. Having

* See pp. 221–222 above.

reached the mouth of the Forth, he put into the port of
Scotland's capital, to wait there for a convoy sailing south
under proper naval protection. In time of war it was not
unusual for ships returning from southern waters to take
this roundabout route to the Thames, and the Dunkirkers
sometimes took British ships as far north as Shetland.*

To a certain type of religious mind Green's arrival
seemed ' providential ' : heaven's justice could now be done.
The English ship had come to Leith like the lamb caught
in the thicket for sacrifice. Roderick Mackenzie, Secretary
to the Darien Company, believing the *Worcester* to be a ship
of the hated East India Company, hired some ' pretty
fellows ' who boarded her disguised as friendly visitors and
seized her by force, under circumstances much nearer to
piracy than anything of which poor Captain Green had ever
been guilty.

All this had been done ' upon reprizal ' for the seizure
of the *Annandale* ; but it then turned out that the *Worcester*,
so far from being an East India Company ship, was an inter-
loper, a ' Separate Stock ship,' as hostile to the tyrant of the
Eastern seas as the Darien Company itself. However, it also
emerged that the cargo she had brought home was valuable
and that her owners, her Captain and most of her crew belonged to the hated English nation. She was detained at
Burntisland on the opposite shore of Forth.

December came, and Mackenzie's lawless claim on the
cargo had not yet been decided upon by law. For four
months the crew of the *Worcester* had been hanging about
the public houses of Leith and Edinburgh. Some of them,
'being pretty mellow with the punch,' had spun yarns to
amuse the terrors of the landsmen, and one or two had
hinted evil things of officers against whom they had a
grudge. Their idle words dropped into the deep soil of

* E.g. *Add. MSS.* 37155, fo. 156. We now know the details of the *Worcester's*
voyage and Captain Green's doings in the Indian seas, from the owner's papers ;
they have been published and excellently analysed by Sir Richard Temple, in
The Papers of Thomas Bowrey (Hakluyt Soc., 1925), and in *The Tragedy of the
Worcester* (Benn, 1930). See also *The Company of Scotland*, by G. P. Insh (Scribner
1932). The affair remains an historic tragedy, but is no longer in any sense an
historic mystery. Green and his crew never committed any act of piracy at all,
either against the *Speedy Return* or against any other vessel. The report of the
trial will be found in *State Trials*, XIV, pp. 1199–1311.

Scottish suspicion, and fructified there like dragons' teeth. The patriotic feeling of the moment, and the greed and knavery of Mackenzie, seized upon these hints to construct a charge of piracy against Green.

A Scottish ship, the *Speedy Return*, had long been missing, and the rumour now spread that Green had met her somewhere in the Indian Ocean, pirated her and murdered her captain and her crew. In fact, she had been seized in Madagascar by a real pirate, John Bowen, and afterwards burned on the Malabar coast. Some of the crew of the *Speedy Return* were already back in England ready to bear witness to the true facts, but this was not known in Scotland till the certainty of Green's guilt was too strongly fixed in the national mind to be shaken by any evidence in the world.

From January to April 1705 Scotland thought and spoke of little else save the charges against Green and his men. Passion blinded judgment in high and low, save in the case of a few of the best minds, like those of the young Duke of Argyle and the still younger Forbes of Culloden.

By order of the Privy Council, Green and his crew were arrested and put on trial. The evidence, except in the case of a perjured Indian, named Ferdinando,* did not even pretend to be more than hearsay ; another Indian and the ship's surgeon had imagined grievances to avenge, and had been worked upon by the prosecution and by the heat of Scottish public opinion to make good what they had been supposed to hint, but did not pretend ever to have seen. The witnesses contradicted each other's statements. There was no vestige of evidence of piracy to be found in the *Worcester* or its cargo, as the Privy Councillors had discovered in January, when they sent over six Lords of their own body to Burntisland to examine and report on every object on board the detained ship. If the evidence of the three hostile witnesses had been sifted, or if the rest of the crew had not been debarred from giving evidence by the prosecutors' device in putting them all in the dock together,

* He died immediately after the trial. It was said that Mackenzie murdered him because he proposed to go back on his tale. But the evidence, though it would have been held good enough to hang Green, is not enough to condemn Mackenzie, rascal though he was.

the truth must have appeared even to a Court drunk with patriotic prejudice. As it was, upon March 21, 1705, Green and fourteen of his crew were condemned to be hanged on Leith sands, in three batches to be turned off on successive weeks.*

The trial in Edinburgh was being closely watched from over the Border. The English were as fully persuaded of Green's innocence as the Scots of his guilt. When it was known that he was to be hanged, there was an outburst of fury in London, and for some days Scottish residents found it wise to stay indoors for fear of insult. Secretary Johnstone wrote home from London :

> This business of Green is the devil and all. It has spoiled all business. I am told it was two hours in the Cabinet. Somers says he knows not the laws of Scotland, but that the proceedings are illegal according to all other laws he knows, for the ship on which the piracy is committed is not libelled. In short, nobody believes it. I was surprised to find people believe that the evidence was suborned, and that those who confess it do it in the dread of torture, or upon promise of life. The Whigs make a Jacobitish business of it and it will be trumped up at all the Elections.†

Should Anne allow the executions to proceed ? She found it as embarrassing to be Queen over two hostile countries as William had found his dual kingship during the Darien affair. If she pardoned the crew of the *Worcester*, as England and as justice demanded, all chance that the Scots would consent to a Union was gone, and war was at the gate. ' If the Queen shall grant them remissions,' wrote Jerviswood from Edinburgh on March 28, ' it will spoil the business of Parliament, and I am afraid will so exasperate the nation as may render it difficult for them to join with England on any terms whatever.'

At her side in London was her new Commissioner for

---

* The case is so fully gone into in Sir Richard Temple's two books that it is enough to refer the reader to them. The visit of the Committee of the Privy Council to Burntisland will be found in the *P.C. Reg. Ed.* Jan. 2 and 16, 1705. The statements in Alexander Hamilton's *New Account of the East Indies* (1727), I, pp. 317–320, are analysed in Temple's *Tragedy of the Worcester*, pp. 126–130.

† *Jerviswood*, p. 70.

Scotland, the young soldier Duke of Argyle, already urging her to get rid of Tweeddale and the *Squadrone* as incompetent poltroons, and trust the whole government of Scotland to himself, Queensberry and the old and tried section of the Whig party. Argyle could raise 6,000 armed men to his own whistle, twice the number Queen Anne had in Scotland. Above all, he had courage, not only in face of the French at Ramillies, but in face of his own countrymen over the Green affair. With all his faults John Campbell was a man, and in the world of Hamiltons, Tweeddales and Roxburghs this counted by contrast. He was convinced that a judicial error was being committed in Edinburgh and was refreshingly ready to say so and abide by the consequences.

He persuaded the Queen that the executions should be delayed pending enquiry. He himself, as the Queen's new Commissioner, wrote a letter to Chancellor Seafield to that effect, but this did not seem warrant enough to the Privy Council at Edinburgh to take their lives in their hands in order to save Green. Moreover, as Hamilton complained, ' Argyle's letter was in such a strain as if he had been writing to one of his chamberlains in Kintyre.' A few days later the Queen herself wrote ordering a reprieve, and the execution of the first batch, due on April 4, was postponed for a week.

The news that the Queen was interfering from London roused the Edinburgh mob to such a pitch of fury as in a later generation sealed the fate of the less innocent Porteous. Indeed the two affairs have many features in common, and if Scott had chosen the tragedy of the *Worcester* as a theme for one of his romances, he would have found it as full of matter suited to his genius as the historical setting of the *Heart of Midlothian*.

Chancellor Seafield was in grave doubt as to Green's guilt. His conduct over Darien had shown that he was not apt to be led astray by popular hallucinations. If the Privy Council had supported him, particularly if the *Squadrone* Ministers had shown the least courage, he would have helped Anne and Argyle to save the innocent men—with what consequences who can tell ? But when he urgently summoned the attendance of Ministers at a meeting of the Privy Council on April 10, the day before the execution,

Roxburgh and nearly all the Queen's servants then in Scotland took care to be absent. Only fifteen Privy Councillors, about half the proper number, attended, and those for the most part holding no office under the Crown.

An express had just arrived from the Queen, dated April 3 ; she said she was studying the report of the trial which the Council had sent her ; the whole tenour of her message presumed that until her further will was known the men would not be hanged. But the Edinburgh mob had decided that hanged they should be upon the morrow. If the Privy Councillors again delayed the execution even by a day, they were in imminent danger of being ' de-Witted.' Moreover, to do them justice, they had also to consider that the pardon of Green would certainly stop the Union and not improbably lead to war. The choice was one which even men of high rectitude and courage might tremble to make.

To add to the discomfort of these not very heroic men, the Queen had sent them, by the same messenger, affidavits of Israel Phippany and Peter Freelands, sailors of the *Speedy Return*, to the effect that their ship had been seized, not by Green, but the pirate Bowen at Madagascar, on a date when the *Worcester* was far distant. This new evidence was April 10 read to the Privy Council and must have further 1705 shaken the faith of several present in the guilt of Green. The last miserable scene shall be given in the authentic words of the manuscript of the Privy Council Register :

Thereon it went to the vote, ' *Grant to the petitioners a reprieve for a short day into the next week till there may be a full council, or not.*' And the rolls being called and their votes marked, there was three of the Council for granting a reprieve ; * and other three not. All the rest present being either *non liquid* [*non liquet*, ' it is not clear '] or refusing to vote, it came to the Lord Chancellor's casting vote. His Lordship [Seafield] declared he was willing to give a vote and sign the reprieve if he knew that a quorum of their lordships would sign the same, without which the order for a reprieve would be insufficient.

---

* The names of the dauntless three who supported Seafield for a reprieve were the Marquess of Lothian, the Earl of Buchan, and General Ramsay. *Jerviswood*, p. 74. *Jerviswood* and the *P.C. Registers* show that this decisive meeting was on April 10, although there was another meeting on April 11, the day of the execution.

And accordingly their Lordships being asked one by one if they would sign the reprieve, and all of them declined, except three besides those [three] who had voted reprieve, and the Lord Chancellor who made but seven, and so not a sufficient quorum for signing a valid reprieve. Wherefore the prisoners were left to the course of justice upon expiring of the former reprieve.

Next morning, Green's doomsday, saw the length and breadth of High Street and Canongate packed with a dense mob. They were armed, some with swords or guns and the remainder with heavy sticks. The peasants for fifty miles round had come in to support the men of Edinburgh, and it was said that 80,000 armed rioters were in the streets. The Privy Council met once more, only eleven strong on this final morning, and, to give 'authority' to their proceedings, adjourned to the Council Chamber in Holyrood. They had to pass thither through the jaws of the mob, whose power and purpose were clear enough. What ' authority ' was left to deliberations so held ? After yesterday's meeting the result was a foregone conclusion. The Privy Council left Green and two of his companions to die that day.

April 11 1705

Chancellor Seafield proceeded back up High Street towards his home, endeavouring to clear his way by telling the mob they would soon have satisfaction. Even so, he was set upon opposite the Tron Kirk, his coach overturned, his servants beaten and himself driven for refuge into a neighbouring house. If he had announced a reprieve he would have been torn limb from limb.

The interest now shifted to Leith sands, where the pirates' gibbet had been set up within the tide mark. The great multitude moved that way, but there was not room for all on the spot, and ' one might have walked on their heads from Edinburgh to Leith sands.' The long road was lined with pitiless faces, when the Englishmen Green and Simpson and their companion Madder, a very valiant Scot, were led that way to die. An eye-witness of the horrid scene heard them—

huzza'd, in triumph as it were, and insulted with the sharpest and most bitter invectives. Being come to the place of execution, good God what a moving sight was it to see those men stand upon the very verge of life, just launching into eternity, and at the same time see the whole multitude transported with joy, some with pleasure asking ' Why their countrymen did not come and save them.' All of which they bore with invincible patience, like innocent men, English men and Christians, and made no other returns than by forgiving them, and desiring their charity and prayers.

As soon as they were dead the mood of the fond many began to change. Some shed tears, and none demanded further victims. The rest of the *Worcester's* crew were shortly afterwards reprieved and quietly released. Not bloodthirstiness but national honour had maddened the crowd. Blood had been let as a sacramental symbol of Scotland's independence, and thereupon sanity began slowly to return. Three men—two Englishmen and one Scot—had died for the nation, for the new nation of Great Britain, which could not have come into existence if their unjust death had been prevented by the hand of power stretched out from London over Scotland. For them no Martyr's Monument stands on Calton Hill or elsewhere, but the names of Green, Madder and Simpson should be remembered with tenderness by all Britons.

The greatest and best of Scottish statesmen of the eighteenth century, Duncan Forbes of Culloden, was then a young law student of twenty. As he listened to the witnesses contradicting one another's statements at the trial of the *Worcester's* crew, he saw where the truth lay. His heart was moved within him, as it always was by injustice and cruelty even when committed by his own side. A generation later, when in the British Parliament he was defending his country's independence from English aggression in the Porteous quarrel, he thus referred to the execution of Green:

I was so struck with the horror of the fact that I put myself in deep mourning and with the danger of my life attended the innocent but unfortunate men to the scaffold, where they died with the most affecting protestations of their innocence. I did not stop here, for I carried the head of Captain Green to the grave.[172]

The English took Green's execution very ill, but the only penalty they could safely exact for it was the removal of the *Squadrone* Ministers, whose cowardly conduct in absenting themselves from the Privy Council at the critical meetings had made them as despicable to Scotland as they were hateful to England. Argyle, the Queen's Commissioner for the coming session of Parliament, demanded their removal and the return to office of the old Whig Ministers under Queensberry and himself. He was supported in his demand by the English Whig Lords, on whom the Godolphin Ministry was becoming every day more dependent. The double failure of the *Squadrone* Ministers in Parliament last summer and in the affair of Green this spring, had destroyed Godolphin's confidence in his favourites ; and the Queen, much as she disliked Queensberry, declaring that he had ' not only betrayed me but tricked me several times,' was compelled to take him into her service again, as Lord Privy Seal, in order to retain Argyle as her Commissioner. Seafield, the adaptable and dependable public servant, remained Chancellor.

These three men were the mainstay of the reconstructed Ministry, and they were the three statesmen in all Scotland most likely, by a combination of their different tempers and talents, to save the imperilled State. It was their task, in the coming summer of 1705, to induce Parliament either to settle the Succession on Hanover, or else to initiate negotiations for a Treaty of Union. The penalty of failure would be the operation of the Alien Act at Christmas, and perhaps war.

Before the Estates met on June 28, and for nearly two months after the session had begun, the Ministry was still divided and uncertain whether to press them to settle the Succession or to treat for a Union. The omens did not seem auspicious either way. The Earl of Mar, not yet a Jacobite, was put up by Government to move that a Commission should be appointed to treat with England for terms of Union. Parliament refused to proceed with his motion, preferring to explore the alternative policy of fixing the Succession on the House of Hanover, with Limitations on the power of the Scottish Crown. But when it came to the point, the House, still distrustful of its own ability to govern Scotland, again rejected Fletcher's

July 20
1705

semi-republican scheme of Limitations. The Succession fell to the ground with the Limitations, and Parliament, late in the session, was forced back to reconsider Mar's proposals for a Union Treaty, as the only way of avoiding the speedy enforcement of the Alien Act by England.

It had been Seafield's opinion that, in throwing all the members of the *Squadrone* out of office, a grave risk was run that they would combine with the Jacobites and obstruct all Parliamentary progress. Queensberry had behaved in that way when he had last been turned out. The imperious Argyle, however, insisted that all the *Squadrone* must go. And, fortunately for the prospects of the Union, they behaved themselves better in opposition than they had known how to do as Ministers. The politic Seafield, their former colleague in office, never wholly lost touch with them. Real consideration for the welfare of Scotland mingled with other motives in the minds of many members of her last Parliament, both within and without the Government circle.[173]

On the last day of August and first of September 1705, a series of important votes decided the conditions upon which Scottish Commissioners should be appointed to treat for terms of Union. Anne, at the request of the Westminster Parliament, would appoint English Commissioners to meet them. If the Commissions of the two countries met and made joint proposals, those proposals would then, in the following session, come before both the Parliaments to be accepted or refused. The Jacobites and the more extreme patriots of the Country party disliked the idea of any negotiations taking place at all, but the general sense of the Estates was less unfavourable to Union, since they had just declined once again to settle the Succession on any other terms. The opponents of Union, therefore, did not directly oppose the appointment of Commissioners to treat with England, but they intended to saddle the negotiation with such conditions as must ensure its failure.

First the Duke of Hamilton moved :

That the Union to be treated on shall not derogate any ways from fundamental laws, ancient privileges, offices, rights, dignities and liberties of the Kingdom.

This was in effect to forbid the Commissioners to treat for an incorporating Union and the merger of the Parliaments. It would confine the possibilities to a loose Federation, and it was known the English would not deal on those terms.

Aug. 31 1705   Hamilton's wrecking motion was lost by only two voices. By such straws are the destinies of nations decided.

Next day the second attack was made. It was moved that no negotiations should be begun until the English Parliament had repealed the Alien Act. The resent-

Sept. 1 1705   ment against the Act was so strong in Scotland that it was regarded as certain that this clause must pass ; and if it passed there would be no Treaty, for the English would not repeal the Alien Act under compulsion. To turn this corner, Government skilfully proposed that instead of the clause taking its place in the Act setting up the Commission, a separate address should be made to the Queen, praying that the Union should not be proceeded with until the unfriendly Alien Act had been repealed. When this amendment was put to the vote, Chancellor Seafield told some English tourists who had been admitted into the Parliament House to hear the proceedings, that the division would decide ' whether England and Scotland should go together by the ears.' Again the Government won by another small majority, and Hamilton's angry gestures betrayed his disappointment and concern.

On that eventful day a story was going round Edinburgh that Hamilton had recently been heard to de- clare ' The bonnet is mine, and, by God, I will wear it.' Cer- tainly, if he aimed at the reversion of the Crown of Scotland, it was his interest to stop the Union. Up to this moment his conduct had been that of fierce opposition, and such it was again next year. But on the evening of the first of September he betrayed his cause and his followers in a manner that has never been fully explained. After the division on the Alien Act, many opposition members had left the Parliament House, thinking that all was over for the day ; but the government benches were still pretty full when the Duke of Hamilton rose, and ' with his usual haughty and bantering air,' moved that the appointment of the Commissioners for Scotland be left to the Queen, and not undertaken by Parliament, which, he declared, was too much ' in heats and feuds ' to be impartial.

He had given no notice to his unhappy followers of this change of front ; indeed he had evaded their enquiries by telling them that the question would not come forward that day.   The Opposition had never doubted that Parliament would refuse to leave the nominations to the Queen, governed as she always was by English advice.   They were equally confident that the Estates would name enough Commissioners hostile to the Union policy to prevent the success of the negotiations.   And now their own leader had come to terms with the government behind their backs, and spoiled a plan that they regarded as being sure of success.

Hamilton, it appears, felt less confident as to the result of a vote in that uncertain assembly.   The government had already won several divisions most unexpectedly, and he feared there would be no majority vote to place him on the Commission.*   He had therefore made a secret agreement with Argyle that, if the choice were left to the Queen, he himself should be one of those named.

The Ministers eagerly supported the Duke's motion, while Fletcher of Saltoun and some of the few Jacobites left in the House denounced his treachery.   Other opposition members did not know what to think or what to do.   The House voted to leave the nomination of the Commissioners to the Queen.†   That night the whole Act for their appointment and instruction was read and approved, for procedure in the Scots Parliament moved quickly when it moved at all.

Sept. 1
1705

' From this day,' wrote the Jacobite Lockhart, ' may we date the commencement of Scotland's ruin.'   At midnight a party of strong Unionists from the Parliament House sat up drinking success to the Treaty, in company with the English visitors who had watched the extra-

---

* There were others who took the same view.   The Whig Sir John Clerk of Penicuik thought that the government majority would have succeeded in keeping all Jacobites and *Squadrone* leaders off the list.   *Clerk* (*Rox.*), p. 57.

† *Crossrigg*, p. 171, says ' by about 40 votes '; *Lockhart*, I, p. 133, says by eight votes ; and *Taylor, Jos.*, p. 118, says four votes.   There is no official record of the figures.

ordinary and fateful proceedings of the day. 'We should now,' they said, 'be no more English and Scotch, but Brittons.' Yet next morning, in the streets of Scotland's capital, the insults to which the same visitors were subjected as the countrymen of Green, and the ballads against English 'pork-eaters' which were everywhere in demand, showed that all was not yet well.   Sir John Clerk of Penicuik, when asked to be one of the Commissioners, was prepared to do his best for the cause of Union, but was convinced their work would be wasted because their countrymen would reject any Treaty they were able to make with the English. Burnet heard from his Scottish correspondents that the Estates were only playing with the negotiation as 'a plausible step, to keep matters yet longer in suspense.' The bark of the Union had already had several miraculous escapes ; its luck would have still to hold if it was ever to reach port.[174]

The dangers, however, would henceforth come all from the side of Scotland.   England had learned her lesson and was prepared to do her part.   South of the Tweed the atmosphere was more favourable in the winter of 1705 than it had ever been before.   During the summer, the General Election* had taken place which routed the High Tories and gave full power to the alliance of Godolphin and the Whigs, who were agreed on the necessity of Union, as the only method left of securing the peaceful accession of the House of Hanover in Scotland.   To give the negotiations a good start, the new English Parliament, in its first session, repealed the Alien Act, in spite of High Tory remonstrance.

Dec.   The Act had served its purpose by inducing the
1705   Scots to treat, and could now be discarded.   'The
English frankness in this affair,' wrote Mar to Carstares, 'by doing more than we ourselves proposed, should make people in Scotland in good humour,'   'This gentle and unforced accord' of England rolled away a great obstacle from the path of the Treaty.[175]

From Christmas till the end of February 1706 the all-important business of choosing the Scottish Commissioners was going forward, not without heart-burning and dispute.

* See p. 31 above.

The Estates had left it to the Queen, and the Queen left it to Queensberry and Godolphin. Queensberry had recovered all his old prestige by his management in Edinburgh during the late session. If Argyle was the stiff backbone, Queensberry was the busy right-hand of the Ministry. And at this moment Argyle was in one of his frequent moods of ill-humour with his colleagues. Anne, advised by Queensberry, declined to nominate as a Commissioner for the Treaty so influential an opponent of Union as the Duke of Hamilton. But Argyle had promised Hamilton that he should be nominated, if only he would leave the choice to the Queen.* When John Campbell found that he could not make good his plighted word, he felt bound to refuse to serve on the Commission himself, and went off instead to the Ramillies campaign, leaving Queensberry in command of the situation.

Others besides Argyle had advised Queensberry to smooth the future path of the Treaty through the Scottish Parliament by placing *Squadrone* nobles and other opposition leaders on the Commission that was to frame it. But Queensberry feared the grit they might put into the wheels of the negotiation in London, and refused to name any but those who had already shown themselves to be good Unionists. There was an exception that proved the rule : on the panel of thirty-one Scots Commissioners, half of whom were in office, sat George Lockhart the Jacobite. Not being a great noble like Hamilton, he felt it would be useless for him to raise a solitary voice against every day's proceedings, so he sat there and suffered in silence, a reporter for his party and posterity.

The English side of the Commission was not appointed till the very eve of its first session in April 1706. Godolphin selected the members on the principles that had governed Queensberry in the choice he had made for Scotland. The only English Commissioner who could be suspected of High Toryism was Anne's favourite ecclesiastic, Sharp, Archbishop of York, deputed, together with Tenison of Canterbury, to hold a watching brief for the Church of England. In fact, Sharp never came to the meetings and did

* See p. 260 above.

not sign the Report, whereas the Whig Tenison attended frequently and signed gladly.   The other Commissioners, some thirty in number, were for the most part Whigs, and the rest Ministerial Tories.   Godolphin, Harley, Hedges and Harcourt were there, together with Wharton, Halifax, Sunderland, Orford, Devonshire, Chief Justice Holt, and, prominent in their counsels, Lord Somers,* whom Anne's prejudices excluded from office, but whose great talents as a constitutional lawyer and constructive statesman were now to be put to their final proof in perhaps the best piece of service that he ever rendered to his country.[176]

On April 16, 1706, the sittings of the Commissioners began, and in nine weeks they had completed the Treaty of Union, which in the end received the assent of both Parliaments and created Great Britain.   The proceedings, inspired from the first by good will and fundamental agreement among the carefully chosen representatives of Unionist opinion in both countries, were guided with more than usual tact and wisdom.

Certain rules of procedure were first drawn up.   The Scottish and English Commissions were to sit apart from each other, in two separate chambers of the building known as the Cockpit in Whitehall, on the opposite side of the street from the Banqueting House.   They sat together only on formal occasions when the Queen was present, except once, when a public debate between the two Commissions was held, on the vexed question of the number of representatives proper for Scotland in the Parliament of Great Britain.   Otherwise all business was conducted by written minutes communicated from one Commission to the other.   It was also laid down that no finding was to be held obligatory till all the articles had been reviewed and accepted together ;   and that all proceedings were to be kept secret until the end of the negotiations.

* Addison was no doubt prejudiced in favour of Somers, but he had inner knowledge.   In his famous character of Somers in the *Freeholder*, No. 39, he writes : ' If he did not entirely project the Union of the Two Kingdoms and the Bill of Regency [see p. 93 above] there is none who will deny him to have been the chief conductor of both these glorious works,' and therefore, in Addison's opinion, the chief contriver of the quiet accession of the House of Hanover.

These were wise provisions, in view of the excited state of feeling outside, particularly in Scotland, whence the Commissioners were being watched with hostile jealousy for any sign that they were falling under English influences in London. Their enemy Lockhart was among them, 'taking notes,' and some day he might 'print them.' All things considered, it was but prudent that, by a mutual agreement, 'none of the English during the Treaty had one of the Scots so much as to dine or drink a glass of wine with them.' *

Both sides knew beforehand the limits of possible negotiation on the main issues. The abortive Commission of 1702–1703 had done preliminary work that now proved of great value.† The Scots Commissioners were well aware, before ever the sittings began, that the English would insist on an incorporating Union and a merger of the Parliaments, and would not even discuss a Federal Union. In those days Englishmen were well acquainted with the federal constitution of the Dutch United Provinces, and they knew its defects. If a Parliament continued to sit at Edinburgh, authority would still be divided and the government of Scotland might be more difficult than ever before.

On the other hand the English by this time realized that they must grant without reservation the right of the future 'North Britons' to trade with the whole 'British Empire.' In ecclesiastical matters the position was even more clear : the Scottish Commission, under the Act that set it up, had no powers to treat on religion. The Presbyterian Establishment was axiomatic. In short, if there was to be a Union at all, there must be one Parliament, one system of trade and taxation, and two Churches.

During the negotiations of 1702–1703 the Scottish Commissioners had themselves proposed an incorporating Union. But, since then, feeling in Scotland had grown more hostile to England, and the present Edinburgh Parliament was more nationalist than the Rump that was sitting in the first year of Anne. In 1706 the Scottish

---

* On a similar principle the Irish Nationalist Members in London, during the long Home Rule controversy of a generation and more, would never accept invitations to the tables of their English allies in Parliament, a very real sacrifice to men living for so long a time away from their homes.

† See pp. 230–232.

Commissioners dared not renew the proposal of their predecessors, though they were ready to accept it under compulsion from the English Commissioners, who therefore made the first move in the game. The famous proposal, drawn up by Somers and sent across from the April 22 English room in the Cockpit to the Scottish room, 1706 ran as follows :

That the two Kingdoms of England and Scotland be for ever United into one Kingdom by the name of Great Britain. That the United Kingdom of Great Britain be represented by one and the same Parliament, and that the Succession to the Monarchy of Great Britain, in case of failure of heirs of her Majesty's body,

be governed by the terms of the English Act of Settlement in favour of the House of Hanover.

The Scots Commissioners, viewing out of the corners of their eyes the sullen face of their colleague Lockhart, and some of them remembering how the mob looked a year ago as it clamoured for Green's blood and chased the Chancellor up High Street, felt it prudent to make a demonstration of patriotic resistance. They sent back counter-proposals for a very loose Federation, under one Monarch, with free trade but no Parliamentary Union. It was a mere manœuvre. The Scottish Commissioners in fact almost all of them regarded such a Federation as an impracticable form of government for two unfriendly peoples. They trusted their English colleagues to reject it, as they very promptly did.

Thereupon the Scots Commissioners, having saved their faces by putting up a sham fight, without more ado agreed to accept an incorporating Union, ' with this pro-April 25 vision, that all subjects of the United Kingdom shall 1706 have full freedom and intercourse of trade and navigation within the United Kingdom and Plantations thereunto belonging.' The English Commissioners replied that they regarded this provision as a ' necessary consequence of an entire Union.'

The foundations of the Treaty had been laid. Because the ground had been well prepared beforehand, and the Commissioners on both sides had been carefully selected for their known opinions, a few days had sufficed, without any serious crisis, to settle the grand affair.[177]

Eight weeks more of arduous labour brought their task to an end. The two Commissions, sitting behind closed doors, decided a number of vexed and angry questions on which agreement could never have been reached in an atmosphere of public discussion.

Though Scotland gave up her Parliament, she was to keep the native part of her laws. The future British Parliament could indeed make new laws for Scotland, either particular to her, or common with England. But her old laws remained in force, except those which contravened the Union Treaty. Her system of law, so different from the common law of England, was left untouched. It remains to this day, a pledge of Scotland's intellectual independence, as the Church of her spiritual. Not only did the Scottish land law retain feudal elements and forms that had disappeared from the English, but the whole law of Scotland, like her religion, moved in an intellectual world of its own, seeking for first principles while the English law sought for appropriate writs and precedents. The mental habits of Scotland, in her golden age which still lay before her, were largely due to the preservation, under the terms of the Union Treaty, of her native law. Her venerable and famous courts, her judges, advocates and writers so racy of the soil, were to remain in Scotland 'in all time coming' and 'no causes in Scotland should be cognisible by the Courts of Chancery, Queen's Bench, Common Pleas or any other Court in Westminster Hall.' Such were the cautious words used in the Treaty. But the House of Lords did not sit in Westminster Hall, and though it was not set down in definite terms, appeals from the Scottish Courts would lie to the supreme tribunal of Great Britain.

The Edinburgh Privy Council was left untouched for the time being, but the Treaty clearly contemplated its abolition, in the words 'until the Parliament of Great Britain shall think fit to alter it.' The Privy Council was little loved in Scotland, and its abolition in 1708 was not resented. Thenceforth the executive as well as the legis-

lative power over Scotland was concentrated in London—
but not the judicial.   Scotland's statesmen have had to be
content with their share in ruling Great Britain, but the
lawyers of Edinburgh long kept alive the native traditions
and the peculiar mentality of the land that bred them.

The heritable jurisdictions, or private law-courts of the
Scottish nobility, were oppressive to the people subject to
them, and were a hateful anachronism in the eyes of English
lawyers and statesmen.   None the less, if the Treaty was to
have a chance of passing the Edinburgh Parliament, the
Nobles must not be offended.   And so these relics of
the feudal age were specially named for survival.   Forty
years later they were abolished by an Act of the British
Parliament, after the suppression of the last Jacobite
rebellion, the last spasm of dying feudalism.

The most difficult point in the negotiation between the
two Commissions was to define the number of Scottish
members to sit in the Westminster Parliament.   Scotland
was entitled by its wealth and share of taxation to thirteen
members in the House of Commons ; by its population to
eighty-five.   After a long wrangle it was agreed to compromise on forty-five.   They were to be elected by the
antiquated and unrepresentative constituencies that had
chosen the Edinburgh Parliament, and they continued to be
so elected until the Reform Bill of 1832.*   The number of
Scottish Peers who were to sit in the House of Lords was
fixed at sixteen, to be chosen by the whole body of Scottish
Nobles.   Scots were also eligible to obtain Peerages of Great
Britain and sit by that right.

The financial arrangements were generous to Scotland.
Her population was reckoned at an eighth, her wealth at
a fortieth of that of England.   And her contribution to the
land tax was fixed at a fortieth.   The taxation and tariff
system of Great Britain was to be one.   But since the
Scottish taxpayer would now help to bear his part of the
national debt that England had contracted before the
Union, Scotland was to be given a handsome ' Equivalent '
for this added burden, in the shape of £398,085 10s.—for
Sir John Clerk had worked it out to the shillings.

* See p. 180 above.

There can be no doubt that the ' Equivalent' helped to win for the Union the grudging assent of the Scottish Parliament. For the Treaty laid it down that the bulk of the money thus handed over to Scotland was to be spent in two ways, highly popular both in the country and in Parliamentary circles. The shareholders of the Darien Company, who never expected to see again the money they had lost in King William's reign, were to get back every penny of their capital and five per cent. annual interest to boot. Many a Scottish home was the brighter for that clause in the Treaty, which was faithfully and fully performed. By putting his hand into his capacious pocket—a gesture to which he was now gradually accustoming himself—John Bull did something to wipe out, if not the memory of the dead who had been so dear, at least the abiding sense of a still unrequited wrong that the word Darien conjured up in every Scottish heart. The tragic accounts of that Company were well wound up, its clerks and secretaries paid off—including Roderick Mackenzie—its books closed for ever. At this hour they lie, those records of a people's agony, locked away in their own old cupboard, opened only by the curious historian, ' all passion spent.'

The other chief use to which the Equivalent money was to be put, according to the express terms of the Treaty, was the payment of the debts of the Scottish government. These debts were chiefly owed to great nobles and government officers. It was difficult for any but a Jacobite to denounce the payment of the national debts as Parliamentary bribery. But the arrangement certainly oiled the wheels of the Union Treaty. Most, though not all, who benefited by this clause, were in fact strong supporters of Union.

On July 22, 1706, the Treaty was signed by all save half-a-dozen out of some sixty Commissioners. Next day they went together from the Cockpit to St. James's Palace, to present their work to Queen Anne, where she sat awaiting them amid a crowd of the ladies of her Court, foreign Ambassadors and other notables. The procession of Commissioners itself contained most of her leading statesmen. They walked into her presence two and two, an Englishman and a Scot in each file. Chancellor Seafield spoke for

Scotland. Lord Keeper Cowper, speaking for England, hesitated, bungled, and finally drew his speech from his pocket and read it, with the imperturbable coolness of a veteran performer, ' while all the audience was in the utmost pain for him.' The Queen made a suitable reply. It was the other great moment of her reign, beside the receipt of the news of Blenheim. The scene has been not unfitly chosen as the subject of one of the frescoes recently set up to adorn the entrance lobby of the present House of Commons, occupying the site of St. Stephen's Chapel, which was in those days the House of Commons itself.[178]

CHAPTER XIV

THE PASSING OF THE UNION TREATY, 1706–1707

Will the Parliaments ratify the Treaty ? Division of opinion in Scotland.
The arguments for and against Union. The Treaty in the Edinburgh
Parliament. Riot and threat of Civil War. Hamilton's weakness.
Queensberry's firmness. Attitude of the Church of Scotland. The
Act protecting her. The Union passes through both Parliaments.
Rejoicings in England. A glimpse into the future.

IT was small wonder that the poor lady, whom two unreasonable nations expected to play the parts of Elizabeth
of England and her rival the Queen of Scots at one and
the same time, had received very graciously the Treaty
proposed by the Commissioners to put an end to the
Dual Monarchy. But it still remained uncertain whether
her subjects, as represented in her two Parliaments, were
prepared to accept the Union. The English Lords and
Commons could be relied on to pass it ; but Ministers
decided not to bring it up at Westminster until it had run
the gauntlet of the Edinburgh Parliament. If it were first
accepted by England, the pride and suspicion of Scotland
would take alarm and regard the Treaty as a piece of English
goods. It had better come before the Estates as the work
of their own Commissioners, before South Britain had the
opportunity of damning it with its approval.

Although the English Parliament usually met in the
winter months, it was the custom of the Scottish Parliament
to meet in the summer. But in the summer of 1706 the
Union Commissioners had been at their work, and the
Estates therefore did not meet till October 3, for what
proved to be the last session of the last Parliament of
Scotland.

The detailed terms of the Treaty had not until then been published, but it had got abroad that the Commissioners had conceded the 'incorporating Union.' Parliament had not been sitting long before the outcry against 'the Treaters, traitors,' rose shrill from half Scotland.

The other half of Scotland shouted less and perhaps thought more. Quiet folk yearned after a settled Succession, colonial trade and the identity of Scotland's interest with that of her rich and powerful neighbour ; they foresaw the dangers to peace and to Presbyterianism that must follow refusal of the Treaty, dangers which the more loud-voiced opponents either ignored, or, if they were Jacobites, secretly welcomed. Among the inducements leading the unwilling Scots towards a Union was the new prestige won for England by Blenheim and Ramillies, and the assertion of her sea supremacy in the Mediterranean and elsewhere. In the autumn of 1706 England was the acknowledged arbitress of Europe : a closer partnership with her appeared more advantageous than at the beginning of the Queen's reign, and defiance of her in league with France more hazardous. The choice was being narrowed down to that.

The Unionists moreover reminded their countrymen of the realities of Scotland's boasted 'independence.' While the benefit from Union would be substantial, the sacrifice would be to a large extent fictitious. For Scotland did not, under the system of the Dual Monarchy, stand fairly upon her own feet as an independent nation. She had no war fleet of her own to save her from invasion.* Her army of 3,000 men was too small either to police the Highlands or to put down a rising in the Lowlands, unless supported by English troops. With no diplomatic representatives and almost no commerce, her voice was unheard in Europe. For America she had ceased to exist since her disappearance from Darien. Even her domestic independence was more nominal than real. Fletcher of Saltoun spoke the bitter truth when he complained that Scotland's Ministers were chosen and dismissed by Godolphin in London, and that

---

* She had two small frigates, occasionally patrolling one on each coast ; their doings are recorded in the Privy Council registers in detail. But the protection of Scotland from invasion was done entirely by the English fleet—as in 1708.

they took their instructions from the English Cabinet. In December 1706 James Johnstone of the *Squadrone*, discussing the Union Treaty with Marlborough, said to him :

> The true state of the matter was whether Scotland should be subject to an English Ministry without trade, or be subject to an English Parliament with trade.[179]

Scotland was not really independent. And if she aspired to attain independence by proclaiming a King of her own, she must become the enemy of England, throw herself into the arms of the Jacobites and France, and in so doing sacrifice her Presbyterian Establishment. If, as was not unlikely, she were then reconquered by England, her state would be worse than before.

These considerations ultimately prevailed in the Parliament House, persuading the *Squadrone*, in spite of their quarrel with Queensberry's government, to cast their score of votes into the balance on the side of the Union Treaty, and so decide the result.[180]   Moreover, these arguments had force out of doors. A warfare of pamphlets,* which in those days did the work now done by newspapers, wireless and political speeches, put the case for and against the Union to the people. No inconsiderable part of the nation, and more particularly of the clergy and leading laity of the Presbyterian Church, were persuaded at least to refrain from joining in the attack upon the Treaty.

Some of the arguments in the opposition pamphlets were false or foolish, but others urged objections of real weight. Not all the fears expressed were unreasonable, although most of them have been happily falsified by the actual course of events.   For example, it was pointed out that, although the Union purported to guarantee certain Scottish institutions, in particular the Presbyterian Establishment, ' in all succeeding generations,' there would in fact be no legal bar to their destruction by Acts of the British Parliament, wherein English ' prelatists ' would always have a very great majority.   There was, doubtless, a strong moral obligation on England never to disturb the main provisions of the

---

* I have had the use, not only of the pamphlets in the National Library, but of a collection kindly lent me by Sir Charles Firth.

Treaty, but this obligation could not be made legally binding on posterity. In a united Great Britain there would be no high judicial arbiter to preserve Scotland's rights, no such Supreme Court as there is to-day in the Federal Constitution of the United States, to judge Bills passed by the Legislature and decide whether they were in accordance with the Treaty of Union or no. The Westminster Parliament was omnicompetent. It had often changed religion in England, and might in the future change it in North Britain. It would be in its power to pass an Act to abolish Presbyterianism in Scotland—and Christianity too, if it so chose.

The question, therefore, was—could Scotland trust her neighbour's good faith? With bitter misgivings she decided to try the experiment.

Her reliance upon England's honour has not been misplaced. It is true that several provisions of the Treaty which were specially marked to be perpetual have been repealed or altered by the British Parliament. For instance, private feudal jurisdictions were abolished in 1747 ; and, in a later age, posts in the schools and Universities of Scotland have been opened to others beside Presbyterians. Whether these were ' breaches of the Union Treaty ' or no, they could be made legally, and, since Scottish opinion assented, with perfect justice. There have indeed been some Acts of the British Parliament which parties in Scotland regarded at the time as violations of the spirit of the pact of 1706; for example, the Whig Treason Act of 1709, and the Tory Toleration Act and Restoration of Church Patronage in 1712. But on the whole England has kept faith for two hundred years, and is not likely to break it now.

The men who opposed the Union, though posterity may think them mistaken on the balance of argument as viewed in the light of subsequent events, had strong patriotic reasons to urge. Their most valid objection was to the sacrifice of the Edinburgh Parliament. This was a real sacrifice, because, since the Revolution, the Scottish Estates were beginning to attract to themselves an interest unparalleled in their long but not very glorious history. Parliamentary life was beginning to stir in Scotland, and the Union killed it in its infancy. Yet the reason why the

Union had become an imperative necessity to Britain was precisely that the Scottish Parliament had become for the first time a reality in the reigns of William and Anne, and that its independent action, however desirable from certain points of view, was rendering the peaceful government of Scotland by an English sovereign impossible on the existing terms.   Therefore there must be a joint government of Great Britain, on economic and religious conditions equitable to Scotland.

Undoubtedly there was loss to set against the gain. The disappearance of the Parliament from Edinburgh nipped in the bud the nascent interest taken by the Scot in politics proper.   Religion, agriculture, trade, literature flourished in Eighteenth-Century Scotland, but not political life.   The Scots took little interest in the doings of their so-called representatives at Westminster.   'The General Assembly,' writes Professor Rait, 'retaining its much more efficient representative machinery, again displaced Parliament as the body which attracted the interest of the nation.' [181]   Scotland for the next hundred years prospered materially and grew intellectually as never before.   But political life only began to revive, painfully enough, at the close of the century, when the agitation for and against Parliamentary Reform, and the hopes and fears aroused by the scent of approaching democracy, raised new parties and new passions.

The debates and votings on the Union Treaty, begun in the Parliament House early in October 1706, went on until the end of January 1707.   Of the few speeches that were published by their authors and have so come down to us, several are well-reasoned arguments and indicate a high level of discussion upon the real issues.   But the most famous of them was the most absurd.   Lord Belhaven's emotional oratory had great vogue when he printed it for consumption out of doors, but it only aroused laughter in the Parliament House, as delivered by the 'rough, fat, black, noisy man, more like a butcher than a lord.'

I think [cried Belhaven], I think I see our ancient mother Caledonia, like Caesar, sitting in the midst of our Senate, ruefully looking round about her, covering herself with her royal garment, attending the fatal blow, and breathing out her last with an *et tu quoque, mi fili.*

To which the Earl of Marchmont made answer :

Behold he dreamed, but lo ! when he awoke, he found it was a dream.[182]

It was soon apparent that a small majority was available for carrying the Union Treaty, clause by clause, through the angry House. The tactful firmness of Queensberry, presiding as Anne's Commissioner, and the disinterested decision of the nobles of the *Squadrone* to support on this great issue the government that had supplanted them, decided the fate of Britain. The majority in favour of the Union was larger among the Nobles than among the Barons and Burgesses, but each of the three Estates recorded a majority on nearly all occasions. About forty members, between a fifth and a sixth of the House, did not vote. It was evident that only pressure from outside could prevent Parliament from passing the Treaty, and the pressure was organized and applied in three forms—addresses, rioting and the threat of armed rebellion.

Ninety addresses were presented against the Union and none in its favour. Yet of thirty-four shires only fourteen addressed ; of sixty-six burghs, only nineteen ; of nine hundred and thirty-eight parishes only sixty ; of sixty-eight presbyteries only three. The members for the protesting shires and burghs in nearly every case voted against the Union, so that there is no clear evidence that on this issue Scotland was seriously misrepresented in the Parliament House. The Convention of Royal Burghs decided to address against the Union by twenty-four votes to twenty, while twenty-two were absent. The Unionists declared that the twenty represented wealth of a far greater taxable value than the rest. The mobs of Glasgow and Edinburgh were indeed hot against the Union, but the wealthier burghers were inclined to favour the change. Opinion in Scotland was divided perhaps not unevenly. But there was more anger and enthusiasm among opponents than among supporters of the Treaty, for even Unionists were

Scots and human, and did but accept the inevitable with a sigh for ' the end of an auld sang.'[183]

The deliberations in the Parliament House were more disturbed by the rioting than by the addresses. For the rioting was, in the most literal sense, at the door. The Edinburgh mob had, ever since its successful activity in the Revolution winter, aspired to hold the government of the country in check, much like the mob of Paris in a later age. It had recently secured by terrorism the execution of Green, and it was now resolved to secure by similar means the rejection of the Union. For if the Union were passed, the political importance of the Edinburgh mob would be gone : the legislature would be moved to London, and in all probability the executive, in the form of the Privy Council, would shortly follow.

But Queensberry and Argyle were not the men to be terrorized, as the *Squadrone* ministers had been terrorized in the affair of Green. In the last week of October, as soon as the first serious riot had proved the inadequacy of the City Guard, who could not prevent the mob hammering on the locked door of the Parliament House, the Government called the Foot Guards down from the Castle, ' His Grace the Duke of Argyle mounted at the head of the Horse Guards,' and the troops occupied High Street and Parliament Close in military form. The opposition in the Estates denounced as tyrannical the protection thus afforded to their debates, and ' it was alleged that it was never known in Edinburgh before.' But the majority of members had no wish to be torn to pieces. Thenceforth the mob had to confine itself to the daily ovation to Hamilton on his way to and from Parliament, and the chase of Lord Commissioner Queensberry's glass coach, as it galloped back to Holyrood with Horse Guards in front and panting footmen behind, before the halloos and stones of the pursuing mob—an undignified but comparatively harmless performance.

Daniel Defoe was living all this while in Edinburgh, as the unofficial agent of the English Government. The long and often alarming reports on Scottish opinion, which he sent to his employer Harley, were passed on to Godolphin, who wrote of them as 'serious and deserving reflection.' Defoe was also in secret conference with the leading Presbyterian clergy, to persuade them, as a representative of the Nonconformists of England, from whom he showed letters, that the Protestant interest in Britain imperatively required the passing of the Union.   He describes himself as 'every day a member of the General Assembly,' and writes that 'every night and morning I have a reverend committee with me to answer their cases of conscience.'   'He was,' wrote Clerk of Penicuik, 'a spy among us, but not known to be such, otherwise the mob of Edinburgh had pulled him to pieces.'   Though his business was not publicly known, he had Englishman written on his face and clothes, and he confessed to Harley that as he walked about— followed by cries of 'No Union,' 'English dog,'—'I cannot say to you I had no apprehensions, nor was Mons. de Witt quite out of my thoughts.' [184]

But destiny had other uses for him than to die in a bicker on High Street.   At that moment, half the world away, in an uninhabited island of the Pacific, a Scottish sailorman was wandering sadly through the brushwood along the high rock ridges, his gun on his shoulder, himself clad in a queer goat-skin hat and suit, the most utterly friendless and for- gotten of all Queen Anne's subjects.   Defoe had never yet even heard the name of Alexander Selkirk, whose story he was to render far more widely known to remote posterity and distant lands than is the tale of Marlborough's battles or the passing of the Treaty that made Great Britain.

Throughout November and December, the critical months when the fate of the Union was decided, Edinburgh was held in awe by the display of military force.   But the army of 3,000 was not enough to keep down all Scotland. In Glasgow, the Town Council had refused to petition against the Union, for Bailie Nicol Jarvie and his like were already dreaming of profitable voyages to the English plan- tations.   Thereupon the mob rose and seized the town. Dumfries was occupied by a regiment of Cameronian rebels from the countryside.   Ayrshire and all the old Covenanting districts were up.   The moment had come

for the opponents of Union to march on Edinburgh and
' raise the Parliament.'

Fortunately for the prospects of the Treaty, its opponents
were even more strongly opposed to one another. The West
was rising to save the Kirk from subjection to a Prelatic
Parliament at Westminster. But it was by no means from
that motive that Episcopalian lairds in the North-East were
saddling their horses and calling out their men ; nor was
it for love of the Kirk that kilted clansmen were waiting in
the glens for the word to march on Edinburgh. Queensberry had his paid agents, Ker of Kersland and Cunningham
of Ecket, at work among the Cameronians. These men first
gained the confidence of the formidable zealots by urging
them on to occupy Dumfries and burn the houses of local
Unionists, and then preached to them the doctrine of the
sin and danger attending all traffick with Papists, Prelatists,
French and Jacobites. Would they make themselves the
Pretender's tools ? In this way Ker persuaded the Western
fanatics to halt in their march upon the capital, and ultimately to disperse. English troops had been moving to the
Border, but with no intention of crossing it unless Edinburgh
were in peril.

Meanwhile the Jacobites of North and East did not
march. They were ready, but no one gave the word. Their
leaders, Hamilton and Atholl, were jealous of one another
and would not concert plans. Enquiry had shown that no
French troops were so much as promised, and that the
English Jacobites refused to stir so long as Queen Anne was
alive. Hamilton, as always, failed those who relied on him
when the crisis came. He loved to figure in Parliament as
the patriot Duke, and in High Street as the idol of the mob.
But from decisive action he was restrained by a combination
of motives—some remnant of political wisdom, fear of civil
strife, thoughts of his English estates, his heavy financial
embarrassments, his want of genuine interest in the Pretender's claim to a throne that he had dreamed of for
himself ; he would not give the word for war. It is even
possible that he had secret misgivings that the Union might
after all be the best way out. He had discussed it as an
open question with Mar in September. And in November,

as the crisis approached, he ' was four hours with the Lord Commissioner in his apartments, and went out as well as came in *incognito*,' and he was ' with the Chancellor very frequently.' Once, when the Opposition had planned to secede in a body from the House as the preliminary to revolution, he had consented to take the lead, but on the morning of action sent word that he was ' seized of the toothache.' When at length his followers had forced him to come to the Parliament House, he refused to act. Under such a leader rebellion proved impossible.

It was, moreover, noted as fortunate for the Unionists that this all-important session had, contrary to custom, been held in the winter. The depth of Scottish roads and the shortness of Scottish days around Yule were strong additional reasons why hesitating men should not leave their firesides for the miseries of campaign.

' There is a tide in the affairs of men . . .' It had ebbed, while they still hesitated to embark. Glasgow had been re-occupied by dragoons, and the mob ringleaders arrested. December 1706 had passed without catastrophe, and with the New Year a new atmosphere prevailed. The Ministers and their friends wrote to their English correspondents that the Treaty was safe.[185]

One of the chief reasons why the national discontent had just not boiled over was that the Presbyterian Church had received in November 1706 important safeguards for her position under the Union. The Scots Commissioners who made the Treaty in London had been forbidden to treat of matters ecclesiastical, which the Edinburgh Parliament reserved for its own consideration. Between November 7 and 12 it debated and carried an ' Act for securing the Protestant Religion and Presbyterian Church Government within the Kingdom of Scotland,' and incorporated it as an essential part of the Union Treaty. This Act preserved the existing privileges and monopolies of the Presbyterian Establishment ' to continue without any alteration to the people of this land in all succeeding generations.' It may be matter of argument whether or not the clauses were so drawn as to render it a breach of faith on the part of the British Parliament in

1712 to pass the Toleration Act and to restore Church Patronage in Scotland. In any case the Church Security Act put the strongest possible moral obligation on the Westminster Parliament to respect the fundamentals of the Presbyterian Establishment.

The incorporation of this Act in the Treaty did much to relieve the fears of the Church. The hot young ministers who, earlier in the autumn, had been preaching against the Treaty as a betrayal of Scotland into the hands of English Prelatists, began, as the winter advanced, to abate their fury. The Jacobite Lockhart mournfully recorded that

no sooner did the Parliament pass an Act for the security of their Kirk, than most of the brethren's zeal cooled.

The General Assembly of the Church was sitting in Edinburgh all this time ; fortunately the judicious Carstares presided as Moderator. The Assembly at first had shown some hostility to the Treaty, but after the passing of the Act to secure the Church in November, it became neutral, if not favourable. The strong, gentle influence of Carstares was now, as always, potent for the good. It was thought that the Treaty would never have won through Parliament, if the Assembly, under worse guidance, had in December passed a vote against the Union. But it voted instead in deprecation of the riots.

Presbyterians had been put on their guard by the over-great zeal of Episcopalians, in and out of Parliament, in warning them that the Union would be the destruction of the Kirk, and vowing that the Act for her security failed to secure her at all. The gentlemen protested too much. It was notorious that their real quarrel with the Union was that it made the Protestant Succession and the Presbyterian Church in Scotland essential parts, for all time to come, of the Constitution of Great Britain.

From the Presbyterian point of view there remained, indeed, one serious blot on the Treaty, the Sacramental Test. The Test of Anglican Communion, however much modified in practice by the possibilities of ' occasional conformity,' * purported to keep out Scottish Presbyterians from those

* *Blenheim*, pp. 277–279.

Ministerial and other offices of Great Britain which were held in England. It was only a partial compensation that the Treaty reserved all offices held in Scotland to Presbyterians, for the centre of political ambition and power, alike for Scots and English, was now to be fixed in London. But in fact the grievance proved more theoretic than practical, because in the latitudinarian atmosphere of the Eighteenth Century, not clearly foreseen in 1706, the Sacramental Test was readily taken by Scots Presbyterians aspiring to British official posts, or else was not in fact offered to them.* But at the time when the Union was passed, great indignation was felt in Scotland at the injustice of the Test. Since, however, it was known that the English would not alter the Test Act in their country even for the benefit of North Britons, it was necessary to endure what could not be cured.[186]

The Scottish Parliament made few alterations or additions to the Treaty as presented by the Commissioners, beyond the addition of the Act for securing the Presbyterian Church. Some amendments were accepted referring to details of trade and taxation, on which great stress was laid in Scotland. But the Ministers, in spite of severe pressure brought upon them, refused all such changes as would have led to dangerous disputes when the amended Treaty appeared before the English Parliament. For example, they successfully rebutted the claim that Scotland should continue to be allowed to export raw wool abroad, contrary to a prime principle of English economic policy.[187]

When in the course of January 1707 it became clear that, contrary to so many expectations, the Treaty was actually passing through the Estates in a form that England would accept, the chagrin of the Jacobites and extreme Nationalists was proportionate to their recollection of a dozen different occasions on which the Union would have

---

* Pitt's friend and Cabinet colleague, the great Henry Dundas, was a Scottish Presbyterian, at one time active in the business of the General Assembly. Yet he said to Dr. Thomas Somerville anent the Sacramental Test : ' Doctor, I did not think you had been so illiberal. Would you scruple to take the sacrament in the Church of England, or join in communion with its members ? ' *Somerville*, p. 232. See also the quotation from Dr. Alexander Carlyle's speech to the General Assembly in 1791, in *Dicey and Rait*, pp. 248–249, 254–256. The growth of Moderatism in Scotland greatly smoothed the working of the Test in practice.

been wrecked by the least turn of chance or by a slightly greater effort of co-operation among its opponents. Jacobites like Lockhart could not forgive Hamilton. Nor could they believe that a wider vision of their country's needs had brought round many to acquiesce regretfully but hopefully in the great change. Lockhart took refuge in the theory that the Union had been passed by wholesale bribery. The fact that he adduced in support of this charge was the advance of £20,000 by the English to the Scottish government, in two instalments, in October and November 1706. It was to be paid back, but exactly how much of it ever was paid back did not emerge from the investigation into the matter by the Tory Parliament of 1712. There was something irregular about the accounting for the transaction. But at most only a small part of it was spent in direct bribery. For the greater part was spent on the purpose for which the sum was ostensibly borrowed, the payment of debts owed by the Scottish government to individuals. No doubt some of these payments were made thus punctually in order to facilitate the passage of the Treaty. Possibly some may have gone to solve the doubts of a few waverers, but most went into the pockets of men who had all along been staunch supporters of the Union. Queensberry had long been clamouring for the settlement of the great sums owed him by government, and when he again took office in 1705 it had been agreed that he should be paid. More than half the £20,000 went to liquidate his claims. How far can payment of debts, justly due, be regarded as bribery?

Lockhart, however, stated that some of the persons so paid had no claims on Government, or else were paid twice over. But he is a strongly prejudiced witness, and he brings no evidence beyond his bare word. There is no proof or disproof in some of the cases. In others, such as those of Queensberry, Marchmont and Roxburgh, the money paid was certainly owing to them from Government. One of the beneficiaries, Atholl, remained a staunch opponent of the Union to the end.

It would be idle to pretend that no money passed to ease the passage of the Union. It would be strange if it had not, for on the most ordinary occasions, both in the English and

Scottish Parliaments, it was the custom of the age for the government to give *douceurs* in one form or another to some of its supporters. Even Opposition parties were held together, not only by hope of obtaining office, but also by more immediate inducements. Opponents of the Treaty had themselves taken French and Papal gold through the medium of their leader Hamilton, and the Scottish Whigs declared that this ' occasioned much difficulty in bringing about the Union.' But that did not prove that the Jacobites and Nationalists opposed the Union because they had been bribed *en masse*. And Lockhart's corresponding theory that the Union was the outcome of wholesale bribery of individuals is equally absurd. The Treaty was carried, as it was also opposed, for grave public reasons earnestly considered by men who were not indifferent to their country's interests, nor, it may be admitted, to their own.[188]

In February 1707 the Treaty as passed by the Scottish Estates was recommended to the English Parliament in a Speech from the Throne. In both Houses the High Tory leaders spoke against the Union, chiefly on the ground of its recognition of the Church in Scotland and admission of a Presbyterian phalanx among the Lords and Commons at Westminster. Nottingham declared that it destroyed ' the very constitution of England.' In the previous Parliament the Treaty would have had heavy going in the Commons, but Sir John Packington now harangued in vain on the impropriety of having two Churches in one Kingdom. It was indeed an anomaly according to the theory and practice of the age, but the queer, flexible patchwork of the British Empire was in future to be sustained by a long series of such anomalies, paradoxes and innovations.

In neither House did the Opposition venture to divide on any but subordinate issues. All the Whigs and governmental Tories were for the Union, and so were the North-Country members irrespective of party, in their dread of renewed Border War and the Scottish occupation of the Tyne coalfields. The majority of the Bishops supported the Treaty. Archbishop Tenison grieved the High Churchmen and placated the Scots by declaring that ' the narrow notions

of all Churches had been their ruin ; and that he believed
the Church of Scotland to be as true a Protestant Church as
the Church of England, though he could not say it was so
perfect.' He introduced a Bill for securing the Church of
England, to be appended to the Union Treaty like the
corresponding Act for the Church of Scotland. Tenison's
Bill gave to existing Acts, which protected the Church of
England in her rights and monopolies, the character of
essential parts of the constitution of Great Britain. The
High Tories declared the security insufficient, but my Lord
Wharton pronounced it unnecessary. He was in high good
humour at the success of the Whig policies, and told the
House in his pleasantest vein that ' the Church was secure
enough without it, since the Scripture had declared it was
built upon a rock and the gates of Hell should not prevail
against it.' Coming from Tenison or Nottingham the sentiment would have been listened to with edification, but when
Noble Lords heard it from Wharton they scarcely knew
what face he intended them to wear.[189]

There was no need again to put the Union Treaty to a
vote of the Scottish Estates. It had been passed by the
English in the form in which they had received it from
Edinburgh ; only the Act securing the English Church had
been added on, in a manner agreed to beforehand by words
in the Treaty as it had passed the Scottish Estates. Queensberry therefore had only to announce at Edinburgh the rati-
fication of the Treaty by England. Before the end of March
he had wound up the business of the last session of the last
Parliament of Scotland.[190]

The First of May 1707, when Great Britain was to come
into existence by Statute, was awaited in England with deep
thankfulness unalloyed by regrets. But in Scotland some
natural tears were shed. The public was disturbed when,
in the last days of April, ' thirty-one whales ' were found
dead on the sands of Kirkcaldie ; their monstrous presence
was regarded throughout the land as an evil omen. On
May 1 itself an Edinburgh correspondent wrote to the Earl
of Mar:

There is nothing so much taken notice of here to-day as the
solemnity in the south part of Britain, and the want of it here. The

first tune of our music bells this day is ' *Why should I be sad on my wedding day ?* ' There being a printed account of the whales come ashore at Kirkcaldie, I send it inclosed to your Lordship.

But meanwhile Queensberry, bringing the Union with him, had been making a triumphant progress through England in the April weather. Southwards from Berwick bounds, he was received with acclamations by the people, and feasted by the magistrates of every city on the London road, while the gentlemen of each shire rode in to do him honour. ' At Barnet he was met by the Ministry of England and most of the Nobility then attending the two Houses of Parliament. Their retinue consisted of forty-six coaches and over a thousand horsemen.' Thus royally accompanied, the last Queen's Commissioner for the Scottish Parliament made entry into London through the shouting streets. The Scots in England for once found themselves popular, and observed ' real joy and satisfaction in the Citizens of London,' who ' were terribly apprehensive of confusions from Scotland in case the Union had not taken place.'

On May 1 all England made holiday. The Queen, accompanied by four hundred coaches, went to yet another ceremony at St. Paul's to give thanks for the greatest of all the victories with which God had blessed her reign.[191]

The one-sided rejoicings over the Union were soon over, and in a few weeks charges and counter-charges were being bandied about between Scots and English. The later pages of this history will record fresh instances of bad blood and misunderstanding between the two now yoked as one ; and the economic prosperity which the Scots expected to reap at once as a result of free trade with the Empire, was long in coming. But the new yoke, though it galled, held fast ; and if prosperity came late, it was one day to come in full plenty as a direct result of the Union. Meanwhile the immediate object of the statesmen who had united the Parliaments was fulfilled upon Anne's death : the House of Hanover succeeded to the throne of Great Britain, and no rival reigned at Holyrood. But, because the terms of the Union had been founded on justice and equality between Scots and English, an even greater measure of success

crowned the work in more distant years—the full reconcile-
ment of the two peoples. The British Empire became much
greater, and in every sense richer than an English Empire
could ever have been with Scotland for enemy—in arms,
in commerce, in colonization, in thought, science, letters
and song.

And yet, though Scotland had lost her Parliament, she
had not lost her soul or her personality as a nation. Indeed
her full development was only rendered possible by the release from poverty and isolation that the Union brought in
its train. The golden age of Scotland was still in the future—
the age of Burns and Scott. Then would be seen a sight
to make Defoe smile and Swift sneer—England coming
to worship at the shrine of Scottish tradition and legend !
The angry reluctance with which Scotland had consented
to the Union was not meaningless ; if she had agreed with
enthusiasm, if she had nourished no resentments and no
regrets, she might have dwindled down into the thing she
was officially to be called—' North Britain.'

CHAPTER XV

The Check to the Allies in 1707

Allied dissension. Marlborough's visit to Charles XII. Marlborough's
Great Design. Peterborough's tour in Europe. Almanza and the loss
of Spain. Fruitless campaign in the Netherlands. Villars breaks into
Germany. The failure before Toulon. The 'half-sinking' of the
French fleet. Death of Sir Cloudesley Shovell.

THE *annus mirabilis* of 1706 had put an end to French
hegemony in Europe and had secured those war aims which
the Grand Alliance had originally been pledged to attain.
But the military events of 1707 were to reveal the limits of
the Allies' power, to show that France was not impotent for
self-defence and that Spain was not, like one of the Provinces
of her Empire, a mere counter with which diplomats could
bargain at the Hague. Almanza, Toulon, the raid of Villars
into Germany and the failure of Marlborough to achieve
anything remarkable in the Netherlands formed a sum total
bitterly disappointing to those over-confident hopes with
which the campaign began.

But, in every field, the failure of the Allies was not more
due to the resistant powers of the French and Spanish
nations than to the jealousies that divided Britain, Holland
and Austria, all the more bitterly now that so large a measure
of safety and success had been secured. The three-cornered
quarrel over the Governorship of Belgium in the previous
summer * bore fruit in 1707 in the supine and selfish conduct by which Austria surpassed herself in Germany and
the Mediterranean, and in the partial relapse of the Dutch
Field Deputies into a surly obstructiveness to Marlborough's

* See pp. 132–135, above. *For this chapter see Map X (Europe), below.*

action in the field, in contrast to the ready co-operation they had displayed throughout the campaign of Ramillies. Marlborough suffered allies more gladly than any other great commander in history, but even his letters in this year of unfulfilled renown speak bitterly of chances thrown away in every part of Europe, chiefly by Austria and in a less degree by the German Princes and by the Dutch. The refusal of the Emperor to come to terms with the Hungarians continued to enrage the English Ministers, and the recent conquest of Italy opened up a whole new series of bitter quarrels between the Duke of Savoy and the Imperial Court. According to Godolphin in June, ' Vienna has not one thought that is not directly opposite to the interest of the Allies'; whereas the Viennese Ministers had the temerity to complain that Austria alone of the Allies was gaining nothing by the war ! [192]

While in the West the enemies of France were held in check by their mutual dissensions, in the East a dark cloud hovered over them in the shape of Charles XII and his victorious army of Swedes, camped in the heart of Saxony and threatening to attack the Empire through its back door. It was well indeed that he had not arrived there before Blenheim and Ramillies.

Charles was the Cœur-de-Lion of Swedish history. He used his country as a base for military operations in the pursuit of glory, and died, like his English prototype, by a shot from the walls of a petty fortress. State policy of the higher sort he had none. Apart from ambition and revenge he had one ideal motive akin to that of the old Crusading King, the desire to do something for the oppressed Protestants of Eastern Europe. In that part of military strategy which consists in prudence he was almost as deficient as in political wisdom, but he was admirable in the discipline of an army and in the tactics of the field. Posterity is familiar with his Spartan figure, without hat, wig or decorations, clad in a plain military frock-coat and topboots. The top-boots seem the essence of the man, for he could not sit still on his throne and govern, but must needs be always on the move at the head of his troops, and Leibnitz in 1707 wrote of him to Lord Raby, that ' his demeanour and dress are those of the troopers of the old school.' *

Charles, having defeated the Russians at Narva and conquered Poland, of which his enemy Augustus, Elector of Saxony, was King, put Stanislaus on the throne in his place, and pursued him across Silesia into his German Electorate. In the autumn of 1706 the Swedish armies took military possession of Saxony, where Charles kept a rough military court at Altranstadt, a few miles from Leipzig. During his year of comparative immobility that followed, the eyes of all warring Europe were turned thither to take note of this meteor of the Northern skies, which it had been impossible to observe with attention so long as it had been flashing without rest over the Baltic fields of battle.

Altranstadt, indeed, became in 1707 the scene of the main diplomatic rivalry of Europe. It was neutral ground where France and her enemies could meet and contend for the friendship of Charles. For some years past no important international business had been transacted between the Western Powers and Sweden, because the King in the field had had little taste for interviews with foreign civilians, and his Ministers had small influence upon his decisions and no authority to deal in his name. The able English Envoy to Sweden, the Reverend John Robinson,† who knew Scandinavia better than any of his countrymen, had sometimes been privileged to speak with Charles in Poland, but to little purpose. In November 1706 he hastened to Altranstadt, where he found the agents of King Louis busily endeavouring to stir up the Swede to invade the Austrian border, so temptingly at hand, and settle all his

* Leibnitz adds : ' The King of Sweden had set out to review his troops dispersed throughout the country [Saxony] and the administrator of Holstein had run more than forty leagues after him without being able to catch him. At the moment when the King returned, I was at Altranstadt, and I saw him at dinner. That lasted a full half-hour, but his Majesty did not say a single word during his dinner, and never raised his eyes but once, when a young Prince of Würtemberg, seated at his left hand, began to play with the dog, which he left off doing the moment he caught that look.' *Kemble*, p. 458.

† Afterwards Lord Privy Seal, negotiator at Utrecht and Bishop successively of Bristol and London. It is because of his double connection with Scandinavia and Oriel that a Runic inscription to this day adorns a quadrangle in his old College.

quarrels with the Emperor by the sword.   If they could
succeed in that, their master might yet recover all that
Marlborough had torn from him on the Danube and the
Dyle.

The matters in dispute between King Charles and
Emperor Joseph would scarcely have been raised between
two friendly princes, or would quickly have been settled ;
but they were not unlikely to cause war between these two
very obstinate monarchs.   The first cause of dispute was
the condition of the Emperor's Protestant subjects in Silesia.
Their churches had been taken from them and their liberties
infringed contrary to certain clauses in the Treaties of
Westphalia, of which Sweden was a guarantor.   Charles
made himself the champion of their cause.   His attitude,
recalling that of Gustavus Adolphus, stirred up the latent
antagonism of the Protestant and Catholic interests throughout the whole body of the Empire.   He had designs for a
League of Protestant Princes in Europe, the formation of
which would have shattered the Grand Alliance constructed
on a different principle.

His other demands on Vienna were more personal and
related to molehills which the unfriendly relation of the two
courts raised into mountains—insulting words spoken of
him by an Hungarian nobleman, and the escape from
Austrian territory of some Russian troops who ought to
have been interned.

It was the part of England and of Marlborough to
appease these discords.   The Emperor must be induced to
do something for the Silesian Protestants, and the King of
Sweden persuaded to leave the other religious problems of
Germany and Europe alone.   Fortunately Charles, though
he detested the Emperor and his Jesuit camarilla, equally
detested Louis as the arch-persecutor of Huguenots.   Moreover he considered that he still had accounts to settle with
the Czar : if only the Emperor would consent to stave him
off with concessions and courtesies, he would disappear with
his army into the depths of the Russian wilderness.

Marlborough was the obvious mediator.   For some
years past it had been known in diplomatic circles that the
mysterious young warrior of the Polish campaigns was ' bon

Anglois,' for in spite of his economic disputes with England over the Baltic trade, he had not forgotten that England's fleet had saved him from his leagued enemies at the beginning of his career.* As early as 1704 it had been said in Eastern Europe that ' the Emperor was obliged to his alliance with Queen Anne for the quiet which his countries enjoyed ' on the side exposed to invasion by Charles. The heir of Gustavus rejoiced in the allied victories over the Revoker of the Edict of Nantes. He was full of generous envy of Marlborough, and boyish inquisitiveness about him, characteristically enquiring whether he led his troops to the charge in person, and declaring that he would be delighted to meet so great a soldier face to face.†

It was in these circumstances that the Duke, at the request of the Emperor and other Allies, undertook a journey to Saxony, before opening his campaign in the Netherlands. Driving by way of Hanover, where he again paid successful court to the Elector, he arrived at Altranstadt in the last days of April. The Swedish Minister, Count Piper, gave him better hospitality than was to be had in the King's own quarters, and took him next day into the royal presence. This meeting of the two famous soldiers, so different in their genius, temper and destiny, has always held the imagination of mankind. Marlborough presented letters from Queen Anne and ' made a short compliment in English, which was interpreted by Mr. Robinson.'

April 28 1707

I present to your majesty [he said] a letter from the Queen, my mistress. Had not her sex prevented her, she would have crossed the sea to see a Prince admired by the whole Universe. I am in this particular more happy than the Queen, and I wish I could serve some campaigns under so great a general as your majesty, that I might learn what I yet want to know in the art of war

No words could have gone more straight to the King's heart. Yet his next campaigns could only have taught Marlborough what every general in Europe except Charles

* In 1700. See *Blenheim*, pp. 9-10.
† P.R.O. (S.P.) 91, 4, Whitworth's letter from Breslau, December 7, 1704 ; *Coxe*, chap. liv. (Grumbkow to Marlborough, January 11, 1707).

already knew, that it is not prudent to lead a great army across interminable leagues of Russian marsh and forest, without proper roads, communications and supplies.

The contact thus happily established in public audience was continued in private conversation. The Englishman was not long in discovering that Charles was rootedly hostile to France and that the very insistence of Louis' agents helped to restrain him from attacking Austria. Marlborough effectively pleaded the common cause of the Allies, and showed the unseasonableness in the Protestant interest of the formation at that moment of a Protestant League. He left the Swede more unwilling to make war on Austria, and more anxious than ever to be off to dethrone the Czar before returning in a more favourable season to settle the affairs of Germany. According to Voltaire's testimony, Sarah in her widowhood told him that her husband, in this famous interview, saw a map of Muscovy on the table, noticed how the King's eyes blazed when he mentioned the Czar, and concluded that his real ambition was to dethrone Peter the Great as he had dethroned Augustus of Poland.

So, having settled English pensions on Charles's Ministers according to the custom of the age, Marlborough got into his coach and drove back again to the West. The influence of his visit on the King had been considerable as a restraint on immediate action against Austria. But it had not been in itself decisive. Until the Emperor gave way, Charles would not budge. It was not till the first week of September that Vienna capitulated on all points. Then and then only Charles broke up his Saxon camp and marched off behind the curtain of the Russian forests, to meet his fate at Poltava.[193]

Charles has much to answer for in history. His restless ambition and revenge, his inability to remain at peace and perform the proper duties of a King, went far to destroy the influence and power of Sweden, that might have been so strong for the good of civilization ; and his headlong attempt to reach Moscow raised up instead, upon the flank of Europe, the barbarous might of the Russian hordes—because Peter the Great, for all his savagery, was a statesman, while Charles XII was only a warrior, and not a wise one,

> A hare-brained Hotspur, governed by a spleen.

Marlborough, as he started back across Germany to the Hague, hopefully revolved the Great Design he had formed and set on foot for the destruction that year of the enemy's power of further resistance. The action in all the seats of war had been planned and timed by his master mind. He did not trust to his own successes in the Netherlands alone. He hoped indeed for a battle there that would bring him within striking distance of Paris. But he knew that the Dutch would be difficult to handle this year ; he knew that the great enemy fortresses, like Lille, Mons and Tournai, lay thickest on the borders of France ; and Louis, by a great effort at recruiting during the winter's breathing space, had concentrated on that frontier a field-army of more than 100,000 men, commanded by the able Vendôme with orders to avoid a battle. Marlborough would not therefore confide in his own success to finish the war. But the very size of Vendôme's army argued that the other fronts had been weakened. The Mediterranean, never far from the Duke's thoughts, should be the scene of the *coup-de-grâce* to the French power.

The year then, as he planned it, should open with an attack across the Alps, to be delivered by Eugene from the newly acquired allied base of the Italian peninsula. Toulon was to be the objective. The forces of Piedmont and Austria, with the German troops paid and supplied by England in that seat of war, would surely suffice for Eugene to take the great French arsenal by a surprise attack, aided by the British fleet under Sir Cloudesley Shovell. If once the allied flags flew over Toulon, Louis must seek peace on his enemy's terms. Moreover, the mere fact of the invasion of Southern France would bring back thither Berwick's army from Spain and leave Madrid open once more to occupation by the armies of England and Portugal.

Such was Marlborough's Great Design. The leading part was without jealousy assigned to Eugene, the comrade-in-arms in whom he always confided, but who failed him on

this one occasion.   If the Allies had become intelligent or
even docile agents in the execution of the plan, Toulon
must have fallen.   But the statesmen of Vienna, if not also
the Duke of Savoy, were half-hearted in their desire to
capture the great naval base for the benefit of the Maritime
Powers.   They failed to consider the war as a whole, and
they neglected the importance of punctual time-keeping
in the elaborate plan laid down for the various actors in
the piece.

While Marlborough was preparing for his wearisome
journey to Altranstadt to secure the safety of Austria, the
Emperor Joseph had been taking steps which upset his
plans and compromised beforehand the chances of allied
success against Toulon and Madrid.   In March the
Emperor concluded a secret and separate Treaty with
Louis for the neutrality of Italy, by which the French
garrisons cut off in the Milanese were allowed to return
home ; in this way some 12,000 veteran troops, who must
otherwise have surrendered, went to swell the forces of
resistance in Spain and Provence.   The Emperor's object
was to put himself as speedily as possible into complete
occupation of the Italian provinces, which the victory of
Turin had laid at his feet.*   To enjoy the immediate full
possession of the Milanese and Neapolitan territories
meant more to Viennese statecraft than to prepare further
blows against France at the bidding of England.   If the
Maritime Powers would not hand over the reconquered
Netherlands to their lawful owners, the House of Hapsburg
would at least help itself to its own Italian property.

By the same reasoning the Emperor saw fit, in spite of
the lively remonstrances of Marlborough and of the British
Ministers, to send an Austrian army trailing down the
length of the peninsula to expel the feeble Spanish garrisons
from Naples.†   This premature and unnecessary assertion

* See p. 144, above.
  † With the disregard to the territories of weak neutrals common to both sides
in these wars, the Austrians marched right across the States of the Church to reach
Naples, gravely alarming the Pope and Cardinals by their passage.   Naples, where
there was strong anti-French feeling, fell without resistance, and the fortress of
Gaeta after a siege.   Sicily, which would have put up little resistance, was not
occupied at once as the English fleet was not co-operating.

of undoubted power delayed for months Eugene's advance
into Provence and weakened its force when at last it took
place.   Marlborough had timed the passage of the Maritime Alps for the early spring, both in order to secure a
surprise attack on Toulon and to relieve French pressure on
Spain.   The Emperor postponed the vital operation until
late summer, and long ere that Spain had been lost for good
and all at Almanza.[194]

In 1706 the Allies had let slip the only real opportunity
they ever had of placing Austrian Charles on the throne of
Madrid with anything like acquiescence on the part of his
subjects.   The strange campaign had ended with the concentration of the bulk of the allied forces on the Mediterranean seaboard, Galway with the army of Portugal having
retreated eastward from Madrid to join the forces of King
Charles in Valencia.*

Early in the new year they received a further accession
of strength.   In the previous autumn Earl Rivers had been
sent out from England in command of more than 8,000
troops.   It had been originally intended that he should
land on the coast of Guienne : he was there to proclaim
that he had come as the friend of French liberty, to restore
the States General and the Edict of Nantes ; he was to
raise the Huguenots of all Southern France in aid of their
brethren of the Cevennes, and so join hands with the attack
to be made from Italy upon Toulon.   But, for a variety of
reasons, the rash project was abandoned, greatly to the
ultimate advantage of the Huguenots and of French civil
and religious liberty, which would not have benefited by the
runaway knocks of foreign powers.   The expedition under
Rivers had thereupon been sent south, first to Lisbon, and
thence by way of Gibraltar to join Galway in Valencia.
There he arrived in February 1707, with little more than
half his original force, the remainder of the unhappy
English soldiers having perished of the miseries of the
protracted winter voyage—the storms of Biscay Bay and the
diseases begotten of the unwholesome conditions of transport.
True to the quarrelsome tradition of allied commanders

* See p. 158, above.

in Spain, Earl Rivers, even before he reached Valencia, had begun a feud with his future colleagues, writing home from Lisbon violent abuse of Galway, whom he accused of treachery and whom he claimed to supersede. The very extravagance of the charges he made told against him. The Ministers at home supported Galway, the more so as the old Huguenot was a great favourite with the Whig Lords. General James Stanhope, often a peacemaker between others though not without a spice of temper himself, succeeded in composing the quarrel between his chiefs, and Rivers in the end went home very decently by his own consent, leaving his troops to be led by Galway to their fate at Almanza.*

In those same first months of 1707 Peterborough returned to Valencia from his Italian holiday,† and took part in the councils of war that decided on the policy for the year's campaign. Galway and Stanhope were for taking the offensive in the rashest form of all—another advance on Madrid. Charles and his generals were for the feeblest and most dangerous of all schemes of defensive warfare—the distribution of the army in garrisons along the eastern coast of Spain. Peterborough took the side of caution, declaring that the war could only be won in Provence, and that till the blow was actually being delivered against Toulon, the Allies should remain on the defensive in Spain. The Franco-Spaniards, he declared, were stronger in the field, particularly in cavalry. After much heated debate the worst possible decision was reached, reflecting the evils of a divided command. Galway and Das Minas went forward with the English, Dutch and Portuguese under their orders, while Charles and his General Noyelles led off their Imperialists and Catalans to garrison the towns of Aragon, Catalonia and the coast. If all had marched forward as a single army, Almanza might perhaps have been won. If all had remained behind, it would never have been fought.

---

* Rivers was a famous rake, but Dr. Johnson was probably deceived by friendship when he believed his friend Richard Savage, the poet, to be the illegitimate son of the Earl.

† See p. 157, above.

Peterborough now received his recall from the home authorities, and in March 1707 took his final departure from Spain.   To Stanhope, with whom he had quarrelled less bitterly than with any other colleague, he wrote, after Almanza, a cheerful letter to the refrain ' I told you so ' :

> You find Spanish horse will beat English foot, and that it was not so easy as you thought the getting to Madrid.   I thank all those that have assisted in sending me to London.

The son of Mercury, released from serious labours, passed a happy summer rushing round the capitals and camps of Europe, persuading the statesmen of Vienna that he was the friend of Charles III and Galway the enemy, and boring or scandalizing each Commander-in-Chief in turn with the volubility of a self-invited guest at headquarters.   Eugene wrote : ' his lordship thinks like a general although he does not always express himself with propriety.'   At Altranstadt he would have been a danger, with his talk against the Emperor and his flattery of Charles XII as the mediator of Europe, had not that silent Prince conceived the strongest distaste for him.   Last of all, in August, it was the turn of the English headquarters in Belgium :

> Lord Peterborough has said all that is possible to me [writes Marlborough in quiet despair], but says nothing of leaving the army. . . . What is worse, the ill weather hinders me from going abroad so that he has the opportunity of very long conversations ;   what is said one day, the next destroys ;   so that I have desired him to put his thoughts in writing.

At last he consented to cross to England, whither he had been ordered to return six months before.   He arrived in London in the autumn, in time to publish the tale of his exploits and his wrongs, and to lead the attack in the next session of Parliament against the Government.   He had much to tell his Peers, for the Ministry that had recalled him from Spain had been punished by the catastrophe that befell our arms in the Peninsula only a few weeks after he had left.[195]

In April Galway moved inland from Valencia with his section of the allied forces.*   He intended to advance on

---

* Nominally the Portuguese General Das Minas was commander-in-chief. But Galway in reality was the leader. *See Map X, end of volume.*

Madrid by turning the upper waters of the Tagus ; but before marching north, he had to secure his communications by reducing certain enemy garrisons in Murcia.   While he was thus engaged the Duke of Berwick approached with an army of 25,400 French and Spaniards.   Galway and Das Minas commanded only 15,500 men, and more than half were Portuguese who proved worse than useless in field operations.   Of Berwick's forces nearly half were French, and though the Spanish foot were of little use save for guerilla purposes, the Spanish cavalry, as Peterborough had forewarned his countrymen, proved formidable even against English troops.

In face of such odds, it was a fatal mistake on Galway's part to seek out Berwick at Almanza and challenge him to battle.   It appears that, owing to the hostility of the countryside, he did not learn till too late that the enemy's force had just been increased by 8,000 men fresh from France.   They had been sent to Spain as a result of the Emperor's grant of free passage to the French garrisons from the Milanese and the excentric movement of the Austrian army of Italy towards Naples.   The Allies were the architects of their own ruin at Almanza.

The great plain, into which Galway had led his forces so deeply that he could not retreat when he realized the immensely superior force of the enemy, afforded no shelter or way of escape for the weaker party.   Having entered the trap, they must break through or suffer complete disaster.

The action began at three in the afternoon.   Both armies set their infantry in the centre and their horse on the wings, as in one of the old battles of the English Civil War.   But the Allies, being weak in cavalry, 'interlined' the squadrons of their left wing with English infantry, after the model of Marlborough's tactics at Blenheim.   On that flank the struggle of all arms was long and fierce.   The only Portuguese who behaved well that day were the squadrons whom Das Minas himself there led into the mêlée : his mistress, who followed him in male attire, was struck dead at his side.   On the same wing of the battle, Galway, entering the thick of the fight without the sword-arm he had lost in the trenches before Badajos, was

Aug. 25
(N.S.)
1707

wounded by a sabre cut over the eyes that put him out of action during the critical minutes of the battle.

In the centre, the English, Dutch and Huguenot infantry, though they began the fight that afternoon exhausted with thirst and long marches, showed all their wonted valour, and drove back superior forces of French and Spanish infantry till they were right under the walls of Almanza. Victory might have been won, or disaster at least avoided, but for the conduct of the Portuguese cavalry, of whom the allied right wing was entirely composed. They fled from the field without striking a blow.

As evening came on, the masses of the enemy closed in on the deserted remnant of the allied army. The disappearance of almost all the Portuguese horse and foot from the field left some 8,000 men to contend against more than 20,000. Das Minas and Galway, if they were neither of them great generals, were both of them gallant veterans, accustomed to keep their heads in the stress of battle and defeat. They succeeded in extricating and carrying into safety some squadrons of cavalry, 1,500 of the infantry of England and Holland, and the English train of six guns. The twenty Portuguese cannon fell to the victors.*

Another column of English, Dutch and Huguenot infantry, variously estimated at 2,000 and 4,000 men, also cut their way out of the ring of foes. Led by General Shrimpton, one of the heroes of the defence of Gibraltar, they retreated that night into the hill country, some eight miles from the field. But next day, too weary to march further, with no food or water and almost without ammunition, they capitulated on the approach of the enemy's cavalry. The decision was not taken till after an angry debate in the council of officers ; there were some present who bitterly resented Shrimpton's surrender. It was said that it was no less fatal and even more unnecessary than the capitulation of the French infantry in Blenheim village. Opinions differed, and on this later occasion the historian has not sufficient information on which to form a judgment.

---

* General Erle, writing to Marlborough on June 26, 1707 (*Add. MSS.* 9099), gives the English and Dutch infantry who escaped at 1,500. Berwick is wrong in claiming to have captured 10,000 men and all the cannon, besides killing 5,000 men ; there were only 15,500 allies in all, and the Portuguese had fled betimes.

The English and allied foot who thus became prisoners
had borne themselves magnificently in the battle on the
previous day. But Galway complained of the conduct of
two ' newly raised ' regiments of English dragoons ' who
did not do their duty ' ; they formed the greater part of the
English horse who escaped with him from the field. The
victors had lost heavily. Berwick, who exaggerated the
allied loss in his *Memoirs*, reported his own at 2,000, which
the Allies considered less than the truth. In any case he
paid but a small price for such a victory ; the last chance
that ' Charles III ' would become King of Spain had now
been destroyed.[196]

A ballad, evidently of contemporary origin though still
circulating many years later, gives some aspects of popular
English tradition that may well have derived from the tales
of private soldiers who took part in the battle :

> Full twenty miles we marched that day,
>   Without one drop of water ;
> Till we, poor souls, were almost spent
>   Before the bloody slaughter.

> Brave Gallaway, our General,
>   Cry'd ' Fight on, while you may ;
> Fight on, brave-hearted Englishmen,
>   You're one to five this day.'

> The Dutch fell on with sword in hand,
>   And that was their desire ;
> Thirty-five squadrons of Portuguese
>   They ran and ne'er gave fire.

> The Duke of Berwick, as I have been told,
>   He gave it out in orders
> That, if the army should be broke,
>   To give the English quarters.

> ' Be kind unto my countrymen,
>   For that is my desire ;
> With the Portuguese do what you please,
>   For they will soon retire.' [197]

The religious and civil strife of that epoch had arrayed
the French army under the English Catholic Berwick, and

the English army under the French Huguenot Ruvigny, Earl of Galway. The High Tories, who made the most of Galway's defeat at Almanza, had a toast to Berwick as ' the brave English general who had defeated the French.'

During the remainder of 1707 the Peninsular War resolved itself into a series of sieges conducted by the victors. The allied army could not take the field again that year, but the courage and energy of Galway were unsubdued by wounds and defeat. He put heart into the remnant of his army, which was seasonably reinforced from England. Effective garrisons of regular troops were put into the cities of Valencia, where all that was left of the Carlist party joined in the defence of their homes, with the desperate valour which Spaniards have so often shown in siege warfare. Under these conditions the capture of Xativa in Valencia and Lerida in Catalonia cost the besiegers dear, and Denia repelled the utmost efforts of the French and Spaniards, who lost over 3,000 men before its walls. An incident in the defence of Denia was exultantly recorded by Archdeacon Perceval of Dublin, from a letter he received from his brother the Major, who was in the thick of the business :

Their grenadiers, sustained by three thousand foot, were again bravely repulsed. The first that entered the breach was a priest in his habit, carrying before him a large cross and crying with a loud voice ' Here enters Christianity.' The grenadiers were all at his back, believing that the Spaniards and Portuguese would not fire at the cross, but they were mistaken, for Major Perceval had planted fifty of his Englishmen at the entrance of the breach, one of which swore a bloody oath that the priest lied, and without any more ceremony shot him dead, and all the officers that entered the breach with him met with the same fate.[198]

Nevertheless the priest represented Spain, no less than the honest soldier who shot him represented England. For the battle of Almanza, following on the allied failure to hold Madrid the year before, had decided the dynastic question in the Spanish mind. Henceforth the struggle was regarded as a national and religious war of the Spaniards and their French allies, to repel the invasion of English and Dutch heretics, joined with German, Portuguese and

Catalan foreigners, who would fain impose a German King upon Spain. Sermons and pamphlets worked up the feeling against the ' Lutheran ' English soldiery, who had sacked churches and convents round Cadiz and Gibraltar. The Carlist or anti-Castilian party in Valencia and Aragon never recovered its hopes after Almanza. The open country of those two provinces was at once overrun by the armies of Philip V. Only Catalonia and those fortresses of Valencia which lay along the coast and were therefore in touch with the allied strength through the English fleet, held out stubbornly, and cost the Bourbon armies much to reduce them over a number of years.

The Allies might well have accepted the decision of Almanza and so given peace to Europe five years before Utrecht. But, just when their chance in Spain was gone, they began to make greater efforts there than ever before. Austrian troops, no longer needed in Italy, were poured into Spain from 1708 onwards. And England went on increasing her war effort in the Peninsula. London and Vienna seemed ready to do anything for Spain—except send either Marlborough or Eugene to that grave of military reputations. Marlborough declared he could not leave the Netherland frontier of France, because if he did, the French would then force their way back into Belgium. And the Emperor refused, in spite of Marlborough's solicitations, to let Eugene go to a scene of action so far removed from Germany. Since all else had failed, there grew up the notion, at once inhuman and ridiculous, of forcing King Louis to dethrone his own grandson, and perform what the Allies were unable to do for themselves. Ere long it was put forward as an essential article of peace that the French armies should compel the unwilling Spaniards to accept the Austrian Prince as their King. The proposal was a measure of the bankruptcy of allied policy in Spain.

When in May 1707 Marlborough took the field on his return from Saxony, the news of Almanza had already struck a damp into the heart of the Dutch and rendered them more timid and alarmist than ever. And the same news, that reduced the Duke's always very moderate chances of success in the Netherlands, dimmed the confident hopes he had entertained for Eugene against Toulon. All the delicately poised, interdependent parts of the clockwork of his Great Design were shaken out of their places by the reverberation of Galway's defeat. Almanza meant not only the loss of Spain but a potential increase in French strength on all other fronts, while the Neapolitan expedition both delayed and weakened the Austrian invasion of Provence. And before the end of May another disaster occurred, further delaying and deranging the allied plans in every seat of war. Villars again demonstrated the genius that set him above the other French Marshals, by breaking through the German watch on the Rhine and forcing the lines of Stolhofen by a surprise attack. The French overran and ravaged great parts of Swabia and Franconia. Their advance parties penetrated as far as the field of Blenheim. Promiscuous plunder, and the systematic levy of immense contributions from the cities and peasants of South-western Germany, enriched the victorious general and his soldiers, and aided the desperate plight of their King's Treasury.

The blame for this fresh misfortune lay with the supine inactivity of Vienna and the German Princes. They had been warned again and again by Marlborough, but had not even condescended to answer his letters, still less to pay heed to his advice.* It might have been expected that things would have gone better that year on the Rhine, for Prince Lewis of Baden had died, but he had been replaced by an even worse general, the Margrave of Baireuth. There had been no lack of troops in South Germany, but they had been scattered about on useless garrison duties, and no one had the sense to concentrate them until after the lines of Stolhofen had been stormed and whole districts of the Fatherland overrun. When at length the German forces

---

* Marlborough writes to Charles III on June 13, 1707, in a very bitter strain on this subject : ' Nous nous voyons reduits a fonder toute notre esperance sur le seul projet d'Italie (= Toulon) par la negligence inouie et la mauvaise conduite qu'on a tenu en Allemagne en laissant passer le Rhyn a Mons. de Villars, quand, selon ses promesses, qu'on nous avoit fait, nous avions plutot lieu d'espérer une bonne diversion de cette cotté là en notre faveur, ayant pris toutes les paines du mond pour exhorter la cour de Viennes et les cercles par des envoyés exprés et de lettres reiteratives pendant 4 mois.' *Add. MSS.* 9093, ff. 11–12.

took the field, the victorious Villars had not, as he tells us himself, the numbers to dare to give them battle. Marlborough insisted that the command should be taken from the Margrave of Baireuth and given to the Elector of Hanover, who was at least not incompetent. The Duke's advocacy of the Elector's claims had the further advantage of pleasing the Whigs at home and securing for himself the favour of his future sovereign.[199]

Almanza and the raid of Villars into Germany went far to discourage the Dutch, who were already for political reasons much less disposed than they had been twelve months before to lend hearty support to Marlborough in the field. The peace party was growing in Holland, and such is the effect of an illogical association of ideas that those who were very reasonably anxious that peace should be made were most unreasonably indifferent to pushing on the war with vigour so long as it lasted. The Dutch had refused as a matter of course to let Marlborough operate on the Moselle this year. And even in the Netherlands their Deputies would not allow him to attack the enemy. In 1707 he was back in the same tutelage that had ruined all his plans of campaign except those of Blenheim and Ramillies.

The situation this year was not indeed likely to produce a chance of victory so obvious as to shame the Deputies to consent to a battle. Vendôme's field army numbered some 100,000 to Marlborough's 80,000, and after Almanza and Stolhofen the French soldiers had recovered their morale, at least to all appearance. Moreover Vendôme was manœuvring amid border fortresses of the first class like Mons, Lille and Tournai, while Marlborough had to cover open or half-open towns like Brussels, Bruges and Louvain, whose inhabitants had been alienated from the allied cause by a year of contact with Dutch administration. Knowing that he had the Field Deputies against him the Duke seemed at times to lose heart and initiative, or at least to be waiting first for the good news from Toulon that never came. This year was singular in Marlborough's campaigns for the absence of any battle won or any place of importance taken. But it still remained true at the end of his career that he

had never fought a battle he did not win, nor sat down
before a place which he did not take.*

In spite of the failures in every other theatre of war,
Marlborough by no means despaired of the year's success
until the master stroke against Toulon had been tried. The
delay of the Imperialists in postponing till midsummer the
attempt which England had wished them to make in the
spring, had been largely responsible for Almanza and
Stolhofen. But if the Allies could even now occupy the
southern arsenal and sea-board of France, victor's terms
might yet be dictated in the winter.

When Eugene and Victor Amadeus, Duke of Savoy,
at length crossed the Maritime Alps at the beginning of
July, the joint Imperial and Savoyard army of invasion
only numbered 35,000 men, insufficient for so great an
enterprise as the conquest of Provence. Eugene had little
zeal for the undertaking. And from first to last the
general sentiment of the Austrian court and army was
that they were being used at the dictation of England to
pull the Toulon chestnut out of the fire for the benefit of
the Maritime Powers.

The eagerness of the English nation for the enterprise could manifest itself only in the co-operation of the
fleet under Sir Cloudesley Shovell. The British and Dutch
fleets accompanied the march of the armies along the south
coast of France, and, by turning the enemy's flank, assisted
them to force the passage of the river Var at its mouth,
where the French attempted a delaying action. Indeed,
throughout this unhappy expedition the co-operation of

* It is needless, after the masterly investigation of Frank Taylor in his *Wars of
Marlborough*, chap. xvii, to argue again in detail against the hypothesis of the
Dutch Deputy Goslinga that Marlborough this year was not playing to win
because he was sulky at not having been allowed to accept the Governorship of the
Netherlands the year before. His correspondence shows him to have been
throughout 1707 the life and soul of every allied effort that was made in any part
of Europe. But it is probably true, as Col. Cranstoun wrote, that he made an
error in his orders (or want of orders) to Count Tilly at Nivelle, and perhaps
thereby lost a chance of the action he so much desired to bring on. And no doubt,
as Cranstoun reported, he was towards the close of the campaign 'much out of
humour and peevish' at the universal want of the allied success which he had planned
for that year. *H.M.C. Portland*, IV, pp. 440–444. See also *ibid.*, 416, 420 ;
H.M.C. Bath, I (1904), pp. 172–173 ; *Coxe*, chaps. lvi–lvii, lx–lxi.

the naval with the land forces was exemplary. The army had to be fed from the ships, and relied on the navy for the cannon and other material for the siege. The forced march to Toulon was made under a broiling sun by not very enthusiastic soldiers, none of them English. Their sufferings were increased by the active hostility of the inhabitants, whom they plundered without restraint. The Allies had been persuaded by the tales of Huguenot exiles into the belief that they would find friends or neutrals in the oppressed subjects of King Louis. When this proved an illusion, the discovery afforded to Eugene yet another reason or excuse for condemning as impossible the enterprise on which they were embarked.

It was a race against time. Toulon, when the allied army started on its march, was almost ungarrisoned and its defences were in a deplorable condition. The French ' army of Italy ' was bivouacked in many different posts along the Alpine frontier, not knowing by what valley their enemies would approach. But the moment Marshal Tessé learnt the route they were taking he divined their objective, and set his regiments racing to Toulon from their various mountain camps. He improvised a new scheme of earthwork fortifications on the hills behind the city, which was carried out with excellent speed, and called the Entrenched Camp of St. Anne. The guns of the Grand Fleet in the harbour were sent ashore and placed in the new line of fortifications, and manned there by naval gunners and officers, who well knew how to handle them. Twenty thousand French infantry reached Toulon just in time to prevent the entry of the Allies. It had been a neck and neck race between them, won by the more eager of the two runners.

Tessé's conduct throughout the whole of this critical summer was energetic and able, in contrast to his recent failures before Gibraltar and Barcelona. The Pasquinading genius of his countrymen, though grateful to him for saving Toulon, could not forbear rhyming it that of course he was successful this time, since he knew so well how sieges were raised. The spirit of France, from Marshal to private and peasant, was roused to surpass itself in defence of the soil.

Arrived before Toulon just too late to find their entry
unopposed, the allied commanders, at their camp of La

Valette, held counsel what they should do. Eugene,
July 26 supported by the Austrian staff, was for returning
(N.S.) at once by the way they had come. He feared that the
1707 French King would concentrate new forces in their
rear and cut off their retreat. The Duke of Savoy and

MAP VI

TOULON
Aug.-Sept. 1707
Scale of 1 Mile
0   ½   1

Mont Faron

+ Croix de Faron
C

La Valette

A
A

←To
Marseilles

TOULON

A

C
St. Catherine

B
B

B

C
La Malgue

HARBOUR

C

FORT ST. LOUIS

GREAT
TOWER

ENGLISH & DUTCH FLEET

N

A. *Trenched Camp of St. Anne*
B. *French Fleet half sunk*
C. *Allied lines*

Emery Walker Ltd. sc.

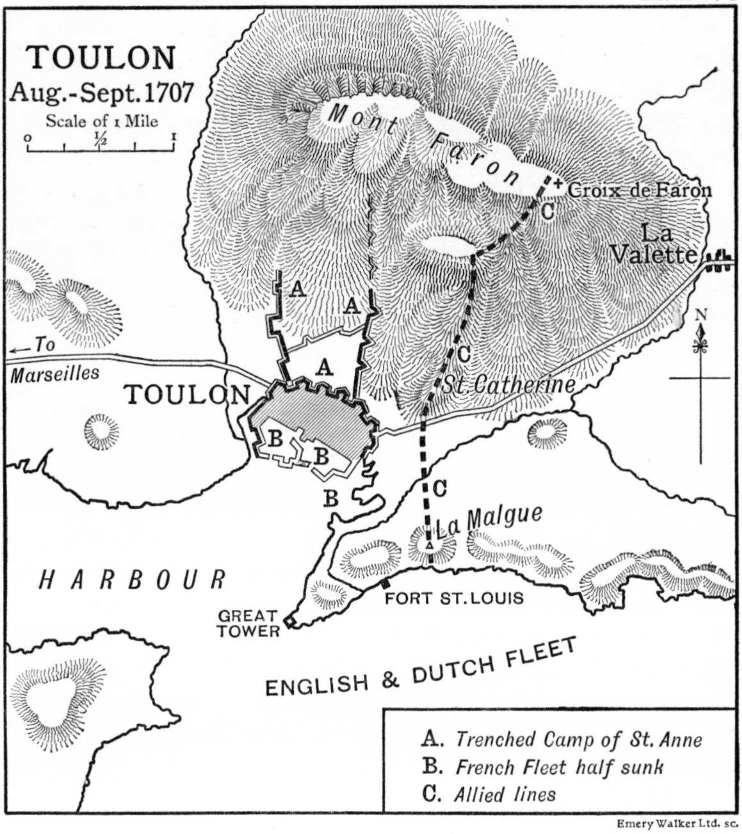

Sir Cloudesley Shovell angrily opposed such a feeble conclusion of so great an effort. Sir Cloudesley, speaking
in the curt phrases that became his character, told the
Prince that England had set her heart on the taking of
Toulon, that his orders from home were peremptory, and
that the attempt must be made. He had the right to use

such language, not only because the army depended for its very food on the fleet, but because most of the troops were paid by English subsidies.   As to Eugene's fear lest their retreat should be cut off, the Admiral declared that if indeed retreat later on became necessary, his ships would carry back all the allied infantry and the horse could ride away. Eugene submitted, but his unwillingness even to attempt the siege was of evil omen for its success.*

Victor Amadeus had urged that the Allies, at the very moment of their arrival, should storm the still unfinished lines that Tessé was constructing over the hills outside the town.   But Eugene insisted that, if the siege were to be undertaken at all, a more formal approach must be made and allied lines must be dug.   The decision not to attack at once may or may not have been right in the circumstances. But those circumstances included a moral factor.   The 20,000 French were full of that spirit of resistance which has so often stood their fellow-countrymen in good stead at Malplaquet, Valmy and the Marne.   The 35,000 Allies had small enthusiasm for their task and were already blaming and abusing one another.   In the previous September this same Eugene and Victor Amadeus had gone straight in, with a force inferior to the enemy's, and stormed the French lines before Turin without waiting to cannonade them.   Now, though the numerical odds were the other way, Eugene shrank from an immediate attack.   For the more important moral factor was reversed.

Even the Duke of Savoy, who had been gay and confident on the march, turned sulky and despaired of success after Eugene's refusal to co-operate with vigour.   He told Sir Cloudesley that he ' never was more concerned or out of humour in his life, no not when the French had drove him out of his country.'   When such was the temper of Savoyard and Austrian, angry with one another, and both

---

* This account is taken wholly from Eugene's own letter to the Emperor of July 29, 1707 (*Feldzüge*, IX, Appendix, pp. 177–178).   It cannot, therefore, be challenged as unfair to Eugene.   English writers, including I am bound to say Julian Corbett, being very excusably in love with the noble Prince and regarding him as Marlborough's *alter ego*, which he was in other campaigns, have not realised his less heroic part in the Toulon affair ; such authors have failed to study the German authorities, *Klopp* and above all the *Feldzüge* of Eugene himself.

now without hope of victory, the siege was half raised before
it was begun.*

Owing to the new lines which Tessé had constructed
over the heights of St. Anne to the north of the town, the
allied army could not blockade Toulon, and could only
attack it from the east. They succeeded in occupying the
crest of Mont Faron above, and in storming the outlying
fort constructed by Tessé on the heights of St. Catherine,
and through those points drew their line of trenches southward to the sea. The fleet landed ship's cannon, ropes and
stores, without which the army could have done nothing.
But during the first fortnight of August Tessé's lines
were strengthened every day, and more and more troops
poured into Toulon from west and north.† The Allies
lost the numerical superiority which had been their only
advantage. Disease raged in their camp, and food was
short when the weather made communication with the fleet
difficult. The soldiers began to desert in crowds to the
enemy. The French took the offensive in successful
sorties. By the middle of the month all agreed that the
siege must be raised. The cannon, sick and
wounded were taken on board the fleet, and the
army marched back by the way it had come.
Stragglers were cut off by the peasants, but the
new French armies which Eugene had feared to find in his
rear did not materialize to intercept the return to Italy.[200]

Aug. 22
(N.S.)
1707

But there was one aspect of the attack on Toulon that
was not so ill. Another serious blow had been struck at the
waning efficiency of the French Grand Fleet, which had for
several years past been concentrated not at Brest but at
Toulon.‡

In the last days of the siege, after the capture of Fort
St. Louis near the entrance of the harbour, the English and
Dutch fleets had been able to come near enough to bombard
the town and docks across an intervening neck of land.

---

* *Byng Papers* (*Navy Records Soc.* 1930), I, pp. 226–227.

† In several ways the conditions of attack and defence were not unlike those of
the Siege of Sebastopol.

‡ See *Blenheim*, p. 406.

The damage done by their bombs was not very great. Yet
French sea power did not escape uninjured. For, on the
first approach of the Allies in July, a measure akin to panic
had been taken by the besieged : the Grand Fleet had been
half sunk at its moorings in shallow water, partly to diminish
the effect of bombardment on the ships, partly to render it
difficult for the Allies to carry them off if Toulon fell.

Owing to this operation, hastily and not very skilfully
carried out, what yet remained of the naval power of King
Louis was seriously crippled for the remainder of the war.
Some of the hulks were wholly under water, but most were
only half sunk in the shallows, so that the upper tier of guns
on the three-deckers were still in action. A few small vessels
had been left afloat. It was intended to raise them all
after the enemy had gone, but the work of salvage proved
longer and more difficult than had been expected. Many
ships were floated again, but were neither so water-tight nor
so seaworthy as before. Six great ships and many second
and third rates were next year scuttled, as being beyond
repair. And many others were of less service and of shorter
life owing to these not very well managed operations, that
required more men, skill and money than could be found.
The fact that King Louis could not afford to spend much
on repairing his fleet rendered the half-sinking at Toulon
a more disastrous affair than a similar undertaking might
have been if conducted by the English at Portsmouth or
Chatham. The Grand Fleet lay in Toulon, for the rest of
the war, starved and neglected by Versailles, licking its
numerous wounds—some of them self-inflicted—leaving
the English undisputed masters of the sea.*

But Sir Cloudesley Shovell, who had from boyhood

---

* The facts of the half-sinking of the Toulon fleet have been variously stated
by English writers from *Burchett*, p. 732, onwards. I prefer to rely entirely on
French authorities. *Pelet* and *Tessé Mém.*, intent on the glory of France, say
nothing about the matter. The contemporary French account, printed in
the English translation, entitled *The Siege of Toulon, collected from the original
Papers*, 1746, p. 183, briefly admits the fact, but minimises the extent and consequence. The detailed account of the affair is to be found in V. Brun, *Guerres
maritimes de la France, Port de Toulon*, 1861, I, pp. 120–126, based on full local
and technical knowledge. It is this authority from which I have drawn my
account, much abbreviated.

served his country in days less fortunate for the English
Navy, never came back another year to show his flag in
triumph round the shores of the Mediterranean.   As he
sailed home that autumn, one of those mistakes that are
never out of the scope of chance even with the best seamen,
misled his fleet on a misty night among the rocks
Oct. 22   of Scilly.   His flagship, *The Association*, and two
1707   more of the squadron were lost.   His body was cast
ashore in Porthellic cove.   He was lying unconscious but
still alive upon the sands, when a woman, who coveted his
emerald ring, extinguished the faint spark of life.   At least
so she confessed thirty years later, showing the ring to a
clergyman.

The Admiral's name has always been dear to his countrymen, especially in association with the charming legend that
he had once been a cabin-boy.   He was buried in the sands
by those who had stripped him, but his body was found
and moved to Westminster Abbey.   The monument over
his grave there is well known, and all the better known for
the criticism of it that Addison wrote in the *Spectator* in
March 1711 :

Sir Cloudesley Shovell's monument has very often given me great
offence.   Instead of the brave, rough English Admiral, which was the
distinguishing character of that gallant man, he is represented on his
tomb by the figure of a Beau, dressed in a long periwig, and reposing
himself upon velvet cushions under a canopy of state.   The Dutch,
whom we are apt to despise for want of genius, shew an infinitely
greater taste of antiquity and politeness in their buildings and works
of this nature.   The Monuments of their Admirals, which have been
erected at the public expence, represent them like themselves ; and
are adorned with rostral crowns and naval ornaments, with beautiful
festoons of seaweed, shells and coral.

One could almost wish these words might be inscribed in
stone and placed beside the monument in the Abbey.[201]

CHAPTER XVI

The Fall of Harley

Town gossip. Abigail Hill. Harley between the Queen and the Government. The Bishoprics question. The first Parliament of Great Britain meets, winter 1707–1708. The attack on the Admiralty. The convoy system. Peterborough as a Tory hero. ' No peace without Spain.' Fall of Harley and triumph of the Whigs. The Secretary's office and Greg's treason.

WAR and politics are the two horses the historian must drive abreast, for they alone can be harnessed to a logical narrative of events. But, as the actual days passed over Queen Anne's London, ' the town ' had many merry matters to think of besides the victories of ' the Duke of Molbery,' the Scots Treaty and what the Swede intended, what the French. There was the Italian Opera, newly come to England to put her native music out of fashion.*

Our famous Nicolini got 800 guineas for his day ; and 'tis thought Mrs. Tofts, whose turn is on Tuesday next, will get a vast deal. She was on Sunday last at the Duke of Somerset's, where there was about thirty gentlemen, and every kiss was a guinea ; some took three, others four, others five at that rate.

Nicolini and Mrs. Tofts, thus sought after by ' the great,' knew how to give themselves airs :

The Dutchis of Molbery [writes Lady Wentworth] had gott the Etallian to sing and he sent an excuse, but the Dutchis of Shrosberry [a sister Italian and of a sprightly disposition] made him com, brought him in her coach ; but Mrs. Taufs huft and would not sing becaus he had first put it ofe ; though she was thear yet she would not, but went away.

* *Blenheim*, p. 87.

Old Lady Wentworth was a dear, good soul, who 'lamented that such a yousles creature as I should outliv soe many fyne young folks'; but she still relished her share of life in the years between Ramillies and Oudenarde, had a keen ear for fashionable and domestic gossip, and retailed it to her son Lord Raby, the British Ambassador at Berlin, in letters spelt as ill as fine ladies were wont to spell in the days of her youth.

> Lady Derringwater's new husband coms every day to the coffy hous in his fyne coach and twoe footmen to wait of him, and the coach waits at the coffy hous, and all elc hear walk to it, soe he is laught at for it.
>
> I am sure could you see my fyer side, you would laugh hartely to see Fubs [the dog] upon a cushin, the cat of another, and Pug [the monkey] of another lapt up al but her face in a blanckitt.

Then, in the cold winter of 1708, poor Fubs goes to join the 'many fyne young folks,' and its mistress is desolated :

> I had rather lost a hundred pound to have saved poor charming Fubs. As it leved soe it dyed, full of lov, leening its head in my bosom, never offered to snap at anybody in its horrid torter, but nussle its head to us and look earnestly upon me and Sue, whoe cryed for thre days if it had been for child or husband . . . so much senc and good nature and cleenly and not one falt ; but few human creeturs had more senc then he had.

When even illiterate old ladies had the wit to write in this style the advent of the *Tatler* and *Spectator* might well be near at hand.

Another event that had excited Lady Wentworth and the town was the trial of 'Beau Feilding' for bigamy. The story breathes the very atmosphere of the 'artificial comedy' of Congreve and Farquhar, whose characters and plots of intrigue, in spite of Charles Lamb's belief in their unreality, faithfully delineated the more corrupt part of the society of that age. Marriage was regarded by adventurers as a financial investment, and was often undertaken after a few hours' or even minutes' acquaintance.

'Beau Feilding,' a Catholic and Jacobite, the 'Orlando' of the *Tatler*, dressed fantastically himself and clothed his footmen in yellow coats with black sashes. He was a gambler and would have been a bully if he had been brave enough. He was as big a fool as Witwould and as handsome and irresistible as Mirabel. His face was his fortune, and he took it twice to the wrong market. He was enticed to marry a woman passed off on him by conspiracy as a great heiress with £60,000 to her fortune. On discovery he beat and discarded her, and in the same month of November 1705 sold his charms in bigamous marriage to no less a person than Barbara Villiers, Lady Castlemaine and Duchess of Cleveland, who had ruled Whitehall in the days of the Merry Monarch. By this time she had little of her beauty left but much of her wealth. She confessed to being fifty, and was more than sixty-four. ' She is fallen in love,' writes Lady Wentworth, ' with this young Feelding and ses she only begs he will be sevell to her, she fears he cannot lov her, though she dus him soe much, and Weding cloaths are making.' Such a loving voyage was only victualled for six months. Then he ' broak open her clossett doar and toock fower hundred pound out '—so Lady Wentworth reports to Berlin; —' there is a paper out about it. He beat her sadly and she cryed out murder in the street out of the windoe, and he shott a blunderbus at the people.' The Beau's other marriage was discovered ; he was tried and convicted as a bigamist, but not severely punished. He ended his life in poverty half a dozen years later, tended at the last by his real wife who had been fraudulently foisted upon him.

What did the ' Duke of Molbery ' think and remember, when the sordid tale filtered through to him, as he marched in triumph through the cities of Belgium in the summer weather after Ramillies ? * It was more than thirty years since the smart young officer, Jack Churchill, not yet

---

* The *Dictionary of National Biography* on Barbara Villiers, Duchess of Cleveland, tells us that ' towards the close of 1677 the Duchess gave the sum of £1,000 to the English nuns of the Immaculate Conception, Rue Charenton, Paris, a nunnery in which she placed as pensionnaire her youngest daughter, Barbara, to whom the Duke of Marlborough was father. This young lady, who was never married, and who subsequently, as " Sister Benedicta," made her profession as a nun, became in 1691, by the Earl of Arran, the mother of Charles Hamilton, and died Prioress of the nunnery at Pontoise on 6th May, 1737.' Questions of the paternity of the Duchess of Cleveland's children were often rather difficult. Another article in the *Dictionary of National Biography* on Charles Hamilton makes, not Marlborough, but Charles II his grandfather ! Who shall decide ?

domesticated by the love of Sarah, had been caught by
King Charles in bed with the royal Sultana—now shrunk
to this despicable old woman, still raking in the cinders
of her inordinate passions, the dupe of a silly Beau who
had himself been duped like the fool in a comedy.[202]

In the summer of 1707 another successful actress makes
her first appearance on the stage of political intrigue.
Abigail Hill, whose Christian name had been singularly
well chosen for the part she was to play in life, belonged to
the large class of humble companions whose profession was
to make themselves agreeable and useful in a patron's family.
Abigail was a distant relation of Sarah, Duchess of Marlborough, who took her into her house at St. Albans and did
many kindnesses both to her and her impoverished relations.
The tall, ragged brother, Jack Hill, was clothed and sent
to school by Sarah, and at her orders the Duke ' made him
his aide de camp and afterwards gave him a regiment,' protesting all the while that ' Jack Hill was good for nothing.'
In an evil hour for herself, the Duchess crowned her
work of good nature by introducing Abigail into an office
in Queen Anne's bedchamber. The new courtier was more
astute and less humble than she had allowed her first
mistress to perceive. In competition for the royal favour
Abigail would have some decisive advantages over Sarah—
Tory politics, a temper perfectly under control, and a readiness to study the thoughts and wishes of those whom she
could not command. Of any higher qualities she never in
her life gave evidence.*

When and by what stages she began to obtain influence
over the Queen, and to act under the secret orders of Harley,
does not appear. But in the summer of 1707 the Churchills
found themselves in the presence of something they had
never known for a quarter of a century past—a rival in the
affections of Anne Stuart.

Here is the first of many memorable scenes, all described

---

* In the MSS. at Althorp, Sarah writes that Abigail had ' no education and no
qualifications, but a little *skill in mimicry*, which served to divert her mistress sometimes, and perhaps incapable of doing mischief if she had not that man [Harley]
for her director in everything.'

by Sarah in the artlessness of an anger that conceals nothing against herself :

Being with the Queen (to whom I had gone very privately by a secret passage, from my lodgings to the bedchamber) on a sudden this woman, not knowing I was there, came in with the boldest and gayest air possible, but, upon sight of me, stopped ; and immediately, changing her manner, and making a most solemn courtesy, *did your Majesty ring?* And then went out again. This singular behaviour needed no interpreter *now*, to make it understood.

In the early summer of 1707 Abigail Hill was secretly married to a Mr. Masham, in the presence of the Queen, but without the knowledge of the Duchess. Humanly regarded, such concealment on the bride's part was ungrateful to her first mistress, to whom she owed everything. Politically it had a deeper significance which the Churchills could not miss. As early as June 3, 1707, the Duke was writing anxiously to Sarah from the field : ' if you are sure that Mrs. Masham speaks of business to the Queen, I should think you might with some caution tell her of it, which would do good. For she certainly must be grateful, and will mind what you say.' On this occasion Marlborough thought too well of human nature, as he soon had reason to confess. In August and September, he, Sarah and Godolphin were in full correspondence with each other and with the Queen and Harley, on the subject of the private influence which Harley had established over Anne through the medium of Abigail Masham.*

---

* The growing confidence of Abigail and growing despair of the Churchills are marked in the following letters :

Abigail to Harley, September 29, 1707 : ' I had a very low courtesy [from Sarah], which I returned in the same manner, but not one word passed between us, and as for her looks, indeed, they are not to be described by any mortal but her own self.' *H.M.C. Portland*, IV, p. 454.

Sarah to Sir William Trumbull, November 13, 1707 : ' 'Tis plain you live in the country by your writing to me to ask a favour of the Queen, to whom I never have the honour to speak of anything but what concerns my own offices, and in that I can't prevail ; all which is compassed by the black ingratitude of Mrs. Masham, a woman that I took out of a garret and saved from starving.' *H.M.C. Downshire*, I, pt. 2 (1924), p. 855.

Marlborough to Sarah, the Hague, November 8, 1707 : ' What you say of Mrs. Masham is very odd. And if you think she is a good weathercock, it is high time to leave off struggling. For believe me nothing is worth rowing against wind and tide, at least when you come to my age.' *Coxe*, II, p. 368.

The situation revealed by these letters in the autumn of 1707 was by no means simple. Marlborough did not wish to rely upon the Whig Junto more than he was already obliged to do. But he was aware that, if Harley replaced Godolphin as the power behind the throne, the Whigs would rebel when Parliament met : either they would throw the Ministry out, or else compel Godolphin to replace all Tories in the Government by Whigs. The Duke dreaded either event. He had no wish to be subservient either to a Tory Cabinet controlled by Harley, or to a Whig Cabinet controlled by the Junto. He was the more indignant with Harley for creating a situation which must lead to one or other of these results. He saw that the Queen was losing confidence in Godolphin, and told her in October that if that confidence were withdrawn from his kinsman at home, he could no longer serve her to any purpose abroad.

Harley, for his part, desired neither a government wholly Tory, nor the dismissal of Marlborough. But he wished to destroy the increasing influence of the Whig Lords over the Cabinet and to continue a Moderate Ministry, relying as heretofore not on either party but on the favour of the Queen and the support of the nation. He was courting the moderate Whigs like the Duke of Newcastle, who were jealous of the Junto ; and he was also courting the more reasonable of the High Tories. The latter, under the tutoring of misfortune, were learning ' conviction of their folly ' and were repenting that they had ever quarrelled with the Queen and her Moderate Tory Ministers. Thus neither Marlborough nor Harley wanted a Ministry completely Tory or completely Whig. But they could no longer act together because Harley now aspired to become the chief man in the Moderate Ministry, by displacing Godolphin in Anne's favour through the new female influence. The quarrel between Harley and Anne on one side and Marlborough and Godolphin on the other, largely personal in its motives, drove these four Moderate Tories apart, Harley and Anne into the arms of the High Tories, Godolphin and Marlborough into the no less embarrassing embrace of the Junto Whigs. In this way the non-party Ministry dependent on the Queen's personal choice began to break up, and party government in the strict sense of the word established itself, in the last half of Anne's reign, as the final form taken by the British Constitution.   Because Abigail encouraged the Queen to assert herself against the Churchills, the Crown ceased to hold the balance between parties and became the instrument of party Ministries, alternately Whig and Tory.   No one of the persons whom this busy woman set by the ears—neither Anne nor Harley, neither Godolphin nor Marlborough— got what they wished out of the quarrel.[203]

The first consequence of the new influence in the bedchamber was to set going in country and Parliament an

Aug.   open struggle for power, that raged all autumn and
1707–   winter until Harley fell and the Whigs triumphed.
Feb.   For six months the contest revolved round an issue
1708   characteristic of the politics of that age—the appointments to certain Bishoprics.   The position and privileges of the Established Church were of so commanding a nature that the control of the Church was of the very essence of political power in Eighteenth-Century England.   Not only would the political character of the Episcopal Bench influence in a thousand ways the direction towards Whig or Tory taken by the clergy as a whole in the rising generation, but in the immediate present the votes of the Bishops might confirm or destroy the small Whig majority in the House of Lords. *

The Whig party, therefore, took grave alarm when they heard in the autumn of 1707 that the Queen had nominated two Tories as Bishops of Exeter and Chester.   It was true that Exeter had been vacated by the promotion of Trelawny to the rich see of Winchester in reward for his desertion of the High Tory standard two years before.†   It was true also that the Queen's new choices, Blackall and Dawes,

* See Appendix D below, *Bishops in the House of Lords.*

† See p. 30, above.   Trelawny was not, however, regarded as a proper Whig, as is shown by Burnet's acid remarks on his promotion to Winchester.   The Cornish Baronet was in high spirits at thus attaining the goal of his ambition, and wrote to Matt. Prior in August 1707 : ' I don't doubt of your having your eye upon the Bishopric of Winchester, but I beg you would not expect it these twenty years.   After that I wish you may have it at least as many more.' *H.M.C. Bath*, III, p. 436.

were proper people to be Bishops, and that Dawes was a very moderate Hanoverian Tory. But Blackall was famous in controversy against Whig champions. The Junto were furious, and, unjustly suspecting Marlborough and Godolphin of having given the advice, threatened to withdraw their support when Parliament met in the winter, if the nominations were not cancelled.

The two kinsmen were on a lee shore, between the wind of Whig indignation and the rock-like obstinacy of the Queen. In truth Anne had not consulted them before permitting Blackall and Dawes in August to kiss hands in the closet as her nominees. But she declared that Godolphin was wrong in supposing that Harley had advised her. As on other occasions, Sharp, Archbishop of York, whom she favoured as much as she disliked Tenison of Canterbury, had been the first to suggest to her the persons selected.*

None the less the situation was governed by the fact that Harley and Mrs. Masham were urging her to be ' a Queen indeed,' and to ' act without her Ministers ' in making appointments, like her Tudor and Stuart predecessors. They fed her with palatable reminders that she was breaking no law, and not even infringing the custom of the constitution as practised by William. Since he and Mary had made Whig Bishops without always consulting their lay Ministers, why should not she make Tory Bishops with a like personal freedom ?

It was indeed a nice constitutional issue between Crown and Ministers, as well as a political battle between High and Low Church. Godolphin and Marlborough, though they dreaded the predominance of the Whig party in the Cabinet, feared still more what it might do if it broke with the Queen's servants. In such a case what might not happen when Parliament met ? And how would the war be carried on if the Ministry fell owing to a hostile vote ? The Queen

---

* Just before Christmas she confided to Sharp that ' she meant to change her measures, and give no countenance to the Whig Lords, but that all Tories, if they would come in, and all the Whig likewise, that would show themselves to be in her interests, should have her favour.' *Life of Sharp*, I, p. 323. Somers wrote to Tenison as early as June 1707 urging him to write to the Queen about Church appointments, ' if the way of talking is difficult,' since ' the Archbishop of York never suffers her to rest.' *Wake MSS. Epist.* 7.

refused to view the question of the Bishoprics in that light. Godolphin saw it in no other :

> The liberties of all Europe [he wrote to her on Sept. 11] and the glory of your reign depend upon the next session of Parliament. This being truly the case, what colour of reason can incline your Majesty to discourage and dissatisfy those [the Whigs] whose principles and interest lead them on with so much warmth and zeal to carry you through the difficulties of the War ? What appearance will it have, that all these weighty matters cannot stand in the balance with this single point, whether Dr. Blackall at this time be made a Bishop, or a Dean or a Prebend ?

That question, however, continued for five months to shake the State, until, at the New Year, some weeks after Parliament had met, it was finally settled. Blackall went to Exeter as Bishop, and Dawes to Chester. But, by way of compensation, the Low Church controversialist, Dr. Trimnel, formerly domestic chaplain at Althorp, was made Bishop of Norwich ; and, owing to the strong personal representations of Marlborough, the Queen reluctantly gave to Dr. Potter, Archbishop Tenison's learned Whig chaplain, the Regius Professorship of Divinity at Christchurch, to the intense disgust of the College and University. The Whig party in Parliament accepted the compromise.[204]

Jan.
1708

The political importance of a Regius Professorship may astonish and amuse a careless posterity. But it was regarded as a key position. Potter rose thence to be a Whig Archbishop of Canterbury under the Georges. The intensity of the political character of University life, when Oxford and Cambridge were valued mainly as supplying the personnel and guiding the thought of the Established Church, can be illustrated by an incident that had just occurred at Cambridge. The musician, Thomas Tudway, had been organist of Great St. Mary's for many years, as also of King's and Pembroke ; in 1705 he was made 'Professor of Music' to the University. He was a strong Tory, and an inveterate punster. He exercised his gift once too often at the expense of the Queen, whom the High Tories accused of being too fond of Dissenters. Tudway was heard to remark that although the Queen had refused an address from the Hertford burgesses, she would have received it ' had it been presented by Daniel Burgess,' the famous dissenting preacher.   Since the dons were fools enough to take such a jest as a serious matter, it offended both Whigs and Court Tories.   For this paltry witticism, the old and honoured servant of the University was in July 1706 brought up before the Vice-Chancellor and Heads and deprived of his Professorship and his three organist's posts. Eight months later he was reinstated, after making a public apology.[205]

When the first Parliament of Great Britain met, shortly before Christmas in 1707, the Whig element in both Houses was increased by the arrival of the Scottish representative Peers and Members.   The Bishoprics question still hung undecided, and the Whigs, led by Wharton and Somers, determined to make their power felt.   They entered into a momentary alliance with the High Tories against the Government.   It was only too easy to attack the administration, for the war that year had been one long disappointment—Almanza, Toulon, and nothing done in the Netherlands.

But the grievance that was first taken up by the Opposition was the bitter complaint of the merchants of England against the Admiralty.   Three years before, the naval administration had been subjected to a full dress attack in Parliament.*   The grievances were old and real, and it was well in the public interest that they should again be ventilated.   But it is probable that this particular subject of criticism was chosen by the politicians, because the Admiralty Board, which governed in the name of the otiose Prince Consort, was in practice controlled by Admiral George Churchill, Marlborough's ultra-Tory brother.   He must be removed, or else Marlborough must save him by making terms with the Whigs.   It was lucky for the administration that Robert Walpole had for some time been on the Admiralty Board, and now defended it loyally before his brother Whigs in the House of Commons.   It was lucky for the administration The brunt of the battle was borne in the House of Lords.

* See p. 19, above.

There the enquiry into Admiral Churchill's conduct on the Board was pressed by Wharton with a zeal that Marlborough took very ill.   The Whig chief was supported by Rochester and Haversham, but it was noticed that while the Whigs attacked only the Admiralty, the Tories denounced the Cabinet.   The High Church opposition, recently crushed under electoral misfortune, again lifted its head ; its members carried down to the country the newspapers and pamphlets in which the Whigs attacked the administration of the navy, and scattered them through the villages to arouse the discontent of the people.   In December the High Tories won a by-election at Leicester against the government candidate.

The City of London sent in memorials to support the Parliamentary inquisition, for discontent had been aroused by the scant consideration that naval commanders too often showed for the feelings of the merchant service and for the interests of those who owned the ships and their cargoes. The perennial grievance against the press-gang, that stripped the crews from outward-bound merchantmen in harbour, was again brought to the notice of Parliament.   But even louder rose the cry against the defects of the convoy system : the delays in sailing, so caused, which took the heart out of commerce ; the imperfections in the network of convoy that gave so many rich prizes to the privateers of Dunkirk and Martinique.   Finally there were certain yet grosser scandals.   On the West Indian station, Commodore Kerr was in the habit of exacting blackmail from merchants before he would grant them protection, and ships had been lost that could not afford to pay his nefarious charges.

All this was true, yet the failure was only relative. While the naval debate was going on, the Jamaica fleet arrived at Torbay under convoy, very richly laden. And it is only fair to remember that this middle period of the war saw the high-water mark of the French privateers, because King Louis had now laid up his Grand Fleet in harbour, and was devoting the whole naval energy of France to commerce-destroying. Greater protection was therefore required, and was before long supplied.[206]

The naval debates in the winter session of 1707–8,

though initiated as a political manœuvre, served the country well. It is true that no immediate change was made in the personnel of the much-abused Board, because the Whigs were placated by the compromise on the Bishoprics, and by the fall of Harley. But Commodore Kerr was disgraced, and

these warm proceedings had a proper effect ; they convinced such as sat at the admiralty-board, that it was dangerous to treat British merchants with contempt ; as on the other hand it taught the officers to know that having friends on the board would not always secure them from punishment. (*Campbell's Admirals.*)

Even at the time the debate took place, we had not, as the Admiralty pointed out, done so badly on the balance. From the outbreak of war in May 1702 to Christmas 1707 we had destroyed or taken over seventy French warships of all sizes carrying 1700 guns,* besides 175 privateers and 1,346 enemy merchantmen ; while we had lost thirty-five warships carrying 800 guns, and 1,146 merchantmen, of which 300 had been retaken.

In the subsequent years of the war, from 1708 to 1712, the protection of our shipping became more effective, or else the enemy's striking power diminished. No more collective complaints were heard from the merchant community after this winter, and in 1712 the tonnage of British shipping clearing outwards was greater by a fifth than when the war began. Taking the war as a whole, the protection afforded was not bad, especially if we remember that, when hostilities were first resumed in 1702, the ports of Italy, Spain and the Spanish Indies had been closed to our shipping, whereas in King William's war they had been at our service to protect us from the weather and the French.† A steady increase of British sea-power can alone account for so tolerable a result under circumstances so unfavourable. Two years before the war ended at Utrecht, Addison, in the second number of his *Spectator*, makes Sir Andrew Freeport, ' a merchant of

---

* Not including those half-sunk by the French themselves in Toulon harbour.
† On the other hand, the statement made by the Admiralty in December 1707 that in William's war as many as 4,000 English merchantmen were lost, was based on no lists or on any good authority, and appears to have been greatly exaggerated. *Parl. Hist.*, VI, pp. 660–661, and G. N. Clark, *Dutch Alliance and the War against French Trade*, pp. 62, 127–128.

great eminence in the City of London,' call the sea 'the British Common.'[207]

Even more pressing than the problem of Admiralty was the question of Spain. The attempt to substitute King Charles for King Philip had failed, and the refusal to recognize the fact was the main obstacle to the immediate conclusion of a satisfactory and even glorious peace. But this view was not yet accepted in Parliament, not even by the High Tory Opposition. Although they used the disasters in Spain to attack and embarrass the Government, they did so not by demanding peace but by urging the transfer of our principal war effort to the Peninsula.

Their informant was Peterborough. Since the Ministers, exasperated by his erratic conduct, had called him home under censure, he had thrown himself into the arms of the Opposition. ' It is a perfect jest,' wrote Swift, who still stood as a neutral observer between parties, ' it is a perfect jest to see my Lord Peterborough, reputed as great a Whig as any in England, abhorred by his own party and caressed by the Tories.' The Opposition spoke of him that winter as the English hero basely sacrificed to the foreigner Galway. His great deeds at Barcelona and elsewhere were held up to the admiration of his countrymen in the famous volume, then first given to the world by Dr. John Freind, who had been his physician in Spain.

Peterborough's advice to his new Tory allies was that, rather than abandon Spain, England should submit to a land tax of ' nineteen shillings in the pound ' ; that, since the Germans would always be useless in Spain, more and more English must be sent there. The second part of the advice was more palatable to the Tories than the first, for the proposal to send English troops from the Netherlands to Spain would be a blow at Marlborough and a blow at the Dutch. Nottingham, reviving a policy he had pursued when in office,* supported Rochester's motion in the Lords that 20,000 men should be withdrawn from the Netherlands and sent to the Peninsula.

Dec. 19
1707

The proposal for once ruffled the imperturbable surface

* See *Blenheim*, p. 303.

of Marlborough's temper, and their Lordships enjoyed the unwonted spectacle of John Churchill in a rage. His speech bears careful consideration. He asserted that if the bulk of the British Army were removed from the Netherlands the French would advance and recover much of what they had lost. This calculation was justified by the events of the ensuing campaign, when Ghent and Bruges were betrayed to the enemy and only won back as a consequence of the victory of Oudenarde. Less convincing was the other part of the Duke's argument, that Spain could be won back by the dispatch of a great Imperialist army of 11,000 men or more under Prince Eugene. Such was not Austria's way. The Emperor positively refused Marlborough's earnest request to send Eugene to Spain as ' la dernière ressource du roi Charles.' The weakness of our policy was revealed by the debate : the government would neither abandon Spain nor produce any practicable plan for its reconquest.

Somers concluded the debate by carrying a motion to assert ' that no peace can be honourable or safe for her majesty and her allies if Spain and the Spanish West Indies be suffered to continue in the power of the House of Bourbon.' As yet the Tories did not oppose the formula of ' No Peace without Spain.' Only one Peer ventured to suggest that we should not commit ourselves too deeply against a partition of the Spanish Empire, which King William had contemplated and which we might yet be forced to accept. This solitary advocate of peace and prudence was Richard Lumley, Lord Scarborough, an honest and independent man, who had been converted from Romanism in the heyday of James II's power, had served William faithfully in war and was a leader of the Whig interest in the North of England.[208]

For another year Scarborough's sage counsel found no support on either side of the House. The war was still popular. Even the Tories proposed only to move the seat of operations from Flanders to Spain. The payers of land tax grumbled less at their burdens now the war was won than a few years back when there had been grave reason to fear it would be lost. They were proud to pay, because they saw more evident return for their money than during

William's barren campaigns. ' Look 'ee, Captain,' says
Justice Balance in Farquhar's *Recruiting Officer*, ' give us but
blood for our money and you shan't want men. I remember
that for some years of the last war our armies did nothing
but play at prison-bars, and hide-and-seek with the enemy.
But now ye have brought us colours and standards and
prisoners.'

The popular craving for peace did not begin till the
following winter. It was the warlike state of opinion that
rendered it possible for the Junto Whigs, in the year now
opening, to overcome the Queen's opposition and form a
Whig Ministry pledged to war *à outrance*.

In January 1708 a stage had been reached, publicly in
the Houses at Westminster and privately in the closet at
St. James's, when Marlborough and Godolphin must choose
between two policies. Either they must fall into line with
the Queen and Harley and revert to a union with the more
reasonable elements in the estranged Tory Opposition ; or
else they must accept the alliance of the Junto on Whig
terms, in order to coerce the Queen into the dismissal of
Harley. The reasons are clear why they chose the latter
course, though Marlborough at least regarded it with regret
and misgiving. In the first place the personal hatred against
himself and Godolphin evinced by the extreme Tory wing
whom they had extruded from power, made them dread the
probable consequences of a High Church revival. In the
second place the Queen confided no longer in them but in
Harley, and therefore any Ministry in which he had a place
would be his Ministry rather than Godolphin's. Finally, the
Tory leaders in the House of Lords had announced their
determination to stop Marlborough's offensive in the Netherlands, and to take the big decisions on European strategy
out of his hands. But the Whigs regarded the great Duke
and his achievements as the chief asset of their party in its
popular appeal ; they thought of the war not only as a
national necessity but as a Whig interest.

The independent position that Marlborough and Godolphin had to some extent enjoyed through the Queen's
favour during the crisis of the war, was gone now that she

had turned away her face, now that the period of national danger was over, and now that the two-party system was reasserting itself in the State. The two noble kinsmen must serve where they had commanded—they must serve either Harley or the Junto. They preferred to serve the Junto as the lesser of two evils.

When the Houses met again at the New Year, things marched rapidly to this consummation. For four years past Henry St. John had been a Marlborough man. As Secretary at War during the years of Blenheim and Ramillies, he had felt all the glamour of personal connection with the great Duke, for whom his pulses quickened with an admiration such as the less mercurial spirit of Harley could never feel. He had offered the Dean of Christchurch £100 to put up a statue of Marlborough ' in the middle of the area of Peckwater.' Ever since he took office in 1704, Highchurchmen had spoken of St. John as ' an errant country gentlemen,' that is to say a bad Tory. But he was now ' growing honest again.' For if he had to choose between his personal connection with Marlborough and his chances of future Tory leadership, he could not hesitate. He was still faithful to the fortunes of Harley, his ' dear master,' who had brought him into the government.[209]

> Jan.–Feb. 1708

At the end of January 1708, St. John, as Secretary at War, laid before Parliament papers which seemed to show that out of 29,000 men whom it had voted last year for the war in the Peninsula only 8,000 had been present on the field of Almanza. What had happened to the rest ? Whigs and Tories, moved as much by patriotism as by desire to embarrass the Ministry, angrily asked the question. St. John made explanations that were at least partially satisfying.* But it was strongly suspected that his original production of the papers in their first damaging form was an underhand attack on his colleagues, inspired by Harley. Whether the suspicion were just or unjust, the rift between Godolphin on one side and Harley and St. John on the other was complete.

* The paper giving the gist of his explanations will be found in *Add. MSS.* 22264, ff. 16–18, an interesting study in the war-wastage and recruiting and depôt methods of the day. It brings the 29,395 who had been voted, down to 11,621 actually in the Peninsula. Each of the English regiments in the list is of one battalion, nominally between 800 and 900 strong.

At the same time, the recent arrest of Harley's secretary, William Greg, on a charge of high treason that proved only too well founded, shook his master's position at the moment of crisis now at hand.

In the first week of February the Queen attempted to dismiss Godolphin, and retain Marlborough as the servant of a Harleian Ministry. St. John acted as inter-mediary between his sovereign and the hero he worshipped, but in vain. The Duke wrote to the Queen in stronger terms than he often employed, denouncing 'the treacherous proceedings of Mr. Secretary Harley to Lord Treasurer and myself,' and declaring that ' no consideration can make me serve any longer with that man.' The two kinsmen resigned, but the Queen and Harley, though disappointed at the Duke's resignation, persisted in their project. ' The back stairs were very much crowded for two or three days,' and Tory hopes ran high. If a moderate Tory Ministry were formed, a General Election, it was thought, would as usual go in favour of the government as the disposer of patronage.

Feb. 1708

But it proved impossible to form a Ministry that could face the existing Parliament or carry on the business of the country even for a week. The middle party among the Ministers, Somerset and Pembroke, refused to act without Marlborough. The Prince Consort, stirred up by Admiral Churchill, deprecated his wife's rashness. When the usual Sunday meeting of the Cabinet took place, the Queen, according to custom, took her seat at the head of the table, and Harley opened the proceedings with a lively air. He was interrupted by the Duke of Somerset, who said ' he could not imagine what business could be done as neither the General nor the Treasurer were there.' He expressed the sense of those present, and the Cabinet broke up in confusion. Two days later Harley had resigned, and Marlborough and Godolphin were back. They had survived, but it was Whigs who had triumphed.

Feb. 9 1708

St. John, Mansell and Harcourt followed Harley out of office. Henry Boyle, a moderate and useful man now associated with the Whigs, replaced Harley as Secretary of State. Robert Walpole replaced St. John as Secretary at

War. John Smith, the Whig Speaker, became Chancellor of the Exchequer. Henceforth no one in the Government would oppose the policies of the Junto.

The Queen had been coerced. She had also been alienated. Henceforth she lived in a perpetual conspiracy to displace the Ministers who had been thrust back upon her. Abigail Masham was still at her side, the real ruler of the closet and the back stairs. By her management, ' while she lived at her Little House over against the gate that goes into Windsor Castle, Harley and his friends saw the Queen as often as they pleased,' wrote Sarah. ' Those that saw the Queen that were not to be known, came in from the Park into the garden, and from thence Abigail carried them a back way to the Queen's closet, which kept this correspondence secret for some time.' [210]

The long-lived ' Godolphin Ministry,' begun in 1702 as a combination of all sorts of Tories, had become in 1704 a non-party group of the Queen's servants, and now in 1708 entered on its final period as a Whig Government. The only thing common to its three phases was the presence at the Treasury of Godolphin, sometimes called ' The Prime Minister,' and his close relation with Marlborough. Round those two planted figures the rest of the Ministerial world came and went like shifting phantoms, now Tory, now Whig. Even the relation of the Ministry to the Crown had altered as often and as completely as any other of the changing circumstances of its being. In 1702 Godolphin and Marlborough had the support equally of the Queen and of the Tory party ; from 1704 to 1706 they depended on her support against both parties ; in 1708 they depended on the Whigs, while their royal mistress had been defeated in her attempt to overthrow their power.

Harley, as the more important of the two Secretaries of State, had conducted the office from which he was now driven in a manner that had reflected his own personality both for good and ill. He had set up an admirable system for gathering information ; secret agents from every quarter of Britain retailed to him, by letter or by word of mouth, the movements of public opinion in England and of the more strange and complicated affairs of Scotland. ' No person,' wrote his brother Edward, ' since the time of Secretary Walsingham, ever had better intelligence, or employed more money to procure it.' The most useful of these reporters, Daniel Defoe, was on such terms with Harley that he ventured in 1704 to send him a Memorial on the conduct of the Secretary's Office, based on the text ' Intelligence is the soul of all public business.' Harley had, moreover, seen the advantages of using the press to put the Government case before the public, and had employed Defoe's *Review* for this purpose.* His love of secrecy, his thirst for information, his sympathy with common folk, had inspired these useful activities in the Secretary. But his less admirable quality, the furtive and slovenly habit of his mind, which made his speech and writing so often unintelligible, and his purposes uncertain to others and sometimes even to himself, led him to conduct the business of the office with haphazard methods and lax discipline.

There was then no standard of civil service routine in the Secretary's Office. The Treasury functioned well under the methodical Godolphin, and in any case the Treasury was developing its own procedure and traditions. But it was otherwise in the office of the Secretary of State, where the clerks were chosen and paid, not as the servants of the Crown, but as the personal employees of the Secretary himself.† When Harley took over the office in 1704, Defoe's Memorial had warned him of its defects :

> I have been in the Secretary's Office of a post night when, had I been a French spy, I could have put in my pocket my Lord Nottingham's letters directed to Sir George Rook and to the Duke of Marlborough, laid carelessly on a table for the doorkeeper to carry to the post.

If these things could be corrected, wrote Defoe, the Secretary's Office, under an active and ambitious chief with a proper system of ' intelligence ' on all subjects, might

---

* After his fall, in 1708, the *Review* supported Godolphin and the Whig Ministry until 1710.

† See pp. 163–167, above, and Mark Thomson, *The Secretaries of State 1681–1782*, pp. 128–130.

become the clearing-house of the nation's business in place
of the Treasury, and ' be thus the only Cabinet. . . .
Here would be a Prime Ministry without a grievance.'
But Harley, though active in collecting intelligence and in
forming secret connections with all sorts of parties and
persons, not excluding his old friends the Dissenters,
neglected that part of Defoe's advice which concerned the
discipline of the office. He was punished by the tragedy
of William Greg.[211]

Greg had been, like Defoe, one of Harley's ' intelli-
gencers,' at one time sent to his native country of Scotland
to report on the Union crisis. He had then, by Harley's
personal choice, been fixed in the Secretary's Office in
London, which proved a demoralizing atmosphere for an
unsteady young man. Owing to the hours of posting,
work was done from eleven at night to four in the morning ;
much of Greg's task was ' perfect drudgery,' for no attempt
was made to discriminate between what we now call ' first
and second division work,' though Greg was one of the most
intelligent men in the office and the only one who knew
French well. The pay was bad, and Greg, a profligate
young fellow according to his own account, was seriously
embarrassed by small debts.

In the autumn of 1707 temptation came in his way.
An English merchant offered him two hundred guineas if
he would secure a French pass for his ship that would
enable her to sail to and fro without molestation by the
privateers. Greg was in charge of the correspondence of
Tallard and the other French prisoners in England, to
which, on account of his linguistic ability, he acted as war
censor. Through that medium he put himself in touch
with Chamillart, the War Minister at Versailles, and offered,
in return for the desired ship's pass, to supply the enemy
with information from the Secretary's Office. Defoe had
already warned Harley how easily a rogue or spy could
sequester important documents, and so it now proved.
Greg sent to Chamillart a letter of Queen Anne's to the
Emperor about the proposal that Prince Eugene should go
to Spain. It happened that just at this time there was
suspicion in Ministerial circles of leakage, chiefly about the

movement of shipping. The French prisoners' post bag was therefore opened and Greg's guilt was at once apparent.

Greg made a full confession and pleaded guilty at his trial. He was therefore condemned to the horrid penalties of treason, without need for the court to enquire fully into the circumstances of the case. The brevity of the proceedings at the Old Bailey justified the House of Lords in seeking further light, to discover whether or no Greg had accomplices. He stated that he had none, but on a matter so important to the public weal there was good reason to test his assertions.

Jan. 19
1708

The fault of the Lords lay in the political character of the Committee they elected to enquire. It consisted of seven Whig noblemen, and no single representative of Harley's side.* Yet the point of the enquiry which for three months fixed the eyes of all politicians on Greg's cell in Newgate was the question whether or not Harley had been cognizant of the treason of the man whom he had chosen as his Secretary. In fact he was perfectly innocent ; and most fortunately for him the poor wretch who had betrayed his country for two hundred guineas would not bear false witness against his chief to avoid the noose and the quartering block.

Greg, indeed, was now in a state of true repentance of his wickedness, and the prison chaplain, Paul Lorrain, of Huguenot origin, exhorted him as he valued his soul not to save himself by accusing the innocent. According to a letter written by Lorrain three years later,† Greg was for weeks beset by men offering him life if he would speak out. He was kept in Newgate a hundred days under sentence, but in the end went to the scaffold, protesting to the last the utter innocence of Harley.

April 28
1708

The Whig Lords had not wished him to give false evidence. They had thought it highly probable that Harley was guilty. To them he was the furtive, treacherous

---

* The Dukes of Devonshire, Somerset and Bolton, Lords Wharton, Townshend, Somers and Halifax.

† It is to be noted that this is not quite such good evidence as a letter would have been if written in 1708. But it cannot be neglected.

' Robin the trickster,' who had deceived them and Marlborough and Godolphin.* Why should he not also have
betrayed his country? In truth they understood little about
him. During the hundred days of Greg's ordeal Harley
showed the best side of his character—perfect calm and
dignity in face of danger that his friends considered
appalling. ' Your brother's head is upon the block,' said
Atterbury to Edward Harley. But Robin, when he heard
of these alarms, only said to Edward, ' I know nothing that
I can do, but entirely to be resigned to and confide in the
Providence of God.' It was the same quiet power of
waiting patiently on events that served him so well when
next his enemies compassed him about, in 1715, when
Bolingbroke's lack of nerve hurried the more brilliant man
to disaster.

The conduct of the Committee of Whig Lords who
examined Greg, or of some of them at least, bears an ugly
look, though it is not necessary to believe all that Swift in
later years wrote about them. Their methods would be
impossible in our day, but in that day they were normal.
We can even note the progress that the passage of a
century had already made. No one touched Harley, and
no one procured false evidence against him. A hundred
years before, if the secretary of a newly fallen Minister of
Elizabeth or James I had been discovered in an act of
manifest treason, the fellow would have been lucky if he
escaped the Tower rack. Even a short generation back
some Titus Oates would assuredly have arisen to seize upon
an opportunity so agreeable to the ancient profession of
witness for the Crown.[212]

* See p. 84, above. An example of the talk against Harley at the time of the
Greg incident is given in Archbishop King's letter to Swift, February 28, 170$\frac{7}{8}$,
about the report of a French invasion : ' The great cry is that this was Harley's
plot and if he had continued three days longer in his place, the French would have
landed at Greenwich.' *Swift's Letters*, I, p. 78.

CHAPTER XVII

THE ATTEMPTED INVASION OF 1708 AND ITS CONSEQUENCES

Ill feeling between England and Scotland after the Union. Custom-house questions. The Scottish Privy Council abolished. Franco-Jacobite intrigues. The invasion launched from Dunkirk. The Pretender at sea. Byng to the rescue. Failure to effect a landing. Consequences of the attempt in Scotland and England. The General Election, May 1708. Triumph of the Whigs.

THE Union of the Parliaments of England and Scotland, which in course of time drew the two peoples together in mutual amity and respect, had no such consequence during the remaining years of Queen Anne. The marriage, which was to prove so long and so happy, had no honeymoon: indeed the first quarrel arose loud at the very door of the church.

Great Britain came into statutory existence on May 1, 1707 : in expectation of that propitious event large consignments of goods had been previously imported from the Continent into Scotland, paying the old Scottish duties, which were in most cases very small. After the Union had come into force, these goods were reshipped to London for the English market, where, after May 1, they would be free of all duty as coming from North Britain. It was a game that could only be played once, but the opportunity was not neglected. A fleet of forty ships from Scotland sailed proudly up the Thames in June 1707, loaded with French and Dutch produce. The sight provoked the fury of the Londoners, who swore that if these foreign manufactures were put on the market duty-free, Englishmen would be undersold and the revenue defrauded. Under the influence of this outcry the custom-house officials, regardless of the new law, seized the cargoes as smuggled goods. The House of Commons supported the seizure, and proposed to give it authority by retrospective legislation.

When the news of these proceedings reached Scotland, all the old Darien anger was stirred up against England's enmity and fraud. The Union Treaty, men said, had been broken already. Fortunately the House of Lords, true to its then customary rôle as pacificator, refused to support the rash action of the Commons' House, and procured delay, till the English had time to recover their tempers and release the goods duty free.

Scotland had won the first round ; but she had to submit to more permanent defeat from the presence in ' North Britain ' of a horde of English custom-house officials, sent there to exact the new duties and to teach their kindly Scots colleagues the more rigorous English methods of administration. Their irritating inflexibility, their belief that their own ways were the only ways, their self-conscious efficiency and rectitude, their contempt for poverty and dislike of dirt angered the Scots as these attitudes have angered many other races since. To throw an English gauger over the cliff seemed a work of mercy.

The custom-house became to the Eighteenth-Century Scot the symbol of a foreign oppression. Angry patriotism and the prospect of great gains combined to make the ' free trade ' a national institution. Fiscal uniformity for the whole island meant that French wine and brandy were due to pay five to eight times what they had formerly paid north of the Cheviots. But the cellars of the ' Caledonian ' gentry continued to be famous for their claret, and not much of it had seen the inside of the custom-house.

The activities of the smuggler were closely connected with those of the Jacobite agent. The same ship carried both kinds of night-birds between France and Scotland. Both acquired a sort of popularity, even with rigid Presbyterians, as enemies of England and of the Union. Till the middle of the century this association of ideas continued to operate, as among the rough population of the Solway coast described in *Redgauntlet* and *The Master of Ballantrae*.[213]

The first Parliament of Great Britain, in its first session, passed an Act that swept away the Scottish Privy Council. To make the Union complete, there should be not merely a single Parliament but a single Privy Council for the whole island. This change had been foreshadowed in the wording of the Treaty of Union,* and was not unpopular in Scotland. For whereas the Edinburgh Parliament had, since the Revolution, stood up for the nation against England, the Privy Council had no such claim on the country's gratitude. Ever since the Union of the Crowns, the Council had been the catspaw of the English Court, and under Charles and James II its torture chamber has been associated with atrocities remembered with a sacred horror in Presbyterian martyrology.

The proposal to abolish the separate Privy Council for Scotland was not therefore resented by the common people as being another attack on the national independence. Scottish politicians of the various Opposition parties hated the Council as the weapon of their successful rivals for office, particularly in the control of elections. For this reason the representatives of the *Squadrone* at Westminster urged the English Whigs and Tories to abolish the Edinburgh Council. A combination of all the Opposition parties of North and South Britain carried the change against the wishes of Godolphin and the Government, who desired to retain the Scottish Council as an instrument of their own authority, pleasantly independent of control by the Westminster Parliament.

The English Whigs, who had not yet brought Godolphin completely under their control, had long been jealous of his personal position as Grand Vizier of Scotland. They still felt uncertain whether he was stout for the Hanoverian Succession in those parts. Moreover, their principles taught them to regard with aversion an irresponsible body like the Scots Privy Council, sitting in secret, subject to no Parliamentary control and liable at any moment to become an instrument of royal despotism. Somers put forward these arguments in a forcible speech. The English Tory Opposition had less theoretic but even more

* See p. 266, above.

practical objection to leaving such an instrument in hands they distrusted. The government was beaten by a large majority in the Commons and by five votes in the Lords, and the Edinburgh Privy Council became portion and parcel of the dreadful past.

It was necessary to make up for this loss of governmental power in Scotland, at a moment when a Jacobite rising and French invasion were instantly feared, and when the difficulty of levying the new customs duties was becoming only too apparent. The English system of Justices of the Peace was therefore extended beyond the Border by the same Act that abolished the Privy Council in Edinburgh. The new magistracy competed with, though it did not yet supplant, the heritable jurisdictions of feudal origin. Neither was this change resented by the Scottish people, who were not as fond of the feudal courts as were the nobles and lairds who had bargained for their continued existence under the Treaty of Union.[214]

Ever since the beginning of the reign of Queen Anne, Pope Clement XI had been urging France to send an army on crusade to restore the Catholic Stuarts in Britain, and he had supplied money to help the design. Although Rome was informed by her agents that the English and Scottish Catholics were not seriously ill-treated, the complaints, only too well founded, which were constantly made by the Irish Catholics of the persecution they suffered contrary to the terms of the Treaty of Limerick, incited and encouraged the Papal Curia to resume against Anne the policy of war and deposition which it had instituted against Elizabeth, although assassination was by this time out of fashion. But in the first years of the century Louis had not attempted the invasion of Britain or of Ireland, and the Papal money had gone instead in Parliamentary bribery, designed to keep a Jacobite interest alive in the Scottish Estates. The Parliamentary habit vied with the physical force policy in the minds of Scottish Jacobites, undermining the warlike zeal for rebellion even of such stalwarts as Lockhart, more than they themselves were perhaps aware. But now the Union had abolished the Edinburgh Parliament, and, unless

Jacobitism was to expire, it must adopt the policy of invasion and rebellion.[215]

The Court of St. Germains supported the representations of the Court of Rome at Versailles, urging the case for a French invasion of Britain, more particularly of Scotland. The Pretender's Ministers pointed out that their master's restoration was the greatest of all French interests. In 1704 they had not been ashamed to use the argument that 'a Catholic King of Britain must always be a dependent on France.'[216] It was the truth of this statement that rendered it impossible for English Tories, least of all for Marlborough and Godolphin, to be real Jacobites. The consideration was of less weight in Scotland, where popular sentiment was neutral between France and England. The unpopularity of the Union made it possible that a French invasion might detach Scotland from Great Britain at least for long enough to restore the waning fortunes of Louis in the European war.

If the French had landed troops in the winter of 1706–7, while the agitation to prevent the passage of the Union Treaty was at its height, the result would have been a very serious insurrection. But for a year after Ramillies the French had had other fish to fry. Their relative success in the subsequent campaign of 1707 put Versailles in a position to consider an invasion of Scotland for 1708. It might at least cause disturbance enough to draw Marlborough's troops back from the Netherlands, and so enable Vendôme to reconquer Belgium with the help of the changing sympathies of the inhabitants of its great cities. To make the invasion of Scotland worth the while of King Louis, it would not be necessary that the Pretender should have any chance of reaching London, or even of maintaining himself permanently in Edinburgh against the might of England. A temporary diversion in Scotland might help France to a good peace on the Continent.

The Ministers of the French Crown explored the ground through the agency of Nathaniel Hooke, who was in Scotland on their behalf from April to June 1707.* He

---

* Hooke, of Irish Protestant origin, seems to have liked running to extremes and was always on the losing side. He was chaplain to Monmouth on his

made it his boast that he acted ' blindly ' on the orders not of St. Germains but of Versailles : at one moment he considered seriously whether, in view of Hamilton's desire to wear the Scottish Crown himself, France should not support his claim rather than that of the Stuarts if by so doing it would be possible to conciliate the Presbyterian interest.

In effect Hooke achieved little. But the detailed accounts of his mission, written by himself and others, throw much light on the state of Scotland in 1707, and the intestine feuds of the various Jacobite and semi-Jacobite factions. On the one hand the modern reader is astonished by the freedom with which the nobles avowed their disloyal sentiments and formed conspiracies to overthrow the State, undisturbed by a government that had neither the troops, the police nor the popular support to suppress the most open treason. But if the Jacobites were formidable in their defiance of external control, within their own body their leaders were half-hearted and divided by personal jealousies and mutual distrust.

Landing in Aberdeenshire, at Slains Castle,* one of the usual Jacobite ports of call, Hooke found himself in the region of the supporters of the Earl of Errol and the Duke of Atholl, whose chief concern was to warn him against trusting the Duke of Hamilton. Hamilton indeed played his usual part, pretending to be too ill to see Hooke, but dealing with him through the agency of a Roman Catholic priest who had assumed the name of Hall. The Dukes of Gordon and Atholl were equally shy of meeting Hooke, or of committing themselves to rise in arms. In the absence of firm leadership, no serious plan was made, although Errol and some of the less important nobles signed an invitation to the Pretender to come over with 8,000 troops. Hooke could do nothing to remove the old difference of opinion between the Scots and the French as to whether the invasion should be the preliminary condition of the insurrection, or the insurrection of the invasion. But he

expedition. He then became a Jacobite and a Roman Catholic, and in 1706 became naturalized as a French subject. See *Hooke (Rox.)*, II, pp. i–xiv.
* *For this chapter see Map of Scotland, p. 177, above.*

was able to tell Louis on his return that no one would move in Scotland unless at least 5,000 French Regulars first landed.

Otherwise Hooke arranged nothing, and obtained little information of value about a country of which he was not a native. He never realized that the strength of the Jacobite fighting force lay in the Highland Clans, about whom he made few enquiries. And he was deceived by the talk he heard into believing that the great body of the Presbyterians would join a French invasion to put a Roman Catholic King on the throne for the benefit of the Episcopalian party.[217]

So passed the summer of 1707, in Jacobite talk without leadership, with growing popular dislike of the Union, but with a growing sense that there was no way of getting rid of it. Meanwhile another arch-conspirator, Ker of Kersland, an impecunious gentleman of the South-West, was exerting his considerable local influence with the extreme Covenanters, whether in the interest of the Jacobites or of the Government no one quite knew. As often happens, the subtle knave had a power over the headstrong zealots which honester men could never obtain. Jacobites and Hanoverians both thought that Ker was leading in their direction the formidable fighting spirit of the Cameronians. According to his own account he was acting in the government interest, and he was certainly in the government pay.

Ker indeed took money wherever he could get it, even from the Whig and Tory Oppositions at Westminster, on the promise of proving the Lord Treasurer to be in league with the Jacobites. The defenceless state of Scotland in the winter of 1707–8, in the face of constant rumours of invasion next spring, had reawakened dormant Whig and Tory suspicions of Godolphin's loyalty to the Revolution Settlement. But in truth, although the Jacobite agents in France and Scotland still had hopes of him and of Marlborough, the two kinsmen were completely loyal to Queen Anne ; only they had chosen to leave Scotland scantily defended, rather than weaken the British military effort on the Continent. They relied upon the navy to ward off invasion, and if necessary to carry troops straight back from

Ostend to any point upon the British coasts that the enemy might threaten.[218]

Such was the state of affairs at home and abroad when in March 1708 Louis at length launched the Pretender at his foes. Six thousand French infantry were put aboard a squadron of nearly thirty sail, commanded by the gallant privateer Commandant, the Comte de Forbin, a true successor of Jean Bart, the uncrowned King of Dunkirk. Forbin was in a position to take a high tone with Versailles, whose Ministers he treated to his Provençal humours, denouncing the whole affair as madness, and insisting that if he was to go on such a fool's errand at all, the slow transports on which it had been proposed to embark the troops must be changed for fast-sailing privateers, of which good store were laid up in Dunkirk, clean vessels, accustomed to outsail the weather-beaten warships of England : otherwise, he declared, the absurd expedition would most certainly go to the bottom, with the loss of squadron, troops and Pretender together. On these altered terms he consented to sail if positively ordered, but still under protest : ' As for me, I risk nothing, I can swim,' he said gaily.

The preparations and even the intentions of the enemy were accurately known to the British government, kept well informed by agents in the Netherlands and spies in Dunkirk. Ever since the middle of February, the mouth of the privateers' harbour had been watched by a formidable extra squadron, equipped by the Admiralty with vigour and dispatch.* In the first days of March the sight of Byng's topsails in the offing caused the French to abandon their design as impracticable, the more so as the Pretender was sick of measles in Dunkirk. All seemed at an end. But in the days of sailing ships everything was subject to the caprice of the winds, and at this moment Byng was compelled by the weather to put back to the Downs, leaving his scouts on the watch. In a moment the soldiers and

---

* Godolphin wanted them to block up Dunkirk harbour with sunken ships, à la Zeebrugge, but the experts showed it was impossible. *Byng Papers*, II, pp. 125–128.

Jacobites got the ear of Versailles. Forbin was overruled ;
the Pretender recovered and was eager to be off ;
March
$\frac{6}{17}$, 1708 the troops were hastily embarked and the expedition
sailed.

Forbin's attitude was one of breezy scepticism about the
chances ; he did not conceal his dislike of the British and Irish
exiles he had to carry, and his pity for their young King
' James VIII ' of Scotland, who in his opinion was the only
Jacobite on board his ship who showed any pluck at all.*
Judging from Forbin's own memoirs, we must suppose that
he was much more intent on the difficult task of bringing
back his squadron unsunk, than on landing either the Pretender or the French regiments on the barbarous mountains
of Scotland. To account for his subsequent conduct, it is
not necessary to believe, as Lockhart and others suspected,
that he had secret orders from Versailles not to put ashore
either the Pretender or the troops. If his orders left him
any discretion, he was safe to be very discreet indeed.

Forbin had started in a brief interval of the heavy
weather that had released him from Byng's blockade. His
voyage to Scotland was made in westerly gales, rain and
snow. The Jacobites were soon very sea-sick : ' it pleased
me,' he wrote, ' to see them so unwell, having fulfilled their
desire to put to sea. *I can do nothing*, I told them. *Your
wine is drawn and you must drink it.*' Some of his ships
were driven back by the winds and returned to Dunkirk
with one thousand of the troops. But if he could throw the
remaining 5,000 ashore anywhere in Scotland the consequences might be serious enough. If he had had either
the instructions or the will to sacrifice his squadron in order
to land the soldiers, a civil war might have been kindled
enough to paralyse Marlborough in the Netherlands. But
he had no such heroic orders, and his personal desire was
confined to the safe return of the French ships.

---

* It was as King of Scotland that he intended to make his appeal on landing.
The proclamation which he had with him on board was the appeal of ' James VIII
to his good people of his ancient Kingdom of Scotland,' to break the Union with
England. He declared in the proclamation that he would leave everything to a
newly elected Edinburgh Parliament. He gave no guarantee to the Presbyterians,
and it is clear that their church would have been destroyed. *H.M.C. Stuart Papers*,
I (1902), pp. 218–219 ; *Lockhart*, I, p. 239.

It had been agreed that the landing should be made if possible in the Firth of Forth. Edinburgh was at the moment almost without defence ; according to Ker ' there was not four rounds in the Castle,' or ' forty effective men,' and indeed Lord Leven was preparing for its evacuation if the enemy landed. According to one of Harley's Edinburgh correspondents, the little Scottish army, such as it was, was ' debauched ' and would join the Pretender as soon as he appeared.*

But from first to last everything went wrong with the invasion. Forbin made his landfall ' six leagues ' too far north, and had to sail back along the coast of Fife, losing hours that the event showed to be invaluable. On the afternoon of March 12 his ships began to draw into the mouth of the Firth of Forth and one of them communicated with the shore at Pittenweem, famous for its witch-hunts.† That night the invaders' squadron lay between Crail and the Isle of May. They showed the concerted signals to attract the attention of their Jacobite friends on land, but there was no reply. The failure to return so important a message confirmed Forbin in his prejudice that the whole of the Jacobite business was moonshine.

Next morning, the light of dawn showed the English squadron at ' four leagues ' distance to the south. Byng had begun the pursuit with twelve hours to make up and with slower ships, but by hugging the coast he had kept pace and came just in time. Though he had sent a detachment to convoy British troops from Ostend to Tynemouth, he had with him thirty-two ships, some of them three-deckers. Forbin was outnumbered and outclassed, and in grave danger of being shut up in the Firth. He fled north before the Union Jack, seeking home by the route of the Armada.

March $\frac{13}{24}$, 1708

* On March 13, while the French topsails were visible in the mouth of the Firth, Leven wrote to Mar : ' Here I am. Not one farthing of money to provide provisions. None of the Commissions yet sent down. Few troops and naked. It vexes me sadly to think I must retire to Berwick if the French land on this side Forth.' *H. of L. MSS.* (1708–1710), pp. ix, 140 ; *Ker*, I, p. 63. Godolphin had been negligent, at least in the matter of Edinburgh Castle. On the Scottish army see *Portland*, IV, p. 466.

† See p. 212, above. See *Map of Scotland*, p. 177, above.

It was a stern chase. The quarry were the picked privateers of France, in excellent condition from cleaning and repairs in harbour. The hounds were the English men-of-war, their bottoms foul with the ceaseless patrol-work that mastery of the sea entails. But the leaders of the chase, the *Dover* and the *Ludlow Castle*, ' the only clean sailing ships we had,' got in among the French fleet and began to cannonade Forbin's flagship. The balls whistled round the head of ' James VIII,' who bore himself like his father in the Dutch sea battles long ago. But some of the exiles were ducking all over the deck, to the glee of the Frenchmen who loved them not. While the cannonade continued, the Jacobites asked Forbin to be allowed to get into a boat with the King, and land on the neighbouring coast. Forbin absolutely refused. He thought they made the proposal out of fear and a cold heart, to get out of the shot of the English ships. But as they were seconded by James himself, whose courage Forbin admits, it is charitable to suppose that his companions wished him to land, even with only a few followers, in order to raise the rebellion, since the chance of his landing with the French troops seemed already to have disappeared. Indeed the plan was itself the height of rashness, and Forbin's refusal would have been justified on that ground alone. Seasick lands-men, especially if they are exiles in sight of home, will want to get ashore at any risk.

All day and all night the chase continued, up the coast of Forfar and Aberdeen. But at dawn on March 14, off Buchanness, Byng saw the enemy's rear so many miles ahead that he abandoned pursuit, and went back to guard the mouth of the Forth against any possibility of their return. The English had captured one of the larger enemy vessels, the *Salisbury* * of fifty guns, loaded with French infantry and a few Irish and Scottish Jacobites, including old Lord Griffin. But fortunately for Anne's peace of mind, her servants had not caught her brother.

He, poor lad, was still for the bolder course. When next day the English pursuit had stopped, he again urged Forbin to make a landing near Inverness. The Jacobites

* She was an English ship, taken in 1703 and used by the French.

and the military favoured the design and at one moment
Forbin consented.   But the weather turned worse, adding
to his fears of losing his squadron if caught in the Moray
Firth by Byng, as it had been nearly caught in the Firth of
Forth.   The storm dispersed the fleet, and the pilots were
ignorant of the coast.   For these reasons all at length
agreed to sail on round Cape Wrath and Ireland, and make
the best of their way home.

After horrible sufferings and the loss of several ships and
many men dead of the hardships of the voyage, the squadron
won back to Dunkirk.   Some English prisoners in the port
witnessed their disembarkation, and thus described it :

The forces relanded out of the ships in a very miserable condition
both in health and clothes, and [we] saw the person called the Pretender land on the shore, being a tall, slight young man, pale smooth
face, with a blue feather in his hat, and a star on his cloak ; at his
first going off they mightily huzzaed him with *Vive le Roi*, but were
very mute at his coming back.*

Marlborough had made his plans for throwing troops
into Scotland, and they moved like clockwork.   None the
less, the clock had been set at least ten days behind what
would have been required in order to garrison Edinburgh
at the moment Forbin was in the Firth of Forth.   He was
there on March 12 (O.S.).   On March 21 there arrived off
Tynemouth the ten battalions of English infantry, sent
there from Ostend under a convoy of ten English and Dutch
warships.   On March 24 another small army began to
march north from the neighbourhood of London.   Some

* My account of the attempted invasion is drawn mainly from *Forbin's* own
memoirs, from the *Byng Papers*, vol. II (an invaluable source), *Burchett*, pp. 740–747,
and *The House of Lords MSS.* (1708–1710), pp. iii–ix and 32–79 (see pp. 41–42 and
48 in particular).   *Hooke*, 1760, pp. 152–163, contains other French and Jacobite
narratives to be compared to Forbin.   To these I should like here to add the
Pretender's own account, taken from his instructions to Charles Farquarson, who
was sent over later in 1708 to raise the drooping spirits of the party in Scotland :
' First you are to assure them of the concern and trouble we are in on their
account as well as our own, that this last enterprise has failed, occasioned by our
sickness, the mistakes of the pilots, and other unforseen accidents which gave the
enemy the opportunity of preventing our landing in the Firth [of Forth] ; while,
on the other side, violent contrary winds, the dispersing of the fleet, the ignorance
we were in of the coasts and want of provision hindered our landing in any other
place,' *e.g.* Inverness.   *Bodleian MSS., Carte*, 180 f. 22.

15,000 seasoned English troops would have been in Scotland in April. Such a force should have sufficed to check and ultimately to suppress any rebellion that might have resulted from a French landing, but it is not likely that the ten battalions could have returned to Ostend in time to save the year's campaign for Marlborough in the Netherlands.

Not being in fact needed, the ten battalions were never landed at Tynemouth at all. After lying off the coast there for some days, they were sent back in plenty of time to help win the battle of Oudenarde. Their experiences at sea had not been pleasant. Over 5,000 of them had been packed in leaky, rotten and pest-ridden transports, while the remaining 1,700 had been crammed into the men-of-war where there was no accommodation for them at all. Stretched on the hard planks without bedding or proper food, the sick died in misery as great as the sufferings of the French troops then tossing off Cape Wrath. Even Marlborough's care for his men had not been extended to improve their conditions when at sea.[219]

When Forbin had been in the mouth of the Firth, the gleeful and vindictive glances of the Jacobites on the High Street of Edinburgh had alarmed the loyal. But it was the opinion in government circles that the Presbyterians would have opposed the Popish claimant and the Episcopalian party, if a landing had been effected : Carstares was congratulated on the loyalty shown by the Church, and Sunderland, as Secretary of State, wrote to the Earl of Leven on March 18 that 'the account we have of the good disposition of the people in and about Edinburgh is very comfortable, and particularly that of the Church, which I am sure deserve all encouragement.' Defoe's analysis of the general feeling of the ' poor, honest, but ill-natured and imposed-upon people ' of Scotland, written from Edinburgh in May for Godolphin's instruction, implies uncertainty as to what would have happened if the enemy had landed :

It began to be said at the time of the invasion ' *It lay between the English and the French ; let them fight it out.*' There was nothing for the honest people, as they called themselves, to do in it. While they were increasing in this temper the French appeared. What temper then began to show itself little judgment can be made, there was so little time between the appearing of the French and Sir George Byng, being but one afternoon [March 12].

And there, with no more certain pronouncement, we must be content to leave speculation on the untried event.[220]

The Privy Council of Scotland, already under statutory sentence of death, spent the last weeks of its existence in preparing against invasion and arresting Jacobite suspects. By the end of March the castles of Edinburgh and Stirling were crammed with lords and gentlemen. Many, who had drunk Jacobite toasts in unwary moments, were glad enough to be thus honourably quit of any moral obligation to risk their necks and estates. Arrests on the eve of a rebellion often gave much secret personal relief to the outwardly indignant victim. Hamilton, who had taken care to be in England when the expedition approached the Scottish shore, was probably glad enough when the Queen's messenger came to serve the expected writ. His rival the Duke of Atholl was at Blair Atholl among his Highlanders, and it was thought prudent to leave him there on his giving a bond of £5,000 to appear if summoned. More deeply implicated were a few gentlemen of Stirlingshire who had been seen ' out ' with their horses and servants incautiously soon. Much indignation was aroused when these and other prisoners were sent up to London to be tried there, or at least examined there by the Ministers.

Fletcher of Saltoun was called before the Edinburgh Privy Council and established his innocence. But poor old Lord Belhaven was sent to London, on the fame of his all too popular speech against the Union.* He was genuinely indignant at being considered disloyal to the Protestant Succession merely because he was an ' Anti-unioner,' and wrote Ministers long letters on the subject, which they passed about among each other as ' comical.' He was bailed out, but the misunderstanding of his political position had gone to the old man's heart, and he died that summer, it was said, ' of chagrin.'

* See p. 274, above.

No one died by the executioner for the affair of the invasion, not even those who were taken in the *Salisbury* in the act of levying war.   One of them, the veteran Lord Griffin, was condemned to a traitor's death as a returned outlaw.   But even he was reprieved ' because the Queen cannot bring herself to let him suffer, whom, she says, she has known so long.'   He died in prison, a few years later. Lord Sunderland was so much disgusted by the clemency of the government to which he belonged that he wrote to Newcastle : ' their late management in relation to the Invasion and in particularly the pardoning of Lord Griffin, is a declaration to the whole world, as far as in them lies, for the Prince of Wales.'

Anne, Marlborough and Godolphin were all humane by nature and moderate in opinion.   But there was a further reason for clemency.   A General Election was coming on—the first to be held for a Parliament of all Britain.*   The government had no wish to lose support in Scotland by undue harshness after so fortunate an escape. Moreover the Whig Lords, half in and half out of the government, were playing a game of their own on Godolphin's flank and against his interest.   Hamilton struck a bargain with the Junto.   He and his friends should be let out of prison to return to their homes at once, if they would support the Whigs against Godolphin's candidates in the coming elections.   The Scottish representative Peers might hold the balance in the evenly divided House of Lords, and their election by their fellow-nobles of Scotland was therefore of prime importance to the English Whigs.   Sunderland, though Secretary of State, was so little loyal to his father-in-law and Godolphin that he wrote to the Duke of Roxburgh while the election was pending : ' I would not have you be bullied by the Court-Party, for the Queen herself cannot support that faction long.'   His anger at the clemency shown by others to Lord Griffin did not prevent him from joining in this intrigue to let out the rest of the Jacobite conspirators on the Whig terms.

Thus, by arrangements made, some with Godolphin

* In the previous session the Scottish representatives had taken their seats at Westminster in the sitting Parliament.

and some with Sunderland and his friends, all the Jacobite suspects were free men before the election in May, except the Stirlingshire gentlemen. Even they were sent back to be tried in Scotland, with a resulting verdict of ' not proven,' as few there were willing to testify even to known facts against them.[221]

The General Election of May 1708 was governed by England's alarm and anger over the attempted invasion in March. When the French were on their way to Edinburgh, a run on the Bank of England had been engineered by its rivals, the goldsmiths and private bankers, led by Sir Francis Child, Tory member of Parliament. Their unpatriotic attempt had been defeated by the efforts of Godolphin at the Treasury and by the Whig monied interest in the City. The incident told heavily against the Tories at election time. Patriotism and the desire for stability ranged themselves on the side of the Whig candidates. On March 31 the Dean of Norwich wrote to a friend :

Had the Bank broke when the run was made upon it, I must have broke too, for I had then £4,000 in it. I reckon the matters that have been of late transacted will, on this baffle, have a great influence on this next election. I wish it do not carry the Whig interest too high, for that is best when well balanced.

On account of the invasion, many supported the Whigs who might otherwise have been inclined to vote for the Tories in hopes of a speedy peace. In the previous winter the country had seemed hardly to know whether it wanted to continue the war or not. In December 1707 Swift had written from Leicester,

This long war has here occasioned no fall of lands, nor much poverty among any sort of people, only some complain of a little slowness of tenants to pay their rents. There is a universal love of the present government.

But only six weeks later he wrote from London :

Preparations for war much slower, so that we expect but a moderate campaign, and people begin to be heartily weary of the war.

In face of such contradictory opinions formed by the same observer it would be rash to pronounce how the election would have gone in May 1708, if there had been no invasion in March. But an attack on our shores was a challenge and a provocation from the French King, not likely to lead a high-spirited people into the path of peace.

The polling took place while folk were talking of nothing but the invasion, and the Whigs endeavoured with some success to turn it against the Tory party as a whole. Their *Advice to the Electors*, said to have been written by ' some eminent members of the Kitkat,' ' excuses the Papists and Non-jurors as inconsiderable, the Whigs as not to be suspected, and lays the whole blame of the late invasion at the poor Tories' door.' [222]

In these circumstances many borough-owners, squires, clergy and freeholders gave their support to Whig candidates whom they more frequently opposed. In spite of division between the Whigs and Godolphin, and the similar coolness between Godolphin and the Queen, the weight of government was once more thrown against the Tory Opposition ; and in Anne's reign the government of the day never once sustained defeat in a General Election. The result was that on May 27 Sunderland wrote triumphantly to the Duke of Newcastle :

I heartily congratulate with your grace upon the Elections throughout England, being so well over as they are. I think one may venture to say it is the most Wig Parliament has been since the Revolution.

Whether it was one of those recurring moments when a Whig Parliament was what England and Europe most required may be questioned. But there was the fact, the natural outcome of the invasion.[223]

Yet governmental influence had not been exerted to the fullest extent on behalf of all the Whig candidates. Neither Godolphin nor the Queen, nor even the moderate-minded Whig Chancellor Lord Cowper, were prepared to sweep all Tory magistrates off the bench to prepare the way for the election. Sarah bitterly complained that her brother had been defeated in his candidature for her own town of

St. Albans, because his Tory opponent ' had been left with the power of justice in the town.' 224

The personal influence of the borough owner, the land-lord, the patron, the official superior in Church or State, played the usual part in this as in all other elections of the reign, and bribery was administered by all sides as unblush-ingly as ever. The House of Commons had dallied with a mild anti-bribery Bill just before the election, but the Lords had thrown it out. If it had passed, it could no more have been enforced in that age than Prohibition in the United States to-day.

We are coming to a Parliamentary Election [wrote Defoe in his *Review*]. It is to no purpose to talk any more about bribing, treating, buying of voices and such things as these, articles now become as necessary to Elections of Parliament men, as bread is to life. . . . Here are two gentlemen in a town on the market day ; there they take up each of them a public-house. The ale-house keeper bam-boosels them and charges all the ale he has in the house twice over, whether tis drunk or no. If his Worship does not like it, he does him wrong, for he has brought in all the customers to vote for him.

The public-house was the necessary headquarters for conquering a popular constituency, followed up by ' two guineas a man ' for the voters, as at Ludgarshall in Wilts. But in close boroughs the Corporation could be bought wholesale, as at Thetford, where ' the election is among the magistracy, and 50 guineas for a vote is their price,' in 1708.225

The Cornish rotten boroughs, which were all of them ' owned,' continued a slow gravitation away from the High Tory monopoly that had existed in those parts at the beginning of the reign. A Cornish Tory correspondent wrote to Harley :

Addison has been brought in at Lostwithiel by an interest carried on in another name and transferred by surprise. Upon the whole these two last elections [1705 and 1708] have made us rather worse than better in this County.

It had been found impossible to procure one of the Cornish seats for Henry St. John, who did not venture to contest his old seat at Wootton Bassett. He prepared for a few years of philosophic retirement, ' a blessing,' he wrote, ' I never yet enjoyed.' And he used the opportune absence from the House to renew his old High Tory friendships and connections at Oxford and elsewhere.

When the new House met, the election petitions were carried by the votes of the House in favour of ' Whigs and Courtiers,' as shamelessly as the Tories had carried them on former occasions. Bishop Burnet, who, strong partisan as he was, had always some sense of decency and fair-play, was shocked at the injustice of his own side. There was no doubt who had won the General Election.[226]

Note on Sir Walter Scott and the Scotland of Queen Anne.

The politics of Scotland during the attempted invasion of 1708 form the historical background of *The Black Dwarf*, where Scott has drawn the least favourable of his pictures of Jacobite society and conspiracy. *The Bride of Lammermoor* is apparently meant to take place in the first few years after the Union; besides its tragic intensity and march of fate, that book has also a secondary value as a picture of Scottish society of the period, such as the great antiquary could draw with such imaginative realism and dexterity out of the fulness of his knowledge.

CHAPTER XVIII

Oudenarde, Lille, Minorca

Campaign of 1708. Ghent and Bruges lost. Battle of Oudenarde. Marlborough's proposal to march on Paris vetoed by Eugene. Siege and capture of Lille. Battle of Wynendael. Recovery of Ghent and Bruges. Leake in the Mediterranean. Sardinia. The Pope. Capture of Port Mahon, Minorca. Some diplomatic repercussions. Admiral Wager's action.

MARLBOROUGH well knew that the failure of the Allies in 1707 to achieve anything in any theatre of the war must not be repeated in 1708, if the struggle was ever to be brought to a good end. Last year's experience had also shown that there was no chance of success except through his own exertions. He determined so to contrive that Eugene should co-operate with him in the field. He had failed to persuade the Emperor to send that Prince to Spain, and since he himself could not leave the Netherlands in face of Belgian disaffection and French numerical strength, he plotted to bring Eugene thither, to win with him another fraternal victory, and make a push through the frontier fortresses into France.

But the projected union of the forces of Marlborough and Eugene had to be kept a secret. The Elector of Hanover was the Imperialist General on the Upper Rhine : though he was not, like his predecessors in that command, incompetent, he was hardly less jealous than Lewis of Baden, and he expected that the other army of the Empire, under Eugene, would be sent to join him. For many reasons Marlborough had no wish to offend the future King George more than was absolutely necessary for the common weal. It was therefore arranged as a compromise that there should be three separate armies : the Elector with 40,000 men should watch the French in Alsace ;

Eugene with 45,000 should operate on the Moselle ; while
Marlborough guarded Belgium with the 80,000 men in
English and Dutch pay.   But it was secretly agreed between the two old comrades of Blenheim that at midsummer
Eugene should march from the Moselle to the Netherlands
and join Marlborough in an attack on the French frontier.
On May 3 the Duke wrote to Godolphin from the Hague :
' as for the joining of the two armies, we thought it best
not to acquaint the Elector with it, so that I expect when that
is put in execution, he will be very angry ; but since the
good of the campaign depends upon it, I know no remedy
but patience.' [227]

Meanwhile the French also had their plans for an offensive that should lead to a ' good peace.'   The events of
1707 had gone some way to restore their fighting spirit, and
though the economic conditions of France made peace imperative, Louis thought he could get it on good terms if
he was again successful in the field this year.

The French plan was to make military capital out of
Belgian discontent with Dutch administration, and out of
the popularity which the Elector of Bavaria had formerly
enjoyed as Governor of the Spanish Netherlands.   His
rule and his person had won the special approbation of
the aristocracy and more particularly of the ladies.   Indeed
Max Emanuel, whom Marlborough's two great victories
had made twice an exile, was a kind of Belgo-Bavarian
' Bonnie Prince Charlie.' *   The hope of restoring him to
power in the Netherlands had been connected with the
attempted invasion of Scotland in March, which was
designed to draw home the whole of the British forces for the
whole summer.   Their departure would have been followed
by a great French advance in co-operation with sym-
pathisers inside the Belgian cities.   The failure of the
Pretender's voyage and the consequent return in April of
the ten English battalions that had been sent to Tynemouth
from Ostend, put an end to the diversion.   But even so the
French attack on the Netherlands was attempted in July
with a fair chance of success.

---

* *St. Simon* (V, chap. xxi) dwells on this.   He remarks that it was, therefore,
a mistake to send Max Emanuel this year to the Rhine, instead of to the Netherlands.

It was to be a grand effort. The days had long gone by when King Louis used to take the field himself to watch the easy capture of a town ; but the Dauphin's son, the Duke of Burgundy, the future King of France if harsh fate had permitted, was to go in nominal command and reap the glory of the campaign. Beside him rode the youth who was already King of England—had his subjects only thought so. In the presence of Princes the French soldiers of that epoch were expected to do battle with even more than their usual ardour. Marshal Vendôme was sent as Burgundy's adjutant or tutor—it was hard to say which. He was an experienced, bold and able soldier, a grandson of one of Henri Quatre's too numerous children, popular with the rank and file of the army, but tainted with vices of a kind which even the courtiers of Versailles found it hard to stomach. He was often sunk in sensual sloth, but could arouse himself to act with energy and courage. The camp was at once divided into the faction of Vendôme and the faction of Burgundy ; the feud was perpetually breaking out in the most violent scenes between the two commanders, and had much to do with the ultimate failure of their campaign.

All, however, went well at first. Early in July the French Generals boldly and ably gave Marlborough the slip, as he stood covering the ill-fortified towns of Brussels and Louvain. Having passed his guard, they appeared in force before the gates of Ghent, which were opened to them by conspiracy within. Bruges followed suit, and the French armies lay safe behind the cover of the Bruges Canal, in Marlborough's very rear. ' The States,' wrote the Duke to Godolphin on July 9, ' have used this country so ill that I no ways doubt but all the towns will play us the same trick as Ghent has done, whenever they have it in their power.' *

Marlborough had been outmanœuvred. He was ill at ease in body and in mind. He suffered constantly from fevers and headaches—' my blood is so heated,' he is perpetually writing to Sarah ; he was troubled by news from home of the alienation of the Queen and the in-

* For this chapter see Map IX, The Netherlands, etc., at end of this volume.

transigence of the Whigs ; he realized to the full the
dangers of the politico-military state of Belgium, and he
decided that nothing but a battle won could restore the
situation. If, by any device, he could bring the French to
action in the field, he would not let slip the opportunity,
even if the delay of a few days would increase his force by
the expected arrival of Eugene's army from the Moselle ;
for he well knew that such an addition to his strength would
render the French much more unwilling to risk a battle.
The Dutch Field Deputies, as a result of last year's fiasco,
had this year been instructed not to interfere with his plans.
In the other camp, Vendôme and Burgundy and their respective factions were highly elated at the capture of Ghent,
but were still somewhat afraid of a return stroke from Marlborough, the ' mortified adventurer ' whom, as they remembered, Villeroi had so rashly despised and challenged
at Ramillies. The French Generals were therefore divided,
each in his own mind, between boldness and caution ; and
they were further divided by jealousy one against the other.
A clear and consistent plan of action was not likely to be the
result. Such was the psychological situation that led to the
clash at Oudenarde.[228]

Leaving strong garrisons in Ghent and Bruges, Vendôme
and Burgundy moved back towards the French frontier.
But instead of marching straight home to the safe cover of
Lille, they lingered on the way, playing with the idea of the
capture of a fortress under Marlborough's nose. They
quarrelled, of course, as to which the fortress was to be.
Burgundy was for besieging Menin ; Vendôme preferred
Oudenarde, and insisted on having his way. He designed
that the army should move from Ghent to Lessines on the
Dender, in order to keep the Allies to the east of that river,
and so cover the siege of Oudenarde. But Marlborough
marched from Herfelingen and was in Lessines before the
French could get there.

Vendôme, thus thwarted, fell back on Burgundy's plans
against Menin. He sought to cover the siege of that place
by crossing the Schelde at Gavre and occupying its left
bank from Gavre up to Oudenarde. Since Oudenarde and
its bridges were in allied hands and Marlborough was

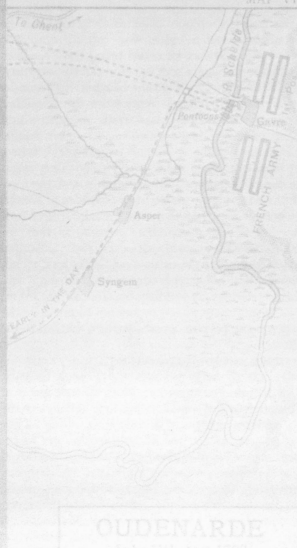

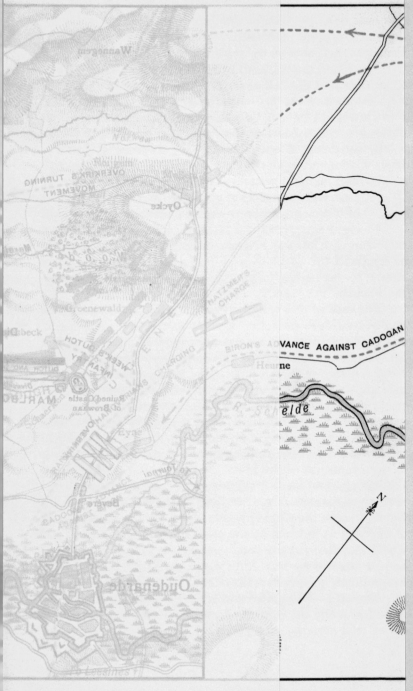

clearly in more active mood than the French generals, the plan was none too safe, as the event proved.[229]

Marlborough had been joined by Eugene. The Prince's army, now on its way from the Moselle, was several days' march in the rear, but neither comrade in arms wished to wait for it at the risk of letting Vendôme escape from the trap into which he had sauntered. Even as it was, the French would escape if they were not outmarched as well as outfought. But Marlborough's men could do both.

Before dawn, at one o'clock in the morning of July 11, Irish Cadogan, again, as at Ramillies, Marlborough's harbinger of victory, started from Lessines. He took with him the vanguard of the army, consisting of a dozen battalions chiefly of British infantry, and eight squadrons of Hanoverian dragoons including their young Electoral Prince—in whose name as George II of England the Seven Years' War was won half-a-century later ; to-day he was to serve his apprenticeship in beating the French.

July 11
(N.S.)
1708

The task of this vanguard was to construct a number of pontoon bridges over the Schelde just below Oudenarde, and hold the approach against all comers, in order to secure the passage of the river by the main army later in the day. After a march of fifteen miles, they reached the edge of the hills above Eename, about ten o'clock in the morning, and suddenly saw below them the Schelde winding through its marshes, and on the further bank the pretty fortress town of Oudenarde. Above its houses rose the tower and high-pitched narrow roof of the church, and the gorgeous architectural fantasies of the Hotel de Ville. But that morning Cadogan had no eyes for such matters ; his gaze was turned northward, where, six miles away, above the heights of Gavre, he saw the whole French army, still on the same side of the river as himself, on the point of crossing it by bridges which they had already laid. He might yet be in time, but he had none to waste. He speedily laid his ' tin boats ' in five pontoon bridges over the Schelde, hard by the town, and the vanguard—horse, foot and artillery—trundled across.

Meanwhile the French also were passing the Schelde at Gavre and moving southward in leisurely and uncertain fashion. If Burgundy and Vendôme had been like Marlborough and Eugene, they would have flung their whole force on Cadogan as fast as they could bring it up ; they might well have driven him into the Schelde, together with the head of Marlborough's supporting columns. If, on the other hand, the French were playing for safety, they could have taken up a fine defensive position on the heights of Huysse, Lede and Wannegem. That long ridge rises, bare and smooth as a glacis, from the bottom of the Norken stream. Marlborough would not have had time to storm the position on the evening after his long march from Lessines : if the French had wished, they could have stolen away in the night ; or, if they so preferred, they could have stood the shock next morning on ground most favourable for the defence. But their quarrelsome commanders were incapable of taking friendly counsel together to arrive at any definite plan. A series of rival orders, given some by Vendôme and some by Burgundy, led the French into a battle wherein they failed either to take active advantage of Cadogan's dangerous position, or to secure the maximum of safety for a defensive action.

From the first moment of crossing the river at Gavre, the enemy's movements were planless and undecided. The bulk of the army moved in the general direction of the Huysse heights, while a detachment under Biron was sent down to occupy Eyne and dispose of Cadogan. The laying of the pontoons, which were to be Marlborough's path to victory, had held the vanguard of the Allies busy beside the river banks, until Biron's Swiss regiments had had time to occupy Eyne.

It was now afternoon and the head of Marlborough's main columns were beginning to appear on the edge of the hills above Eename. The pace at which the great army had moved from Lessines, whence it started about seven o'clock, had been a measure of the enthusiasm of all ranks. Everyone was burning to wipe out the stain of Ghent and Bruges, lost by ' treachery,' as they all said. The French had stolen an advantage and had begun to crow about it ; they must be put in their place again, as in the Ramillies year. Marlborough's presence made every man confident of victory.

English, German, Dutch, Scandinavian, Huguenot, they
marched under many flags, but they had faith in one man.
He had set them to race against time, and they all knew it.
The day's march would be arduous, but evening would
bring the battle for which they thirsted. The unlucky files
who had been detained to guard the baggage deserted their
inglorious post, to join in the rush of their comrades to
Oudenarde. Cheerfully swearing and singing in a dozen
different tongues, they pounded along the dusty highway
in the poplar shade. Even dour Colonel Blackader was
moved to a sombre joy : ' My thoughts were much on the
103rd psalm,' he wrote, ' which I sung (in my heart)
frequently upon the march.' When, after fifteen miles
of it, they reached the edge of the Eename hill and saw the
shining river and the white coats of Louis's Grand Army
beyond, they doubled their pace. The leading squadrons
went ' at a full trot ' over the pontoons which Cadogan had
laid so well. Behind them the blue-coated Prussian infantry ' ran ' across the swinging highway, and after them
more redcoats. Marlborough and Eugene, riding side by
side, crossed in this eager company.

At first sight of the approach of these succours, Cadogan
had moved forward from the riverside and attacked Biron in
Eyne. He had brought with him in his vanguard the pick
of the English infantry. They advanced on the village in
line with shouldered muskets, never firing a shot, or even
bringing their bayonets to the charge till they were within
pistol-shot of the Swiss. The mountaineers were among
the best troops the French had, but three battalions laid
down their arms in Eyne, and the Hanoverian dragoons cut
the fourth to pieces as it attempted to retreat, together with
three more battalions coming up too late from Heurne.
The Hanoverian horsemen, elated by their easy victory over
the enemy's foot, followed their General Rantzau to fresh
adventure, and crashed into twenty squadrons of French
cavalry near Heurne and scattered them in rout. In this
brilliant charge, performed in presence of the two approaching armies, the Electoral Prince George distinguished
himself. His horse was shot under him, and for a moment
men thought that England must seek another heir. But

the choleric, spirited little gentleman was up and on again. The English ballads of Oudenarde hawked through the country that summer told of his prowess against ' Jack Frenchman.' It was a point gained for the Hanover Succession. The Pretender, too, behaved well that day, but he was fighting against England.

Such was the prelude, of happy augury for the Allies, to the main encounter, that could not now be avoided, between the two great hosts of 60,000 men or more on each side. The strength of the French army was on or near the Huysse heights, but at sight of Biron's discomforture and Marlborough's approach, it began, too late, to move down in successive detachments by way of Roijgem mill, across the Marollebeck, to crush Cadogan and Rantzau at Groenewald. Marlborough speeded on the Prussians and other troops of the main army, as fast as they crossed the pontoons, to hurry to the support of the adventurous vanguard. As the regiments on either side arrived upon the scene, the battle was joined on an ever wider front, spreading out like an opening fan. First the line was set from Herlejem to Shaerken ; and later in the afternoon along the banks of the Diepenbeck south-westward from Shaerken, as far as the moat surrounding the ruined Castle of Browaan, the left wing of the allied position. Along a line more than two miles long, one of the severest infantry actions of the war raged for hours without intermission, until night put an end to the slaughter.

The French, through their dilatory tactics, had thrown away their chance of driving Cadogan and the Hanoverians and Prussians into the Schelde before the rest of the allied army could cross ; but they did their best to make good their fault. The English declared the enemy had never fought better : certainly they had fought worse at Ramillies. Vendôme had sulkily acquiesced in the *fait accompli* of the descent from the Huysse heights, initiated by Burgundy without his knowledge. Now, however, he was fighting at Groenewald, a half-pike in his hand, no longer the slothful debauchee, but the descendant of the victor of Ivry ; and the best infantry of France thronged after him into the mêlée.

But the Allies, though they had marched more than fifteen miles that day, were more than a match for the enemy, both commanders and men. As a special compliment to Eugene, who was present without his army, Marlborough put him in command of the right wing, where the danger was greatest, and where the British soldiers fought. The Guards and that famous regiment that was even then known as ' the Buffs,' from their yellow facings, were proud to fight under Eugene. Argyle was their immediate commander, in the very thick of it, as he was in the thick of every great action in Flanders.

Oudenarde differed from Blenheim and Ramillies in its general character. There was no ranging of the two hosts in proper order of battle, on positions previously explored and selected. It was an ' encounter action.' The regiments came up happy-go-lucky, and were thrust into the gaps of the firing line as fast as they could arrive. The battle was not set, it grew. In such an affair, rarer in those days than in later warfare, a General must have an eye for rapid calculations of time and distance, a brain to make and execute plans on the spur of the moment. And at Oudenarde Marlborough showed himself as great a master of this game of catch-as-you-can as of the prearranged tactics of forcing the enemy's reconnoitred positions at Blenheim and Ramillies. As each battalion hurried up from the bridge head, he flung it in wherever it was most needed. At one moment he moved Lottum's brigade bodily from the left wing, where it had begun the fighting, to go to the support of the hard-pressed Eugene ; while he himself led the latest arrivals, Dutch and Hanoverian foot, across the Diepenbeck, driving back the enemy's right. This elaborate and nice manœuvre, carried out in the heat of such an action, shows what complete mastery he had in his mind over the course of the battle.*

There was a further difference between Oudenarde

* Marlborough had another superiority over the French commanders in better knowledge of the character of the ground, where some of his troops had recently been camped. Burgundy made an error, possibly fatal to the event of the day, in stopping a movement which Vendôme had ordered to envelope Eugene's right, under the mistaken belief that the ground over which they were to pass was too boggy for passage.

and the Duke's other two great victories in the lesser
importance of the part played by the cavalry, owing to the
nature of the ground. The decision was reached by the
infantry. There were indeed two very effective and useful
charges made by the allied horse, the first by Rantzau's
Hanoverians at Heurne as already described, the other
later in the evening by Natzmer and his Prussian troopers
on the outside of Eugene's right flank, which they saved
from being turned, plunging deep into the heart of the
approaching French forces. But in the essential fighting,
on the two-mile line from Herlejem village to Browaan
Castle, only infantry were engaged, because the ground
there did not admit of charges of horse. Even the artillery
played a less part than usual because of the difficulty of
bringing up the guns in time through the enclosures.
The French left their whole artillery in the rear, and so
saved it intact when disaster fell on the forces actually
engaged. But Marlborough made good use of his artillery
in the centre of the firing line.

Chance had directed that the main encounter of the two
armies should take place in a region of enclosed ground, the
petite culture and woodlands of the villages along the Marollebeck and Diepenbeck. On every side of this enclosed
region the Flemish landscape wears its usual aspect of open
rolling corn-lands, fit for cavalry operations ; and over such
ground the Hanoverian and Prussian charges were made.
But the infantry were disputing for villages, hedges,
orchards, rows of poplars, scattered cottages and cabbage
gardens straggling along the becks and the irrigation
channels connected with them. John Marshall Deane,
who fought as a ' private sentinel ' in the Foot Guards that
day, thus describes the action in which he took part :

> The fight was very desperate on both sides and continued from five
> in the evening as long as there was any light ; in which time the
> enemy was beat from hedge to hedge and breastwork to breastwork,
> that one would have thought it impossible for them to have lost the
> battle, they having had time to secure themselves of strong ground as
> they always do, getting into villages, possessing themselves of houses,
> and making every quickset hedge a slight wall that we cannot come
> at them.

The upshot was that Eugene, thanks to the valour of the Prussians and the deadly platoon firing of the English, held his ground against the superior force of French foot on that wing, while Marlborough, with the Dutch and Hanoverian infantry on the allied left, pushed the enemy back at the bayonet's point from the Diepenbeck, and advanced in earnest as the evening shades began to show the flash of each musket shot. 'We drove the enemy,' wrote an eye-witness, 'from ditch to ditch, from hedge to hedge, and from one scrub to another, and wood, in great hurry, disorder and confusion.'

Nor was this all. Marlborough, so far from being per-plexed by the urgent details of the encounter action as it developed from moment to moment, had planned a great enveloping operation. Not all his army had crossed by the pontoons. His friend among the Dutch Generals, the veteran Overkirk, led a strong force of Dutch cavalry and infantry across the fortress bridges of Oudenarde, right through the town, and up the Oycke hill, which the French had left unoccupied, though it dominated their own right flank and rear. At a certain point Overkirk detached General Week and his Dutch infantry to fall on the flank of the battle behind the Castle of Browaan ; while he him-self took the cavalry through the village of Oycke on the heights, and round behind Oycke wood towards Roijgem to envelope the whole rear of the French army. The arrival of Week's foot aided Marlborough to drive back and sur-round the enemy's right wing. But Overkirk had not time to complete his own operation before darkness had fallen, and it was under cover of darkness that the enemy's left wing and supports escaped from the field. Another hour of evening light would have made Oudenarde a Sedan. And more than an hour had been lost by one of those unforesee-able accidents that play so large a part in the history of war. When Overkirk had been passing the Schelde at Oudenarde, the fortress bridge gave way and, according to Eugene, two hours had been lost in repairing it sufficiently for the passage to proceed.*

That strange last evening hour, while the blanket of the

* *Feldzüge*, II, i, p. 352, and Appendix, p. 155.

dark was mantling the locked combatants, and extinguishing the battle at its very height and climax, deeply struck the imagination of those who witnessed it. The French saw the circle of flame, spitting around them ever more clearly as blackness fell, and knew themselves surrounded. Marlborough, fearing lest his regiments, coming now from opposite directions, should volley upon each other in the night, gave orders to cease fire. His men pressed in to take their prisoners with the bayonet. Whole companies and battalions of the enemy's right wing threw down their arms. Cottages and ditches were gone through with the steel for hideaways. The French Huguenots played a trick on their persecutors : their drummers marched about beating the French retreat, while their officers cried aloud the names of the regiments engaged, '*A moi, Picardie*,' '*A moi, Roussillon*,' till groups of bewildered men came running through the darkness to the familiar summons, and were captured as they came up. It was a pitch-black night, and rain began to fall, adding to the misery of the wounded, whose groans were ' very dolorous.' The victors stood with bayonets fixed all night, gathering in and guarding the thousands of prisoners, while the left and reserve of the French army crept off and disappeared in the direction of Ghent. And so, as a Scottish private sang in rough rhyme,

> In hedges and dykes they lay like dead tikes
>   As the dark night began to draw near.
> For fear of alarms we stood to our arms
>   Until the day light did appear.

Marlborough had been suffering from fever and headache, but he and Eugene spent the dark hours on horseback upon the field with the troops, ' in a very soaking rain.' At muddy dawn, all the French who had not fled to Ghent overnight were found and secured, and pursuit was sent out after the rest. Captors and captives then left the sodden battlefield to the surgeons and their fatigue parties, and tramped off to Oudenarde to recuperate. The prisoners were ' coming by droves into the town for many hours,' by the open track across the fields from Shaerken. In the market place, beneath the towering Hotel de Ville, Marlborough

and Eugene at length dismounted—sick, famished, tired
and happy—amid the chaff and cheering of their troops
in like case with themselves. Around stood and lay the
prisoners, their white uniforms stained with blood and dirt ;
already 6000, including 700 officers, had been brought into
the town, and in a day or two the total captured had risen to
9000 by further desertion or successful pursuit. A hundred
' standards and colours ' were trophies of the completeness
of victory.

Between killed, wounded, prisoners and deserters,
' Oudenarde,' as the Duke reckoned, ' has lessened their
army at least 20,000 men.' ' But our greatest advantage,' he
wrote, ' is the terror that is in their army.' ' We could beat
them with half their numbers, especially their foot.' For
the moment the French were shut up again behind the
Bruges Canal, where Marlborough could not get at them.
Their chiefs were quarrelling violently, and many officers
threatening to desert Vendôme. He kept his head and
maintained his courage. Indeed he behaved well under
trying circumstances in every respect except in sending a
most dishonest report of the battle to King Louis, which
failed to deceive him as to the real situation.

The Allies reckoned their own killed and wounded at
3000, and declared that this number had been made up
within a week of the battle by ' Germans, Switzers and
Savoyards,' enlisted from the ranks of prisoners and
deserters. In any case the Allied losses at Oudenarde were
very small compared to what they lost in the four months
they afterwards spent before the city and citadel of Lille,
when a single night's work once cost them 4000 casualties
and the whole siege 15,000.

Oudenarde had just failed to be a Sedan. But it had
annihilated the enemy's right wing, broken the fighting
strength of the French field-army for the rest of the campaign, restored the moral superiority of the Allied forces,
rendered possible the grand operation of the capture of Lille
and effective progress against the frontier of France. A third
name had been added to Blenheim and Ramillies. ' No envy
or faction can reach a man that has gained three such
battles,' wrote Mr. Maynwaring to the Duchess on receipt

of the news. 'And if he brings home a peace next winter, it will be as impossible for his enemies to hurt him, as for the wind to blow down Mr. Vanburgh's thick walls.' But he did not bring home a peace, and even before Mr. Vanburgh had finished laying his ' heavy load ' upon the earth at Blenheim, ' envy and faction ' had taught the English to forget for awhile the gratitude due to their deliverer.[230]

After a necessary day's rest for his utterly exhausted army, Marlborough sent a detachment under Lottum, from the field of battle, to seize and level the earthwork Lines which the French had constructed from Ypres to the Lys. Lottum arrived on July 15 in time to prevent Berwick from being there before him. The Lines were destroyed and the way across the French border and the approaches to Lille were thus secured by promptitude in following up the victory. Next day Marlborough wrote : ' We are now masters of marching where we please, but can make no siege till we are masters of Ghent, from whence only we can have our cannon.'

Such were the Duke's first thoughts on the strange situation created by Oudenarde and by the French retreat behind the Bruges canal. The arrival of Eugene's army after the battle raised the Allied field force to 100,000 men, elate with victory, commanded by the two greatest soldiers of the age, united in a friendship that knew no touch of jealousy. So formidable an instrument of conquest had never before taken the field in the history of warfare. No important body of troops lay between it and Paris. But behind the Allies, if they moved forward, would lie an army almost as large as their own, though by no means so good or so well commanded. And meanwhile Vendôme, by his occupation of Ghent, prevented the siege train in Dutch territory from being sent to Marlborough's camp by the usual water route, up the Schelde or the Lys. If, therefore, the Allies undertook the siege of Lille, the greatest masterpiece of Vauban's engineering skill, they would conduct the operation under conditions of peculiar danger and disadvantage. But their road to Paris lay open.

It was in these circumstances that the Duke conceived,

in the week after Oudenarde, the design of marching straight
into the heart of France. He would mask Lille, occupying
the channel ports so as to obtain a new and shorter line of
communications with England, threaten the capital and
perhaps dictate that winter a Treaty of Versailles.*

It has been observed, in defence of Marlborough's
project of marching on Paris after Oudenarde, that, after
Waterloo, Wellington and Blücher adopted the plan with
success, masking or disregarding Lille and the frontier
fortresses. But the political state of France gave Wellington
a greater opportunity, and he had not an enemy force of
80,000 men behind his back. One objection to Marlborough's scheme, which the Dutch were certain to feel
acutely, was the question what Vendôme might attempt if
Marlborough left him behind in the Netherlands. It is
indeed highly probable that he would have come racing
after the Allies to save Paris, and in that case they might
have brought him again to battle, which above all else
they desired.

The second objection to an invasion of France was the
problem of provisions. Such an advance made by a great
army, with no proper base of supply, and with the enemy's
chief force left behind on the line of communication, was
clean contrary to all the rules of war as then recognised.
No doubt it would have been hazardous. But it would not
have been as foolish as the blind plunge of Charles XII
across the Russian forests that year, for Marlborough
trusted to establishing new communications through the
Channel ports with England as his supply base ; and
meanwhile he looked to the rich lands of Artois and Picardy
to feed his men, as the invaded lands often fed Napoleon's
armies on like errands. Already before the end of July ' all
the hussars were ravaging into the heart of Picardy,' having
been sent thither ' to play the devil for twice twenty-four

* The design is by itself enough to destroy the ridiculous charge brought
against Marlborough by the Dutch Deputy, Goslinga, and by some of the more
malignant English Tories, that he was seeking to protract the war indefinitely for
his own ambition and avarice. He may have been—I myself think that he was—
unduly stubborn not to make peace except on such terms as only complete victory
could have secured. But complete victory, at the earliest possible moment, was
his aim from first to last, as his every action and every letter indicate.

hours.' France was beginning to feel and to feed her invaders, and could be made to do so on an ever more extensive scale.

But Eugene could not rise to quite so bold a flight. His veto on an immediate invasion of France, which Marlborough accepted with quiet good-temper, prevented the question from being even propounded to the Dutch. On July 26, 1708, the Duke announced to Godolphin the all-important decision, in his usual calm and unemphatic way of recording things as they are :

> I have acquainted Prince Eugene with the earnest desire we have for our marching into France. He thinks it impracticable, till we have Lille for a *place d'armes* and magazine. And then he thinks we may make a great inroad, but not be able to winter, though we might be helped by our fleet, unless we were masters of some fortified town.

The same day he wrote to Halifax :

> Your notion of entering France agrees very well with my own inclinations, and were our army all composed of English, the project would certainly be feasible, but we have a great many among us who are more afraid of wanting provisions than of the enemy.

If he had been in complete command of his own army, as were Cæsar, Cromwell and Napoleon, he would have done on this occasion as Cæsar, Cromwell and Napoleon would have done, and as he himself had done when he marched to the Danube, shifting his base and communications as he went. If Eugene had heartily agreed, it is possible that Dutch opposition could have been overcome and the Allies would have advanced into France without first besieging Lille.[231] What then would have happened, no one can pretend to tell.*

So, instead of the march on Paris, began the famous siege of Lille, one of the chief cities of France and the strongest fortress in Europe, defended by 16,000 French

---

* If anyone's opinion on the subject is worth hearing, it is Lord Wolseley's. Shortly after he had been engaged in the study of Marlborough's life he talked to me one day about it, and I took notes of what he said. He was strongly of the opinion that Marlborough would have got to Paris after Oudenarde if Eugene had agreed to the attempt.

under the experienced and courageous Marshal Boufflers, assisted from without by the two armies of Vendôme and Berwick, amounting together to 100,000 men, the main body of them lying right across the proper communications of the besiegers.   It was a task in some respects more difficult than the invasion of France would have been.   If no one but Marlborough would have dreamt of invading France, no one but Marlborough and Eugene would have dreamt of besieging Lille under such conditions.   It was by far the greatest operation yet undertaken in the war ;   it lasted four months and all the other incidents of the great campaign were subsidiary to it.

The first thing was to bring up the siege train from Holland.   The usual waterways were blocked by the enemy's occupation of Ghent, and the cannon could only be sent from Holland by boat as far as Brussels.   The roads of Belgium were very different then from what they are now, and to take a heavy siege train any distance overland was regarded as almost impossible.   But, in the circumstances, it was necessary to traverse seventy odd miles of road from Brussels to Lille ;   16,000 horses dragged the 100 great siege guns, 60 mortars and 3,000 waggons laboriously across the land, ' under the nose of an army of eighty-thousand men,' as Feuquières the French military critic complained, ' which might have been assembled to stop this prodigious convoy, stretching over at least fifteen miles of road.'   But such was the fear established by Oudenarde, that rather than risk an encounter, Vendôme allowed the clumsy cortège to arrive at its destination.   By the middle of August the siege of Lille had fairly begun.

Eugene conducted the siege and Marlborough the vast covering operations ;   both tasks were in the highest degree difficult.   The fear that the Allies had established among their foes in the field had found no place among the garrison of Lille, and the arts of defence were practised to perfection in that superb fortress by Boufflers and his engineers.   The attacks were by no means all of them successful.   The mined breaches, the ' hellish invention of throwing bombs, boiling pitch, tar,' and all the casual slaughter of ' this murdering siege ' cost more lives than the

Allied commanders had reckoned to lose—in the end five times as many as their losses at Oudenarde. But, contrary to the expectations of the French, the siege went on, the supplies continued, though with great difficulty, to be brought up, and Marlborough's protecting guard could nowhere be pierced. The letters exchanged between King Louis, Chamillart, Burgundy, Vendôme and Berwick display them at once agitated and planless in face of a situation full of great opportunities that they were unable to grasp. For they could not trust their troops to face the Allies in battle, and were, therefore, powerless spectators of a drama in which the world expected them to be chief actors. The moral situation created by Oudenarde still overruled the strategic.

Not more than five British battalions took part in the actual siege under Eugene, but they lost 1,600 men,* over a third of their number. The total Allied loss before Lille was twelve to fifteen thousand. The great body of the English had been kept by Marlborough for his own service in the lines of contravallation which he held against the relieving armies, and in the vital work of convoying the supplies through the zone of French activity.[232]

Towards the end of September the siege reached a dangerous crisis. Eugene had been wounded and Marlborough, though in very poor health, had for a time to take over the siege itself as well as the covering operations. It was just as well that he did, for he writes to Godolphin :

> Upon the wounding of Prince Eugene, I thought it absolutely necessary to inform myself of everything of the siege ; for before I did not meddle in anything but the covering of it. Upon examination I find that the engineers did not deal well with the Prince, for when I told him that there did not remain powder and ball for above four days, he was very much surprised. I own to you that I fear we have something more in our misfortunes than ignorance. Our circumstances being thus, and the impossibility of getting a convoy from Brussels, obliged me to take measures for getting some ammunition from Ostend, which we could never have attempted but for the good luck of the eight English battalions there.

The French had closed the route from Brussels by which the besiegers had at first been supplied from Holland. But

* *Millner*, p. 249.

Ostend, the direct sea route from England, made good the deficiency. It would indeed be a shorter line of communications if it could once be established. But the crisis in the last days of September was acute. If the train of ammunition then on its way from Ostend had been intercepted, the siege must have been raised at once.

The convoy on which the success of the campaign depended was under the immediate protection of Major-General Webb and 6000 infantry. He had no artillery and practically no cavalry—150 sabres. He was attacked by General La Motte with a force of all three arms, amounting to 12,000 men. The disparity between the two forces was more than the difference in numbers of two to one, for it was all three arms against infantry alone. Webb, undismayed, sent the convoy on its way and occupied a passage through woods at Wynendael, placing an ambush in the brushwood on either side of the enemy's approach to his front line. La Motte's artillery, unanswered, bombarded the recumbent allied infantry all afternoon without shaking their nerve ; as the shades of evening began to fall, the French horse and foot delivered their attack. The double crossfire of the ambush surprised them, and they were repelled after a stiff fight, in which Webb lost nearly a thousand killed and wounded, and La Motte many more. The French officers were unable to induce their men to march again to the assault, in spite of the difference in strength. The moral superiority of the Allies was emphasised even more than at Ramillies or Oudenarde. The French Generals and writers fully admitted that their men had behaved ill. In Holland the cry was that the Deputies should never again prevent Marlborough attacking whenever he wished, for no one could resist his troops. Not more than two or three British battalions had been present among Webb's band of brothers, but Dutch, Hanoverians and Prussians had all fought in Wynendael wood as became ' Marlborough's men.'

Sept. 28 (N.S.) 1708

But the hero of the day was Webb himself. Cadogan had been in general charge of the arrangements for the passage of the convoy, and had done well in that capacity, but he had only arrived at Wynendael with reinforcements

after the battle had been won.   Unfortunately the first news
in the *London Gazette* spoke of Cadogan and not of Webb.
The error was speedily corrected in later issues, but the
harm had been done.   It was said that Marlborough was
jealous of a rival.   The Tories took up the cry, and Webb,
a fine, honest soldier but not without vanity, allowed himself
to conceive a permanent grievance and to become the puppet
of our factious politicians.   *Esmond* has immortalized his
legend.   Yet, as early as September 29, Marlborough had
written to him :

> Mr. Cadogan has just now arrived and has acquainted me with
> the success of the action you had yesterday in the afternoon against
> the body of troops commanded by M. de la Motte at Wynendael,
> which must be attributed chiefly to your conduct and resolution.
> You may assure yourself I shall do you justice at home.

The same day the Duke wrote to Sunderland ascribing the
victory to Webb and not even mentioning Cadogan.*   And
he continued to urge the Queen to promote Webb to
Lieutenant-General, as she did in the following winter.   On
December 13 the Whig House of Commons unanimously
voted thanks to Webb ' for the great and eminent services
performed by him at Wynendael,' but in the debate the
Tory speakers sneered at Marlborough.   The mischief was
afoot and it became an article of faith in some Tory quarters
that the Duke had been bribed by the French to allow
Webb's convoy to be cut to pieces by a superior force, so as
to have an excuse for raising the siege of Lille.[233]
    If Marlborough had been in search of reasons to rise
up from before Lille, he had plenty to hand without treating
Webb as David treated Uriah the Hittite.   The
next move of the French was to cut the dykes and
swamp a great area round Ostend, rendering land
passage for supplies impossible for some miles.   Cadogan
fitted out a fleet of flat-bottomed boats which ' is troublesome, but will do,' as Lord Stair wrote.   Then the French

October
1708

---

* But on September 21 (O.S. October 2, N.S.) Sunderland writes to Marlborough of ' the news of Major General *Cadogan* having defeated M. la Motte's
party ' ; this was before Sunderland received Marlborough's letter of September 29
(N.S.), as his next letter (September 24, O.S.) shows.   *H.M.C. Marlborough Papers*
(1881), p. 33.

let in more water, deep enough to float galleys which they launched on the flooded meadows to waylay the allied flotilla. The besiegers of Lille would have been starved, had they not been able to recoup themselves by raids into Artois at the expense of the French peasantry. Even so they went hungry, and it was none too soon for them when on October 22 Boufflers surrendered the great city and retired into the Citadel of Lille.[234]

It was November, well past the usual time for going into winter quarters, but Marlborough and Eugene would not relax the hold upon their prey. Vendôme made a last effort. He marched on Brussels, hoping to draw the Allies away from Lille to its relief. But when the French appeared before Brussels, it was not betrayed from within as Ghent and Bruges had been betrayed. Marlborough, by a great effort of strategy on his own part and by forced marches on the part of the English Guards, came to its rescue just in time, while Eugene still battered the Citadel of Lille.*

Nov. 28
1708

On December the 9th Boufflers surrendered the Citadel. Lille had fallen.

Yet even now, though winter had come, Marlborough was not content till Ghent and Bruges had been recovered, for 'without them,' as he wrote, 'we can neither be quiet in our winter quarters or open with advantage the next campaign.' His army, which had never forgiven the French for taking these two towns ' by treachery,' was prepared to keep the field in the bitter Christmas weather, contrary to all the customs of war, in order to recover them. Vendôme, for his part, wished to remain with a portion of the Grand Army behind the Canal all winter, to save Bruges and Ghent ; but Louis, advised by the jealous Burgundy, called him home and bade leave the two towns to be defended by their garrisons under the incompetent La Motte.[235]

When Marlborough drew near, the dykes and moats were thick with ice over which his troops could march.

---

* Pious Colonel Blackader, recording a day of thanksgiving for the ' relieving of Brussels ' (date given wrong in *Blackader*, p. 335), notes ' The Duke never fails to give thanks after victory and success. But these things are mocked and ridiculed in our army.' ' Atheists,' he finds, ' despond most.'

The resistance made was poor and half-hearted. Round about the New Year of 1709 he crowned the longest and perhaps the greatest of all his campaigns by the recovery of Ghent and Bruges. The fickle citizens of Ghent cheered him obsequiously and illuminated their town in his honour, and though the troops ' believed this joy to be fictitious,' the Duke prudently accepted it at its face value. ' This campaign,' he wrote to Godolphin, ' is now ended to my own heart's desire.' [236]

In January 1709 the military situation, which had not been so bad for France twelve months back, had turned against her once more. Her economic condition for some years past had been terrible. And now came on a winter that killed her vines and froze her seed-corn in the earth. The fierce cold fixed its jaws upon warring Europe, destroying the strength of Charles of Sweden's army, lost in the Russian forests, and killing the starved French peasants in their hovels. Even the Grand Monarch felt pity for his people and was ready to cast off his pride and become a suppliant for peace. The time had come for the Allies to make up their minds what terms they would exact.

In September another success had attended the arms of Queen Anne, more easily achieved than the capture of Lille, but of no less consequence for the future of Britain. Port Mahon, in the island of Minorca, had been taken. Its deep, long, land-locked harbour, just not too narrow for the largest ships of the sailing era, enabled our war-fleets to winter and repair there as they could not in the more open roadstead of Gibraltar. Mahon, from its island situation, was as impregnable as the Rock itself, so long as England held the sea. ' And, could we keep it in time of peace,' wrote Lord Raby, ' 'twould be better than Tangier ever could have been to serve our Turkey trade.'* It used to be a saying in those latitudes that ' June, July, August and Port Mahon are the three best harbours in the Mediterranean.' † With Gibraltar, it made England mistress of

---

* Raby to Robinson, October 30, 1708, *Add. MSS.* 22198, f. 99.
† ' Junio, Julio, Agusto y Puerto Mahon
     Los mejores puertos del Mediterraneo son.'

the inland sea in the Eighteenth Century, as Malta in the Nineteenth.

It was not by chance that Minorca fell into our hands. In 1708 all the advantages which its possession would bring to England were fully understood by Marlborough, Leake, Stanhope and Sunderland, the Secretary of State in charge of our affairs in Southern Europe. It was a commonplace in their correspondence that since Toulon had not been taken, it was essential to have a harbour where a squadron could winter near at hand to watch the relics of the Toulon fleet, and that such a harbour could be found to perfection in Port Mahon. It was indicated alike by the needs of the moment and the hopes of the more distant future. After the failure of 1707, the war on the east coast of Spain could only be carried on if the English ships could winter in close proximity. For this reason ' Charles III ' urged his Allies to occupy for him his island of Minorca, as could so easily be done from the bases of Barcelona and Majorca already in their hands. The Englishmen agreed with the ' King of Spain's ' arguments, secretly determining that Port Mahon should remain not in his hands but in England's, when the war was over.

In June 1708 the Council of the Admiralty reported that the fleet ought to winter in the Mediterranean and that Port Mahon was the place required for the purpose ; and Sunderland on the 25th wrote to Marlborough, ' Indeed I believe they are right, that it can be with no safety but at Port Mahon.' Thereupon, two days after Oudenarde, Marlborough wrote to Admiral Leake in the Mediterranean the model of what a soldier's and statesman's letter to a sailor should be :

You have the copy of the letter from the Admiralty to the Earl of Sunderland about the wintering of the squadron in the Mediterranean. I send it only for your information, . . . for it is certain our sea-officers are the best judges of what may be done with safety in this case.

And then came a postcript, written in the Duke's own hand:

I am so entirely convinced that nothing can be done effectually without the fleet, that I conjure you if possible to take Port Mahon.

Thus, while leaving freedom of choice to the Admiral on the spot, the Duke indicated as strongly as possible his own opinion that Minorca should be taken at once.[237]

Early in August Leake was occupied in reducing the island of Sardinia to the obedience of Charles III, thereby scoring an important point for the Allies in the coming peace negotiations. Its capital town of Cagliari sur-

Aug. 13 (N.S.) 1708

rendered to the English fleet after a short bombardment, though one of our Captains described it as ' a City much stronger than Barcelona.' Leake himself wrote of it that ' five or six hundred might defend it against an army of 20,000.' [238]

Leake then turned his attention to the Pope, whom he had Sunderland's orders to call to account. He addressed to Clement XI a letter in the following terms :

Holy Father,—My royal mistress, the Queen of Great Britain, being assuredly informed that your Holiness did not only promote and encourage the late intended invasion of Her Majesty's dominions by the pretended Prince of Wales, assisted by the French, but also advanced a considerable sum of money for that end, and in the most public and insolent manner ordered prayers in the Churches of Rome for the success of the expedition. . . . Her Majesty has commanded me to demand of your Holiness the sum of four hundred thousand crowns, and to acquaint Your Holiness that, if this demand is not instantly complied with, your country will be put under military execution. . . .

I am, Holy Father,
Your Holiness's most, etc.,
J. LEAKE.

The Admiral was preparing to follow up this missive by an attack on the Papal port of Civita Vecchia, when a felucca arrived in the fleet, bringing dispatches from Barcelona, in which General Stanhope and King Charles III besought Leake to co-operate with them at once in the seizure of Port Mahon. At a council of war Leake and his Captains wisely determined not to let slip the moment when allied soldiers from Spain were available for a purpose so dear to the heart of the senior service. The Pope was left to think over his future conduct in relation to the mistress of the seas, and Leake and Stanhope brought their combined forces to the reduction of Minorca.

Again, as on so many other occasions in the War of the Spanish Succession, the co-operation of army and navy was admirable. The problem was the reduction of Fort St. Philip, about two miles from the town of Mahon, commanding the narrow entrance of the envied harbour. First of all Stanhope landed with a small party at some distance from Fort St. Philip, and marched up to the town of Mahon, where he was welcomed by the inhabitants. Philip V had deprived them of their ancient privileges, and the Minorcans were Carlists to a man. They even raised a few militia who aided the Allies in the subsequent operations. The fleet sent ships round the island and reduced with little loss the other two places of importance, Civadella and Fornelles, the latter being a fort commanding a harbour second only in excellence to Mahon itself.*

Sept. 14 1708

But all was of no avail unless they could reduce Fort St. Philip, with its hundred cannon and its garrison of 500 French and 500 Spanish troops. Stanhope commanded about 2000 soldiers, some half of them English, and 500 English marines lent by the navy. Leake himself had sailed home, having made every arrangement that Stanhope could desire, and leaving a squadron, chiefly English and partly Dutch, under Admiral Sir Edward Whittaker to co-operate in the reduction of the island.†

The first operation of any real difficulty was the landing of the siege guns. Before the British occupation of the island there were practically no roads ; the first of any pretension was constructed a few years later by General Kane, the 'roadmaker' of Minorca. The ground near Port Mahon was hilly and covered with rocks and brushwood, making it altogether unfit for the transport of cannon. It was therefore necessary to shorten the distance by landing them as

---

* After the reduction of Minorca, Stanhope wrote to Sunderland : ' I hope the want of Ports will no longer be an objection to wintering a squadron here, Her Majesty being now Mistress of the two best Ports in the Mediterranean, this [Mahon] and Fornelles in the same island.' *Byng Papers*, II, p. 301.

† Stanhope was not generous in his account of the naval co-operation, as emerges from *Leake* (*q.v.*). Mr. Basil Williams in his *Stanhope*, p. 78, holds the balance even.

near as possible to Fort St. Philip, and this was a delicate operation. The first attempt was prevented by fire from the fort, so that ' we were forced to remove our landing to a cove further off, from whence we immediately made a very good road for the cannon.' * This indispensable work of disembarking forty-two cannon and fifteen mortars, transporting them over difficult country and mounting them in the batteries, was principally done by the sailors.

At length, some ten days after Stanhope had first set foot on the island, his batteries were ready, having been erected by arduous labour under a severe fire. The outer works of Fort St. Philip consisted of a drystone wall, some nine feet high, with four towers on it each carrying cannon. The British bombardment began, breaches were made, and the cannon in the towers were silenced or dismounted—but not before the death of Stanhope's well-loved brother Philip, Captain of the Milford galley, had saddened his comrades. He had ' been very instrumental in engaging the seamen in this enterprise,' as his brother reported. He had gone up to the enemy's wall, and made two of his sailors hold him up so that he could look over it, where a shot in his forehead ended a promising career and struck grief into all the camp.

Sept. 23
1708

Brigadier Wade, afterwards the roadmaker of the Highlands, commanded the right of the besiegers. Some of his Grenadiers, without waiting for orders, rushed forward to seize the battered wall, and it was thought fit to support them with the rest of the army. Stanhope rode his horse over the breach, under a hot fire. The whole outwork was captured, together with the small town that lay between it and the Citadel of Fort St. Philip. The Citadel would still have been hard to take, for it was well stored with food and ammunition. But its commandant, La Jonquière, surrendered to Stanhope's threats of the slaughter that would result from further resistance, and his offer of good terms of capitulation. The presence in the Fort of a large number

---

* See the excellent account by Stanhope's aide-de-camp, John Cope, afterwards the ' Johnnie Cope ' of Preston Pans, in the somewhat mutilated letter *Add. MSS.* 22231, f. 78. It was near the point where the guns were landed that the ' First Camp ' was formed, as marked in the contemporary map. (*Map VIII, opposite.*)

MAP VIII

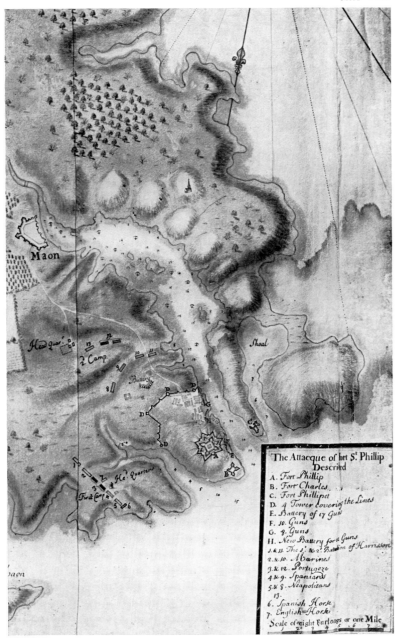

The Attacque of brt St. Phillip
Descrid
A. Fort Phillip
B. Fort Charles
C. Fort Phillipet
D. A Tower covering the Lines
E. Battery of 17 Guns
F. 10. Guns
G. 8. Guns
H. New Battery for 6 Guns
1. & 11. The 1.t & 2.d Battalion of Garrison
2. 8. 10. Marines
3. & 12. Portugeze
4 & 9. Spaniards
5. & 8. Neapolitans
13.
6. Spanish Horse
7. English Horse
Scale of eight Furlongs or one Mile

THE CAPTURE OF FORT ST. PHILIP, PORT MAHON, MINORCA, 1708.

(*From a contemporary map at Boughton, by kind permission of the Duke of Buccleugh.*)

of wives and children of the Spanish garrison is thought
to have weakened the wish for further hostilities.   When
La Jonquière returned to France he was tried and sent to
prison.[239]

Thus on the last day of September 1708 the Union
Jack waved undisputed over the whole island of Minorca,
not to be hauled down for half a century, when the son of
Queen Anne's Admiral Byng paid so dear a penalty for
its loss.

As the tidings spread through Europe that England had
taken Port Mahon, men knew that she had come to stay
in the Mediterranean, no longer as a yearly visitor but as
a resident with a house of her own.   The permanent
presence of an English squadron with a base between Italy
and Spain had many consequences.   The first was to
' terrify the Italian Princes and States from engaging in
the Pope's quarrel,' as Sunderland wrote.   It helped
indeed to frustrate the endeavours that King Louis was
making to build up again a French party in Venice, Tuscany
and Genoa under the leadership of the Pope, in defiance
of the Austrian armies in Naples and Milan.   Clement XI,
Francophile as he was, had no wish to receive the postponed
visit of the English fleet ;   and he was put under even
stronger pressure from the occupation of the northern part
of the Papal States by an Imperialist army and the threat of
its advance on Rome.   With bitter reluctance he abandoned
the French alliance that lay so near his heart, and in January
1709 recognised Charles as King of Spain, a great point
gained for the Allies in the approaching peace conference.
Admiral Whittaker, who had been preparing to attack
Civita Vecchia, was told to desist, as the Pope had changed
sides.   Henceforth, instead of fomenting French invasions
of Great Britain, Clement joined with Austria in perfectly
proper remonstrances to the British Ministers against the
treatment of the Roman Catholics in Ireland, with which
Vienna was wont to counter English complaints about the
treatment of Silesian and Hungarian Protestants.[240]

The Minorca question added fresh fuel to the discords
of the Allies.   The English were determined to keep it for

themselves, and Stanhope, the man on the spot, was the most determined of all. He was a soldier-statesman of strong will, as the features of his countenance betokened, and of a very pure zeal for his country's interests. He saw the full importance to England of Port Mahon, in peace and in war, and wrote home constantly urging that money should be spent on making it impregnable, and unselfishly offering to ' stay and live there himself three or four years to put it in order.' ' All our seamen,' he wrote, ' agree that it is in all respects the most convenient harbour in Europe.' No wonder that, when in the next reign he was made a Peer, he took the title of Lord Mahon.

But even Stanhope felt obliged, in the first instance, to name a Spanish Governor of the Island to act for Charles III. He was careful, however, to leave none but English soldiers and marines in Fort St. Philip, and to instruct their commander to take no orders save from British authorities. He then turned his attention to securing from Charles III the formal cession of Minorca to Great Britain. In that he was supported by Marlborough and Sunderland, though they were more alive than he to the diplomatic difficulties, which presented themselves with even greater force to Godolphin.

In the first place the negotiation had to be concealed from the Dutch, who thought that the continued presence of the British in Port Mahon in time of peace would do a serious injury to their own rival trade interests in the Mediterranean. Vryberg, one of their leading diplomats, declared that ' Minorca in English hands would be as hazardous to the Republic as Ostend.' Under these circumstances at the Hague, Stanhope's work at Barcelona of extorting Minorca from Charles III had to be conducted in secret. Charles for his part was most unwilling to render himself odious to his potential Spanish subjects by giving away such a jewel of the Crown. But the hold the English had over him was very strong. He was deeply in their debt for subsidies which he could never hope to repay, and if they withdrew support he could not carry on the war in Spain a single month. For the Dutch were weary of it and were reducing their quota of men, money and ships.

Already Charles had been compelled in January 1708 to make a secret treaty with Britain, consigning to her the trade with Spanish America when the war was over. An Anglo-Spanish company was to be formed to enjoy the monopoly. That, too, was an ugly secret kept back from the Dutch.

So, when Stanhope pressed Charles to cede Minorca, making it the condition of further British support in the Peninsular War, he dared not refuse point blank, but by evasions, promises and compromises kept the negotiations spinning out through the whole year 1709. In the autumn Heinsius got wind of it, and was helped by the knowledge to extort better terms in his famous Barrier Treaty which he was then making with the English Government.

Meanwhile the French had intercepted dispatches which revealed Stanhope's harsh pressure on Charles to obtain Minorca. In January 1710 they published the facts in Amsterdam with explosive results on all other negotiations then on foot. To appease the anger of the Dutch people, the British Ministers disingenuously threw over Stanhope, repudiating the negotiations for the cession of Minorca which they had officially authorised him to undertake. But, treaty or no treaty, Port Mahon remained in the power of the English garrison of Fort St. Philip, and the whole island was legally acquired at Utrecht, together with Gibraltar, the more easily because it was no longer Charles the ally but Philip the enemy who was acknowledged to be King of Spain.[241]

Meanwhile in the West Indies and off the Spanish Main the rival claims of King Philip and King Charles further confounded the confusion of those lawless and romantic coasts. The doubt as to who was king enabled Spanish colonists who saw their interest in trading with the English, to do so with some show of legality, and a brisk commerce sprang up under the cannon's mouth.* But

* In August 1708 we read: ' Some trading sloops came from the Spanish coast [to Jamaica] five or six days ago. And there are now going out to Porto Bell ten or twelve sloops under convoy of two men of warr, with the manufactures of Great Britain and the prize goods lately brought in here.' *C.S.P. Am.* (1708–9), p. 56.

the English privateers, who interpreted their commissions as giving them leave to rob all French and Spaniards indifferently, compromised the more peaceful efforts of those of their countrymen who were trying to establish a trade.

The power of the English flag in Spanish-American waters grew greater each year as the war went on, but rather by the increase of the privateers than of the Royal Navy. For in colonial waters, captains of men-of-war were not permitted to recruit as at home by means of the press-gang, although their crews were perpetually deserting to the easier and more lucrative life on board a privateer. Captains thus rendered shorthanded had orders to return to England. The natural lawlessness of the region that was the native home of the buccaneers was increased by this crippling of the Royal Navy for the benefit of privateers who were often half pirates. Even the avowed pirates were active and formidable enough to negotiate with both belligerents; though commanded by a Frenchman, the ruffians scorned the proffered French alliance and sought the protection of Queen Anne.[242]

In the last days of May 1708 occurred Admiral Wager's action against the Spanish treasure-galleons from Porto Bello—the most celebrated event of the whole war in those regions, with the possible exception of Benbow's action.* In both cases the commanders of the other English ships deserted their Admiral, leaving him to fight an heroic battle almost single-handed against the enemy squadron. But Wager was more fortunate than Benbow. Though the odds against him were great they were not, as against his predecessor, utterly impossible, and his own and his crew's courage won him a victory which made him famous and rich for the rest of his long life.

The wealth of the South American mines, that was to have put King Louis and King Philip on their feet again for another year of war, lay stored chiefly in the hold of the enemy admiral's galleon of sixty-four guns, in bars and pieces of eight to the value of several million sterling, variously computed. In a midnight battle Wager's flagship, the *Expedition* of seventy guns, was firing broadsides into her at pistol-range

* See *Blenheim*, pp. 252-254.

when the great treasure-ship blew up, almost sinking the *Expedition* and scorching her men with burning planks and timbers. The great galleon 'sunk immediately, with all her riches, which must have been very great,' and seven hundred soldiers and seamen besides. Salvage was impossible and Wager at once attached himself to the second great galleon, and after three hours' fighting captured her with a smaller quantity of treasure. A third galleon escaped into Cartagena. A fourth, of forty guns, was chased ashore, where the Spaniards blew her up. All the serious fighting against the squadron of fourteen enemy sail had been done by Wager's *Expedition*. The captains of the two recalcitrant English men-of-war were afterwards court-martialled and broke, though many thought they should have been shot like those who had deserted Benbow.

The wealth captured was great ; the wealth destroyed was enormous. 'This must in all probability,' wrote Sunderland to Marlborough, ' prove a fatal blow to France, for I believe this was one of their last resources for carrying on the war.' It can be imagined how the news stirred the greed and imagination of our forefathers. As the visitor enters Westminster Abbey by the north door, he will see, hard on his right, overlooked by Chatham from his monument, the tomb of Admiral Wager, whereon a bas-relief records in marble the forms of those old ships, battling for the treasure in the tropic midnight, at the moment when the great galleon bursts asunder in flame and smoke, and disappears from before the startled eyes of its English enemies.[243]

Whether in the Mediterranean or off the Spanish Main or in home waters, the triumph of England at sea had been made manifest in 1708. The shipowners no longer, as in the last winter session, complained to Parliament that they were insufficiently protected. This year ' the merchants were better served with convoys and no considerable losses were sustained.' At sea, as on land, the enemy's strength was giving out.[244]

CHAPTER XIX

The Failure to make Peace

The Queen, Sunderland and his kinsmen. Tory reunion and the question of Peace. Death of the Prince Consort. The Junto gains possession. The new Parliament meets, winter 1708–9. The Scottish Treason Bill. The Third Secretary of State. The Great Frost of 1709. Negotiations for peace. Marlborough and Berwick. Torcy at the Hague. The 'Preliminary Articles' of May 1709. Causes and consequences of the failure to make peace. The era of Party Government in Great Britain.

The Whigs had forced Harley out of office at the beginning of 1708 and had won the General Election in May,* but even in the autumn they were not yet admitted to the inner-most counsels of Queen Anne and her two chief servants. The Lords of the Junto were an external power with whom Godolphin and Marlborough had at every important step to come to terms, but they were not the government itself. It is true that Sunderland was Secretary of State, but, as he constantly complained, his influence was not paramount. He was closely related by marriage to the Churchills and through them to the Lord Treasurer, but as a statesman he thought more of party than of family, and he was more faithful to his colleagues of the Junto than to his colleagues of the Cabinet. Throughout the year of Oudenarde he spoke of the political conduct of his two kinsmen with more suspicion and bitterness than the gay Wharton or the prudent Somers. In October he wrote to the Duke of Newcastle, a less fiery Whig than himself, that it was impossible for the party—

with any reputation to themselves, or safety to the publick, to go on any longer with the Court, upon the foot things are at present, for that if one looks round every part of the administration, the manage-

* See pp. 328, 349 above.

ment of the fleet, the Condition of Ireland, the Proceedings in Scotland, the management of the late Invasion, the disposall of Church Preferments, etc. ; they are all of a Piece, as much Tory, and as wrong, as if Ld. Rochester and Ld. Nottingham were at the head of every thing, under the disguise of some Considerable wigs, in some considerable places, but with so little creditt or to so little purpose, that they can neither obtain any right thing to be done, nor prevent any wrong one.

This is the language of exaggeration, more befitting an Opposition orator than a Secretary of State. No wonder Queen Anne disliked Sunderland. In June she had demanded his dismissal, because he had acted in avowed opposition to the Government of which he was a member, in forming a separate party against his Cabinet colleagues in the Scottish elections : *

I cannot but still resent this usage [she wrote to Godolphin] ; though I have not yet taken the seals from him. I cannot forbear putting you in mind of the promise you made to me when I first took this person into my service, which was that if he did anything I did not like, you would bring him to make his leg and take his leave.

But Sunderland's relations, however little pleased by his public conduct, were in no position to dismiss him. They understood, and tried in their letters to make the Queen understand, that after the Whig success in the General Election there must needs be not fewer but more Whigs in the Cabinet. Only they were willing to put off that evil day so long as they could, in other words till the meeting of the newly elected Parliament in November 1708.[245]

The Queen, secretly receiving Harley's advice through Abigail Masham,† was every month more deeply alienated from Sarah ; but she remained during the summer of Oudenarde on tolerable epistolary terms with Marlborough. In her letters to him she still asserted that her aim was independence of both Whigs and Tories :

The parties are such bug-beares that I dare not venture to write my mind freely of either of them without a cypher for fear of any accident. I pray God keep me out of the hands of both of them.[246]

Her prayer was not to be answered.

* See p. 348 above.   † See p. 329 above.

Meanwhile a rumour was afloat in political circles that Marlborough intended to cut out the Whigs in the favour of the House of Hanover, particularly with the young Electoral Prince who had served under him with such distinction at Oudenarde. Harley was informed, with what truth it is hard to say, that :

The Duke will next winter bring him or his grandmother [Dowager Electress Sophia] over hither, in such manner that they shall have the obligation neither to Whigs or Tories, but entirely to himself and Lord Treasurer. . . . The Whigs are much alarmed and swear the Duke shall not run away with the credit of so popular a thing.

The Whigs, it was said, intended to get in before Marlborough and Godolphin, by themselves moving, next session, that the Electoral Prince be invited to visit the country. Lord Haversham had the face to go to Anne and complain that the Whigs intended to advocate the very policy which he and his High Tory friends had formerly proposed at the price of losing her royal favour.* Thus warned, the Queen repeated her objection to a visit from any member of the Hanover family with such bitter emphasis that both Marlborough and the Whigs abandoned the plan, if in fact they had ever entertained it. In October 1708, therefore, the Tories were able to flatter themselves with the belief that :

There are great discontents at Hanover. That Court is exceedingly dissatisfied with our two Kings,† who now again are grown very cold towards them, and say nothing more of the invitation upon which they were so hot last spring.

Meanwhile Sunderland continued sourly to suspect his two kinsmen of meditating a Jacobite restoration on the Queen's death, though it is probable that their thoughts were then less inclining to St. Germains than on various other occasions, both before and after.[247]

The Tories, on the other hand, accused the Duke of aiming at sovereignty himself, and muttered of ' Cromwell.'

* Pp. 91–92 above.
† At this time ' The two Kings of Brentford ' was a cant phrase for Marlborough and Godolphin.

A friend wrote to Harley :

> History furnishes many examples of men who from the command of less force [than Marlborough's army] have aspired to sovereignty. But I believe there is no instance that ever any man who had tasted of absolute power could ever retire to a private life and become a good subject.[248]

Fear of the British general was already in the summer of 1708 operating as one among several reasons why the Tories were turning towards a policy of immediate peace and disarmament, even at the price of Spain.

Other circumstances were drawing the party in the same direction. The forced recruiting of the unemployed into the army was unpopular, and the proposals of the Government for a larger measure of conscription, denounced by all Tories and some Whigs as French militarism, failed to pass into law. The original objects of the war had been attained. War taxation was felt as an increasing hardship by the mass of the people. The national expenditure was more than twice what it had been in the years of peace and disarmament at the end of William's reign, and was soaring higher and higher as the operations of the war increased each year in magnitude, and as each year Britain's share of the burden became proportionally larger than that of her allies. The Land Tax could not be further increased without such a mutiny of squires as would sweep the Tories back into power. But the attempt to assess all incomes for a general Income Tax had failed, for want of a proper civil service machinery,* and Godolphin therefore had to go on increasing indirect taxation, much of which fell on the poor or on the ordinary middle classes, and made the war generally unpopular as a burden bearing heavily on all. The Treasurer's other expedient was borrowing through the Bank of England, with the loyal support of the rich City men who were mostly Whigs. Every year that the war went on increased the National Debt, and increased Godolphin's obligations to the Whigs and the monied interest.[249]

For these reasons even the more moderate Tory leaders were in 1708 veering round to a policy of peace. If Harley

---

* See *Blenheim*, pp. 292–293, on taxation ; and pp. 218–219, on Recruiting Acts.

and St. John, the ' war Tories,' now demanded peace, it would be easy for them to recover the leadership of the High Tories who had always disliked the war. Every considera- tion, partisan and patriotic, was pushing them in that direction. Peace would now be a popular cry, and to stop the war would be to check the control exercised by the Whig monied interest over government. St. John in October wrote to Harley urging him to be reconciled to the High Tories, on these terms :

What can redeem us from more than Egyptian bondage ? There is one person [Anne] who with a fiat resolutely pronounced might do it ; but when I recollect all I heard and saw last winter I despair of any salvation from thence. There is no hope, I am fully convinced, but in the Church of England party, nor in that neither . . . without more confidence than is yet re-established between them and us. Why do you not gain Bromley entirely ? . . . *You broke the party, unite it again.* . . . This hollow square will defend you who seem to be singled out for destruction.

And then again, on November 6, on the eve of the meeting of the new Parliament, he writes to Harley in anticipation of the measures likely to be proposed by the war ministry :

That they should think of raising sixteen regiments more, and of mortgaging either land or malt, is to my apprehension downright infatuation and what I am glad of. They hasten things to a decision, and our slavery and their empire are put upon that issue. *For God's sake let us be once out of Spain !*

At last he had said it. The exigencies of party had driven St. John to pronounce the forbidden word of common sense which was to prove the ' open-sesame ' for England and for Europe.[250]

As the time for the meeting of Parliament drew near, the Lords of the Whig Junto pressed their claims for fuller representation in the Cabinet and admission to the inner- most counsels of government. Moderate Whigs, such as Newcastle and Devonshire, lent them their full support. The party had won the election in the summer and claimed power as a consequence. It might be a novel doctrine, but it was slowly and surely working its way into the theory of the Constitution, because it was not to be resisted in practice. Marlborough and Godolphin, though they would in their hearts have preferred Anne's time-honoured principle that the servants of the Crown were above party, knew that if they did not appease the Whigs by giving office to their chiefs, supply would not be carried through the new House of Commons.

The Queen was all the harder to move because the Whigs demanded the substitution of the Earl of Pembroke for her beloved husband, Prince George, at the head of the Admiralty. The Prince Consort, though not himself a strong partisan,* was under the personal influence of Marlborough's brother, Admiral George Churchill, a hot Tory, and had at his instigation opposed the claims of Somers to office, and helped to foment his wife's prejudices against him. Marlborough, hoping to placate the Whigs without removing the Prince, told his brother to resign from the Board. But the Whigs were not satisfied and claimed that the Prince also must go. Their object was to give his post to Pembroke, in order that the two posts that Pembroke then held—the Lord Lieutenancy of Ireland and the Presidency of the Council—might be given to Wharton and Somers respectively. To save her husband Anne might have surrendered on other points, but, just as the crisis was coming to a head, the Prince removed all difficulty by dying, a fortnight before Parliament was due to meet.

Oct. 28
1708

The disappearance from the scene of this dull and kindly man, who had neither used nor abused his position in England, made everything easy for a settlement. A new Lord High Admiral had to be chosen, and Pembroke, the most Whiggish of moderate Tories, was politically unobjectionable at the Admiralty. Nor was Queen Anne in a state any longer to resist the other Whig demands. For some weeks she was prostrate with grief, locking herself up in Prince George's room from the two women who were wrangling for her favour, each of whom tortured herself

---

* The Earl of Westmorland, who knew him well, declared he would, if he had lived, have used his influence with his wife against the High Tory reaction of 1710. H.M.C. *Westmorland*, p. 50.

with the belief that the other was secretly at their mistress's ear.* She had good reason to mourn. The death of her husband and the quarrel with Sarah had made a desert of her private affections. The mean-souled Abigail could be a servant and humble companion to Anne Stuart, but hardly a true friend.

Unable for some weeks to attend to business, Anne gave her indifferent consent to the new arrangements. The Lords of the Junto marched into the conquered citadel of power. Wharton was sent to govern Ireland, where Whig and Tory factions among the Protestants were growing as bitter as in England. Somers became Lord President of the Council, with an influence over great decisions, domestic and foreign, equal to that of Godolphin and Marlborough.

It was not long before Somers exerted over the Queen the personal charm of his wise and courteous speech. Hitherto she had only known him by the reports of his political rivals. He soon conquered her prejudices against him, as Peel, when Prime Minister, overcame the similar prejudices of Queen Victoria. Moreover Somers, alone of the Junto Lords, maintained excellent relations with Marlborough and Godolphin. What unity and stability the new Cabinet had, came from the good understanding of the new Lord President with the Treasurer and the General. Halifax and Sunderland never ceased to show their hostility and suspicion of all who had ever borne the name of Tory. Sarah was up in arms on behalf of her husband and her friend Godolphin. Before many weeks were out, she was writing to Marlborough in terms as abusive of the Whigs as any she had formerly found for the Tories. Since Marl-

---

* 'When, upon the death of the Prince,' wrote Sarah (*Conduct*, pp. 222-223), 'one would have thought that her Majesty's real grief would have made her avoid every place and every object that might sensibly revive the remembrance of her loss, she chose for her place of retirement his closet and for some weeks spent many hours in it every day. . . . The true reason of her Majesty's chusing his closet to sit in, was that the back stairs belonging to it came from Mrs. Masham's lodging.'

On the other hand, Mrs. Masham wrote to Harley, eleven days after the Prince's death : ' Since the misfortune, the Lady Pye [Sarah] has hardly left her so long as to say her private prayers, but stays constantly with her. My lady's friends say it is fit she should, to keep that jade my cousin Kate [Mrs. Masham] away from her.' *H.M.C. Portland*, IV, p. 511. I deduce that the poor Queen really shut herself up with her grief away from both these importunate comforters.

borough also was deeply incensed by the personal attitude of his Whig colleagues, husband and wife at last saw eye to eye on domestic politics. That must have been a great consolation, for nothing else had ever divided them, and times were coming when the joint philosophy of husband and wife would be put to the test.

Even Somers failed to propitiate Sarah.

I was a martyr upon his account [she long afterwards wrote], pressing the Queen so much to comply in that matter. And I remember just before I got him in, I met him upon the road as I was going to Windsor, and he did a thing very uncommon upon the sight of me. He stood up in his coach, when the custom was only bowing as one passes by. But after he was in possession of his employment he never made me but one visit, but employed himself wholly to worship Abigail.*

It is untrue that he paid any court to Abigail, at least until 1710, but it is possible that, owing to lack of encouragement, his visits to Sarah were few. At any rate the new Whig-Marlborough alliance, though consummated, had little in it of mutual affection. Its want of inward cohesion made it the more vulnerable to attempts from outside to divide it by intrigue or overthrow it by open attack.[251]

At the time of these Cabinet changes following on the death of the Prince, the Reverend Jonathan Swift was enjoying the privilege of interviews with the Whig chiefs. He was already a person with whom ' the great ' liked to consort, though they did not yet perceive that his company could only be safely enjoyed upon his own terms. He was over from Ireland on one of his periodic missions on behalf of the interests of the Irish Church Establishment, to which he was heart and soul devoted against either Presbyterian or Papist. He wrote to Archbishop King at Dublin, describing the change in the English government and its possible effect upon his fortunes :

There is a new world here. . . . Although I care not to mingle

---

* *Althorp MSS.*, the interesting letter of Sarah to Mr. Mallet, September 24, 1744, a month before her death. As she grew older, Sarah grew more ' impossible.' But she was always capable of generous friendship where there was not opposition. The account of her real kindness to Lady Hervey at this time (March 1709) is pleasant reading : ' so much tenderness that she would not have done or said more to any child she has.' *Hervey, L. B.*, Vol. I, pp. 240–241.

public affairs with the interest of so private a person as myself, yet upon such a revolution, not knowing how far my friends may endeavour to engage me in the service of the new government, I would beg your Grace to have favourable thoughts of me on such an occasion ; and to assure you that no prospect of making my fortune shall ever prevail on me to go against what becometh a man of conscience and truth, and an entire friend of the established Church.

Since he did not agree with the Whigs on ecclesiastical questions, he would prefer, rather than engage as pamphleteer to the new government, to go out as Queen's Secretary to Vienna. The Ministry, he declares, had promised him the post. If they had either held their promise or engaged him as pamphleteer on suitable terms, the history of English literature and politics might have been different. ' The author of the *Tale of a Tub* goes Queen's Secretary to Vienna,' Harley had been told. But it was not so. And the fact that Swift was thus in common parlance designated by his authorship of that unconventional defence of the *via media*, stood across the path of his chances of Church promotion under the pious and simple Queen. His time was not yet.[252]

Since the meeting of the new Whig Parliament synchronised with the entry of the Whig chiefs into office and power, the session was one of the easiest. At Westminster the Tories put up no serious resistance in either House, although in the country the unseen tides of opinion were noiselessly changing. The only heats of that session were not between Whig and Tory but between England and Scotland, anent the Treason Bill, which bore the question-begging title ' An Act for improving the Union of the Two Kingdoms.'

Nov.
1708–
March
1709

The recent escape, in the Scottish courts of justice, of the Jacobite gentlemen of Stirlingshire * had aroused alarm in governmental and Whig circles. The English supposed that it resulted from some defect in the Scottish law of Treason, though in fact it had been caused by the temper of Scottish opinion. The new Government introduced into

---

* See pp. 347 and 349 above.

the new Parliament a Bill to have one law of Treason for the whole island, and that to be the English law. In a moment all Scotland, without distinction of party, was in a blaze of indignation. Every Scot in either House of Parliament, not excluding Queensberry, Argyle and Bishop Burnet, denounced a measure which seemed to infringe on the judicial separateness promised to Scotland in the Union Treaty. The opponents of that Treaty had always warned their countrymen that its interpretation would lie with the English, and so indeed it was proving. The Scots at first had the House of Commons with them against the Treason Bill, but the party tie and Government pressure eventually carried it through both Houses, with some slight modifications to placate Scottish opinion.

Whether the English or the old Scottish law of procedure in treason trials was the best on the balance is perhaps an open question. Each had strong and weak points. Marchmont, a former Scottish Lord Chancellor now in retirement from public life, wrote to Somers in the following July :

I have ever been of opinion that the laws and trials relating to treason were safer in England than in Scotland. I mean that innocent persons were more safe and the guilty as obnoxious.

One memorable change was effected in Clause VIII of the new Treason Act, which declared :

that no person accused of any capital offence or other crime in Scotland shall suffer or be subject or liable to any torture, except in the case of pressing to death as permitted by the English law in the case of persons indited for felony who refuse to plead.

The use of the ' boot ' and the ' thumbikins,' already obsolete in practice, was thus forbidden by law.

But, whatever the merits or demerits of the Act in itself, the overriding of the unanimous opinion of Scotland by the English Whig majority at Westminster formed a precedent for the action of the English Tory majority a few years later in questions affecting the Kirk. The sum total of these proceedings, and the spirit of indifference to Scottish opinion that they revealed, very nearly caused the repeal of the Union in the last years of Anne and was a principal cause of danger in the Rebellion of 1715.²⁵³

In May 1708 the Duke of Queensberry had been created Duke of Dover, so that he could sit in the House of Lords in his own right as a British Peer, not as an elected representative Peer of Scotland; and the same independence had been conferred on Argyle, as Earl of Greenwich. But Ministers paid no attention to the protest against the Treason Act of these, the two chief supporters of the Whig and Government interest in North Britain. By way of compensation, perhaps, a Third Secretaryship of State was created, principally to deal with the affairs of Scotland ; and Godolphin, against the wishes of his Whig colleagues, named Queensberry the first holder of the office.* He became at once engaged in a quarrel with Sunderland for a proper share of the Secretaries' fees. Till Sunderland fell he was unsuccessful in his claim, but when in 1710 the Tory Government was formed, they secured Queensberry's adhesion by continuing him in the office, and attaching to it a full share of secretarial fees, together with charge of British relations to Russia and the Baltic Powers.²⁵⁴

Feb.
1709

While Parliament was sitting, Thames was freezing. The great cold began the night before Christmas Day, and by January 3, 1709, people were putting up tents on the river for an ice fair, where a few days later Swift ' ate ginger-bread in a booth by a fire on the Thames.' Dear old Lady Wentworth † wrote to her brother :

My ink is fros, and tho I writ with it as it comes boiling from the fire, it's white. If I might tell you all the stories are daily brought in of accidents accationed by the Great Frost I might fill sheets, as children drown upon the Thames, post-boys being brought in by their horses to their stages frose to their horses stone dead, and we are obliged to the horses for having our letters regular.

Marlborough, meanwhile, had retaken Ghent and Bruges by crossing the ice,‡ and some of his English corre-

---

* See *Blenheim*, p. 290, on the two other Secretaries of State (Northern and Southern). See Appendix B, p. 410 below, list of offices and their holders.
† See p. 313 above.   ‡ See pp. 373-374 above.

spondence was held up for weeks, because the messenger ships were frozen in to the port of Harwich.   The staple of conversation of all classes in town and country was comparison with the well-remembered Great Frost of 1683–4,— since which how much had happened !   The Great Frost of the Merry Monarch's day was voted to have been the kinder of the two.   It had been shone upon by a bright sun, and followed by a dry summer and a good harvest.   The Great Frost of 1709 was accompanied by dark clouds and comfortless cold ; and went on, with intervals, for an interminable time, while cattle, sheep and birds perished.   It was followed by prolonged rains, and a thin harvest that doubled the price of corn in England, and reduced France to starvation.   In both countries these natural disasters stimulated the craving for peace by greatly increasing the miseries of war.[255]

It was during this cold February of 1709 that Epworth Rectory, with its thatched roof, was burnt down, for the second time in the Queen's reign, and the Reverend Samuel Wesley, stern and perplexed sire of that strong brood of sons and daughters, was once more houseless and well-nigh ruined.   In the hurry of escape, his son John, then five years old, was almost forgotten, ' till I was taken out of the nursery window,' as he afterwards testified, ' by a man strangely standing on the shoulders of another, . . . a brand plucked out of the burning.'   The history of religion sometimes turns on straws, no less than the history of war and politics.[256]

At the beginning of 1709 the war against France had been won.   The soldier and sailor had done their part, and it was the golden moment for the statesmen to garner the gains. Louis was beaten to his knees and was ready to buy peace at almost any price.   But the Allies failed to seize their opportunity, because Austria, Holland and England equally misunderstood the situation in one important respect.   They thought there was only one war, against Louis, and that they were its victors.   But there were in fact two wars: the great war against France which they had won, and the lesser war against Spain which they had lost.   The net result of five years' fighting in the Peninsula had been to attach the Spanish people to Philip V, no longer as the French candidate but as the Spanish King. In 1702 Louis could have withdrawn his grandson from Spain by a word. At midsummer of 1706 he could still have said that word with effect. But in 1707, and still more in 1709, no orders from Versailles would have sufficed to make Philip abdicate, and all Europe could not compel the Spaniards to accept King Charles. The reason why the negotiations for European peace broke down in 1709 was that the Allies refused to admit these facts, and still insisted, several years after it had ceased to be possible, in trying to dispose of the throne of Spain by a treaty with France alone. Louis knew he could not deliver the goods in that form, and he said so. The war was therefore allowed to proceed on its aimless, endless way, until a revolution in English politics placed in power the Tory party, whose chiefs had already, in November 1708, been privately writing to each other, ' For God's sake let us be once out of Spain ! ' *

During the years 1707 and 1708 there had been no serious negotiations for peace. But a certain neutral diplomat named Petkum, envoy of the Duke of Schleswig-Holstein at the Hague, had been keeping up an indirect correspondence between the Dutch and French statesmen as to possible terms. The chief interest of this correspondence is an expression of opinion by the Marquis of Torcy, Louis' able Foreign Minister who eventually negotiated the Treaty of Utrecht. As early as October 1707 he wrote to Petkum a letter which shows that he had already grasped the new situation in Spain, which the allied statesmen still declined to recognise more than two years later :

> As to there being no need to consider the views of Spain [wrote Torcy], I differ. So long as the war was carried on in Italy, France had a determining voice in the matter. But now the King of Spain is defending his kingdom by his own troops paid by himself, and I was speaking two days ago to a well informed man, who comes from Madrid, and who answered me that the King would rather die than give up Spain and the Indies.[257]

* See p. 388, above.

During the siege of Lille in 1708 Marlborough opened a secret peace correspondence on his own account with his nephew, the Duke of Berwick, Marshal of France. He always kept in friendly touch with his Jacobite nephew, partly, it may be supposed, to be sure of a powerful friend in case Berwick's half-brother, James, should ever chance to sit on the throne of Britain. The negotiation came to nothing, because the advisers of Louis were still hoping that Marlborough would fail to take the citadel of Lille or to recover Ghent and Bruges ; they therefore showed curiously little eagerness for peace that autumn, compared to their desperate pursuit of it in the following spring. Berwick, who at no time suffered from illusions as to the military situation, was vexed at the failure of Versailles to make the most of his uncle's offer, and declared that ' it was a chief cause of the aversion the Duke of Marlborough ever afterwards showed to the making of peace.'

Be that as it may, the interest of this abortive negotiation lies in the fact that it was initiated by Marlborough in person, desirous of procuring peace for Europe, though he failed so miserably next year to discover a method by which it could be attained. But most curious of all is a single sentence in Marlborough's initial letter to Berwick of October 30, 1708 :

> You may be sure that I shall be heartily in favour of peace, not doubting that I shall find the proof of goodwill [*l'amitié*] which was promised me two years ago by the Marquis d'Alègre.

It cannot be doubted that he refers to a transaction in the winter of 1705–6, when the Marquis d'Alègre had been instructed by Louis to offer him two million *livres* for peace, on terms which, however, he considered inadequate to England's interests.* The money which he had then refused as a bribe he was now fishing for as a *douceur*, which he saw no harm in accepting if he negotiated a peace on terms agreeable to Britain. His conduct, both before and after, shows that he had no intention of being bribed to betray his country's interests, but he hankered after the French gold with a cupidity that can only be partially

* See p. 60, note, above.

excused by the bad customs of the age in which he had been brought up.

When, in the following spring, Louis on his own account sought peace from the Allies at the Hague, he gave instructions that Marlborough should be offered four million *livres* if he could obtain Naples and Sicily for Philip as an inducement voluntarily to quit Spain. The Duke, though he again talked to Torcy significantly about the ' Marquis d'Alègre,' did not take the bribe. ' When I mentioned his private interests,' wrote Torcy, ' he blushed and seemed desirous of changing the topic of conversation.' He had good reason to blush. Behind the façade of his impenetrable reserve and godlike calm, strange debates were too often being held between his baser and his nobler self.[258]

It was early in November 1708 that Louis had rejected the proposal to negotiate made to him through Berwick. In a few weeks he had ample reason to repent. The fall of the citadel of Lille, followed by Ghent and Bruges, still more the horrors of that Russian winter, the destruction of the vines of France, the starvation of her peasants, who swarmed into the towns in search of food and died in the streets because none was to be had, all these accumulated misfortunes made a crisis in the land without precedent in memory and converted Louis into a sincere and almost abject suppliant for peace.

Throughout the early and middle part of 1709 the negotiations for a general pacification went actively forward at the Hague, whither Torcy had been sent to act for Louis. Point after point he and his master were forced to concede. In their desperate need for peace they refused nothing asked that it was in their power to give. The King of France did not stand out to keep his grandson in Spain, but he understood, what the Allies refused to recognise, the difficulty of compelling him to give up the throne which the Spaniards wished him to keep. Louis therefore proposed that Philip should be given some inducement to abandon Spain by the offer of a compensation elsewhere, for instance Naples and Sicily. But neither Austria nor England would consent to establish a Bourbon anywhere in Italy, and the proposal was rejected on the ground that there must be no partition of the Spanish Empire.

After much negotiation, the Allies at the end of May drew up their demands in forty 'Preliminary Articles,' which the plenipotentiaries of Austria, Great Britain and the States General signed and presented as an ultimatum to France. To all these Articles save one Louis eventually gave his consent. The whole Spanish Empire in all continents was to be surrendered to Charles, barring such places as might be reserved for Holland or Britain. Louis also ceded to the Dutch the great French fortress town of Lille, together with Menin and Maubeuge. As surety of good faith he was at once, on signature of the preliminaries, to surrender to them the places he still garrisoned in the Netherlands, such as Tournai, Ypres, Mons, Namur, Charleroi and Luxemburg. He was at once to surrender Strasbourg and its fort of Kehl, and to abandon many of his rights in Alsace.* He undertook, moreover, to destroy the fortifications of Dunkirk and to leave that bugbear of English merchants as an undefended harbour. Newfoundland and all French rights in it were to be ceded to Britain. Portugal and Savoy were to get the readjustment of boundaries for which they had stipulated. Louis even undertook in general terms, by Article IV, to co-operate with the Allies for the coercion of his grandson if he refused to quit Spain.

The only Article which Louis refused to sign was the famous Thirty-seventh, which declared that the cessation of arms could be brought to an end if the whole monarchy of Spain was not delivered up and yielded to Charles III within two months. This meant that if Philip refused to quit Spain and could not at once be driven out, the Allies could renew the war against his grandfather and invade France from the bases of Strasbourg, Tournai and the other frontier fortresses that would be already surrendered to them under the Treaty. Good faith and strict fulfilment of the terms on the part of Louis could not secure him against a renewal of the war under military conditions rendered far worse for him by his attempt to conciliate the

Note marginal date: May 1709

---

* Next year, 1710, he offered to give up Alsace entirely. *Torcy*, II, p. 74.

Allies. He refused to sign Article Thirty-seven. The negotiations were broken off on that point alone in the summer of 1709, and the campaign, which had already been resumed, went forward to Malplaquet.

I must confess [wrote Torcy to Petkum in July] that the more I seek a solution as to Article Thirty-seven, the less able I am to find it. We need not have been troubled by it, had we arranged the partition that I demanded for the King of Spain. By insisting on leaving him without States you drive him to fight for his crown and deprive the King of France of any means of influencing him for peace.

Great was the sorrow and surprise of Europe at the resumption of the long war, which men had all that spring regarded as being over at last. The first result was to rouse France to a last effort of desperate patriotism, on behalf of a king who had offered to make such immense sacrifices to give his people peace, and had offered all in vain to the insulting enemy. The fighting spirit of the armies defending the border of France rose from the level of Wynendael to the level of Malplaquet. The shock of disappointment in England was less immediate in its consequences, but in a year's time it had, in conjunction with the Sacheverell affair, aroused a passionate demand for peace, and a great anger with the statesmen who had refused the offer of such terms.

That, however, was not the immediate reaction. The bulk of the English people in the spring of 1709 believed that they had won the war, and they had long been taught to regard the cession of the whole Spanish Empire to Charles as the prize of victory.

The root trouble was that no diplomatic agreement with France could secure Spain for Charles, not even the clumsy and barbarous machinery of Article Thirty-seven. Godolphin thought that even if Louis accepted the ' Preliminaries ' entire, the situation would be full of danger for England. For if once the Dutch obtained possession of the Netherland towns to be ceded by Louis under the Treaty, they would not, the Treasurer thought, engage in another war with France ; if, therefore, war were to be renewed under Article Thirty-seven it would be a war fought by England, very little aided by the other allies, against France and

Spain. For these reasons Godolphin was not sorry when the negotiation was broken off and the war continued as before.*

His conclusion against peace was wrong, but his premises were right. He correctly saw the difficulty of winning Spain by a treaty with France. The right conclusion which he did not see was that Spain should be left to Philip and the Empire partitioned as William III had desired to partition it ; that conclusion could be drawn only by the Tories. Neither the Whigs nor Marlborough nor Godolphin would yield the point, and it was therefore in the interest of Europe that their newly formed Ministry should, as speedily as possible, be overturned.

Marlborough and Eugene had both acted in these negotiations with a feebleness that betrayed their embarrassment and their inability to formulate any practical plan. Neither of them made an effort to alter the preposterous character of the Preliminaries, yet both, immediately after the failure of the negotiation, privately confessed how preposterous they were. On July 10 Marlborough wrote to Heinsius, ' If I were in the place of the King of France I should venture the loss of my country much sooner than be obliged to join my troops for the forcing of my grandson.' But he had done nothing to find a way out of the *impasse*, being content to shift the responsibility, in part at least, on to the shoulders of the Whigs, the new men who understood the real difficulties less than he, and could therefore feel happy so long as they could continue to repeat the slogan of ' No peace without Spain.' To that formula Marlborough and Godolphin still adhered, though without any clear knowledge how to give it effect. It was indeed they, and not the Whigs, who had originally forced upon the Allies the dogma of the indivisibility of the Spanish Empire. They had first asserted it in the Treaty which

---

* *Geikie*, pp. 129–130. Godolphin was not the only person in England who had these fears of the insufficiency of the Preliminaries. Thus on June 3, 1709, Secretary Boyle wrote to Townsend: ' no cautionary towns are of much significancy in this case, unless such as are maritime and essential towards reducing Spain by force. It seems very plain that the French King does not intend the whole Spanish Monarchy.' *R.H.S. Diplomatic Instructions, France* (1925), Wickham Legg, p. 16. Even Marlborough's chaplain, Francis Hare, wrote in August 1709, ' A Spanish war may prove very troublesome as well as expensive, and the load will lie entirely upon England, when the other Allies have got all they want.' *H.M.C. Hare*, p. 228.

they and Nottingham had made with Portugal in 1703, and they had confirmed it by their insistence with the recalcitrant Dutch in 1705–6.

In 1709 the Dutch themselves, encouraged by the tide of victory, strongly supported the cession of Spain and the Indies to Charles. They did so partly in order to justify and earn their own claims to a large part of the Netherlands by way of 'Barrier,' to be obtained by the help of the Barrier Treaty which they were negotiating with the English Whigs to the detriment of the sovereignty of Charles in Belgium. But the Dutch had other and more direct reasons for supporting the claims of Charles to Spain and the Indies. As a trading nation they, like the English, believed that their commerce with Spain, Italy and America would be safer under the House of Austria than under the House of Bourbon.* The responsibility for the failure to make peace may fairly be divided between the statesmen of England, Austria and Holland, none of whom made any such effort as that made by Torcy and his master to find a solution to the very real difficulties of the case.[259]

One reason for the unpractical character of British statesmanship at the Hague in 1709 was that the war party had been put into office in the previous November, at the very moment when the question of the hour was the problem of peace. If the Whigs had been given power four years earlier—as they might have been if Anne had so willed—the change would then have been suited to the nature of the time, while the exorbitant power of France had still to be reduced. In fact the war had only been won because the Whigs, while kept on the outskirts of office, had consented to support the war ministry against High Tory recalcitrance and defeatism. The victories of Marlborough, the Regency Act and the Union with Scotland were due to the active support of the Whig party outside the circles of government. The services of the Whigs to the country, while they were being rendered, had been indifferently rewarded owing to Queen Anne's objection to a party

* On this as a chief motive of the Dutch attitude in the negotiations of 1709 see *Geyl*, pp. 14–20.

government. At length, in November 1708, the Junto
had forced its way through the Queen's resistance into
power, largely owing to the General Election of that
summer, itself to some degree the chance result of the
attempted Jacobite invasion in the spring. The Whigs
were established in office at the very moment when they
could do least service and most harm.

The two great services which the Whigs could render
to the country in this epoch were the reduction of the power
of France and the securing of the Protestant Succession. On
both these questions the Tory party was divided. But they
were the two questions of prime importance. If the power
of Louis as it stood in 1704 had not been reduced by war,
or if the Roman Catholic Stuarts had returned to the throne,
our country would have been thrown back into the internal feuds and external weakness of seventeenth-century
England, from which the Revolution had done so much to
rescue her. The prosperity, unity and power of Great
Britain in the eighteenth century would not have been
realised without the victories of Marlborough and the
accession of the House of Hanover. In the early years of
Anne the Whigs had enabled Marlborough to win the war ;
in the last months of her reign their firm stand amid the
frightened and divided counsels of their opponents secured
the peaceful accession of King George. But in the year
1709 the need was neither the war nor the succession, but
the peace. And that the Whigs could not give.

They were sincerely convinced of the necessity, in the
interest of British trade and security in the coming era, of
depriving the House of Bourbon of the whole Spanish
Empire. But they had no idea how to accomplish it, except
by interminably continuing the war against France. That
did not seem to them so great an evil as it should have done.
Their enemies said of them, with some measure of truth :

The party that is founded upon war and a senseless jargon of
France, Jesuits and an invisible army of 100,000 pilgrims mounted
upon elephants, have not yet acquired power enough to support themselves in that most difficult and slippery state of peace.*

* Thomas Harley to Edward Harley, December 30, 1708. *H.M.C.
Portland*, IV, p. 516.

Half-consciously the Whigs hoped that, as long as the war
went on, their power would be safe ; and it is not impossible,
though I know no proof of it, that a further consideration
helped to reconcile them to the continuance of a state of war
with France.   If Anne died while we were still fighting the
Pretender's patron, the accession of our Hanoverian ally
would be certain and unopposed.   England would not go
to the enemy's camp for a King.

At any rate the Whigs were useless as peacemakers.
And Marlborough and Godolphin were no better.   Moreover the confusion of British counsels at the Hague in
1709 was worse confounded by the fact that Marlborough was pursuing a different line of policy from
the Lords of the Junto.   The Whigs had sent over to
Holland their own emissary, Charles Townshend ; he was
in close touch with Somers, Halifax and Sunderland, but
he was not in the confidence of Marlborough.   Townshend's
instructions were to drive to a speedy conclusion the Barrier
Treaty with the Dutch Government, by which Britain
would guarantee a long list of Barrier towns in the Netherlands to Holland, and Holland would engage, in case of
need, to send over troops to secure the accession of the
House of Hanover in Scotland or England.*   Marlborough wished these negotiations to be spun out incon-
clusively, as he feared the Allies would give Holland too
much, particularly as Charles III still promised him that he
should enjoy the governorship of the Spanish Netherlands
after the peace, and he had therefore personal as well as
public reasons to deprecate their dismemberment.

Not only, therefore, was the Duke alienated from his
old friend Heinsius, but he was not really in the confidence
of Townshend and the Junto, both on account of party and
personal rivalries at home, and on account of the Barrier
question.   This division between the English negotiators
at the Hague prevented them from taking reasonable
counsel together on the terms to be demanded of France
and the famous Article Thirty-seven.   Neither Marlborough nor the Whigs were likely to take effective action
to compel the other Allies to make peace, but the fact that

* See pp. 138–140, above.

they were not on intimate terms with each other rendered it doubly impossible that the British delegates could do any good at the Hague.[260]

And so the war went on. Even before Malplaquet some of Marlborough's men began to feel, what they had never felt before, that their lives were being wasted. In August Colonel Revett wrote home from before Tournai :

> I am so great a lover of peace and the good of my country, that I among the majority wish that there had not been any cause for the loss of so many good men and officers that have fallen at this siege.

The writer was a brave soldier and no politician : he was killed at Malplaquet next month.[261]

In these circumstances it was inevitable that the British army should become increasingly divided, the peace party against the war party, Tory against Whig, the partisans of Argyle or of Webb against those of Marlborough. These threefold divisions, though not exactly corresponding, strengthened one another ; and the army, recently a band of brothers, was torn by feuds and factions. So when the Queen, as she presently did, began to make promotions without consulting Marlborough, discipline was seriously affected. The Duke was soon writing to Godolphin :

> If it be the intention of the Queen that I should serve her, which I am ready to do with all my heart, she must, in order to bring the dissipline of the army back to that happy posture in which it was some time ago for the service, let me have in my power to oblige the officers, and not to have anybody incoraged to think thay can meet with preferment by others.*

Meanwhile, at home, the failure of the negotiations of 1709 gave the Tories their cue for an agitation for peace and disarmament, coupled with an attack on the Whigs and Marlborough as militarists aiming at another Cromwellian regime. The national dislike of a standing army and the dread of a redcoat appealed to many instincts and traditions besides the Cavalier tradition of the Tories themselves. These feelings were exploited in the cause of High

---

* From a letter in my possession, undated but of 1710 probably, addressed ' for yourself ' [Godolphin] in Marlborough's handwriting, though without signature.

Church and Sacheverell.   Ned Ward, the Tory public-
house poet and pamphleteer, published in 1709 *Mars
stripped of his Armour*, a ferocious attack on the army
beginning :

An army is the reverse of a Church, for as we learn piety in the
first, 'tis ten thousand to one but we are taught prophaneness in the
other.   As all religions concur and meet together in Amsterdam, so
all vice in an army.   A regiment is a corporation which consists of
individuals detached from Bridewell, the Queen's Bench, Fleet,
Newgate and the Counters.

The cry against soldiers as such, singularly ungrateful
after the unparalleled services they had just rendered to
England, was raised as loud as the cry against Dissenters.
Both must be suppressed, or Marlborough, another Cromwell, would lead on the redcoats, the Whigs, the ' fanatics '
and the monied men to destroy the Church and the Monarchy
and make him perpetual dictator.   The abject nonsense of
such cries, with which England was to be filled for the next
few years, was a measure of the terrible mistake that had
been made by the opposite party in refusing peace.   The
nonsense did its appointed work, according to the wont of
political England, and produced in good time the Treaty of
Utrecht, a blessing to Britain and to the world.   Then the
nonsense went raging on till it became dangerous and, at the
Queen's death, reached in its turn its appropriate calamity.

In spite of Queen Anne, Harley, Godolphin and Marlborough, and partly through the defects of their respective
qualities, the attempt to govern England on non-party lines
had come to an end, after a not inglorious period of trial.
Party henceforth was to rule in alternate manifestations of
Whig and Tory ; but the foundations of Great Britain and
her constitution and her place in the world had been well
and truly laid, if party could be wise enough to treat them
with respect.   The temptations to violence in public life
are always great, but of the two parties that one which
should first recover its temper and walk in the ways of
prudence would be the winner in the end, and would be
the true successor of the great traditions of patriotic government which had been established under the ministry of
Marlborough and Godolphin.

APPENDICES

APPENDIX A

Marlborough's Letters to Heinsius, 1705

As in the appendix to my earlier volume, *Blenheim*, here again I print some of the letters of Marlborough to his coadjutor in the Alliance, Heinsius, Grand Pensionary of Holland ; they are taken from MSS. in the Rijks-archief at the Hague. They are written in English, in the Duke's own hand. Later letters of this correspondence, from 1706 onwards, have been printed by Vreede and are available for students. These letters of 1705, which are here printed for the first time, illustrate the crisis of Marlborough's struggle for emancipation from the control of the Dutch Generals and Deputies in the field (see pp. 55–57, above) ; they also show that the principle of ' No Peace without Spain ' was enunciated as a slogan of British statesmanship, even before Ramillies (see pp. 59–60, above).

1705. July 30 [N.S.]. Meldert. Since my last to you, I prevailled with the Generall, to consent that we shou'd march as we did this last night to try if we cou'd pass that River before the french cou'd know it. I did promise them that if the ffrench army shou'd be there I wou'd not attempt the passage, til I had there consent. . . . I am afraid this was known to Mons. de Villeroy, otherwis I do not think he wou'd have ventur'd to be there. But God forgive those that are better pleased when any thing goes ill then when wee haue success.

Aug. 2. Meldert. I am very uneasy in my own minde to see how every thing here is like to goe, notwithstanding the superiority and goodness of our Troupes, which ought to make us not doubt of success. However it is Certaine that if affaires Continue on the same foot thay now are, it is impossible to attempt any thing considerable with success or advantage, since Councils of War must be called on every occasion, which intirely destroys the Secrecy and dispatch, upon which all great undertakings depend ; and has unavoidably another very unhappy effect, the private animostys between so many Persons to be assembled being so great, and their Inclinations and Interest so different, as allways to make one part oppose what the other advise and consequently never agree.

I do not say this because I have the honour of being at the head of the army, but it is absolutely necessary that such a power bee lodg'd with the General as may enable him to act as he thinks proper according to the best of his Judgment, without being oblig'd either to communicate what he intends further than he thinks convenient.   The success of the last campane [1704] with the blessing of God was owing to that Power, which I wish you would now give for the good of the Publique, and that of the States in particular, and if you think anyone can execute it better than myself, I shal be willing to stay in any of the towns here, having a very good pretext, for I really am sick.   I know this is a very nice point, but it is of the last importance, for without it noe general can act offensively.

Aug. 13.   Meldert.   We shall march on Saturday, and the troupes are so good that if it were possible to haue secresy, and obedience, with the blessing of God, I think we haue a much fairer prospect then we had this day twelfmonth [Blenheim day, Aug. 13]; but we have tempers here that are never pleas'd, but when they are sowing dissention. . . . I must own that my patience is very much tryed.   I have write again to Vienna to presse that Court to lose no time in sending more troupes to Prince Eugene, but I foresee that when ever those orders are given Pr. Lewis of Baden will make difficulty, by which there will be time lost.

Aug. 19. . . . On this occasion I can't forbear saying that if your Generals wou'd have allow'd of our attacking the enemy, you might in my opinion have been in a condition of proscribing to ffrance what Peace you pleased. . . . I wish I cou'd be with you for one hour that I might talk freely to you, as to what is propos'd for the Preliminaries to the treating for a Peace.   I do before God declare to you that I am persud'd that if Slanenbourg [= Slangenberg] had not been in the army at this day we might have prescribed to ffrance what peace we had pleas'd.   But as the circumstances now are I agree with you that it will be very difficult to persuade ffrance to consent to such conditions, as are absolutely necessary to make the Peace lasting.   You know as well as I, that England can like no peace, but such as puts King Charles in the possession of the Monarke of Spain ; and as for yourselves, I think you ought to have garrisons in Antwerp, Namur, and Luxembourg, besides I think the Duke of Savoy shou'd be our particular care.   And if wee will have a lasting Peace and the blessing of God, we must do somthing for the advantage of Protestants.

Aug. 18, 1705.   [A letter from Godolphin to Marlborough sent on enclosed to Heinsius.]   Since you desire my thoughts upon the extract of a letter from the Pensionary which you were pleased to send mee, I must beg the freedome to tell you if England had lost a battell at sea and another at land, I think they would still despise such a peace, and I believe you may depend upon it they will never consent to any peace that leaves Spain and the Indies or either in hands of the Duke of Anjou.   Nor will they be pleased with the Treaty of partition, tho' that bee not altogether so bad as this proposall.   Godolphin.

The remainder of the letter shows that the Partition Treaty here referred to is the Second Partition Treaty (1699).   This correspondence shows that even in the winter before Ramillies Marlborough and Godolphin were determined to have ' no peace without Spain ' for the Austrian candidate.

Aug. 27. Marlborough to Heinsius. Mr. Slenenbourg [Slangenberg] hitherto has oppos'd everything that has been propos'd by mee. So that I have taken a resolution of not exposing my own honour, nor the Publick good, by making any schem, but went that very afternoon I receiv'd yours, to beg of the deputys that they wou'd speak to Mons. Slanenbourg, and such other of their Generals as they thought fitt, to know what they thought might be done for the Publicke good and the particular Interest of the States, and did then asssure them, and did desire thay wou'd lett their Generals know that I wou'd joyn in what ever they thought might be done ; for I have so good an opinion of this army that I think they are able to execut what ever their Generals will resolve, besides we have yett two months before we ought to think of winter quarters. I beg you will beleive and assure others that for the remainder of this Campagne I will with all cherfulness endeavour to make everything succed that shall be propos'd to mee ; by which I hope at last Mons. Slanenbourg will be brought to do me the Justice to beleive that I act by no other principle but that of the Publicke good.

Sept. 5. Tirlemont. Marlborough to Heinsius. I have receiv'd a letter from Pr. Lewis of Baden to acquaint me of his having forced the Lyns of Hagnau, this Confers me more and more in the opinion I have, that the ffrench will always be forced when ever they are attacked. I am very glad to find by your last letter that there was no designe to mortefie me. What is thought for the good of the publick, it is very fit I shou'd bare itt, and shall from henceforward endeavour not to trouble my friends with complaints. The resolution I have taken of being governed by your Generals the remaining part of this Campagne gives me a great deal of quiet, so that I am now drinking the Spaa watters.

APPENDIX B

PRINCIPAL OFFICERS OF STATE IN THE GODOLPHIN MINISTRY, 1705–1708

(*Whigs are printed in italics.*)

	1705	1706	1707	1708
Lord Treasurer	Sidney, Lord Godolphin	Created Earl of Godolphin, Dec. 1706		
Lord President of the Council	Thos. Herbert, Earl of Pembroke			Nov., *Lord Somers*
Lord Privy Seal	John Sheffield, Duke of Buckingham. *Succeeded by John Holles, Duke of Newcastle*			
Chancellor of the Exchequer	Hon. Henry Boyle*		Apr., *John Smith*	
Lord Keeper of the Great Seal	Sir Nathan Wright *Succeeded by Sir William Cowper*	*Created Lord Cowper, Dec. 1706*		
Lord Chancellor			*Lord Cowper, becomes Lord Chancellor*	
Secretary of State (Northern Department)	Robert Harley			
Secretary of State (Southern Department)	Sir Charles Hedges	Dec. *Charles Spencer, Earl of Sunderland*		Feb., Hon. Henry Boyle*

APPENDIX B—continued.

PRINCIPAL OFFICERS OF STATE IN THE GODOLPHIN MINISTRY, 1705–1708

	1705	1706	1707	1708
Secretary of State	(Third Secretary, created Feb. 1709 chiefly to deal with Scottish affairs, see p. 394, above)	.	.	Feb. 1709, *Duke of Queensberry.*
Lord Lieutenant of Ireland	James Butler, Duke of Ormonde	.	.	Nov., *Thomas, Earl of Wharton*
Lord High Admiral	Prince George of Denmark, Prince Consort	.	Thos. Herbert, Earl of Pembroke	Nov., Thomas Herbert, Earl of Pembroke, on death of the Prince
Secretary at War	Henry St. John	.	.	Feb., *Robert Walpole*
Master-General of the Ordnance	Duke of Marlborough	.	.	
Comptroller at the Household	Thomas Mansell	.	.	*Earl of Cholmondeley*
Master of the Horse	*Duke of Somerset*			
Lord Chamberlain	*Henry Grey, Marquess of Kent*			
Lord Steward	*Duke of Devonshire*			

* Henry Boyle, always a Moderate, and a friend of Harley, may perhaps be said to have become a Whig during this period.

APPENDIX C

Sunderland's Letters to Newcastle. Relations of the Junto to Marlborough and Godolphin in 1708

The following letters of Sunderland to the Duke of Newcastle (never, I think, printed before) are from the *Lansdowne MSS*. in the British Museum, 1236, ff. 242–253. They show the degree to which Sunderland, while Secretary of State, was incensed against the Lord Treasurer Godolphin ; they show the suspicion he entertained in the summer of 1708 that not only Godolphin but even his own father-in-law, Marlborough, had been playing into the hands of the Jacobites in the affair of the attempted invasion of Scotland in March (see pp. 340, 343 note, above). The belief of the Junto clearly was that the Hanoverian Succession was not safe unless the Whigs had full power in the State.

The later letters show how, using the lever of the Whig majority in the Commons secured at the General Election in May, the Junto in the autumn pressed for a more completely Whig administration ; how the opposition of the Queen, and in a less degree of Godolphin and Marlborough, to the removal of the Prince Consort from the Admiralty to make room for Whig control, was only overcome by the Prince's death. (See p. 389 above.)

Whitehall May 27. 1708.

My Lord.

I was very sorry, I had the misfortune of missing of y^r Grace the night before you went out of town, but I happen'd to come in to My Ld. Steward's [Devonshire's], the minute you were gone, I hope you have already found benefitt, by the Country air, which onely can make amends for our loosing you here ; I hope y^r Grace will pardon my giving you this trouble now, but it is at the desire of My Ld. Steward, Ld. Sommers & Ld. Halifax, who think this matter of the D. of Queensberry's Patent, [see p. 394 above] of so very great consequence, that they have desir'd me to lay their thoughts before you, that since you have told y^r opinion of this matter to the Queen, in the honest, plain, & noble way, you have done it, whither it would nott be right, before you putt the Privy Seal to it, to write a letter to the Queen once more, to represent this matter & its fatall Consequences to her. with this view, that in case she continues obstinate in her resolution, (as I take for granted she will) that at least you have done all in y^r power, which justifies you sufficiently afterwards, in putting the seal to it, & in acting afterwards in relation to this affair in Parliament, as you shall judge proper ; these are the thoughts of y^r humble servants here upon this subiect, the other Lds. I mention'd would have writt themselves, but that they thought one letter would be lest troublesome; I am so much of this opinion my self, that if the Queen had thought fitt, to have order'd me to prepare the warrant, (as she did Mr Boyle) I should have took this method, that I might have had the Copy of my letter by me, upon occasion ; y^r Grace I am sure will pardon this liberty, since it's mean't purely for y^{rs} & the Publick service.

I heartily Congratulate with y^r Grace upon the Elections throughout England, being so well over as they are, I think one may venture to say, it is the most Wig Parliament has been since the revolution, so that if our friends will stick together, & act like men, I am sure the Court must, whither they will or no, come into such measures, as may preserve both us & themselves ; I Beg my most humble service to My Lady Dutchess, & am allways with the greatest respect

My Lord, Y^r Grace's most obedient humble servant

SUNDERLAND.

The Lords abovemention'd
have all charg'd me with
their Compliments to y^r Grace

Althrop Aug. 9th 1708.

My Lord.

I Believe Lord Sommers, & Ld. Halifax have acquainted y^r Grace, with the unlucky accidents, that have prevented our waiting you at Welbeck, however I should have done my self the honour to have gone alone, butt that since my Coming here, I have had the ill luck to sprain my foot, which has putt me to a great deal of pain and trouble, but is now something easier, I own I am extreamly Concern'd at this disappointment for besides the pleasure of waiting upon y^r Grace, it would have been of use to have talk'd together, of the present posture of our affairs, which tho' they are very fortunately and unexpectedly mended abroad, by our success in Flanders, and in the West Indies [Oudenarde and Wager's action] ; yett seem to grow worse and worse every day at home ; for without running over all the Particulars, such as the villainous management of Scotland, the state of the fleet which is worse than ever, the Condition of Ireland in which the Protestant interest is lower, and the Popish higher than ever ; their late manage-ment in relation to the invasion, and in particular the pardoning Ld. Griffin, is a declaration to the whole world, as far as in them lies for the Prince of Wales, & against the Protestant succession, these are such proceedings that if there is not a just spiritt shewn in Parliament we had as good give up the game, & submitt to My Ld. Treasurer's & My Ld. Marl-borough's bringing in the Prince of Wales ; My reason of troubling y^r Grace, with all this, is to Conjure you, nott to deffer Coming to town too long, till just the Parliament meets, for whatever is proper to be done, must be Con-certed before hand, & that cannott be done without y^r presence & influence :

I know you are very averse to Coming to town before y^r time, but three weeks or a month, sooner or later I hope will break no squares, & it is so absolutely necessary, that it is the joynt request of y^r friends & humble servants, & indeed our all is at stake, for if next sessions of Parliament does not redress the mischiefs, there's an end of the Revolution & the Protestant succession.

I hope y^r Grace has y^r health well in the Country, & beg you to believe that I am with the greatest truth and respect

My Lord

y^r Grace's most obedient humble servant

SUNDERLAND.

London, Oct. 19th 1708.

My Lord.

I give y^r Grace this trouble, at the desire of the Duke of Devonshire, the Duke of Bolton, Ld. Dorchester, Ld. Orford, Ld. Wharton, Ld. Townend, Ld. Sommers, & Ld. Halifax, to give you an account of what has pass'd between them & Ld. Treasurer, in relation to the present posture of our affairs, in which they hope, what steps they have made will meet with y^r approbation ; they have upon the best Consideration among themselves come to this resolution & opinion, that it was impossible for them with any reputation to themselves, or safety to the publick, to go on any longer with the Court, upon the foot things are at present, for that if one looks round every part of the administration, the management of the fleet, the Condition of Ireland, the Proceedings in Scotland, the management of the late Invasion, the disposall of Church Preferments, &c ; they are all of a Piece, as much Tory, & as wrong, as if Ld. Rochester & Ld. Nottingham were at the head of every thing, under the disguise of some Considerable wigs, in some considerable places, but with so little creditt or to so little purpose, that they can neither obtain any right thing to be done, nor prevent any wrong one ; they Consider'd, that the management of the fleet, as it is of the greatest Consequence, so it is under the most scandalous management of all & that this is never to be cur'd, but by the Prince's quitting, for that whatever Councill he has, George Churchill will in effect be allways Ld. high Admirall ; so that they have in a body declar'd to Ld. Treasurer, that if this is not immediately done, they must lett the world & their friends see they have nothing more to do with the Court; the man they propose to be Ld. high Admirall, is Ld. Pembroke, (which would open a redress for Ireland, & what is much desir'd by all honest people, the President's place, for Ld. Sommers.) My Ld. Treasurer seem'd to agree with them in opinion, (as his way allways is in words) but at the same time pretends great difficulties & that when Ld. Marlborough comes all will be sett right, which by the way can't be much before Christmass; to this the Lords told him, that they could no longer rely upon Promises & words, & that therefore they must take their measures, till this thing was actually done, as if it never was to be done & they told him therefore plainly that they would & must oppose the Court, in the choice of the Speaker, that being the first point, to come on, for that they had no other way left to lett the world see, & all their friends that they were upon a different foot; to this, he was pleas'd to make a proposall, which was as ridiculous, as it shew'd the unsincerity of their intentions, to do any thing that was right, & that was, y^t there should be an act of Parliament obtain'd to allow the Prince to continue Ld. high Admirall, & to empower his Councill to act for him, it would be tedious to repeat all the objections the Lords made to this proposall, as absurd, ridiculous, & ineffectuall, & what no Parliament ever would hear off. I will onely mention one Particular, which is very remarkable, & pretty extraordinary, that Ld. Treasurer told them, that he had mention'd this proposall to Ld. Chancellour [Lord Cowper], & that he had entirely approv'd of it. Ld. Chancellour since has been told what Ld. Treasurer said, & he dos positively affirm that he dos nott remember, that ever Ld. Treasurer spoke to him, or he to Ld. Treasurer of any such proposall. This extraordinary proceeding has been a further Confirmation to these Lords of the reason they have to declare against the Court, which they are resolv'd to do in this first point of the Speaker, by setting up Sr Peter King, & I am Confident when the Court see this, that the wigs will no longer be fool'd, they will then do all reasonable things, which they will never do, whilst they hope that words & promises will pass ; I must nott forgett telling you that this day, unexpectedly without any body knowing any thing of it, Sr James Mountague has been made Attorney Generall, & Mr Eyres Sollicitour, which I believe, has been owing to the vigour, with which those Lords spoke to Ld. Treasurer, & confirms them in their opinion, that if they go on in their resolution & stand together, the other more essentiall things will be also done ; My Ld. Steward to morrow, is to speak to Ld. Chancellour, to acquaint him with the resolutions they have taken, & to try to perswade him to act, with spirit & vigour, with the rest of his friends. I Beg a thousand pardons for this long long letter, but as I have been forc'd to omitt a great many particulars for fear of being too tedious, so I was very desirous my self, as well as at the Command of these Lords, to explain this whole affair to y^r Grace as well as I could hoping you will approve of what they have done, for in our present Condition all depends on our acting of a piece & in Concert, & if we do so, we must carry our point, & save our Country, which indeed I think, is in as great danger as ever I knew ; I must add the request of all these Lords to y^r Grace, that you would lett them have y^r Company, & assistance here in town as soon as may be ; I am ever with the greatest respect My Lord

Y^r Grace's most obedient humble servant

SUNDERLAND.

London Oct. 26th 1708.

My Lord.

I have the honour of y^r Grace's letter, & am heartily sorry y^t any accident should have happen'd to occasion a delay in y^r coming to town, for indeed it is of the last Consequence, to have all our friends together, at this juncture, & I am sure there's none whose Presence is of so much Consequence & weight as y^r Grace's ; so that you will give us leave to depend upon y^r hastening all you can ; I am now desir'd by those Lords y^r h^{ble} servants, that I mention'd in my last, to beg you would either speak or send to Mr Jessop about this matter of the Speaker, to engage him for Sr Peter King, & that he would

take what pains he can among the Northern Members, among whom he has
a generall acquaintance, besides the weight in using y^r name; they beg too
that you would write upon this occasion to Mr Monkton & Mr Peyton; I
beg a thousand pardons for this trouble & am ever with great truth & respect
My Lord Y^r Graces most obedient humble servant
SUNDERLAND.

I have obey'd y^r Commands to Ld. Halifax & Sr James Mountague, who
present their h^{ble} service & are truely sensible how much they owe, to y^r
kindness in this affair.
To his Grace the Duke of Newcastle Lord Privy Seal
at Welbeck

SUNDERLAND   Nottinghamsh̄

London Nov. 4th 1708.

My Lord.

Since I writt last to y^r Grace, & had the honour of y^r Answer, the Death
of the Prince, has made so great an alteration in every thing, & particularly
in what was most at every Body's heart, the affair of the Admiralty, that as
soon as it happen'd, those of our friends of the house of Commons, that were
in Town, & that were the most zealous with us, in setting up Sr Peter King,
begun to Press us to accommodate the matter, & nott to make a Division,
since by this accident, there was room, to have every think [sic] sett right;
since that My Ld. Treasurer has acquainted us, that the Queen had agreed
to make Ld. Pembroke Ld. high Admirall, Ld. Sommers President & Ld.
Wharton Ld. Lieutenant of Ireland. Ld. Sommers is out of Town, so that
whither he will be perswaded to accept of it, or no, I can't tell, but he would
be so much in the wrong, if he should nott, that I won't doubt, but he will;
These Proposalls are so great in themselves, towards putting things upon a
thorough right foot, that those Lords in whose names I writt last to y^r Grace,
have desir'd me to acquaint you with it, & that their thoughts upon it are,
that since these main things are like to be done, it would by no means be right
to venture a division of our friends upon the first point of the Speaker, & therefore they have allready spoke with Sr Peter King, in order to endeavour to
make him easy in it, so that if y^r Grace is of the same mind, & approves what
they have done, you will please to lett y^r friends of the house of Commons
know it, in the manner you shall judge properest; we are in expectation of
seeing you here every day, however these Lords directed me to acquaint you,
with it as soon as possible; I am ever with the greatest truth & respect
My Lord, Y^r Grace's most obedient humble servant
SUNDERLAND.

APPENDIX D

Bishops in the House of Lords

IN Queen Anne's reign a hard-working and conscientious Bishop—
and such nearly all the Bishops were—was expected to reside in
London from November to April inclusive in order to perform his
duties in Parliament. Contemporary opinion, clerical as well as lay,
Tory as much as Whig, regarded that as the first charge on a Bishop's
time in the winter and spring months. Such was the conception of
the close relations of Church and State, and the importance of the
Upper House of Parliament, where the Bishops' votes were still
liable to be decisive, and where their influence was not so very much
less than it had been in mediæval times. Modern critics, usually
unjust to the eighteenth-century Church, have neglected this
important fact in judging of episcopal habits of residence. Pre-
occupation at Westminster was the chief reason why even the most
active Bishops, like Wake of Lincoln, found it difficult to get round
their dioceses, geographically so enormous, on visitations which had
to be carried out on the bad roads of the day, either in the heavy
coaches of the period or on horseback, as most episcopal visitations
were performed. The Bishops of William's and Anne's reign were
not sluggards, and were at least up to the level of their predecessors.
On this whole subject see the very interesting work of Professor
Norman Sykes, who is becoming the historian of the eighteenth-
century Church. In his article on *Episcopal Administration in
England in the Eighteenth Century*, in the *Engl. Hist. Rev.* for July
1932, he writes :

In passing to the consideration of the activities of the Bishop, it is
essential to remember continually one fundamental factor, that of the long
residence each year in London required of an eighteenth-century prelate.
The secular English tradition of the association of the Episcopate with affairs
of State suffered a change of form rather than of principle with the Reformation settlement. And towards the end of the seventeenth century in particular, the rise of the two rival political parties of Whig and Tory had given a

new turn to that position by emphasizing the importance of the attendance of the Bishops upon their duties in the Upper House of Parliament. In addition to their period of waiting upon the court, their presence in the debates and divisions of the House of Lords was of great importance to the successive party administrations of Anne and of the early Hanoverian kings. In the conventional [modern] complaints of the non-residence of eighteenth-century prelates, this aspect of their office is commonly aspersed, though esteemed highly by contemporary opinion.

ABBREVIATIONS USED IN THE NOTES

MSS.

Add. MSS. = British Museum, *Additional MSS.* (*B.M.* = British Museum, other collections).

Althorp MSS. = MSS. belonging to Earl Spencer in Althorp House, Northants. Some papers of Sarah, Duchess of Marlborough among others.

Bodleian MSS. = MSS. in the Bodleian, Oxford.

Boughton MSS. = MSS. belonging to the Duke of Buccleugh, in Boughton House, Northants. Papers formerly belonging to the Dukes of Montagu and Shrewsbury.

Heinsius MSS. = Letters of Marlborough to Heinsius in the Rijks-archief at the Hague (see Appendix A, above, for some excerpts).

P.C. Reg. Ed. = *Privy Council Registers, Scotland,* in Register Office, Edinburgh.

P.R.O. = Public Record Office (S.P. = State Papers ; Tr. = Transcripts).

Wake MSS. = Archbishop Wake's MSS. in the Christ Church Library, Oxford.

PRINTED MATTER

Abbey = Chas. Abbey. *The English Church and its Bishops 1700–1800* (1887).

Acts Parl. Scot. = Vol. XI of the *Acts of the Parliaments of Scotland* (1824).

Agnew = Sir Andrew Agnew. *The Hereditary Sheriffs of Galloway*, 1893.

Argyle, Int. Letters = *Intimate Society Letters of the Eighteenth Century.* Ed. by the Duke of Argyle, 1910.

Atkinson = *Marlborough*, by C. T. Atkinson (*Heroes of Nations* series).

B. Williams, Stanhope = Professor Basil Williams, *Stanhope* (Oxford 1932).

Ballard = General Colin Ballard. *The Great Earl of Peterborough*, 1929.

Berwick = *Mémoires du maréchal de Berwick*, ed. 1778.

Blackader = *Life of Col. Blackader of the Cameronian Regiment*, 1824.

Burchett = Josiah Burchett. *Transactions at sea*, 1720.

Burnet = Bishop Burnet's *History of his own time*, ed. 1823 (figures in brackets refer to pagination in some earlier editions).

Burt = *Letters from a gentleman in the North of England* (Ed. Burt, *circa* 1726), ed. 1815.

Burton, Anne = *History of the Reign of Queen Anne*, by John Hill Burton, historiographer royal for Scotland, 1880.

Burton, Scotland = *History of Scotland 1689–1748*, 1853, by the same author.

Byng Papers = *The Byng Papers* (Navy Records Soc., 1930–31).

Calamy = J. T. Rutt's *Life of Edmund Calamy*, 1830.

Carleton = *Memoirs of Captain Carleton*, 1929, ed. by C. H. Hartmann (see his Introduction on the question of authenticity).

Carstares Letters = *State Papers and Letters addressed to William Carstares*, 1774.

Chambers = W. and R. Chambers, *Domestic Annals of Scotland*, 1861.

Clerk (Rox.) = *Memoirs of Sir John Clerk of Penicuik* (*Roxburghe Club*, 1895).

Colonie = de la Colonie. *Chronicles of an old Campaigner 1692–1717* (1904).

Conduct = *Account of the Conduct of the Duchess of Marlborough* (by herself), 1742.

Corbett = Julian Corbett. *England in the Mediterranean*, ed. 1917.

Cowper = *Private Diary of William, 1st Earl Cowper* (Rox. 1833).

Coxe = Archdeacon Coxe, *Memoirs of Marlborough* (page references are to the ed. of 1818).

Crossrigg = *Diary of proceedings of Parl. and P.C. of Scotland, 1700–1707,* by Sir David Hume of Crossrigg, 1828 (Bannatyne Club).

C.S.P. = *Calendar of State Papers* (*Dom.* = Domestic ; *Am.* = *America and West Indies* ; *Tr.* = *Treasury,* 1702–1707).

Culloden = *Culloden Papers,* 1815.

Cunningham = Cunningham, *Growth of English Industry and Commerce,* ed. 1903.

Defoe = Defoe's *Tour through Great Britain,* ed. 1 ; reprint by G. D. H. Cole, 1927.

Defoe, Union = Daniel Defoe, *History of the Union between England and Scotland,* ed. 1786.

Dicey and Rait = *Thoughts on the Scottish Union.* Late A. V. Dicey and Prof. Rait.

Dispatches = *Marlborough's Dispatches,* ed. by Sir G. Murray, 1845.

Dowell = St. Dowell. *History of Taxation in England,* ed. 1884.

Drake, Mems. = *Memoirs of Capt. Peter Drake* (Dublin, 1755).

Dunbar = C. D. Dunbar, *Social Life in former days* (Scotland), 1865–1866, 2 vols.

E.H.R. = *English Historical Review.*

Edgar = Rev. Andrew Edgar, *Old Church Life in Scotland* ; I = 1st series, 1885 ; II = 2nd series, 1886.

Feiling = Keith Feiling, *History of the Tory Party,* 1924.

Feldzüge = *Feldzüge des Prinzen Eugen,* Wien, 1879, Serie I.

Fortescue = Sir John Fortescue, *Hist. of the Br. Army,* I, 1899.

Foulis = *Foulis of Ravelstone's account book, 1671–1707* (Sc. Hist. Soc., 1904).

Freind = *An account of the Earl of Peterborough's conduct in Spain* (Anonymous, but by Dr. John Freind), 1707.

Galway = *The Earl of Galway's Conduct in Spain and Portugal,* 1711.

Geikie = *The Dutch Barrier,* by R. Geikie and Mrs. Montgomery, 1930.

Geyl = *Nederland's Staatkunde in de Spaansche Successieoorlog,* Prof. Geyl, 1929.

Goslinga = *Mémoires de Sicco van Goslinga,* 1857.

Graham = H. G. Graham, *Social Life of Scotland in the Eighteenth Century,* 1899.

Hervey, L. B. = *Letter-Books of John Hervey, first Earl of Bristol,* 1894.

Hill = *Diplomatic Correspondence of Richard Hill,* 1845.

H.M.C. = *Historical MSS. Commission* (e.g. *H.M.C. Marchmont and Seafield* = *Historical MSS. Commission,* 1894, *14th Report, Part III, Marchmont and Seafield MSS.*). R. 5 = *Report 5,* and so forth.

H.C.J. = *House of Commons Journals.*

H.L.J. = *House of Lords Journals.*

H. of L. MSS. = *MSS. of House of Lords,* printed under authority of the *H.M.C.*

Hooke, 1760 = *Secret History of Col. Hooke's negotiations, written by himself,* 1760.

Hooke (Rox.) = *Correspondence of Col. N. Hooke* (Roxburghe Club), 1870.

Hume Brown, Scotland = P. Hume Brown, *History of Scotland,* 1909.

Hume Brown, Union = Hume Brown, *The Union of England and Scotland,* 1914.

Jerviswood = *Correspondence of Baillie of Jerviswood* (Bannatyne Club), 1842.

Kemble = *State Papers.* Edited by John Kemble, 1857.

Ker = *Memoirs of John Ker of Kersland,* ed. 1727.

Kirke = Thomas Kirke, *A Modern Account of Scotland written from thence by an English Gentleman,* 1679.

Klopp = Onno Klopp, *Fall des Hauses Stuart,* Wien, 1875–1888.

Künzel = Heinrich Künzel, *Das Leben des Landgrafen Georg von Hesse-Darmstadt*, 1859.
Leadam = *Longmans' Political History*, Vol. IX, by J. S. Leadam.
Leake = *Life of Sir John Leake* (Navy Records Soc., 1920).
Lediard, N. H. = Thomas Lediard, *Naval History*, 1735.
Lediard, Marl. = Thomas Lediard, *Life of Marlborough*, 1736.
Legrelle = A. Legrelle, *La diplomatie française et la succession d'espagne*.
Lockhart = *The Lockhart Papers* (ed. 1817).
Luttrell = Narcissus Luttrell, *Brief relation of State Affairs*, ed. 1857.
Mackinnon = James Mackinnon, *The Union of England and Scotland*, 1907.
Macky, Scotland = *A Journey through Scotland*, John Macky, 2nd ed., 1732.
Macpherson = James Macpherson, *Original Papers*, 1775.
Marchmont = *Papers of the Earls of Marchmont*, 1831.
Martin = *Life of Capt. Stephen Martin* (Navy Records Soc., 1895).
Mathieson = *Scotland and the Union*, William Law Mathieson, 1905.
Miller = O. B. Miller, *Robert Harley, Earl of Oxford* (Stanhope Essay, 1925).
Millner = John Millner, *Journal of Marches, etc.*, 1733.
More Culloden = *More Culloden Papers*, edited by Duncan Warrand.
Morer = Thomas Morer, *Short Account of Scotland*, 1702.
Noailles = *Mémoires politiques et militaires*. Duc de Noailles, ed. 1777.
P. to St. = *Letters of Peterborough to Stanhope in Spain* (from the originals at Chevening ; not published and only 50 copies printed), 1834. Most of these letters are reprinted as an appendix to Vol. II of Col. Frank Russell's *Peterborough*, 1887.
Parker = Capt. Robert Parker's *Memoirs*, 1746.
Parl. Hist. = Cobbett's *Parliamentary History*, Vol. VI.
Parnell = Col. Arthur Parnell, *The War of the Succession in Spain*, ed. 1905.
Pelet = General Pelet, *Mémoires militaires relatifs à la succession d'espagne* (the French official military correspondence of the period), 1835.
Priv. Corr. = *Private Correspondence of the Duchess of Marlborough*, 1838.
R.H.S. = *Royal Historical Society* publications.
Rox. = *Roxburghe Club* publications.
Remembrance = *The Remembrance*. A metrical record of the Flemish campaigns by a Scottish private soldier, *Scots Brigade in the service of the United Netherlands*, Vol. III, 1901.
Ridpath = *Proceedings of the Parliament of Scotland*, 1703, printed in 1704. By George Ridpath.
Rogers = Charles Rogers, *Social Life in Scotland*, 1884.
Rosebery Pamphlets = Collection of pamphlets, formerly belonging to Lord Rosebery, now in the National Library, Edinburgh.
Russell = Col. Frank Russell, *The Earl of Peterborough*, 1887.
Salomon = F. Salomon, *Geschichte des letzten Ministeriums Königin Annas*, 1894.
Scot. and Scot. = *Scotland and Scotsmen in the Eighteenth Century*. Ed. by Alexander Allardyce, from the MSS. of John Ramsay of Ochtertyre, 1888.
Seafield 1912 = *Seafield Correspondence 1685–1708*, Scottish Hist. Soc., 1912.
Seafield 1915 = *Letters relating to Scotland by Seafield and others*, Scot. Hist. Soc., 1915.
Somerville = Thomas Somerville, *My own Life and Times, 1741–1814* (1861).
Somerville, Q. Anne = Thomas Somerville, *History of Great Britain during the Reign of Queen Anne*, 1798.
Stebbing = William Stebbing, *Peterborough* (*Eng. men of action series*), 1906.
Swift, Letters = *Correspondence of Jonathan Swift*, edited by F. Elrington Ball, 1910.
Sykes' Gibson = *Edmund Gibson, Bishop of London*, by Rev. Norman Sykes, 1926.

Taylor = C. W. Taylor, *The Wars of Marlborough*, 1921.
Taylor, Jos. = *A Journey to Edinburgh in* 1705, by Joseph Taylor, ed. 1903.
Terry, Chev. = *The Chevalier de St. George*, C. S. Terry, 1915.
Tessé Mém. = *Mémoires et lettres du Maréchal de Tessé*, 1806.
Tessé Lettres = *Lettres du Maréchal de Tessé*, 1888.
Tindal = Tindal's continuation of Rapin's *History of England*, ed. 1744.
Turberville = A. S. Turberville, *House of Lords in the Eighteenth Century*, 1927.
Vernon = *Letters addressed to the Duke of Shrewsbury by James Vernon*, ed. 1841.
Wodrow Corr. = *Correspondence of the Rev. Robert Wodrow*, 1842.
Wodrow Anal. = *Analecta*, by the Rev. Robert Wodrow (*Maitland Club*, 1842–1843).

NOTES

CHAPTER I

[1] P. 1. *H.M.C. Downshire* (1924), p. 841.
[2] P. 2. *Coxe*, Chap. XXX, i. p. 339, ed. 1818.
[3] P. 3. *H.M.C. Coke* (1889), p. 52. For the so-called ' four-shilling land tax ' see my *Blenheim*, pp. 292–293. For the big farmers' dislike of a ' swinging crop ' and consequent low price of corn, see Vanburgh's letter of July 3, 1703, Dobree and Webb's *Vanburgh*, IV, p. 8.
[4] P. 4. *Feiling*, p. 375 ; *Vernon*, III, pp. 267–270 ; *H.M.C. Portland*, IV, pp. 146–149.
[5] P. 6. *Coxe*, Chap. XXX, i., pp. 343–346 ; *H.M.C. Portland*, II, pp. x–xi, 184–190 ; IV, p. 150 ; Miller, pp. 12–13.
[6] P. 6. Boyer's *Queen Anne*, ed. 1735, p. 177, note (a) ; *Coxe's Walpole*, II, p. 5 ; *H.M.C. Lonsdale*, p. 118.
[7] P. 7. *Memorial of the Church of England*, 1705, p. 5 ; *H.M.C. Bath*, I, pp. 63, 76.
[8] P. 8. *B.M. Lansdowne MSS.* 825, ff. 120–121 ; *Coxe*, Chap. XXX, i. p. 341 ; for Marlborough's letter of May 1705, quoted, see *H.M.C. Buccleugh*, I (1899), p. 354.
[9] P. 11. *Coxe*, Chaps. XXX, XXXI ; *H.M.C. Portland*, II, p. 62 ; IV, pp. 150–151, 157 ; *H.C.J.*, XIV, p. 501 ; *Life of Archbishop Sharp*, I, pp. 403–449 ; *Abbey*, I, pp. 105–106 ; *P.R.O.* (S.P.), 84, 224, ff. 5, 32, 448–452 ; (S.P.) 90. 1 and 90. 3 *passim* ; *Add. MSS.* (*St.*), 7061, ff. 121, 141 ; 7070, f. 153 ; 7073, ff. 164, 166 ; Hill, I, pp. 466–480.
[10] P. 13. *H.L.J.*, XVII, pp. 567, 579 ; Burnet, V, 183 (405) ; Boyer's *Queen Anne*, ed. 1735, p. 165.
[11] P. 14. *H.L.J.*, XVII, pp. 574–575 ; *H. of L. MSS.* (1704–1706), pp. xix–xx and no. 2029.
[12] P. 16. *Feiling*, pp. 376–377 ; *Parl. Hist.*, VI, pp. 359–367 ; *H.C.J.*, XIV, p. 437 ; *Coxe*, Chap. XXXII, i. p. 361 ; *H.M.C. Bagot*, p. 338 and *H.M.C. Bath*, I, p. 64, for the Fountain Tavern meetings ; Burnet, V, pp. 176–178, 183 (401–405) ; on Tackers and Sneakers, see *Poems on State Affairs*, IV (1707), pp. 1–5, and *B.M. Stowe MSS.*, 354, f. 161 ; *Somers Tracts*, XII, pp. 469–486.
As to the suggestion that Harley secretly prompted the Tack in order to discredit the High Tories (*Parl. Hist.*, VI, p. 359), I agree with *Feiling*, p. 376, that no proof exists of it and that it is inherently improbable. It is true that Defoe, with characteristic over-ingenuity, wrote to Harley on Nov. 2 that it would be a

good thing to ' blacken and expose ' the High Tories by ' bringing an Occasional Bill upon the anvil,' ' by trusty hands,' and ' blast it at last ' (*H.M.C. Portland*, IV, p. 148). What Harley thought of this sufficiently macchiavellian proposal we do not know, but not even Defoe had suggested that the Tack should be proposed. Moreover, the letter of Godolphin to Harley on Nov. 16 (*H.M.C. Bath*, I, p. 64) shows the reasons why the Triumvirate were annoyed that either Bill or Tack had been brought forward in the House of Commons at all.

[13] P. 17. *H.M.C. Portland*, IV, p. 152.

[14] P. 18. *Burnet*, V, pp. 179 and 220, Darmouth's notes ; *Vernon*, III, pp. 279–280 ; *H.M.C. Portland*, IV, p. 154 ; *Bod. MSS., Ballard* 7, Dec. 23, 1704, Smalridge's letter on Tory decline in the House of Commons.

[15] P. 19. Pamphlets on the subject of Place Bills in Trin. Coll. Library Cambridge (I. 3. 21). See *Blenheim*, p. 275 ; *Burnet*, V, p. 196 (412) ; *H.C.J.*, XIV, pp. 489, 499 ; *Vernon*, III, p. 275.

[16] P. 19. *H. of L. MSS.* (1704–1706), pp. vii–xiv, 383–387. By 1710 the Navy debt had grown to four millions and a half, and had ' much affected the credit of the Navy,' see the report of the Commissioners of the Treasury in *B.M. Lansdowne MSS.* 829, f. 128.

[17] P. 21. *Burnet*, V, p. 192 (Onslow's note), 224 (429) ; *Blenheim*, p. 211, Sir John Guise's statement.

[18] P. 21. *Parl. Hist.*, VI, pp. 255–257.

[19] P. 25. *H. of L. MSS.* (1702–1704), pp. xxvi, 259–262 ; (1704–1706), pp. xxi–xxii ; *Parl. Hist.*, VI, and *State Trials*, XIV, sub loc. ; *H.L.J.*, XVII, pp. 676 *et seq.* ; *H.C.J.*, XIV, pp. 443–445, 569–576 ; *Turberville*, pp. 58–71 ; *Wharton, Life* (1715), pp. 44, 50–55 ; Pickthorn, K., *Some Historical Principles of the Constitution*, pp. 126–127 ; Holdsworth, *Hist. of Engl. Law*, VI, pp. 271–272 ; Amos, M., *English Constitution*, p. 25 note ; *Add. MSS. (L'H.)* 17677 *AAA*, ff. 161–165 ; *Burnet*, V, pp. 112–116, 187–192 (367, 408) ; Sir Humphry Mackworth *Vindication of Right of Commons of England* (1704), pamphlet.

[20] P. 26. *Add. MSS.* 4743, f. 32 ; *H.M.C. Coke* (1889), pp. 54–55.

[21] P. 26. *Add. MSS. (L'H.)* 17677 *AAA*, ff. 210–212, 233, 271 ; *Feiling*, pp. 377–378 ; *Coxe*, Chap. XXXIII.

[22] P. 27. *Verney Letters* 18th *cent.*, I, pp. 241–242. This volume and the *H.M.C. Coke* (1889) give an instructive picture of the relation of the ordinary life of quiet country gentlemen to party and politics.

[23] P. 28. *H.C.J.*, XV, pp. 276–278 ; *H.M.C. Portland*, IV, pp. 187–190, 213, 320 ; Foxcroft's *Burnet*, pp. 417–419 ; *Add. MSS. (L'H.)* 17677 *AAA*, ff. 310–311 ; *H.M.C. Ailesbury* (1898), pp. xiii, 190 ; *Return of M.P.s Blue Book* (1878) ; Hearne's *Collections*, I, p. 117 ; *Rehearsal* and *Observator*, passim, May–June 1705.

[24] P. 29. Monk's *Bentley* (1833), I, pp. 183–184 ; *Parl. Hist.*, VI, p. 496 ; Brewster's *Newton* (ed. 1855), II, pp. 215–218 ; *H.M.C. Portland*, IV, pp. 188–189.

[25] P. 30. *E.H.R.*, April 1930, Mr. Norman Sykes' remarkable article ; *Portland*, IV, p. 177 ; *Burnet*, V, pp. 185–186 (406–407) ; *H.M.C. Portland*, IV, p. 214.

[26] P. 31. *Add. MSS. (L'H.)* 17677 *AAA*, ff. 322–323 ; *H.M.C. Portland*, IV, pp. 248, 291 ; for number of Tackers returned, *cf.* list of Tackers in *Parl. Hist.*, VI, p. 362, and *Return of M.P.s (Blue Book)*, Pt. II for 1705. *Stowe MSS. (B.M.)*, 354, f. 161*b*, give another curious analysis of the New Parliament, on a ' confessional ' basis.

[27] P. 32. *Coxe*, Chap. XXXII, pp. 373–375, and Chap. XL, pp. 482–484 ; *Burnet*, V, pp. 219–220 (426) ; Campbell's *Chancellors, Cowper*, Chap. CXIV ; *Add. MSS.* 28070, ff. 12–13 for the Queen's letter of July 11.

CHAPTER II

[28] P. 35. *Künzel*, pp. 465–466, 469–470, 516, 524–525, 553–554 ; *Parnell*, pp. 79–86 and notes ; *Wentworth Papers* (1883), p. 40 ; *Corbett*, II, pp. 536–537 ; *Leake*, I, pp. 228–229.

[29] P. 37. *Tessé, Mem.*, II, p. 147 ; *Leake*, I, pp. 195–197, 215 and *passim* ; *Künzel*, pp. 502–503. *Corbett*, Chap. XXXII ; *B.M. Add. MSS.* 5440–5441, correspondence of Methuen, Hesse and Leake ; 5441, f. 26, after final relief of Gibraltar, Hesse writes to Leake : 'it is only to you the public owes and will owe the many great and happy consequences of it.'

[30] P. 43. Berwick, *Mémoires, sub* 1704–1705 ; *Tessé, Mem.*, II, pp. 136–138, 154–156 ; *Tessé, Lettres*, pp. 219–238 ; *Noailles*, III, pp. 251–253, 269–275. For the Princess des Ursins, the two good and recent books are those by Madame Taillandier and Miss Maud Cruttwell.

[31] P. 47. For the siege of Gibraltar see *Corbett*, Chap. XXXII, and *Leake*, Vol. I. See also Hesse's correspondence in *Künzel*, and Tesse's in *Add. MSS.* 9773, ff. 140–143 ; 9774, ff. 60–61, 72, 88, 109, 147, 155, 186, 204, 214, 246 ; and in *Tessé, Mem.* and *Lettres* ; and Shrimpton's correspondence in *Add. MSS.* 9115, ff. 14–16 ; *P.R.O.* (S.P.), 89, 18, ff. 165, 171–182, 239, Hesse, etc. ; *Add. MSS.* 5442, f. 90, 92–94 ; 5441, ff. 1–38 on Methuen's part ; 28916, ff. 149, 169 ; *Fortescue*, I, pp. 446–450 ; *H.M.C. Portland*, IV, pp. 149–150, a letter by an English engineer, perhaps Captain Bennet ; *Galway*, pp. 4–5 ; *H.M.C. Chequers* (1900). pp. 177–179 ; Allister Macmillan, *Malta and Gibraltar* (1915), pp. 429–430 ; Drinkwater's *Gibraltar* (1790), pp. 9–14 ; Sayer's *History of Gibraltar*, pp. 130–139 ; *Parnell*, Chap. X ; Berwick's *Mémoires, sub* 1704–1705 ; *Burchett*, Bk. V, Chap. XVII ; *Noailles*, III, pp. 252–253, 270–277 ; De Ayala, *Hist. of Gib.*, translated by Bell, 1845, pp. 149–155 ; Monti, *Historia de Gibraltar*, pp. 93–102, 192 ; Montero, *ditto*, pp. 290–291. Monti contains much valuable detail on the Spanish side, but is unfair to the French and badly confuses the date of Susarte's escalade of the precipice.

I have also had the advantage (in 1928) of going over the ground carefully under the guidance of Lt. (now Captain) E. G. M. Goodwin, and of discussion with Col. Goldney at the Engineers' House, Gibraltar. Both of them were most kind and helpful to me. The map on p. 40, above, has been constructed from observations then made, off a large-scale eighteenth-century map in the Engineers' House, Gibraltar, of which Col. Goldney most kindly had a tracing made for me, and off Col. Harcourt's contemporary plan of Gibraltar, 1705 (*Fortescue*, I, p. 450) ; also from the contemporary maps of this first siege reproduced in *Leake*, I, p. 232, and *Fortescue*, I, p. 450. The map in *Tindal*, III, p. 664, gives a totally wrong impression, for 1704–1705, of the size of the inundation and the situation of the enemy trenches, because it refers to the later siege of 1727, and was only drawn in 1738.

CHAPTER III

[32] P. 49. *H.M.C. Coke* (1889), p. 51.

[33] P. 49. *Dispatches*, II, p. 5 ; *Portland*, IV, p. 186.

[34] P. 50. *Coxe*, Chap. XXIX, i. pp. 330–336 ; *Atkinson*, pp. 241–243 ; *Taylor*, I, pp. 246–251 ; *Parker*, p. 98 ; *Dispatches*, I, p. 518 ; *Pelet*, IV, pp. 648–673.

[35] P. 51. *H.M.C. Portland*, IV, pp. 186–187 ; *Add. MSS. (St.)* 7059, ff. 65, 67, 69–70 ; *Coxe*, Chap. XXXIII.

³⁶ P. 52.   *Coxe, Taylor* and *Atkinson, sub loc.*; *Lediard, Marl.*, I, pp. 480–489; *Pelet*, V, pp. 383–480; *Villars Mémoires, sub ann.* 1705; *H.M.C. Portland*, IV, p. 250.

³⁷ P. 55.   *Coxe, Taylor* and *Atkinson, sub loc.*; Millner, pp. 155–158; *Lediard, Marl.*, I, pp. 492–503; *Parker*, pp. 103–106; *E.H.R.*, April 1904, pp. 311–314 (Orkney); *H.M.C. Hare* (1895), pp. 201–203; *Blackader*, p. 254; *Pelet*, V, pp. 52–58, 574–586; *H.M.C. Portland*, IV, pp. 251–253 (Major Cranstoun on the happenings in Tirlemont).   See also *The Cavalry Journal*, July 1931, Major Stacke's article on Elixem, especially for Bavarian uniforms.

³⁸ P. 57.   *Taylor* and *Atkinson, passim.*   *Coxe*, Chaps. XXXVII–XXXVIII; Marlborough's *Letters to Heinsius*, Appendix, p. 409, above; *H.M.C. Downshire*, I, 2 (1924), pp. 841–842; *H.M.C. Hare*, p. 205; *H.M.C. Coke* (1889), p. 64; *Lediard, Marl.*, I, pp. 511–522; *H.M.C. Portland*, IV, 230, 237, 253–255.   For popular feeling in Holland see *H.M.C. Buccleugh*, II, 2 (Shrewsbury, 1903), pp. 710, 796; *Coxe*, I, p. 445 (Marlborough's letter of Aug. 31); *Priv. Corr.*, I, p. 11.

³⁹ P. 57.   *Pelet*, V, pp. 75, 90, 608.

⁴⁰ P. 60.   *Coxe*, Chap. XLI; *Geyl*, pp. 8–10; Marlborough to Heinsius, Nov. 14, 1705, *Rijks-archief MSS.*; *Atkinson*, pp. 275–280.

CHAPTER IV

⁴¹ P. 64 note.   *P.R.O.* (S.P.) 89, 19, no. 41 Milner to Hedges after Methuen's death in 1706, a criticism of Methuen; *Add. MSS.* 28916, ff. 208, 213, 220–228; 9115, ff. 1–3; *Galway*, pp. 5–27; *P.R.O.* (S.P.) 89, 18, ff. 239–240, 331, for Methuen's own views of the Portuguese army; *Parnell*, Chap. XI.

⁴² P. 66.   *Add. MSS.* (*Coxe*) 9097, f. 1, letter of Sept. 3, 1706.

⁴³ P. 67.   *Burchett*, pp. 684–686; *Galway*, pp. 15–16; *Leake*, I, pp. 273–280; *Künzel*, pp. 571–577; *B.M. Stowe MSS.* 471 (*Richards Papers*, Vol. XXV), pp. 12–13; *cf.* also *Parnell, Russell, Ballard, Stebbing, Carleton, sub loc.*

⁴⁴ P. 70.   *Leake*, I, pp. 280–287; *P.R.O.* (S.P.) 94, 75; *Künzel*, pp. 656–666; *Add. MSS.* 8056, f. 323; Richards' narrative in *B.M. Stowe MSS.* 471, pp. 13–15; *cf. Parnell* and the other secondary authorities.

⁴⁵ P. 70.   *Künzel*, pp. 656–658; the date of the letter given is clearly an error.

⁴⁶ P. 76.   As regards the capture of Monjuic, I have given in the *Cambridge Historical Journal* for 1931 my reasons for preferring Richards' evidence, as both unbiassed and first-hand, over that either of the seamen on one hand, or of Carleton on the other.   I have printed in the Appendix to Chap. IV, pp. 79–80, above, the most important part of Richards' narrative, from the *B.M. Stowe MSS.* 467 (diary) and 471 (narrative).

The other authorities for the taking of Monjuic and Barcelona are: *Leake*, I, Chap. IX, *Martin*, pp. 82–84, both prejudiced against Peterborough but safe for the action of the fleet; *Künzel*, p. 666, for Charles III's letter.   Künzel's narrative is too much based on *Carleton*, who should be read but distrusted (on the authenticity but limited value of *Carleton*, see review in *History*, July 1930); *P. to St.*, p. 5, on Major du Terme; some documents printed in *Russell*, Chap VIII.   *Add. MSS.* 28056, ff. 329, 373; 5442, ff. 102–108; *P.R.O.* (S.P.) 94, 75, the letter of Charles III to Queen Anne; *Burnet*, V, pp. 209–215 [420–422] for some evidence of Stanhope at second-hand, and I am sure incorrect in detail. *Freind* is valueless except for the documents, which can be found elsewhere now See also the second-hand narratives in *Parnell, Stebbing, Russell, Ballard* and B. Williams' *Stanhope.*

CHAPTER V

[47] P. 84. Campbell's *Chancellors*, IV, pp. 296–300 ; *Cowper*, p. 30 ; *Burnet*, V, pp. 243–244.

[48] P. 84. *Cowper*, pp. 15–16, 25, 33, 36, 39 ; *H.M.C. Bath*, I, pp. vii, 72–73.

[49] P. 86. *Coxe*, Chap. XLII, i. p. 515 ; Nichols' *Lit. Anecdotes*, I, p. 134 ; *Cowper*, pp. 35–36, 39 ; *London Gazette* Nov. 18, 1706 ; *Luttrell*, VI, pp. 36, 57, 107.

[50] P. 86. *H.M.C. Portland*, IV, p. 268 ; *Coxe*, Chap. XL, i. p. 485 ; *Add. MSS.* (*L'H.*) 17677 *AAA*, pp. 487–489, 496–498 ; *Hearne's Collections*, I, p. 59 ; *Parl. Hist.*, VI, p. 460 ; *Burnet*, V, p. 223 [428] ; Oldmixon, *Hist. of England*, 1735, p. 345 ; *Remarkes in the Grand Tour of France and Italy, performed by a person of quality in 1691*, 2nd ed. 1705.

[51] P. 87. On the Cabinet, Godolphin and the Queen's Speech, see *H.M.C. Bath*, I, pp. 65, 78–79, and E. R. Turner, *Cabinet Council of England*, I, pp. 456–457 ; *Parl. Hist.*, VI, pp. 451–454 ; *Coxe*, Chap. XL, i. p. 490 ; Newspapers in *B.M.*, *passim*, e.g. *Review*, no. 116, Dec. 1705 ; *Flying Post*, March 20, 1705 ; *Rehearsal*, *passim*, e.g. no. 28 ; *Add. MSS.* (*L'H.*) 17677 *AAA*, ff. 513–514.

[52] P. 88. *H.C.J.*, XV, pp. 37–39 ; *Burnet*, V, p. 224 (429) ; *Add. MSS.* (*L'H.*) 17677 *AAA*, ff. 531–532, 550–551 ; *Add. MSS.* 4743, f. 50.

[53] P. 90. *Cowper*, p. 17 ; *Burnet*, V, pp. 238–239 (436) ; *Add. MSS.* (*L'H.*), 17677 *AAA*, ff. 521–524, 529–533, 551–552, 571–574 ; *The D . . . Deputies, A Satyr* 1705 (*Rosebery pamphlets, Edin.*).

[54] P. 91. *H.M.C. Atholl R.* 12, Pt. 8 (1891), p. 63.

[55] P. 91. *Correspondence of Clarendon and Rochester* (1828), II, pp. 459–460 ; A. W. Ward's *Electress Sophia*, p. 382 ; *Burnet*, V, p. 233 (Onslow's note).

[56] P. 93. *Burnet*, V, pp. 225–229 and notes by Dartmouth and others ; *Conduct*, pp. 150–160 ; *Add. MSS.* (*L'H.*) 17677 *AAA*, ff. 521–524, 529–533, 571, 582 ; *Cowper*, p. 15 ; *J.H.L.*, XVIII, p. 19.

[57] P. 94. *Parl. Hist.*, VI, pp. 519–532 ; *Burnet*, V, pp. 228–235 (432–434) and notes ; *Ward*, Electress Sophia, pp. 379–394 ; *Add. MSS.* (*L'H.*) 17677 *AAA*, f. 582 ; *H. of L. MSS.* (1704–1706), pp. 321–328 ; *Klopp*, XII, pp. 5–19 ; *Life of Archbp. Sharp* (1825), I, pp. 307–311.

[58] P. 97. *H.C.J.*, XV, pp. 132–133, 153 and *passim* ; *H.L.J.*, XVIII, pp. 94–96 and *passim* ; *Burnet*, V, pp. 234–235 (434) ; *Add. MSS.* (*L'H.*), 17677 *AAA*, f. 583, *BBB*, ff. 80–81, 95.

[59] P. 99. *P.R.O.* (S.P.) 81, 161, Poley's letters of 1704, *e.g.*, April 4, June 27 ; Ward, *Electress Sophia*, *passim* ; Foxcroft, *Life of Burnet*, pp. 429–430, 458–460 ; *H.M.C. R. 9 Morrison*, p. 468, Halifax' letters ; *H.M.C. Stopford-Sackville* (1904), p. 33 ; Macpherson, *Original Papers*, II, pp. 26–73 ; *Klopp*, XII, pp. 22–32.

[60] P. 99. *Kemble*, p. 451.

CHAPTER VI

[61] P. 103. *Coxe*, Chap. XLIV ; *B.M. Add. MSS.* 7062, ff. 231, 235–243 (Raby from Berlin) ; *Priv. Corr.*, I, pp. 17–22, II, pp. 235–236 ; *Dispatches*, II, pp. 475–485, 510, 514, 521 ; *Klopp*, XII, pp. 73–74 ; *Add. MSS.* 4741, f. 239 on Calcinato ; *Taylor*, I, pp. 366–370 ; *Pelet*, VI, pp. 617–620, the intercepted letter of Count of Maffei, March 5, showing origin of the idea of Marlborough going to Italy.

[62] P. 105. *Dispatches*, II, pp. 517–521 ; *Pelet*, VI, pp. 16–30, 40 ; *Taylor*, I,

pp. 370–373 ; *Coxe*, Chap. XLIV, i. pp. 17–18 ; *St. Simon, Mém.*, Chap. XXII ; *Klopp*, XII, pp. 74–75 ; *B.M. Add. MSS.* 7062, ff. 235–238.

[63] P. 106. *Drake, Mems.*, p. 82, on the three-bore guns ; he was in the French army at Ramillies ; *Burnet*, V, pp. 261–262 (450–451) ; *Colonie*, p. 305 ; *Pelet*, VI, pp. 30–31 ; *Millner*, pp. 170–171 ; *Remembrance*, p. 376 ; *Coxe*, Chap. XLV, ii. p. 30, and Chap. XLVI, ii. p. 37, letter to Godolphin.

[64] P. 110. For the operations on the northern half of the field, see *Pelet*, VI, pp. 33–34 ; *Goslinga*, pp. 4, 19 ; *E.H.R.*, April 1904, p. 315 (Orkney) ; *Millner*, p. 173 ; *Parker*, p. 111 ; *Colonie*, p. 306 ; *Boyer, Annals* (1707 ed.), V, p. 79, reproduced in *Lediard, Marl.*, II, pp. 16–17 ; *H.M.C. Coke*, p. 72 ; cf. *H.M.C. Portland*, IV, p. 310 ; *H.M.C. Bath*, I, pp. 82–83, 96 ; *H.M.C. Hare* (R. 14, pt. 9), p. 211.

[65] P. 111. *Colonie*, pp. 306–316 ; *Pelet*, VI, pp. 31, 35–36, 38 ; Feuquière, *Mémoires* (1741), IV, p. 17 ; *Tindal*, III, pp. 747–748 and map, useful, though in both text and map Taviers is wrongly called Franquenies.

[66] P. 112. *Millner*, p. 172 (for *Javieres* read *Tavieres*, another form of *Taviers*) ; Taylor, I, p. 383 ; *Parker*, p. 112.

[67] P. 113. *H.M.C. Portland*, IV, pp. 310–311 ; *Lediard, Marl.*, II, pp. 17–18 ; *Pelet*, VI, p. 35 ; *H.M.C. Clement (Molesworth)*, pp. 233–234 ; *B.M. Newspapers, passim*, e.g. *Observator* ; *Taylor*, II, pp. 383–384 ; Kane's *Campaigns* (1745), p. 66 ; *Parker*, pp. 110–112 ; *Colonie*, pp. 312–313 ; *Millner*, p. 173 ; *Goslinga*, p. 20 ; *Coxe*, Chap. XLV, i. pp. 30–31 ; *Luttrell's Diary*, VI, p. 49 ; Picture in map in Boyer's *Annals* (ed. 1707), of the Bringfield incident.

[68] P. 114. *H.M.C. Portland*, IV, pp. 309–310 ; *Lediard, Marl.*, II, p. 27 = Boyer, *Annals* (ed. 1707), V, p. 83 ; *Remembrance*, pp. 378–379 ; *Goslinga*, p. 21 ; *Pelet*, VI, p. 36.

[69] P. 116. *Pelet*, VI, pp. 37, 63 ; Boyer (ed. 1707), pp. 81–82, or *Lediard Marl.*, II, pp. 20–21, 38 ; *Millner*, pp. 173–174 ; *Taylor*, I, pp. 384–385, II, pp. 383–387 ; *Goslinga*, pp. 21–22 ; *Drake, Mems.*, p. 83 ; *Tindal*, III, p. 748. *H.M.C., R.* 5, p. 348.

[70] P. 117. *H.M.C. Portland*, IV, p. 311 ; *Lediard, Marl.*, II, p. 19 ; Millner, p. 174 ; *H.M.C., R.* 5, p. 348.

[71] P. 118. *Goslinga*, p. 22 ; *Millner*, p. 174 ; *Parker*, p. 113 ; *E.H.R.*, April 1904, p. 316, Orkney's letter, dated from 'Braunchein,' which cannot be, as the editor says Branchon, near Ramillies, but must be Beauvechain (*alias* Bavechien), west of Tirlemont : see *Taylor*, I, p. 392, and *Dispatches*, II, pp. 521–522.

[72] P. 119. *Drake, Mems.*, p. 84 ; *Pelet*, VI, p. 38 ; *Villars, Mém.*, sub 1706 ; *Lediard, Marl.*, II, p. 29 = *Boyer* (ed. 1707), V, p. 85 ; *Millner*, p. 177 ; *Parker*, p. 114. It will be seen that the losses on both sides were variously computed.

[73] P. 120. *Add. MSS. (L'H.)* 17677 *BBB*, ff. 287, 294 ; *Observator*, May 18–22 ; and English newspapers generally for May ; *Hardwicke State Papers*, II, p. 467 ; *Coxe*, Chap. XLV, ii. pp. 29–30. Marlborough wrote *Bingfield*, but the real name was *Bringfield*, as the tomb in Westminster Abbey and other evidence proves.

CHAPTER VII

[74] P. 123. *Coxe*, Chap. XLVI, ii. pp. 37–40 ; *Blackader*, pp. 280–282 ; *Memoirs of Ailesbury (Rox.)*, II, pp. 602, 604.

[75] P. 126. L. P. Gachard, *Documens inédits concernant l'histoire de la Belgique* (1835), Vol. III, pp. 219–236 ; ditto, *La Belgique sous Charles VI* (1838), I, pp. lxliii–lxliv ; ditto, *Hist. de la Belgique au commencement du 18 siècle* (ed. 1880), Chaps I–IX ; *Dispatches*, II, pp. 529–531 ; *Pelet*, VI, pp. 56–57 ; *Parker*, p. 114 ;

Taylor, I, pp. 392–396 ; *Coxe*, Chap. XLVI ; *H.M.C. Coke*, p. 72, on the entry into Antwerp.

[76] P. 127. *Coxe*, Chap. XLVI ; *Lediard's Marl.*, II, pp. 85–93 ; *Remembrance*, pp. 386–387 ; *Millner*, pp. 181–185. There are good maps of the siege of Ostend in Tindal's *Rapin* (1744), III, p. 749, and in *Description of the Seats of War*, 1707, p. 322.

[77] P. 128. *Parker*, p. 115 ; *Millner*, pp. 185–190 ; *Remembrance*, pp. 387–389 ; *Blackader*, pp. 284–285. There are good maps of the sieges of Menin, Dendermonde and Ath in Tindal's *Rapin* (1744), and in the Atlas of *Pelet*. On the changed attitude of Prussia after Ramillies see *Add. MSS.* 7070, ff. 200, 216, and 7062, f. 243.

[78] P. 128. Richard Cannon, *Historical Records of the Scots Greys* (1837), pp. 40, 50 ; but *Dispatches*, III, p. 105, gives the date of Lord John's death more correctly—Aug. 25, not 15.

[79] P. 129. *Coxe*, Chap. XLVIII, ii. pp. 75–77 ; *Lediard's Marl.*, II, pp. 108–111 ; *H.M.C. Hare*, pp. 212–215 ; *Blackader*, pp. 285–287 ; *Add. MSS.* 37155, f. 158 ; 28057, f. 316.

[80] P. 130. *Pelet*, VI, p. 125 ; *Dispatches*, III, p. 160 ; *Remembrance*, p. 391; *Blackader*, pp. 288–290 ; *Coxe*, Chap. XLVIII, ii. pp. 78–79.

[81] P. 132. *Coxe*, Chap. L, ii. pp. 111–113 ; *Geyl*, pp. 13–15 ; *H.M.C. Bath*, I, p. 105. Marlborough writes, 1706, Oct. 7, N.S., to Harley : ' For the good of Europe I think this war must continue another year.' *Klopp*, XII, pp. 85–87 ; Vreede, *Correspondance Marl. et Heinsius* (1850), pp. xxix–xxxii and *passim*.

[82] P. 137. *Add. MSS.* (*St.*) 7058, ff. 65–66 ; 7075, f. 44 ; 7064, ff. 5, 8, 62 ; 28916, f. 252.

[83] P. 138. *Add. MSS.* (*St.*) 7064, f. 25 ; 7058, f. 62 and *passim* ; *Geikie*, Chap. I and pp. 56–57 on the *Condominium* ; on the sufferings of Belgium after 1706, and the sacrifices of Holland to maintain the war there, see *Geyl*, p. 11 and *passim*, and the Dutch Apology of 1712, *P.R.O.* (S.P.) 87, 4, ff. 202–208, bearing out Ailesbury's words ; *Klopp*, XII, pp. 86–96.

[84] P. 140. *Geikie*, pp. 38–89 (for Harley's double-dealing see p. 82–83 and note.); *Add. MSS.* (*St.*) 7058, ff. 64–66 ; 7064, ff. 25–26, Dec. 1706, for the objections of Marlborough, Halifax and Stepney to the inclusion of Ostend and Dendermonde in the Barrier ; *H.M.C. Bath*, I, pp. 105–107 ; *Dispatches*, III, pp. 166, 168, 194, 223.

[85] P. 141. *Add. MSS.* (*St.*) 7064, ff. 1, 5, 8, 62 ; 7059, ff. 101, 103.

[86] P. 142. *Hill*, II, pp. 695–699 ; *P.R.O. Ven. Transcripts* 112 (Mocenigo), ff. 30–31 ; *P.R.O.* (S.P.), 99, 57, Consul Broughton, Venice, April 30, 1706 ; Horatio Brown, *Studies in Venetian History*, I, pp. 360–364.

[87] P. 144. *Coxe*, Chap. XLIX, i. pp. 82–84 ; *Pelet*, VI, pp. 188–288, 655–685 ; *Feldzüge*, VIII, pp. 240–270 ; Pietro Fea, *L'Assedio di Torino* (1905), *passim* (pp. 164–165 on the Waldensian episode) ; Carutti, *Storia di Vitt. Amedeo*, chap. xvi ; *Add. MSS.* 4741, ff. 241, 243, 245.

CHAPTER VIII

[88] P. 145. *Tessé, Mém.*, II, pp. 210–218 ; *Tessé, Lettres*, pp. 271–272 ; B.M, *Add. MSS.* 9776, ff. 1–175, 250, an important collection of Tessé's letters, Jan.–March 1706 ; *Berwick*, I, p. 196.

[89] P. 147. *Add. MSS.* 28057, ff. 93–94.

[90] P. 150. For the siege and relief of Barcelona in 1706 see *B.M. Add. MSS.* (*Coxe*) 9115, ff. 6–9, 20–31, 74–76 ; *Add. MSS.* 9776, ff. 176–271 (Tessé's letters) ; 5438, ff. 47–55 (Peterborough to Leake) and ff. 70–72 (Charles III to Leake from Barcelona ; *B.M. Stowe* 471, ff. 32–35 (Richards) ; *P.R.O.* (S.P.), 94, 75, Stanhope on

May 9, and 89, 19 Paul Methuen on May 9 ; also Paul Methuen's letter of May 26, printed in Marlborough's *Dispatches*, II, pp. 571–574, note ; *Boyer, Annals* (ed. 1707), V, pp. 114–131 journal of the siege ; *P.R.O. (Tr.)*, 14, 46, letter in French from Barcelona, May 12 ; *Klopp*, XII, pp. 62–71 ; *Tessé, Mém.* II, pp. 215–225 ; *Tessé, Lettres*, pp. 277–280 ; *Leake*, Book II, Chap. XII ; *Kemble*, pp. 443–445 ; *Burchett*, pp. 692–693 ; *Martin*, pp. 94–95 ; *Camden Misc.*, VIII (*Haddock Corr.*), pp. 49–50 ; *H.M.C. Hare* (1895), pp. 209–210 ; *H.M.C. R.* 5 (*Cholmondeley*), p. 348 ; *H.M.C. Chequers*, pp. 192–193 ; *Byng Papers*, I, pp. 99–101 ; *B. Williams' Stanhope*, pp. 45–49 ; *Burton, Anne*, II, pp. 150–152 ; *Freind, Carleton, Parnell, Russell, Stebbing*, etc., *passim*.

⁹¹ P. 154. *P.R.O.* (S.P.), 89, 19, Methuen July 9, and Milner July 27 ; 94, 76, Stanhope's letter of July 24 ; and Peterborough's of Sept. 3 ; *Galway*, pp. 49–54 ; *Berwick*, I, pp. 213, 222 ; *B.M. Add. MSS.* 5438, ff. 66–67, Peterborough to the Admirals ; 9115, ff. 9–10 ; 22200, f. 3 ; *Cruttwell, Des Ursins*, pp. 191–198 ; *Taillandier, Des Ursins*, pp. 125–134.

⁹² P. 156. *B.M. Stowe MSS.* 471, ff. 35–45, Col. John Richards' narrative, most important ; for Peterborough's letters to Leake see *Add. MSS.* 28058, f. 23 ; 5438, ff. 59–68 ; for his correspondence with Stanhope at Charles's court, *P. to St.*, pp. 10–34 ; *P.R.O.* (S.P.), 94, 76, Stanhope's letter of July 24, 1706 ; *H. of L. MSS.* (1706–1708), pp. 470–492, cf. to *Klopp*, XII, pp. 140–146, 543–549. The story told in *Add. MSS.* 9115, ff. 10–11, of the fatal effect of a message from Galway bidding Charles come by Aragon may be true, but needs confirmation ; that was one of Peterborough's statements, see *Add. MSS. (St.)* 22200, ff. 2–3.

⁹³ P. 158. *Berwick*, I, pp. 223–239 ; *H.M.C., R.* 9, II (1884), *Morrison*, p. 468 ; *Add. MSS.* 28057, ff. 194–307 ; 28058, f. 25 ; *Add. MSS. (Coxe)* 9115, ff. 11–13 ; 9097, f. 1 (Marlborough to Godolphin) ; 28058, ff. 23–26 ; *Add. MSS.* 5438, ff. 65–67 (Peterborough to Leake) ; for an example of the letters of complaint by which he had wearied Marlborough, see *Add. MSS.* 34518, f. 45 ; *Leake*, II, Chaps. XIII–XV ; *Parl. Hist.*, VI, pp. 986–988 ; *Galway*, pp. 63–69 ; *Priv. Corr.*, I, p. 24 ; *Coxe*, Chap. XLIX ; *Swift, Conduct of the Allies* ; *Corbett*, II, p. 550 ; *Klopp*, XII, pp. 140–149 ; *B. Williams Stanhope*, pp. 50–52 ; *Kemble*, pp. 452–454 ; *Carleton, Freind, Parnell, Russell, Ballard, passim*.

CHAPTER IX

⁹⁴ P. 166. *Dunbar*, II, pp. 131–137.

⁹⁵ P. 171. *Coxe*, Chap. LI–LII ; *Althorp MSS.* for some unprinted letters of Sarah to the Queen ; *Priv. Corr.*, I, pp. 43–65 ; *Conduct*, pp. 160–173. For Harley's position at this time see *H.M.C. Bath*, I, pp. 109–111 ; *H.M.C. Portland*, II, p. 195 ; *Somerville, Q. Anne*, p. 622–625 ; for Prior, see Wickham Legg's *Matthew Prior*, pp. 128–137.

⁹⁶ P. 173. *Coxe*, Chap. LIII ; *H.C.J.*, XV, pp. 200–219 ; *Parl. Hist.*, VI, pp. 543–552 ; *Burnet*, V, p. 294 (469) ; *Strype's Stow's London* (1720), Book III, p. 173 ; *Add. MSS. (L'H.)* 17677 CCC, f. 111.

CHAPTER X

⁹⁷ P. 175. See Th. A. Fischer's *Scots in Sweden, Scots in Germany* and *Scots in Prussia* ; John Davidson and Gray, *Scottish Staple at Veere* and *Caldwell Papers* (*Maitland Club*), I, p. 177 on Scots in Holland. The literature of Scottish Jacobites in France and Italy is too large for citation. On Scots lawyers at Leyden see *Culloden*, p. viii, and Hill Burton's *Lovat and Forbes*, p. 280.

⁹⁸ P. 175. *Taylor, Jos.*, p. 95.

[99] P. 176. *Calamy*, II, p. 204 ; *Morer*, pp. 2–3, 19 ; *North Eng. and Scotland in 1704* (ed. 1818), pp. 53–54 ; *Kirke*, p. 15.

[100] P. 176. *Taylor, Jos.*, pp. 95–99 ; *Burt*, II, pp. 6–10. Burt made his observations from his residence in the Highlands in George I.'s reign ; I know no English account of travels in the heart of the Highlands in the reign of Anne.

[101] P. 178. *Calamy*, II, pp. 156, 199.

[102] P. 178. My account of the English travel in and attitude to Scotland is taken from so many places I cannot refer to them all. But see *Swift, passim* ; *Hue-and-cry after East India Goods* (1701), pp. 3–5 ; The *Rehearsal, passim* ; *Observator's New Trip to Scotland* (April 24, 1708) ; *Kirke* ; *Taylor* ; *A Description of Scotland and its Inhabitants*, by E. B., 1705 ; *North of England and Scotland in 1704*—journey by an unknown author, published 1818. More friendly are *Morer* and *Calamy*, ii, Chap. vii.

[103] P. 180. The best book on the Scottish Parliament is Rait's *The Parliaments of Scotland* (1924). On the county vote see introduction to Elphinstone Adam's *Political State of Scotland in the Last Century* (1887).

[104] P. 180. For curious evidence on the power of the Nobles see *Scot. and Scot.*, II, pp. 46–49.

[105] P. 182. *Graham (Social Life of Scotland in 18th Century)*, I, pp. 4–5, 16, 195–196. I take this opportunity of recording my debt to that most valuable work ; its fault is that Graham did not verify his references properly, with the result that the pagination in his footnote references is often wrong ; he also sometimes puts into inverted commas what are really paraphrases. See also *Scot. and Scot.*, II, pp. 92–108, and other references too numerous to cite.

[106] P. 182. *Graham*, I, pp. 7–13 ; *Somerville*, pp. 329 note, 331–337, 369 ; *Culloden*, pp. xx–xxi ; *Dunbar*, I, pp. 194–195 ; *Scot. and Scot.*, II, pp. 75–79 ; *Foulis*, p. 327, July 2, 1703.

[107] P. 183. *Dunbar*, I, pp. 42–46 ; *Clerk (Rox.)*, p. 63 ; *Foulis*, pp. xxv–xxvii ; *Seafield Corr. (S.H.R. 1912)*, p. 381 ; *Essays on Ways and Means of Inclosing* (Edin., 1729), p. x.

[108] P. 183. *Scots Kitchen* (Marian McNeill, 1929), p. 20 ; *Fiennes*, p. 171 ; *Scot. and Scot.*, II, p. 68 ; *Chambers*, III, p. 353.

[109] P. 183. *Dunbar*, I, p. 128 ; *Culloden*, Introd. *passim* ; *Scot. and Scot.*, II, p. 73 ; *Graham*, I, pp. 27–28 ; *Burt*, II, pp. 206–207.

[110] P. 184. *Scot. and Scot.*, I, pp. 6–7, II, pp. 52–53, 60 ; *Rogers*, II, pp. 356–359 ; *Graham*, II, pp. 12–14. In *Caldwell Papers* (Maitland Club, 1854), I, pp. 259–272, will be found some very interesting ' remarks on the change of manners in my own time ' by Miss Elizabeth Mure, 1714–1795, on the life of Scottish gentry and gentlewomen. It bears on much that I have written above.

[111] P. 185. *Scot. and Scot.*, II, pp. 57–59 ; *Graham*, I, pp. 21–22 ; Swift, *Essay on Modern Education* ; Defoe, *Compleat Gentleman* (1890), p. 117 ; *Seafield*, 1915, Introd., p. vii ; *Culloden*, p. ix.

[112] P. 186. James Grant, *Hist. of the Burgh Schools of Scotland*, Chap. XIII and *passim* ; *Graham*, II, pp. 149–168 ; Morgan (A. M.), *Rise and Progress of Scottish Education*, Chaps. V and VI ; *Edgar*, II, pp. 63–66, 73–79, 120–121 ; James Campbell, *Balmerino and its Abbey*, ed. 1899, p. 448, inaccurately cited in *Graham*, II, p. 155.

[113] P. 188. *Calamy*, II, pp. 152–153, 157–159, 186, 216–219 ; *Carstares* (R. H. Story), pp. 92–95, 272–280 ; John Watson, *Scot of the Eighteenth Century*, Chap. IV, *Wodrow Corr.*, I, pp. 1–2, and *Seafield*, 1915, p. 21 on Carstares' influence; *Graham*, II, pp. 182–203 ; *Culloden*, p. viii ; *Scot. and Scot.*, I, pp. 225–227, 288 ; *Dunbar*, I, pp. 1–4 ; *Proposals for the Reformation of Schools and Universities*, 1704 ; *Scots Kitchen* (McNeill), pp. 14–15 ; *Morer*, p. 50, bears out *Calamy* (II

219) on Ministers' incomes : 'They have greater equality in their benefices than the C. of E., few exceeding £100 sterling, and as few below £20.'

[114] P. 188. *Bodleian MSS. Carte Papers* 197, pp. 96–103, Memorial by W. Logan of Logan on Scottish feudal jurisdictions, 1707.

[115] P. 189. *Graham*, I, pp. 4–6, 162–166. The *Economic History Review* (Jan. 1931, p. 128) speaks of Graham's 'vivid and gloomy account' of Scottish agriculture at this period as 'so far unchallenged save in minor details and in *obiter dicta.*' *Dunbar*, I, p. 93 ; *Scot. and Scot.*, II, pp. 188–190, 200 ; *Essays on Ways and Means of Enclosing*, 1729, p. vi ; Lindesay's *Interest of Scotland*, 1733, p. 38 ; *Foulis*, p. xi ; *Seafield*, 1912, p. 428.

[116] P. 190. *Graham*, I, pp. 5–7, 16, 169, 195–200 ; *Defoe*, II, pp. 696–698 ; *Scot. and Scot.*, II, pp. 103, 105, 116–121 ; *Barony of Stitchill* (Sc. Hist. Soc.), p. 153 ; *Calamy*, II, p. 182 ; *Morer*, p. 4 ; *Kirke*, p. 3 ; *Ways and Means of Enclosing* (1729), pp. xlvii–xlix ; *Macky, Scotland*, p. 272 ; W. Hamilton Wishaw, *Sheriffdoms of Renfrew and Lanark compiled in 1710*, pp. 52–55, 65, 67, 71, 143.

[117] P. 191. *Agnew*, II, p. 186, 190 ; *Calamy*, II, p. 177 ; *Scot. and Scot.*, II, pp. 201–202 ; *Graham*, I, pp. 180–185; II, p. 16 ; *Burt*, I, pp. 86–89 ; *Morer*, pp. 18–19 ; *Taylor, Jos.*, pp. 134–135 ; *North Eng. and Scot. in 1704*, p. 53 ; *Observator's trip to Scotland* (1708), for the brutality of English contempt for Scottish housing.

[118] P. 192. *Scot. and Scot.*, II, pp. 192–193, 198, 202–203 ; *Rogers*, I, pp. 205–209 ; *Scots Kitchen*, pp. 18–19 ; *Barony of Stitchill*, pp. xvii–xviii ; *Graham*, I, pp. 152–158, 171 ; *Agnew*, II, pp. 184–185 ; Adam Smith, *Wealth of Nations*, Bk. I, Chap. XI, pt. 3.

[119] P. 193. *Graham*, I, pp. 146–152.

[120] P. 194. *Scot. and Scot.*, II, pp. 68–69, 203, 222 ; Guy Miege's *State of Scotland*, 1707, pp. 25–26 ; *Graham*, I, pp. 155, 175–176 ; *Annals of Visc. Stair*, I, pp. 254–255 ; *Morer*, pp. 3, 19 ; *Hooke (Rox.)*, I, p. 426 ; *Agnew*, II, pp. 182–186, 203–204 ; *Defoe*, II, pp. 733–738 ; Adam Smith, *Wealth of Nations*, Bk. I, Chap. XI, pt. 3.

[121] P. 195. *Graham*, Chap. VII ; *Edgar*, II, pp. 3–10, 22, 32–33, 51, 61–62 ; on the English poor law see *Blenheim*, pp. 19–21.

[122] P. 195. Thomas Johnston, *History of the Working-classes in Scotland*, pp. 69–81 ; *New Mills Cloth Manufactory* (Scot. Hist. Soc. 1905), pp. xiv–xv, 37, 264 ; *Graham*, II, pp. 264–267.

CHAPTER XI

[123] P. 196. *Acts Parl. Scot., passim, e.g.* Sept. 1–3, 1703 ; *Defoe*, II, pp. 701, 704, 782–784 ; *Dunbar*, I, pp. 55, 144 ; *Scots Kitchen*, pp. 20–21 ; *Chambers*, III, p. 353 ; article by W. R. Scott in *The Union of 1707* (Glasgow Herald publica. 1907), pp. 93–103 ; *Interest of Scotland considered*, 1733, pp. i–iv and 146–147 ; *New Mills Cloth Factory* (Scot. Hist. Soc. 1905), pp. li–lv, lxxx–lxxxii ; Scottish pamphlets of 1704–5 in National Library, Edinburgh, on badness of trade and on the question of export of raw wool.

[124] P. 197. *Mathieson*, pp. 86–87, 90 ; *Portland*, IV, pp. 70–71 ; *Burnet*, V, p. 95 (357).

[125] P. 197. Denholm's *Glasgow*, ed. 1804, pp. 110–111, gives the population figures, but adds that there may be a defect in the parochial records that show a decline in the population since 1660. But the famine and distress in William's reign might account for it. *Graham*, I, pp. 127–129 (Graham is not as good or as full on trade and industry as he is on agriculture) ; *Glasgow, its origin and development,*

John Gunn, editor, 1921, pp. 8, 40, 43 ; *North Eng. and Scot. in 1704*, pp. 47–49 ; *Defoe*, II, pp. 744–747.

[126] P. 198. *Macky, Scotland*, p. 65. See also the admiration of *Burt* (I, p. 17) for the High Street.

[127] P. 198. *Scot. and Scot.*, II, p. 61 ; *Wodrow Corr.*, I, p. 5. On Dr. Pitcairn and on Hell Fire Clubs see *Graham*, I, pp. 93, 111 ; *Wodrow Anal.*, I, p. 323, III, p. 309.

[128] P. 201. *Defoe*, II, pp. 710–711 ; *Graham*, I, pp. 81–126 ; *Burt*, I, pp. 16–20 ; *Morer*, pp. 70–73 ; *North Eng. and Scot. in 1704*, p. 43 ; *Description of Scotland*, by E. B., 1705, p. 4 ; *Kirke*, p. 6 ; *Taylor, Jos.*, pp. 100–101, 107, 130–131 note, 134–135 ; *Culloden*, p. 27 on the ' babells.'

[129] P. 202. Scottish newspapers in the National Library ; *Edinburgh Periodical Press*, W. J. Couper, 1908, I, pp. 40, 86–98.

[130] P. 203. *Wodrow Corr.*, I, pp. 49–50, 165, 167 ; *Anal.*, p. 344 ; *Scot. and Scot.*, II, pp. 24–25 ; *North Eng. and Scot. in 1704*, pp. 54–55 ; *Graham*, I, p. 161, II, pp. 20–25, 82–83 ; *Morer*, p. 53 ; Alex. Carlyle, *Autobiography*, pp. 4–5 ; *Edgar*, I, pp. 18–20.

[131] P. 204. *Scot. and Scot.*, I, pp. 219–223 ; *Burt*, I, pp. 169, 172 ; *Graham*, II, pp. 8–11 ; Defoe, *Memoirs of the Ch. of Scotland*, 1717 (ed. 1843), p. 105 ; John Watson, *Scot. of the Eighteenth Century*, pp. 138–158.

[132] P. 205. *Graham*, II, pp. 13–14, 18–19, 28, 55–60, 65–66 ; Maitland's *Edinburgh* (1753), p. 282 ; *P.C. Reg. Ed.*, *passim* ; *Edgar*, I, pp. 193–223 ; Arnot's *Trials*, p. 311 ; *Foulis*, pp. xxxiv–xxxv ; Thomas Mair, *Records of the Presbytery of Ellon*, *passim*, e.g., p. 207 ; *Burt*, I, pp. 182–185 ; *Kirke*, pp. 7–8 ; Scott's *Fasti* (1867), I, pt. ii, p. 657 ; Cramond's *Illegitimacy in Banffshire*, p. 9 ; Cramond's *Parish of Ordiquill*, pp. 21–22.

[133] P. 206. *Causes of the Decay of Presbytery in Scotland*, 1713, pp. 3–4 ; *Right of Church members to choose their own overseers*, by James Hogg, minister at Carnock, 1717, and other tracts on patronage ; *Calamy*, II, pp. 153–154, 214 ; Th. Johnston, *Working Classes in Scotland*, p. 87 ; *Wodrow Corr.*, I, p. 15–16 ; *Edgar*, II, pp. 367–369.

[134] P. 207. *Graham*, II, pp. 5–7, 12–14, 48 ; Carstares reckoned the ' episcopal ministers continued in churches under the protection of the law ' at 154 in 1703 (*H.M.C. Portland*, VIII, p. 113), while Defoe reckoned them at 165 in 1707: see Defoe, *Mems. of Ch. of Scotland*, p. 103. The pamphlet, *Presbyterian persecution examined*, 1707, gives the complete list of them, 165 ; Th. Mair, *Presbytery of Ellon* (1898), pp. 240–245 ; *Scot. and Scot.*, II, pp. 51–52 ; *P.C. Reg. Ed.*, *passim*, e.g. April 25, 1704, the assault on the Presbyterian Minister of Dingwall ; *Wodrow Corr.*, I, p. 216 for another such affair ; *Somers Tracts*, XII, pp. 360, 366–367 ; *Add. MSS.* (H.F.) 29588, ff. 496–500, Athol to Nottingham.

[135] P. 208. *P.C. Reg. Ed.*, *passim* ; *P.R.O.* (S.P.) 54, vol. 3, subscriptions for Scottish episcopal clergy collected in England, on appeal of Bp. of Glasgow ; *Life of Archbishop Sharp* (of York), I, pp. 387–388, on Burnet's gift ; *Graham*, II, p. 10 ; Dunlop, *Anent old Edinburgh*, pp. 28–29 *re* the Edinburgh ' baxters ' ; Foxcroft's *Burnet*, pp. 421, 451.

[136] P. 209. *H.M.C. Mar.* (1904), pp. 227, 241 ; *Mathieson*, pp. 190–193 ; *Wodrow Anal.*, I, pp. 13–17 ; Boyer's *Queen Anne* (1735), pp. 27, 54–55 ; Cunningham, *Ch. Hist. of Scotland*, II, pp. 209–210 ; *Hooke* (Rox.), I, pp. 21–22 ; *Lockhart*, I, p. 66 ; the controversy between Sage and Meldrum, *passim* (*Works of Rt. Rev. John Sage*, vol. i, pp. li–lii ; Meldrum's *Sermon against Toleration of Episcopacy*, preached May 16, 1703 ; Sage's *Reasonableness of a Toleration*). It was not till 1712 that Carstares wrote his *Scottish Toleration Argued*, the most nearly reasonable statement of the case against Toleration. See also *H.M.C. 3rd*

Report (Webster), p. 421, Stair's letter of 1703 ; and *5th Report (Erskine)*, p. 638 (37), shows many of the Episcopal clergy will not pray for Queen Anne, as their own champions are forced to allow.

[137] P. 209.   Story's *Carstares*, pp. 274–275 ; *Wodrow Anal.*, I, p. 13 ; *Calamy*, II, p. 153 ; *H.M.C. Marchmont*, p. 153 ; *Mackinnon*, pp. 79–81.

[138] P. 210.   *The Nonconformists' Vindication*, 1700 (Cameronian Tract) ; *Hooke (Rox.)*, II, pp. 308, 371, 477 ; *Ker*, I, pp. 14–16, 28–37, 58–65 ; *H.M.C. Laing*, II (1925), pp. 101–109 and *Clerk (Rox.)* pp. 54–55, for abortive attempts in 1705 to reconcile the Cameronians to the Church.

[139] P. 211.   Arnot's *Edinburgh* (1779), pp. 266–267 ; *Morer*, pp. 118–120 ; *Wodrow Corr., passim*, for General Assemblies from 1709 on ; *Dict. of Nat. Biog.*, *sub* George Meldrum ; Cunningham, *Ch. Hist. of Scot.*, II, p. 210 (ed. 2).

[140] P. 213.   *P.C. Reg.*, June 13 and Oct. 3, 1704 ; *Dunbar*, I, pp. 261–273, and *Chambers*, III, pp. 298–302, are based on *Letter from a gentleman in Fife*, but should be compared with *Just reproof to the false reports* and *Fasti. Ecc. Scot.*, 1925, *sub* Pittenweem on Cowper's conduct.   There are half a dozen pamphlets on both sides in the National Library.   *Graham*, II, pp. 62–65 ; *Burt*, I, pp. 222–226, 265–269 ; Arnot's *Celebrated Trials*, pp. 366–367 ; *History of Galloway*, II, p. 343 note.

[141] P. 214.   *Graham*, I, pp. 187–193 ; *Scot. and Scot.*, Chap. XIV ; *Edgar*, I, pp. 269–270 ; *Wodrow's Anal., passim*, e.g. I, pp. 51–52, 57, 105.

[142] P. 217.   *Scot. and Scot.*, Chaps. XIII, XIV, XV ; *Graham*, I, pp. 184–185, 224–225 ; D. of Argyle, *Scotland as it was and as it is*, 1887, *passim*, e.g. I, pp. 217–221, II, pp. 1–79 ; *Defoe*, II, pp. 838–839 on Highlanders in ' Irish ' regiments in French service ; *Home Life of the Highlanders, 1400–1746*, Maclehose, 1911, *passim*, especially on the music, poetry and superstition.   *Burt*, I, pp. 45–49 and vol. ii, *passim*.

[143] P. 218.   *H.M.C. Portland*, VIII, pp. 373–374, the report to Harley ; Cunningham, *Ch. Hist. of Scot.*, ed. 2, II, pp. 211–212 ; Wm. Mackay, *Sidelights on Highland History*, 1925, pp. 119–123 ; *Moral Statistics of the Highlands and Islands*, Inverness, 1826, *passim* and pp. 14–17 ; *Wodrow Corr.*, I, pp. 73, 216, *Anal.*, III, p. 357, IV, p. 235.   Many pamphlets and broadsheets in the National Library deal with this movement.   Miss Cunningham's recently published work, *The Loyal Clans* (= the Jacobite clans) contains, as one would expect, much interesting matter ; but I confess that I do not think she has proved that the root of Highland Jacobitism was objection to feudal jurisdictions.

CHAPTER XII

[144] P. 223.   *Mathieson*, p. 71 ; *Ridpath*, p. 319 ; *H.M.C. Marchmont* and *Seafield*, pp. 154–155 ; *Wodrow Anal.*, I, pp. 14, 17 ; examples of excellent Scottish pamphlets in favour of Union, written soon after the Darien experience, are *The Interest of Scotland*, 1700 (anon. by Sir William Seton of Pitmedden), and *Parainesis Pacifica or a persuasive to the union of Britain*, Edinburgh, 1702.   Sir Charles Firth kindly lent me his collection of Union pamphlets.

[145] P. 224.   *H.M.C. Marchmont, Seafield*, p. 199 ; *Macpherson*, I, pp. 601, 606, 628 and *passim*, Q. Anne's reign ; *P.R.O.* (*Tr. France*), 190, ff. 56–57, 73–79 ; *Hooke (Rox.)* and *Ker, passim*.

[146] P. 224.   *Carstares, Letters* (1774), p. 714 ; *Lockhart*, I, p. 43.

[147] P. 225.   *Lockhart*, I, p. 58 ; *Letter from one of the country party to his friend in country*, March 1704.

[148] P. 226.   *Ker*, I, p. 22 ; *Hooke (Rox.)*, I, p. 24 ; *Lockhart*, I, pp. 54–56, 58 and *passim* ; *Macpherson*, I, pp. 623–628, 645.   For Jacobite and French suspicions

of Hamilton's own designs on the throne see Hooke, *Negociations* (ed. 1760), p. 40 ; *Legrelle*, pp. 298–299 and note. See also Hume Brown, *Scotland*, III, p. 81, and *Union*, pp. 27–28, 71 note ; Lord Rosebery, *The Union of England and Scotland*, 1871, is good on Hamilton. Salomon, *Königin Anna*, p. 328, for the Pretender's final belief in his loyalty.

[149] P. 228. *P.C. Reg. Ed.*, letter from members of Sc. P.C. then in London, March 8—division and decision of P.C. at Edinburgh, March 13—May 12, war declared ; *Crossrigg*, pp. 80–82 ; *Mathieson*, pp. 75, 88 ; *Jerviswood*, p. 2 ; *Burnet*, V, pp. 20–23 (320) ; *Dicey and Rait*, pp. 154–157 ; *Letter from a member of Parliament of Scotland to his electors*, 1703, good on the illegality of the Parl. in June 1702.

[150] P. 229. *Dalrymple Memoirs*, 1790, III, Pt. IV, p. 257 ; *Lockhart*, I, p. 276 ; *Mathieson*, p. 75 and note ; *Crossrigg*, p. 83 ; *Acts Parl. Scot.*, p. 5 ; *Marchmont*, III, pp. 240–241 ; *Burnet*, V, pp. 23–24. Burnet, a Scot by birth and upbringing, understands Scottish affairs ; moreover, being a Whig but not a Presbyterian, he is not so complete a party man in Scottish affairs as in English.

[151] P. 229. *Lockhart*, I, pp. 47–51 ; *Acts Parl. Scot.*, pp. 18–28.

[152] P. 230. *Marchmont*, III, pp. 243–250 ; *Acts Parl. Scot.*, p. 28 ; *Carstares*, *Letters*, pp. 714–716 ; *Lockhart*, I, p. 48 ; *Mathieson*, pp. 75–76 ; Hume Brown, *Union*, pp. 39–43 ; *Ker*, I, pp. 21–22 ; *P.R.O.* (S.P.) 54, vol. i, letter of June 30, 1702 ; *Defoe, Union*, pp. 75, 85.

[153] P. 232. For the proceedings of the Commissioners see *P.R.O.* (S.P.) 54 (*Scotland*), vol. ii, also *Defoe, Union*, pp. 728–751 (Appendix) ; Burton, *Anne*, I, pp. 142–148 ; *Mathieson*, pp. 77–79, 114, 117.

[154] P. 233. *P.R.O.* (S.P.) 54, vol. i, Mr. Keith's letter of Aug. 7, 1702, on influences at the coming elections. *Ridpath*, pp. 1–20, 42 ; Boyer, *Queen Anne*, 1735, pp. 52–53 ; *Mathieson*, pp. 79–81 ; Hume Brown, *Scotland*, III, pp. 85–87, *Union*, pp. 50–56 ; *Lockhart*, I, pp. 50–58.

[155] P. 234. For the 'riding of the Parliament,' see *P.C. Reg. Ed.*, Order of May 3, 1703 ; *Acts Parl. Scot.*, pp. 104–107 ; *Lockhart*, I, pp. 57–68 ; *Ridpath*, pp. 28–52 ; *Add. MS.* 29587 (H.F.), f. 146 ; 29588, ff. 496–500 ; *Mathieson*, pp. 81–82 ; *Stair, Annals*, I, pp. 203–208, should be compared to Lockhart's complaints on the question whether the Jacobites first deserted Queensberry, or Queensberry the Jacobites. For Godolphin's views see *Stair, Annals*, I, pp. 380–381, and *H.M.C. Atholl* (1891), p. 61.

[156] P. 235. *Dicey and Rait*, pp. 157–158 ; *Clerk* (Rox.), p. 49 ; *Stowe MSS.* (B.M.) 222, f. 216, intercepted Jacobite letters.

[157] P. 237. *Speeches by a Member of the Parliament which began 6th of May, 1703*, Edin. 1703 (=Fletcher's speeches), pp. 5–9, 39–41, 73 and *passim*. Several of these speeches are also in *Ridpath, q.v., passim* ; *H.M.C. Laing*, II (1925), pp. 25–28 ; *Acts Parl. Scot.*, p. 68 ; *Hooke* (Rox.), I, p. 23 ; *Seafield, 1915*, pp. xviii, 2 ; for Queensberry's and Godolphin's views on accepting the Act of Security see *Add. MSS.* 29589, f. 97.

[158] P. 237. *Macpherson*, I, p. 630.

[159] P. 237. *H.M.C. Annandale* (1897), p. 120.

[160] P. 238. *Add. MSS.* 20311, ff. 38–45 ; 31249, f. 15.

[161] P. 238. *Macpherson*, I, pp. 673, 676.

[162] P. 239. *Macpherson*, I, pp. 629–632, 639–681 ; *Terry, Chev.*, pp. 23–27 ; *Lockhart*, I, pp. 72–73, 79–84 ; *Hooke* (Rox.), I, p. 24, speaks of Atholl as '*Jacobite déclaré*' already in 1704 ; see also *Major Fraser's Manuscript* (1889), I, pp. 142–144 ; for Atholl's correspondence with Godolphin in 1703, and his desire for alliance with Marlborough, see *Add. MSS.* 28055, ff. 25–72, especially f. 39, and *H.M.C. Atholl* (1891), pp. 60–61.

[163] P. 240. *H. of L. MSS.* (1702–1704), pp. 300–308 ; *Turberville,* pp. 46–50 ; *Mackinnon,* Chap. V ; *Tindal,* III, pp. 629–639 ; Boyer, *Queen Anne* (1735), pp. 104–118 ; W. C. Mackenzie's *Simon Fraser* (1908) makes the best of a bad case for Fraser ; it is a valuable study.

[164] P. 240. *Add. MSS.* 31250, f. 46 ; *Macpherson,* I, pp. 641–671.

[165] P. 241. *Lockhart,* I, p. 97 ; *Clerk (Rox.),* p. 48 ; *Marchmont,* III, p. 328.

[166] P. 241. *Clerk (Rox.),* pp. 47–53 ; *Marchmont,* III, pp. 263–267 ; *Lockhart,* I, pp. 92–97 ; Mathieson, pp. 91–96 ; *Burnet,* V, pp. 166–169 [396].

[167] P. 243. *Crossrigg,* pp. 136–151 ; *Acts Parl. Scot.,* pp. 127–137 ; *Lockhart,* I, pp. 98–107 ; *Burnet,* V, pp. 169–174 (397–400) ; *Seafield,* 1912, p. 377 ; *Add. MSS.* 28055, f. 90 ; Hume Brown, *Union of England and Scotland,* pp. 174–183, Johnstone's letters ; *H.M.C. Marchmont and Seafield,* p. 204.

CHAPTER XIII

[168] P. 245. *Jerviswood,* p. 14.

[169] P. 246. *Vernon,* III, pp. 279–280 ; *Jerviswood,* pp. 14–23 ; *Somerville, Q. Anne* (1798), p. 618 ; *Burnet,* V, p. 179 and Dartmouth's note ; Hume Brown, *Union,* pp. 75–78 ; *Turberville,* pp. 78–79 ; *Parl. Hist.,* VI, pp. 369–374; *Boughton MSS.,* letter of Vernon to Shrewsbury, Jan. 10, 1705 ; *Add. MSS.* (*L'H.*) 17677 *AAA,* ff. 513–514, 539, 570–571.

[170] P. 248. *H.M.C. Coke* (1889), p. 53 ; *Ridpath,* pp. 258–260 ; *Acts Parl. Scot.,* p. 137 ; *Hooke (Rox.),* I, p. 159.

[171] P. 249. *Add. MSS.* (*L'H.*) 17677 *AAA,* ff. 63, 69 ; *H.M.C. Marchmont and Seafield,* p. 207 ; *Hooke (Rox.),* I, pp. 166–167, 203–207.

[172] P. 256. G. P. Insh, *The Company of Scotland* (1932) ; Sir R. Temple, *Papers of Thomas Bowrey* (Hakluyt Soc. 1925) and *The Tragedy of the Worcester* (Benn, 1930), especially the latter, *passim* ; *Seafield,* 1915, pp. 17–28 ; *Seafield,* 1912, pp. 386–398 ; *Add. MSS.* 28055, ff. 154–155 (Seafield's letter) ; f. 158 (Roxburgh's) ; *Jerviswood,* pp. 64–75 ; *H.M.C. Bagot* (1885), p. 339 (Hamilton's letter April 8) ; *More Culloden,* II, p. 5 ; *H.M.C. Portland,* VIII, pp. 178–179 ; *H.M.C. Hope Johnstone of Annandale* (1897), p. 121 ; Defoe, *Union,* pp. 80–82 ; *Argyle, Int. Letters,* I, p. 11 ; *Taylor, Jos.,* pp. 121–126 ; *P.C. Reg. Ed.* ; *State Trials,* XIV, pp. 1199–1311. Numerous pamphlets, broadsheets and poems in the Nat. Lib., e.g. *A Pill for Pork Eaters* and *Observations made in England on the trial.*

[173] P. 258. *Argyle, Int. Letters,* I, pp. 1–32 ; *Lockhart,* I, pp. 108–124 ; *Jerviswood,* pp. 70–113 ; *Seafield,* 1912, pp. 395–397 ; *Seafield,* 1915, pp. 16–17, 32–33, 37, 47, 52–64, 76–77, 82–83 ; *Add. MSS.* 28070, f. 10, the Queen on Queensberry ; 28055, ff. 158, 162, 168, 172, 357–362 ; Hume Brown, *Union,* pp. 189–190 (Annandale's letters) ; Mathieson, pp. 105–109 ; *Crossrigg,* pp. 152–164 ; *H.M.C. Johnstone of Annandale* (1897), p. 122 ; *H.M.C. Laing,* II (1925), pp. 114–116, Queen's instructions to Argyle as Commissioner of the Scottish Parliament, June 1705.

[174] P. 261. *Acts Parl. Scot.,* pp. 235–237 ; *Crossrigg,* p. 171 ; *Lockhart,* I, pp. 126–137 ; *Seafield,* 1915, pp. 82–88 ; *H.M.C. Mar and Kellie* (1904), p. 235 ; *H.M.C. Laing,* II, pp. 118–122 ; *Taylor, Jos.,* pp. 112–127 ; *Burnet,* V, p. 221 (427) ; *Clerk (Rox.),* pp. 57–58 ; *Add. MSS.* 28055, ff. 360–363.

[175] P. 261. *H.C.J.,* XV, p. 69 ; *H. of L. MSS.* (1704–1706), pp. 318–319 ; *Marchmont,* III, p. 290 ; *Carstares, Letters* (1774), pp. 738–740, 742 ; *Stair, Annals,* I, p. 210 ; *H.M.C. Mar and Kellie,* pp. 239, 243 ; *Defoe, Union,* p. 92.

[176] P. 263. Hume Brown, *Union,* pp. 108–109 ; Mathieson, pp. 112–113 ; *Marchmont,* III, pp. 288, 293 ; *Lockhart,* I, pp. 136, 152–153 ; *Stair, Annals,* I,

pp. 211–212 ; *Jerviswood*, pp. 144, 147 ; *H.M.C. Mar and Kellie*, pp. 240, 242. *Burnet*, V, pp. 273–274 [458], is quite wrong in saying that the policy had been adopted of naming enemies to government and the Union on to the Commission : the opposite was the case. The full list of the Commissioners, with their attendances and proceedings, will be found in the Appendix to *Acts Parl. Scot.*, XI. For Somers' part, see Hardwicke's note to *Burnet*, V, p. 287.

177 P. 266. *Acts Parl. Scot., Appendix*, pp. 165–166 ; *Carstares, Letters*, pp. 743– 744 ; *Defoe, Union*, pp. 115–120 ; *H.M.C. Mar and Kellie*, p. 271 ; *Lockhart*, pp. 152–156 ; *Clerk (Rox.)*, pp. 59–60.

178 P. 269. *Clerk (Rox.)*, pp. 61–63 ; *H.M.C. Mar and Kellie*, p. 271 ; *Defoe, Union*, pp. 194–196 ; the Union Treaty and the Commissioners' Signatures will be found in *Acts Parl. Scot., Appendix*, pp. 201–205. For the question of Commissioners' attitude to the right of appeal to the House of Lords, see *Dicey and Rait*, pp. 192–193, and *Defoe, Union*, 158–161.

CHAPTER XIV

179 P. 272. *Jerviswood*, p. 177 ; *Mathieson*, pp. 121–123.

180 P. 272. That the Squadrone were honestly persuaded by such arguments as these to support the Union, in spite of their little love for Queensberry's government, emerges from *Jerviswood, passim, e.g.*, 141, 152, 174–177 ; *Marchmont*, III, pp. 328–320 ; *H.M.C. Mar and Kellie*, p. 371 ; *Mathieson*, pp. 125, 129–130 ; *Seafield*, 1915, pp. 99, 101 ; *Burnet*, V, pp. 278–280 (460).

181 P. 274. *Rait, Parliaments of Scotland*, p. 124.

182 P. 275. *Defoe, Union, passim* for speeches, pp. 317–328 for Belhaven's speech and Marchmont's answer ; also *H.M.C. Mar and Kellie*, p. 309 ; for Belhaven's personal appearance, '*Macky's*' (?) *Characters*, p. 135, Roxburghe Club, 1895.

183 P. 276. *Defoe, Union*, pp. 245–246 ; *Mathieson*, p. 132, *cf.* Rait, *Parliaments of Scotland*, p. 121 ; *Burnet*, V, p. 282 [462]. For the division lists throughout this Parliament see *Acts Parl. Scot.*

184 P. 277. *Clerk (Rox.)*, p. 64. Clerk is wrong in thinking Defoe was employed by Godolphin—his employer was Harley, to whom he wrote his reports from Edinburgh, afterwards shown to Godolphin, see *H.M.C. Portland*, IV, pp. 340–341, 352, 374, 382, and *passim* ; see also *Defoe, Union*, pp. 236–241 ; *Crossrigg*, pp. 176, 184 ; *Argyle, Int. Letters*, I, pp. 42–43, 50–52, 58 ; *H.M.C. R. 9 (Morrison)*, p. 469.

185 P. 279. For Hamilton's dealings with the Ministers, see *H.M.C. Mar and Kellie*, p. 278, and *H.M.C. Portland*, IV, p. 347 ; for the ' toothache ' and his other failures see *Lockhart*, I, pp. 200, 212–214, and *passim* p. 194 *et seq.* ; *Ker*, I, pp. 25– 39 ; *Dict. of Nat. Biog.* on Ker ; *H.M.C. Portland*, IV, pp. 362–380 ; *Defoe, Union*, pp. 266–281 ; *Somerville, Q. Anne* (1798), pp. 219–220 and notes. *Hooke (Rox.)*, I, pp. 208–214, II, pp. 85–93, and *Lockhart*, I, pp. 147–149, on Jacobite communications with France and England.

186 P. 281. *Lockhart*, I, pp. 173–175 ; *Marchmont*, III, p. 305 ; Story's *Carstares*, pp. 291–301 ; *Carstares, Letters*, pp. 754–756 ; *H.M.C. Mar and Kellie*, pp. 278, 315 ; *Mathieson*, pp. 130, 187–188 ; *H.M.C. Portland*, IV, pp. 340, 343, 346–348, 365, 382–383 ; *Crossrigg*, p. 195 ; *Clerk (Rox.)*, p. 245 ; *Rait and Dicey*, p. 228 ; *Defoe, Union*, pp. 338–342, 469, 557–561 ; *Acts Parl. Scot.*, pp. 314–322 ; *Letter from a gentleman in Scotland to his friend in England against the Sacramental Test*, London, 1708, pp. 4–7 and *passim* ; *Seasonable warning of the Pope and King of France* (Edinburgh ?), 1706, p. 15 and *passim* ; *Add. MSS.* 7078, ff. 237, 241–243 ; *(L'H.)* 17677 CCC, ff. 38, 46.

NOTES 437

P. 281. *Marchmont*, III, pp. 433–434 ; *H.M.C. Portland*, IV, pp. 368–369 ; *Mathieson*, pp. 136–137 ; *Add. MSS. (L'H.)* 17677 *CCC* ff. 38, 46.

P. 283. *Lockhart*, I, pp. 262–272 ; *Parl. Hist.*, VI, pp. 1110–1115 ; *H.C.J.*, XVII, pp. 207–208 ; *Marchmont*, I, pp. xcviii–cxxxiv ; *Mathieson*, pp. 144–147, 148 note, 157–158 ; *Somerville, Q. Anne*, pp. 222–223 and note ; *Jerviswood*, p. 160, on Roxburgh's claim on government, contradicting Lockhart's statement ; *Jerviswood*, pp. 55, 82–83, on Queensberry's desire for a speedy liquidation of his claims ; *Hume Brown, Scotland*, III, pp. 126–127 ; *Dicey and Rait*, pp. 227–228.

P. 284. *H.C.J.* and *H.L.J.*, *sub loc.*; *Parl. Hist.*, VI, pp. 551–578 ; *Add. MSS.* 7078, f. 245 ; *Carstares, Letters*, pp. 759–760 ; *Burnet*, V, pp. 285–288 [463–465] ; *Feiling*, p. 391 ; *H.M.C. Marchmont and Seafield*, pp. 158–159.

P. 284. *Acts Parl. Scot.*, pp. 446–491 ; *Defoe, Union*, pp. 522–523.

P. 285. *H.M.C. Mar and Kellie*, p. 389 ; *Clerk (Rox.)*, pp. 67–69 ; *Seafield, 1912*, p. 432.

CHAPTER XV

P. 288. Besides letters of 1707 printed in *Coxe* and elsewhere, see *Add. MSS.* 9093, ff. 11–12, Marl. to Ch. III ; 9099, f. 120, Godolphin to Marlborough, June 1 ; and, for the Austrian complaints, Prince of Salm's and Wratislaw's letters to Marlborough, 9098, ff. 21–24 and 53–54. The latent ill-feeling behind this interchange of courtesies must have been very strong. For the Hungarian question, see *Add. MSS.* 17677, xxx, ff. 273, 277–278 ; for Savoy *v.* Austria see *ditto*, f. 306 and *passim*.

P. 292. *Coxe*, Chaps. LIV–LV and letters of Aug. 1 and 5–16 in Chap. LIX ; *Diplomatic Instructions, Sweden (R.H.S.* 1922), pp. 14–15, 30–38 ; A. E. Stamp, *Meeting of Marl. and Charles XII* in *R.H.S.* 1898 ; *Dispatches*, III, pp. 347, 350, 357–9 ; *Klopp*, XII, pp. 383–390, 419–446 ; *Add. MSS.* 9099, ff. 120, 171, 180 ; *Lediard, Marl.*, II, pp. 157–179 ; *Voltaire, Hist. de Charles XII*, livre 3, compare *Tindal*, IV, pp. 15–19 and notes ; F. W. Head, *Fallen Stuarts*, pp. 120–121.

P. 295. *Klopp*, XII, pp. 295–325 ; *Dispatches*, III, pp. 326–330, 340–342 ; *Add. MSS.* 9093, f. 8 ; 9098, ff. 162–165, 201–202 ; *Tindal*, IV, pp. 3–4, 21–25 and notes ; *Corbett*, II, pp. 550–553.

P. 297. *Parnell*, Chaps. XXIII–XXIV ; B. Williams' *Stanhope*, pp. 52–58 ; *H.M.C. Bath*, I, pp. ix–x, 146–150, 154–155 ; *P. to St.*, p. 51 ; *Marchmont*, III, pp. 453–460 letters of Rivers and Galway ; *Add. MSS.* 7058, f. 87 ; 9099, f. 156 ; Russell's *Peterborough*, II, pp. 121, 145–157 ; *Coxe (ed. 1818)*, II, pp. 235–238, 295, 298, 305–306, for Peterborough's European tour ; *Tindal*, IV, pp. 4–6 ; *Parl. Hist.*, VI, p. 616 (Feb. 18, 170$\frac{7}{8}$) on losses of Rivers' men on the voyage, and pp. 985–993 on Galway *v.* Peterborough ; see also *Galway*, pp. 75–81, and *Freind*, pp. 178–187.

P. 300. For the whole battle, and particularly for Shrimpton's surrender, see the eye-witnesses' account in *Tindal*, IV, pp. 5–10 ; *Berwick*, I, pp. 251–254 ; Stanhope's *Succession*, pp. 230–235 ; *Historical Records Sixth Regiment of Foot, 1837*, pp. 42–45 ; *Galway*, pp. 82–85 ; *Add. MSS.* 28057, f. 338 ; 31134, ff. 399–400 ; and 9099 (General Erle, June 26, 1707) ; *Klopp*, XII, pp. 284–288 ; for Galway's dispatch of April 27 describing the battle to Sunderland, see *Coxe*, Chap. LVI. Paul Chamberlen's *History of Queen Anne* (1738), pp. 260–262, gives another good account of the battle. He blames Shrimpton's surrender as 'most dishonourable,' and made 'upon a false report that the enemy was surrounding them.' But how this may have been I cannot tell. In the *Relacion de la gran victoria en el campo de Almanza*, Seville, 1707, Shrimpton's surrender is described as being made to cavalry alone.   The same pamphlet contains a map of the battle purporting to mark each regiment in both armies.

[197] P. 300.   W. H. Logan's *Pedlar's Pack*, pp. 82–83.

[198] P. 301.   *H.M.C. Egmont* (1909), II, p. 223.   For the sieges of 1707 see *Parnell*.

[199] P. 304.   *Pelet*, VII, pp. 185–280 ; Villars' *Mémoires*, sub 1707 ; *Klopp*, XII, pp. 492–505 ; *Dispatches*, III, pp. 327, 392, 396 ; *Add. MSS.* 9093, ff. 11–12 ; *H.M.C. Portland*, IV, p. 441.

[200] P. 309.   For the siege of Toulon see *Pelet*, VII, pp. 109–153 ; *Tessé, Mem.*, II, chap. xi ; *Feldzüge*, IX, pp. 96–132, 335–347, and Appendix, pp. 175–188 ; *Klopp*, XII, pp. 326–349 ; *Byng Papers* (Navy Records Soc. 1930), I, pp. 195–235 ; *Tindal*, IV, pp. 25–28 (Chetwynd's journal) ; *Siege of Toulon collected from the original papers and personal knowledge of some gentlemen concerned* (from French sources), 1746 ; V. Brun, *Guerres Maritimes de la France, Port de Toulon*, 1861 ; *Burchett*, pp. 731–732 ; *Coxe*, Chap. LXI.

[201] P. 311.   *Burchett*, p. 733 ; *Spectator*, no. 26 ; above all Professor Laughton's article on Shovell in the *Dict. of Nat. Biog.* ; Campbell's *Lives of the Admirals* gives the old traditions, not reliable.

CHAPTER XVI

[202] P. 315.   *H.M.C. R.* 7 (*Egmont*, I), p. 246 ; *Wentworth Papers* (1883), pp. 39, 50–51, 58–59, 61–62, 64, 66 ; *State Trials*, XIV, pp. 1327–1372 ; *Tatler*, nos. 50–51 (1709), and notes in 1789 ed.

[203] P. 318.   *Conduct*, pp. 177–211 ; *Coxe*, II, chaps. LXII, LXIII *passim*, for the correspondence, Aug.–Nov. 1707 ; see also Marl. Papers in *H.M.C. R.* 8, p. 41, which should be read with knowledge of the cipher : 4=Harley, 10=Godolphin, 40=Marlborough, 17=the Queen, 41=Sarah ; *H.M.C. R.* 9 (Morrison Papers), pp. 469–470 ; *H.M.C. Portland*, IV, pp. 448 (Newcastle to Harley), 454 (Abigail), 426 (High Tories repentant) ; *H.M.C. Bath*, I (1904), pp. 180–181 ; *Miller*, pp. 16–17 ; *Burnet*, V, pp. 326–330 ; *Feiling*, p. 397.

[204] P. 320.   *H.M.C. R.* 8 (Marlborough Papers), p. 41 ; *Coxe*, II, chaps. LXII, LXIV, pp. 337–338, 343, 348, 380–381 ; *Feiling*, p. 399 ; *Burnet*, V, pp. 328–330 [488] ; *Conduct*, pp. 174–176.

[205] P. 321.   *H.M.C. R.* 4 (Emmanuel College Papers), p. 419 ; see also *Dict. of Nat. Biog.* under Tudway.

[206] P. 322.   For the evidence behind the attack on and defence of the Admiralty see *H. of L. MSS.* (1706–1708), pp. xv–xxi, 99–334, and *H.L.J.*, Vol. XVIII, under Dec. 17, 1707 ; Jan. 9 and Feb. 17, 170⅞ ; *Parl. Hist.*, VI, pp. 597–600, 612–613, 619–662 ; *C.S.P. (Am. and W.I.)*, 1706–1708, pp. 602–603 ; *Burnet*, V, pp. 332–338 [489–492] ; *Coxe*, II, pp. 370–374 ; *Feiling*, p. 398 ; *Taylor*, II, pp. 61–64 ; *Klopp*, XIII, pp. 2–3 ; Defoe's *Review*, Feb. 24, 170⅞ on Whigs and Tories.   For the Leicester election see *H.M.C. Portland*, IV, p. 464.   For the Jamaica fleet's arrival see *Add. MSS.* 7078, f. 247.

[207] P. 324.   *H.L.J.*, XVIII, pp. 410, 420–422 ; G. N. Clark in *Ec. Hist. Rev.*, Jan. 1928, pp. 263–264 ; *Chalmers' Estimate*, printed in *Cunningham*, p. 932 ; Campbell's *Lives of the Admirals* (ed. 1817), IV, pp. 27–28 ; *Parl. Hist.*, VI, pp. 645–646, 660–661 ; *C.S.P. Dom.* 1703–1704, pp. 496–497 on prizes.

[208] P. 325.   *Swift, Letters*, I, pp. 67, 73 ; *Freind*, ed. 1707 ; *Coxe*, II, pp. 370–378 ; *Parl. Hist.*, VI, pp. 605–608 ; *H.M.C. Egmont*, II (1909), pp. 220–221, perhaps the best account of the debate ; see also *Vernon*, III, pp. 300–301 ; *Burnet*, V, p. 338 [492] ; B. Williams' *Stanhope*, pp. 66–67.

209 P. 327. *H.M.C. Portland*, VII, p. 68 ; *H.M.C. Downshire*, I, pt. ii (1924), p. 862.

210 P. 329. *Feiling*, pp. 399–401 ; *Swift, Letters*, I, pp. 74–76 ; *Burnet*, V, pp. 339–345 ; *Portland*, V, p. 647 ; *Noorden*, III, p. 220 ; *Portland*, IV, pp. 477–478 ; *Klopp*, XIII, pp. 25–26 ; *Conduct*, p. 212 ; *H.M.C. Bath*, I, pp. 188–190 ; *Coxe*, II, chap. LXIV, pp. 385–388 ; *Althorp MSS.*, Duchess of Marlborough's letter to Mallet, Sept. 24, 1744.

211 P. 331. For Defoe's paper on the Secretary's office in 1704 see *E.H.R.*, Jan. 1907, pp. 130–140 ; *H.M.C. Portland*, V, p. 647, Edward Harley.

212 P. 333. *H.L.J.*, Feb. 9 and March 18, 170$\frac{7}{8}$; *H. of L. MSS.* (1706–1708), pp. xxxvi–xxxvii, 548–551 ; *State Trials*, XIV, pp. 1371–1396 ; *H.M.C. Portland*, IV, pp. 481–484, 488 ; V, pp. 647–649 (Edward Harley) ; *Burnet*, V, pp. 341–348 ; *Report of the House of Lords, being the Trial and Confession of W. Gregg*, 1708 ; *H.M.C. Bath*, I, p. 177. Lorrain's letter of 1711 will be found in *State Trials*, XIV, p. 1390, also in *Secret Transactions, etc.*, by Francis Hoffman, 1711 ; see also Hoffman's *More Secret Transactions*, 1711, and Swift's *Remarks upon a pamphlet entitled A Letter to the Seven Lords*, 1711. Also *Swift, Letters*, I, pp. 75–76. For modern writers cf. *Leadam*, pp. 132–133, to *Taylor*, II, pp. 76–92. I think Taylor trusts too much to what Swift wrote against the Whig Lords in 1711.

CHAPTER XVII

213 P. 335. *Burton, Scotland*, II, pp. 15–20 ; *Mathieson*, pp. 277–280 ; *Defoe, Union*, pp. 567–578, 582–585 ; *Burnet*, V, pp. 289–291 [466] ; *Parl. Hist.*, VI, pp. 579–580 ; *Lockhart*, I, pp. 223–224 ; *H.M.C. Mar and Kellie* (1904), p. 394.

214 P. 337. *Somerville, Q. Anne*, pp. 296–298 ; *Parl. Hist.*, VI, pp. 666–667 ; *Mathieson*, pp. 280–283 ; *Burnet*, V, pp. 348–352 [498–499] ; *H.M.C. Lonsdale* (1893), pp. 117–118, where the letters dated Nov. 1705 should be Nov. 1707. *Burton, Scotland*, II, pp. 20–24 ; *Carstares, Letters*, pp. 767, 770–771 ; *Defoe, Union*, pp. 696–697 ; *Somers, Tracts*, XII, p. 624.

215 P. 338. F. W. Head, *The Fallen Stuarts*, pp. 128–140, 335–345 ; *Add. MSS.* 20241 ff. 18–19, 20242 f. 23, Gualterio Papers ; *Add. MSS.* 20311 ff. 68–74, 31248 ff. 139–142, Irish appeals, 1705–1707. For the contrast of treatment of Catholics in England and Scotland to their treatment in Ireland, as reported to Rome, see *P.R.O.* (Tr.), *Rome*, 101, and *Blenheim*, p. 57 ; *Carstares, Letters*, p. 766.

216 P. 338. *Macpherson*, I, pp. 683–684.

217 P. 340. *Hooke* (Rox.), II, *passim*, especially pp. 347–409 ; *Hooke*, 1760, *passim*, especially pp. 14–91 ; *Lockhart*, I, pp. 227–238 ; *Terry, Chev.*, pp. 36–82.

218 P. 341. *Ker*, I, pp. 40–64 ; *Lockhart*, I, pp. 238, 302–309 ; *Hooke*, 1760, pp. 43–47 ; *Macpherson*, II, pp. 26, 84 ; *H. of L. MSS.* (1708–1710), pp. ix, xiv.

219 P. 346. *H. of L. MSS.* (1708–1710), pp. 44–46 ; *Byng Papers*, II, pp. 96–99, 108–109, 118 ; *Taylor*, II, pp. 96–99 ; *Parker*, pp. 119–120 ; John Deane, *Journal of Campaign in Flanders*, pp. 4–6 (see *Blenheim*, p. 228, for quotation from Deane's account of lying off Tynemouth).

220 P. 347. *Add. MSS.* 9101 f. 187 ; cf. Defoe's *Review*, April 29 and May 4, 1708 ; *H. of L. MSS.* (1708–1710), p. 45 ; *Lockhart*, I, pp. 243–244 ; *Carstares, Letters*, pp. 764–765.

221 P. 349. *P.R.O., S.P.*, 54, Sunderland's letter of March 9 and Dodswell's of March 30 on the arrests show the first initiative came from ' the Councill of Great Britain ' at London ' for the seissing of 31 persons suspect.' *Lockhart*, I, pp. 248–249 ; *H.M.C. R. 8* (*Marlborough Papers*), pp. 34, 41–42 ; *H.M.C. Marchmont Seafield* (1894), pp. 159–161 ; *H.M.C. Portland*, IV, p. 489 ; *Marchmont*, III, pp. 331–335 ; *H. of L. MSS.* (1708–1710), pp. x–xiv,

79–262 *passim* (144–146 on Belhaven) ; *Chambers*, III, p. 345, for a curious incident at the trial of the Stirlingshire gentlemen ; *The other side of the Question*, 1742, p. 380, for Sunderland's letter to Roxburgh ; for his letter about the pardon of Ld. Griffin see Appendix C, p. 412, above.

²²² P. 350. *Letters of H. Prideaux* (Camden Soc., 1875), p. 199 ; *Swift, Letters*, I, pp. 62, 71 ; *H.M.C. Downshire*, I, pt. II (1924), p. 858. Andréadès, *Hist. of Bank of England*, pp. 120–121, and *Leadam*, p. 137, for the run on the Bank.

²²³ P. 350. See Appendix C, p. 413, above.

²²⁴ P. 351. *Priv. Corr.*, I, pp. 116, 130, where 'Mr. Gapp' means John Gape, who got in for St. Albans this election.

²²⁵ P. 351. *H. of L. MSS.* (1706–1708), pp. xxxix, 563–564 ; Defoe's *Review*, May 4 and June 8, 1708 ; *Prideaux's Letters* (Camd. Soc.), p. 200 ; *H.M.C. Ailesbury* (1898), p. 199, for Ludgarshall.

²²⁶ P. 352. *H.M.C. Portland*, IV, pp. 489–490 ; *H.M.C. Downshire* (1924), p. 862 ; *H.M.C. Bagot*, p. 341 ; *Burnet*, V, p. 385 [517].

CHAPTER XVIII

²²⁷ P. 354. *Coxe*, Chap. LXVI (II, p. 415 for the letter) ; *Taylor*, II, pp. 103–105.

²²⁸ P. 356. *Taylor*, II, pp. 116–124 ; *Coxe*, Chaps. LXVIII, LXIX (see his letters to Godolphin of July 9 and July 12, 1708) ; *Pelet*, VIII, pp. 3–34, 381–385, 388–390 ; *H.M.C. Hare*, pp. 217–218 ; *St. Simon*, if he cannot be trusted on details of what befell in the field, is evidence of the bitterness of the open quarrels between Burgundy and Vendôme ; *Priv. Corr.*, I, p. 132.

²²⁹ P. 357. *Pelet*, VIII, pp. 29–34 ; *Coxe*, Chap. LXIX (II, pp. 465–466) ; *Lediard, Marl.*, II, pp. 257–258.

²³⁰ P. 366. For the battle of Oudenarde, see *Feldzüge, Serie* 2, *Band* I, pp. 339–363 and Appendix, 151–156 ; *Pelet*, VIII, pp. 31–38, 388–391 (most dishonest accounts as regards the result of the battle, as Louis seems to have suspected, see p. 399) ; even *Berwick*, II, p. 8, admits the loss of 9,000 prisoners (see also *Dispatches*, IV, p. 137), and speaks of the 'débris' of the army after the battle ; *Lediard, Marl.*, II, pp. 260–293, with some valuable letters from French officers ; *Taylor*, Chap. XX ; *Coxe*, Chap. LXIX, and letters of July 23 and 26, in Chap. LXX ; J. M. Deane, *Journal of Campaign in Flanders* (ed. 1846), pp. 11–16 ; *H.M.C. Hare*, p. 218 ; *Parker*, pp. 122–125 ; *Priv. Corr.*, I, p. 135 ; *Remembrance*, pp. 410–413 ; *Dispatches*, IV, pp. 102–104, 137 ; *Millner*, pp. 214–220 ; *St. Simon* for court gossip as to quarrels of the generals ; *Historical Records of the Buffs*, by Richard Cannon, 1837, pp. 153–157 ; *The Fighting Forces* for Sept. 1924, pp. 489–497, *Oudenarde, the Missing Order of Battle*, by C. T. Atkinson ; Atkinson's *Marlborough*, Chap. XIV ; *Col. Blackader* (1824), pp. 317–320 ; Dr. Francis Hare's *Thanksgiving Sermon* preached before House of Commons for Oudenarde, Feb. 17, 170⅞ ; *Goslinga*, pp. 52–61, though the Dutch Field-Deputy's account of how he snatched victory from defeat when Marlborough had lost his head is only worthy of the treatment it receives in *Taylor*, II, pp. 144–147, as another example of Bill Adams winning the battle of Waterloo.

²³¹ P. 368. *Coxe*, Chap. LXX ; *Dispatches*, IV, p. 129 ; *Taylor*, II, pp. 152–160 ; *Feldzüge, Serie* 2, *Band* I, p. 375 ; *H.M.C. Hare*, pp. 219–220. There is a good discussion of these issues in *Burton, Anne*, III, pp. 23–31, and *Atkinson*, pp. 345–350. Mr. Atkinson's military opinions are always worth noting.

²³² P. 370. *Feuquières, Mémoires*, ed. 1741, IV, p. 119 ; *Pelet*, VIII, pp. 40–168, 393–533 ; *Berwick*, II, *sub. ann.* 1708, and letters of 1708 at end of vol. ;

Atkinson, Chap. XV ; *Taylor*, Chaps. XXI–XXII ; *Coxe*, LXXII–LXXIII ; *Feldzüge, Serie* 2, *Band* I, pp. 364–495 ; *Remembrance*, pp. 418–457.

[233] P. 372. *Pelet*, VIII, pp. 103–106, 444–449 (La Motte's dispatch) ; *Dispatches*, IV, pp. 242–243 ; *Coxe*, Chap. LXXIII, Vol. II, pp. 552–559 ; *Atkinson*, pp. 357–360 ; *Taylor*, II, pp. 206–215 ; *H.M.C. Round*, p. 331 ; *Parl. Hist.*, VI, pp. 760–761 ; Boyer's *Queen Anne*, ed. 1735, pp. 362–363.

[234] P. 373. *Dispatches*, IV, pp. 266–269 ; *H.M.C. Mar and Kellie*, pp. 465–467 (Stair's letter) ; *Coxe*, ii, pp. 562–565 (Chap. LXXIII).

[235] P. 373. *Pelet*, VIII, pp. 151–154.

[236] P. 374. *Lediard, Marl.*, II, p. 419 ; *Coxe*, Chap. LXXIV.

[237] P. 376. *H.M.C. Marlborough Papers*, p. 33 ; *Dispatches*, IV, p. 108.

[238] P. 376. *Leake*, II, pp. 254–270, 279 ; *Rapin*, IV, pp. 94–95 and notes.

[239] P. 379. *Add. MSS.* 22231, ff. 78–80, John Cope's narrative letter ; *Leake*, II, pp. 271–306 ; *Byng Papers*, II, pp. xxi–xxii, 299–303 (Stanhope's dispatch ; *Burchett*, pp. 752–754 ; *Tindal*, IV, pp. 95–97 ; Boyer's *Queen Anne* (1735), pp. 349–351 ; *H.M.C. Marlborough Papers*, p. 35 ; and two excellent secondary authorities, *Corbett*, II, pp. 555–564, and *B. Williams, Stanhope*, pp. 71–78 ; for the naval value of Minorca see also Admiral Sir H. Richmond in *The Study of War* (ed. Sir G. Aston), p. 77.

[240] P. 379. Boyer, *Queen Anne* (1735), p. 351 ; *Tindal*, IV, pp. 98–100 ; *H.M.C. Marlborough Papers*, p. 35 ; *Klopp*, XIII, pp. 93–106, 256–273, 547–550 ; *Dispatches*, IV, pp. 460–462.

[241] P. 381. *B. Williams, Stanhope*, pp. 79–85 ; *Geikie*, pp. 147–154, 180–182 ; *Klopp*, XIII, pp. 278–281 ; *Dispatches*, IV, 409, 562.

[242] P. 382. *C.S.P. Am.* (1708–9), pp. xi–xiii, 56, 486.

[243] P. 383. *C.S.P. Am.* (1706–8), pp. xii, 753 ; (1708–9) pp. xi, 38–40, 56, 95 ; *Burchett*, pp. 705–707 ; *Lediard, N.H.*, II, pp. 835–838 ; *Tindal*, IV, pp. 101–102 ; *H.M.C. Marlborough Papers*, p. 33, Sunderland's letter wrongly dated May 2 ; Laughton's article on Wager in the *Dict. of Nat. Biog.*

[244] P. 383. *Tindal*, IV, p. 101.

CHAPTER XIX

[245] P. 385. Appendix C., p. 414, above, for Sunderland's letters to Newcastle ; *H.M.C. Marlborough Papers*, pp. 42–43

[246] P. 385. *H.M.C. Marl. Papers*, p. 42.

[247] P. 386. Sunderland's letter, App. C., pp. 413–414, above ; *H.M.C. Portland*, IV, pp. 490–491, 507 ; *H.M.C. Bagot* (1906), p. 341 ; *H.M.C. Marl. Papers*, p. 42 ; *Conduct*, pp. 151–153.

[248] P. 387. *H.M.C. Portland*, IV, p. 506.

[249] P. 387. *R.H.S.* 1910, pp. 22–25, *The Finance of Lord Treasurer Godolphin*, by I. S. Leadam ; *Dowell*, II, pp. 67–84 ; *English Taxation 1640–1799*, William Kennedy (1913), *passim*, on the principles underlying taxation at this period. *Parl. Hist.*, VI, pp. 784–787, borrowing operations sanctioned Feb. 1709.

[250] P. 388. *H.M.C. Bath*, I (1904), pp. 191–194.

[251] P. 391. *Coxe*, Chaps. LXXV and LXXVII ; Addison, *Freeholder*, no. 39, on Somers and the Queen ; *Althorp MSS.*, Sarah's letter of Sept. 24, 1744, to Mr. Mallet. It has been asserted that Wharton had evidence of Godolphin's correspondence with St. Germains and used the threat of disclosure to force an entrance for himself and his colleagues into the Cabinet at this period (Charles Hamilton, *Transactions during the Reign of Queen Anne*, 1790, p. 110–121, and, from same source, James Macpherson, in his *Hist. of Gr. Britain*, tells the same story).

It may or may not be true, but no such explanation is necessary. The Parliamentary situation suffices to explain the entry of the Whigs into the Ministry.

[252] P. 392. *Swift, Letters*, I, pp. 116–117, 120; *H.M.C. Portland*, IV, p. 502.

[253] P. 394. *Stats. of Realm* (1822), vol. IX, pp. 93–95; *Parl. Hist.*, VI, pp. 794–799; *Marchmont*, III, p. 354; *Burnet*, V, pp. 389–397; *Hume Brown, Scotland*, III, pp. 142–145.

[254] P. 394. *The Secretaries of State*, Mark Thomson, pp. 31–32, 164–166; *Tindal*, IV, 119; *Wentworth Papers*, pp. 72–73.

[255] P. 395. *Tindal*, IV, p. 119; *Geikie*, p. 101; *Wentworth Papers*, p. 68; *Swift, Letters*, I, p. 134.

[256] P. 395. J. Nichols's *Literary Anecdotes 18th Cent.*, V, p. 233 (Wesley gets the dates and his own age wrong).

[257] P. 396. *H.M.C. Round* (1895), p. 322, 327 (pp. 317–359 for the Petkum-Torcy correspondence 1706–1711).

[258] P. 398. A. Legrelle, *Une négociation inconnue* (1893), *passim*, p. 22 for Marlborough's letter of October 30; *Torcy's Memoirs* (Engl. translation 1757), I, pp. 300, 303–304, 316; *Berwick*, II, pp. 34–35; *Atkinson*, pp. 371–373; *Taylor*, II, pp. 228–233.

[259] P. 402. For the negotiations of 1709 see *Torcy's Memoirs*, Vol. I; *Legrelle*, IV, pp. 459–504; *Klopp*, XIII, pp. 214–256; *Geyl*, pp. 14–20; *Coxe*, Chaps. LXXVIII–LXXIX; *H.M.C. Round*, pp. 338–343; *Geikie*, pp. 127–132, especially on Godolphin's and Marlborough's views.

[260] P. 405. *Geikie, passim*, Chap. IV; *Taylor*, II, pp. 303–304, 318–319; *Coxe*, II, pp. 548–549 (end of Chap. LXXII).

[261] P. 405. *H.M.C. Chequers Court* (1900), pp. xx, 199.

INDEX

States General, Holland, *see* Dutch
States of the Church, 294 *n.*, 379
Steele's *Tatler*, 47
Stepney, George, English Minister at Vienna, 51, 136, 141 ; Minister at Brussels, 136, 137, 140
Stirlingshire Jacobites, 347, 348, 392–3
Stolhofen, 303, 304, 305
Strasbourg, 399
Sun, symbolic eclipse of, 149
Sunderland, Third Earl of (Charles Spencer), 31, 167 *n.*, 168, 263 ; and the Secretaryship of State, 167–71 *passim*, 372, 375, 376, 383, 384 ; attitude to party, 348, 384, 390 ; Queen's dislike of, 168, 385 ; and the Jacobite invasion, 346, 348 ; and Whig intrigue with Jacobites, 348, 349 ; relations with his kinsmen, 348, 384–5, 386, 412 ; and taking of Minorca, 375, 377 *n.*, 379, 380 ; and Queensberry, 394, 412 ; letters of, to the Duke of Newcastle, 350, 384, 412–16 ; mentioned, 11, 28, 404
Susarte, Simon, 39
Sutton, Rector of, 85 *n.*
Sweden, 289 ; and the Austrian claims in Spain, 60 *n.* ; and Baltic trade, 291
Charles XII, 10, 62, 288–93, 297, 367, 374 ; attitude to Louis XIV, 289, 290, 291, 292 ; and Austria, 290, 291, 292 ; and England, 291 ; meeting with Marlborough, 291, 292 ; and Peterborough, 297 ; design for a Protestant League, 290, 292
Gustavus Adolphus, 290
Swift, Jonathan, 7, 185, 286, 324, 333 *and n.*, 349, 391–2, 394 ; and Lord Peterborough, 65, 158 ; and Vienna secretaryship, 392 ; *Tale of a Tub*, 392
Swiss regiments (Biron's), in French service, 106, 111, 358–9 ; in allied service, 113
Sykes, Professor Norman, *quoted*, 417–18

TACK, the, *see* Occasional Conformity Bill
Tackers, the, 15, 26, 31 ; Marlborough and, 15 ; election policy of, 27

Tallard, Marshal, 11, 104, 113, 242, 331
Tarazena, Marquis of, Spanish Governor of Antwerp, 125
Tarragona, 70, 71
Taxation, 164, 165, 166, 167, 387 ; and the Treasury, 166
Taylor, Frank, *Wars of Marlborough*, 305 *n.*
Tea in Scotland, 182
Tenison, Archbishop, 262, 263, 319 *and n.*, 320 ; and Union Treaty, 263, 283–4
Tessé, Marshal of France, besieges Gibraltar, 37, 43, 45, 46 ; besieges Barcelona, 145–52 *passim* ; defence of Toulon, 306, 308, 309
Test Act and the Presbyterians, 280, 281 *and n.*
Thackeray's *Esmond*, 224, 372
Thames frozen, 394
Theatre, the: complaints as to, in Convocation, 89 *n.*
Thetford, 351
Thionville, 49
Tilly, Count, 305 *n.*
Tofts, Mrs., 312
Toland, John, 97
Toledo, 153
Toleration Act, 88, 89 *n.* ; Scotland, 206, 209, 233, 234, 273, 280
Torcy, Marquis of, 396, 398, 400, 402
Tortosa, 70
Torture, 393
Tory party, 403 ; split by the 'tack' proposal, 15 ; views on Cabinet control, 167 ; implications of the word Tory, 183 ; High Tory attitude to the war, 13, 326, 388 ; attitude of aversion to Scotland, 178, 244 ; and Act of Security, 244, 245 ; toast after Almanza, 301 ; and the war in the Peninsular, 324–5 ; attitude to Godolphin and Marlborough, 326 ; and Scots Privy Council, 336 ; suspicions of, on Godolphin's attitude to the Succession, 340 ; sneers at Marlborough after Wynendael fight, 372 ; accuse Marlborough of aiming at sovereignty, 386–7 ; fears of Marlborough, 387, 405 ; Party

Printed in England at THE BALLANTYNE PRESS
SPOTTISWOODE, BALLANTYNE & CO. LTD.
Colchester, London & Eton

MAP IX

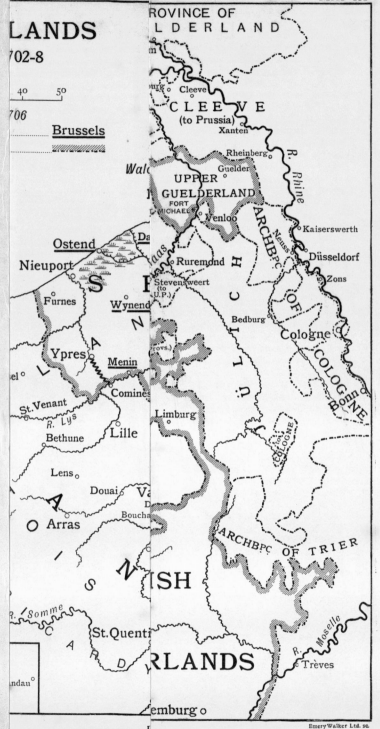

LANDS

702-8

40   50

706

Brussels

PROVINCE OF
ELDERLAND

burg   Cleeve

CLEEVE
(to Prussia)
Xanten

Rheinberg

R. Rhine

Wal   Guelder

UPPER
GUELDERLAND
FORT
MICHAEL   Venloo

Neuss   Kaiserswerth

Da   ARCHBPC   Düsseldorf

Ostend   Ruremond   Zons

Nieuport   Stevensweert
(to
U.P.)

S   N   Bedburg

Furnes

Wynend   OF

Cologne

provs.)

Ypres   COLOGNE

Menin   Bonn

el   L   Comines

St.Venant   Limburg   COLOGNE

R. Lys

Bethune   Lille

Lens

Douai   Va   ARCHBPC OF TRIER

Bouch

Arras

A   N   S

R. Somme

ISH

St.Quentin

C   A   R   D

RLANDS

ndau   Moselle

emburg   R.   Trèves

Emery Walker Ltd. sc.

THE NETHER[LANDS]

Campaigns of 1[...]

English Miles

Places taken by Marlborough in [...]
after Ramillies, underlined thus:
Boundary of Spanish Netherlands

Margate

ENGLAND

Goodwin
Sands

The Downs

Dover

Str of Dover

Dunkirk

Calais

Boulogne   St. Omer

Aire

THE MOSELLE
1704-5   Coblentz

Trarbach

Treves

Luxemburg

Sierk
Thionville   Saarlouis

Metz